CYBERSECURITY

**Protecting Critical Infrastructures
from Cyber Attack and Cyber Warfare**

CYBERSECURITY
Protecting Critical Infrastructures
from Cyber Attack and Cyber Warfare

Edited by
Thomas A. Johnson
Webster University
St. Louis, Missouri, USA

CRC Press
Taylor & Francis Group
Boca Raton London New York

CRC Press is an imprint of the
Taylor & Francis Group, an **informa** business

CRC Press
Taylor & Francis Group
6000 Broken Sound Parkway NW, Suite 300
Boca Raton, FL 33487-2742

First issued in paperback 2020

© 2015 by Taylor & Francis Group, LLC
CRC Press is an imprint of Taylor & Francis Group, an Informa business

No claim to original U.S. Government works

ISBN-13: 978-1-4822-3922-5 (hbk)
ISBN-13: 978-0-367-59936-2 (pbk)

Visit the Taylor & Francis Web site at
http://www.taylorandfrancis.com

and the CRC Press Web site at
http://www.crcpress.com

For her sage counsel,
generous advice, and assistance,
this book is gratefully dedicated to my wife,
Colleen Rose Johnson.

Contents

Contents

Preface

The World Economic Forum regards the threats to cybersecurity as one of the top five global risks confronting nations of the world today. The vulnerabilities of financial loss ranging from cybersecurity breaches to theft of intellectual property are a growing problem. Cyber threats are increasingly targeting the core functions of the economies in nations throughout the world, as well as their governments on local, regional, and national levels. The potential for cyber attacks to disrupt critical services of both the private enterprise and nongovernmental agencies is growing at an alarming rate.

Cybersecurity is now regarded as one of our nation's top concerns, as the potential for motivated groups or individuals to disrupt critical services, attack any one of our 16 critical infrastructures, and induce a range of damage from major economic disruption to massive physical destruction is becoming more difficult to defend against. Even more alarming is the possible threat of cyber attacks on our nation's Department of Defense and military assets, as cyber attacks could severely disrupt or disable our military command and control systems, as well as our communications, intelligence, and joint command systems, which could jeopardize our national security. The threat of cyber warfare is on the horizon, and the development and creation of cyber weapons are being pursued by many nations.

Our book addresses these issues by first examining the historical reference points in the development of the computer industry and, in particular, the dark side, which has seen the development of worms, viruses, Trojans, and a threat landscape that has created the need for an emerging field of cybersecurity. The concern for protecting our nation's critical infrastructure is examined through the programs and actions introduced by Presidents Bill Clinton, George W. Bush, and Barrack Obama, all interested in the development of programs to protect our critical infrastructures and key assets from becoming a target-rich environment for potential adversaries. The protection and engineering design issues in our critical infrastructures are discussed in terms of protection design goals.

The protection of national security issues requires a vigilant cyber intelligence capability not only to address cyber conflicts but more importantly to be able to prevent or defend against cyber warfare. The discussion of cyberspace and cyber battle space is necessary to understand the factors that enable cyber war in terms of both offensive and defensive operations. The key issues in formulating a strategy of cyber warfare and rules of engagement for the use of cyber weapons are an area in need of both analysis and further research. The potential for nation-state cyber conflicts and the Tallinn Manual on International Law and cyber warfare is another emerging worldwide issue that will continue to grow in both importance and necessity for guideline developments. The expanding role of an international comprehensive cybersecurity strategy will also be on the forefront of development as the United States, the United Nations, the North Atlantic Treaty Organization, and the European Union are all beginning discussions as to the legal aspects of the growing problem of cyber attacks and appropriate policies and legal point of control.

Since the cost of cybersecurity has also become a growing burden on the corporate community, we present the results of several important industry-based economic studies of security breaches that have occurred within many nations and also provide a global perspective for comparative purposes. The recent emergence of cybersecurity insurance plans and programs available from the insurance community is another sign of the growing depth of the cybersecurity concerns and economic costs involved in this area. However, the challenges of current cybersecurity models are probed in terms of the audit and compliance model as being based on a reactive posture, when a need for more proactive cybersecurity strategies is being explored for wider application.

If the challenges of cybersecurity were not enough by themselves, we now are experiencing a major set of industry-wide transformational changes that will exacerbate the problems confronting the entire field of cybersecurity. These transformational challenges are occurring as a result of virtualization, social media, the Internet of Things, cloud computing, structured and unstructured data, big data, data analytics, and big data applications. The potential impact that these transformational changes will have on the field of cybersecurity will be enormous and will create a need for additional training and educational courses. More specifically, additional research in the field of cybersecurity will have to assess the impact that these transformational challenges will have on the personnel and practices within the field today and what the future will require to absorb these challenges in the most positive manner possible.

Acknowledgments

This book is the result of many dedicated colleagues who have contributed their wisdom and a great deal of their time to make this book possible. It is with a deep sense of appreciation that I thank each of my contributing authors for their excellent chapters and for their years of service to our nation.

Our publisher, CRC Press, Taylor & Francis Group, has provided us the support and opportunity to once again work with their excellent personnel. Carolyn Spence and the team she assigned to work with us are not only consummate professionals who have offered assistance and encouragement but also the most skilled and thoughtful colleagues, and for this, we are grateful.

Finally, the guidance, wisdom, and support offered by my wife, Colleen, as she worked with each contributing author and myself on a range of issues from constructively critiquing our manuscript to her editorial assistance, have been critical to the preparation of this book. We are indebted to her for her tireless effort and her knowledgeable insights, advice, and support.

Thomas A. Johnson
Webster University
St. Louis, Missouri

Editor

Dr. Thomas A. Johnson currently serves as the associate vice president and chief of Strategic Initiatives for Webster University, St. Louis, Missouri. He serves as a member of the Board of Directors of the SANS Technology Institute. He earned his bachelor's and master's degrees from Michigan State University and his doctorate from the University of California–Berkeley.

Dr. Johnson has developed programs in cybercrime and forensic computer investigation and also founded the Graduate National Security program offered at two of our National Nuclear Security Administration laboratories in California and New Mexico. As program leader for the graduate cybersecurity degree for Webster University, Dr. Johnson worked with 20 colleagues to implement the program at multiple military locations and several regional metropolitan sites, as well as the main campus in St. Louis. In addition, he and Dr. Fred Cohen lead the development of the private cloud cyber laboratory team. Together, they also cofounded the California Sciences Institute, a graduate nonprofit educational institution.

Dr. Johnson serves as a member of the Federal Bureau of Investigation Infraguard program and is a member of the electronic Crime Task Force, New York Field Office, and San Francisco Field Office, U.S. Secret Service. The U.S. Attorney General appointed Dr. Johnson a member of the Information Technology Working Group, and he served as chair of the Task Force Group on Combating High Technology Crime for the National Institute of Justice. Dr. Johnson was also appointed an advisor to the Judicial Council of California on the Court Technology Task Force by the California Supreme Court.

Dr. Johnson has published 7 books and 13 refereed articles and holds copyright on 4 software programs, and his chapter "Infrastructure Warriors: A Threat to the U.S. Homeland by Organized Crime" was published by the Strategic Studies Institute of the U.S. Army War College ("…to insure domestic tranquility, provide for the common defense…" Papers from the Conference on Homeland Protection, 2000). In addition to lecturing at the U.S. Army War College, Carlisle Barracks, he has also lectured at the Federal Law Enforcement Training Center and numerous universities.

Dr. Johnson has appeared in both State and U.S. Federal courts as an expert witness and was a member of the Select ad hoc Presidential Investigative Committee and consultant to the American Academy of Forensic Sciences in the case of Sirhan B. Sirhan regarding forensic and physical evidence concerning the assassination of U.S. Senator Robert F. Kennedy.

Contributors

Dr. Fred Cohen is best known as the person who defined the term "computer virus," is the inventor of most of the widely used computer virus defense techniques, and the principal investigator whose team defined the information assurance problem as it relates to critical infrastructure protection. He is a seminal researcher in the use of deception for information protection and is the leader in advancing the science of digital forensic evidence examination. He is regarded both nationally and internationally as a leading information protection consultant and industry analyst. Dr. Cohen has authored more than 200 invited, refereed, and other scientific and management research articles, and has written several widely read books on information protection.

As a consultant and researcher for the U.S. government, Dr. Cohen was the principal investigator on seminal studies in defensive information operations and on the national information security technical baseline series of reports. Dr. Cohen founded the College Cyber Defenders program at Sandia National Laboratories that ultimately led to the formation of the Cyber Corps program, and led projects ranging from "Resilience" to "The Invisible Router." He has also worked in critical infrastructure protection with law enforcement and with the intelligence community to help improve their ability to deal with computer-related crime and emerging threats to national security.

All told, the protection techniques Dr. Cohen pioneered now help to defend more than three quarters of all the computers in the world. Today, Dr. Cohen is the CEO of Fred Cohen & Associates, and also serves as the acting director of the Webster University Cyber Laboratory. He earned his BS in electrical engineering from Carnegie-Mellon University. He received his MS degree in information science from the University of Pittsburgh and his PhD degree in electrical engineering from the University of Southern California.

Julie Lowrie's chapter "Cybersecurity: A Primer of U.S. and International Legal Aspects" is extremely timely as the legal framework to guide nations in matters regarding cyber breaches, cyber attack, and cyber warfare is becoming critical to the safety of all nations. Julie Lowrie's excellent background in both the legal and forensic investigative areas allows her to offer incisive comments in this newly developing area of scholarly inquiry. She has served as a senior investigator for the U.S. Department of Labor and is an associate corporation's investigator for the California Department of Managed Health

Care. Lowrie has more than 21 years of experience conducting more than 50 complex financial and economic crime investigations involving health care, pension, and bank and bankruptcy fraud. Her investigations have entailed unraveling complex financial transactions in which the dollar amount of losses ranged from approximately $100,000 to $50 million. She received the U.S. Attorney's office Outstanding Achievement Award in 2009 and the U.S. Attorney's office Exceptional Achievement Award for her work in the *United States vs. James Graff* conviction in 2007.

Julie Lowrie's educational background includes a BA degree from the University of California–San Diego; a law degree from the American College of Law; and two MS degrees, one from Utica College in economic crime management and the second one from the California Sciences Institute in advanced investigations. Lowrie is currently an adjunct professor teaching in the cybersecurity program at Webster University's George Herbert Walker School of Business & Technology, St. Louis, Missouri.

Historical Reference Points in the Computer Industry and Emerging Challenges in Cybersecurity

1

THOMAS A. JOHNSON

Contents

1

1.1   Introduction

James O. Hicks Jr. provides a fascinating outline of the early developments in the data processing field by noting the abacus as the first known device capable of making calculations, something so fundamental to the development of today's computer industry. Whereas the Greeks and Romans used the abacus in ancient times, the Chinese made significant improvements to it. The next major introduction into the field of calculations occurred in 1642, when a French mathematician, Blaise Pascal, developed a "gear-driven" mechanical calculator capable of addition, subtraction, and multiplication. Twenty-nine years later, in 1671, a German mathematician, Gottfried Leibnitz, improved upon Pascal's design, and his new mechanical calculator could offer both division and the ability to determine square roots.[1] The concept of performing calculations from beads to abacus to the use of mechanical wheels was fundamental to the modern computer industry's development.

The next major historical contributions occurred in the early 1800s, when Joseph Jacquard developed a loom for production of fabric and clothing. Significant to the eventual emergence of a modern computer industry was Jacquard's use of "punched cards" as the control mechanism in his loom. By sequencing the punched cards, the loom could produce a cast number of patterns and designs. When the punched cards for a particular pattern were repeated, the same pattern would automatically be repeated. Thus, in effect, Jacquard's punched cards were the program for the loom. In 1812, Charles Babbage, an English mathematician, visualized that many of the principles of Jacquard's loom and its use of punched cards could be applied to numerical computation. Babbage's very important observation focused on the use of punched cards as computing steps that were stored on the card in advance of computation, and this allowed a machine to process data totally unaided. Babbage's observation and work were responsible for the first development of the concept of the "stored program" for data processing. This is precisely the capability that differentiates computers from calculators, and Babbage called his first machine a difference engine and designed it to calculate logarithm tables. The major components of Babbage's analytical engine were as follows:

- Input and output devices
- An arithmetic unit to perform calculations
- A memory (punched cards) to store the calculations

As a result of his work, many regard Charles Babbage as the first person to propose the concept of the computer.[2]

An important contributor to Babbage's research was Augusta Ada Byron, the daughter of Lord Byron, the renowned English poet. Ada Byron was an accomplished mathematician, and she analyzed and improved many of Babbage's concepts. As a result of her work in developing and programming the mathematical tables for Babbage's analytical engine, she has been recognized as the first programmer. In fact, the programming language ADA is named in her honor.[3] It is interesting to note that years later, the U.S. Department of Defense favored a substantial number of their applications to be based in what obviously was an improved ADA programming system.

Additional improvements in the punched cards were forthcoming by the late 1870s, and Henry Metcalfe discovered a need to reorganize a cost-accounting system that would take records out of the leather board folios in use at the time and allow a more effective way to retrieve information from the ledgers by transferring accounting records from ledgers to punched cards. These cards could be sorted and information more easily and quickly obtained than by the conventional accounting ledgers. Metcalfe developed a coding scheme and unit records to specify the flow of data. Ten years later, in 1880, Herman Hollerith, a statistician at the U.S. Census Bureau, followed Metcalfe's ideas and began experimenting with punched cards for their use in data processing for the 1880 U.S. Census. Hollerith designed a tabulating machine that used the machine-readable punched cards, and within six years, he founded a company that, by 1911, merged with three other companies forming the Computing Tabulation Recording Company, known then as CTR. In 1924, the CTR Company was renamed as the International Business Machines Corporation and emerged as IBM.[4]

The next refinement occurred in 1908 by James Powers, who refined Hollerith's machine by developing a sorting machine with tabulators that were used in the 1910 Census. Powers also formed a company he named the Powers Accounting Machine Company, which, in 1926, merged with the Remington Rand Corporation and then merged with the Sperry Gyroscope Company to form the Sperry Rand Corporation, and they produced UNIVAC computers. Eleven years later, in 1937, the MARK I digital computer was built by Howard Aiken and IBM engineers, and Grace Murray Hopper programmed the MARK I. Grace Hopper became an Admiral in the U.S. Navy and was an important contributor to various computer languages, especially COBOL.[5]

In 1939, at the University of Pennsylvania, John Mauchly and J. Presper Eckert Jr. led a team of engineers who developed the first electronic digital computer named ENIAC. The ENIAC computer was completed in 1946 and used vacuum tubes. The ENIAC weighed over 30 tons and covered 1500 square feet of floor space. In 1945, the binary number system was developed by John Von Neumann, a Princeton University mathematician. This number system used zeroes and ones as on–off and magnetized and not-magnetized as states that ultimately facilitated the design of electronic computers and formed the fundamentals for today's electronic computers.[6]

The emergence of the microcomputer or PC was a major advancement, especially with user-friendly software and graphic terminals.[7]

1.1.5 Personal Computers

The evolution of the PC, known as the personal computer, profoundly changed the entire computer industry. While the fourth generation of computing actually made possible the achievement of the PC, its interface was responsible for propelling us into the fifth generation of computing. First, we will review the more salient developments in the era of personal computing, which can be marked by the following developments:

1975—The ALTAIR 8800 became the first PC
1977—The Apple I, II, and Commodore Computers
1981—The IBM-PC Home Computer
1983—Apple Lisa Computer
1984—Apple MacIntosh Computer

The above PCs emerging in this decade required software, and the operating system of most significance was Microsoft's MS-DOS system. However, the interesting feature was how the ALTAIR 8800 computer, which had little to any application capability, did in fact inspire many hobbyists to acquire it. Foremost among these hobbyists were Steve Jobs and Steve Wozniak, and they would, within two years, introduce their Apple I and II computers. This computer proved to be an enormous hit with all those watching this new PC industry; however, some skepticism remained regarding these new PCs, that is, until 1981, when IBM released its new PC-Home computer, and this had the effect of legitimizing this new industry. After all, IBM virtually owned the entire computing industry with its worldwide mainframe dominance. The world took notice of the possibilities of personal computing because IBM entered this market.

IBM's entrance into the personal computing market was made with several major strategic decision failures. First and foremost, IBM made the decision to outsource the development of the PC's operating system, and they offered the contract to Microsoft, which developed the MS-DOS operating system. The second major mistake IBM made was in their failure to restrict the licensing of the MS-DOS operating system to IBM-Home PCs. Even more incredible, IBM possessed the personnel, skills, money, and capabilities by which they could have developed their own operating system and did not need to contract this to Microsoft. A third major mistake IBM made was to use off-shelf parts to construct their PC, and when small new companies discovered this fact, they were able to do the same by simply buying off-shelf parts and then license the MS-DOS operating system from Microsoft, which had no restrictive licensing to only sell to IBM. In effect, IBM's presence enabled all unknown small companies to enter this market because of the world respect for IBM.

A fourth major error IBM made upon their entrance into the PC market was a total judgment error in terms of the future of the PC. IBM estimated that the total worldwide production of PCs over their entire lifetime would be 250,000 units. In fairness to IBM, they were selling mainframes in the million dollar cost structure to business corporations throughout the world, and they simply could not envision this "hobby or toy" culture emerging to compete with major corporations, especially since at the time of their ill-fated decisions, software applications for the PC did not yet exist. In short order, these software applications did emerge in the form of the following:

1978—VISICALC spreadsheet software
1979—WordStar software

Each of these products was improved by other companies, and Lotus 1-2-3 emerged as an industry-wide spreadsheet. Also, WordPerfect would become an important part of the eventual word processing Microsoft Office Series.

The historical emergence of the computer industry through the 1970s would be propelled by an incredible acceleration of growth as a result of the Internet and, ultimately, the World Wide Web.

1.1.6   Advanced Research Projects Agency Network, Internet, and World Wide Web

The Advanced Research Projects Agency Network (ARPANET) began operation in 1969 with four nodes (sites) as a result of the Advanced Research Projects Agency experiment by the Defense Advanced Research Projects Agency. This experiment expanded to 37 nodes by 1973, and in 1977, it started using the Internet protocol (IP), a universal connector of networks. By 1997, after the ARPANET was founded, the Internet counted over 20 million computers and 50 million users. The Department of Defense began work on an experiment in communications and resource sharing in the 1950s, an era of concern due to the growth of intercontinental ballistic missiles. The Department of Defense was concerned about the ability of the United States to survive a nuclear first strike and decided that research on a communication network should be supported. Paul Baran of the Rand Corporation was the principal designer and force behind the creation of this new communication system and the following features guided its development:

1. Redundant links;
2. No central control;

3. All messages broken into equal size packets;
4. Variable routing of packets depending on the availability of links and nodes; and
5. Automatic reconfiguration of routing tables immediately after the loss of a link or node.[8]

Larry Roberts of the Massachusetts Institute of Technology's Lincoln Laboratory and J.C.R. Licklider of the Defense Department's Advanced Research Project Agency focused on building networks that made sharing of computers and data both economical and cost effective. In 1965, Larry Roberts and Donald Davies of the National Physical Laboratory in England proposed a packet switched computer network using telephone lines to process messages in speeds from 100 kilobits per second to 1.5 megabits per second and switching computers that could process 10,000 packets per second with interface computers connected to mainframe hosts. Leonard Kleinrock of the University of California, Los Angeles produced analytic models of packet switched networks that were critical to the guide design. In 1968, the Advanced Research Projects Agency awarded a contract to Frank Heart at Bolt Beranek and Newman to build the first interface message processors to connect mainframes and their operating systems to the network. The fact that networks now had to be connected together resulted in Vinton Cerf designing a new protocol that would permit users to interconnect programs on computers in different networks. In 1977, Cerf completed his design of what would become the Internet as most people know it. Vinton Cerf designed a matched set of protocols called transport control protocol (TCP) and IP. The IP protocol routed packets across multiple networks and the TCP converted messages into streams of packets, reassembling them into messages.[9]

The massive investment in research by the U.S. government led by both the Department of Defense and the National Science Foundation enabled the creation and growth of the Internet from 1969 until 1989. The work of many research scientists proved both important and invaluable as their efforts resulted in unifying many networks and ultimately provided a stable and valuable community of networks. By 1989, the ARPANET was officially disbanded, and finally, the backbone of the management of the Internet was transferred to commercial Internet service providers (ISPs) from the National Science Foundation in 1996.[10]

Tim Berners-Lee of CERN, the Zurich-based Research Center for High-Energy Physics, designed the Universal Resource Locator to name documents and the hypertext transfer protocol (HTTP) to transfer the documents. His design included the hypertext mark-up language (HTML) to identify text strings that were active hyperlinks within a document. He named this system of Internet-wide linked documents the World Wide Web, and it was received in 1990 with wide acclaim and usage. Additionally, Marc Andreeson's work at the University of Illinois' National Center for Super Computing Applications brought Tim Berners-Lee's World Wide Web into even greater prominence as Andreeson designed the Mosaic browser as a simple, easy-to-use multimedia interface for the HTML documents and the HTTP protocol. In 1992, this design accelerated the Internet throughout the world.[11]

1.1.7   Fifth Generation—Emerging Technologies

The continuing development of technologies and refinement of software have resulted in remarkable advances and inventions. The transition from an analog world to a digital world has provided unparalleled convergence of communications, publishing, entertainment, and capabilities delivered through devices ranging from cell phones to a wide range of appliances and computers. The advance in multimedia, virtual reality, artificial intelligence, and robotics is challenging all aspects of human behavior. In the process of this fifth generation and emerging technologies, we see governments being challenged as their control of information and communication systems is in fundamental change. Additionally, the issue of privacy and its sense of loss to the individual is growing daily by the very presence of social media and the number of applications developed for a range of devices being created throughout the world.

Researchers and scientists are working on a number of interesting technologies, and at the same time, commercial firms are also pursuing their next design for products they hope will be a "breakthrough" revenue producer.

1.1.8   Fifth Generation—Challenges and Game Changers

Big data
Predictive analytics
3-D printing
Cloud computing
Wearable user interfaces
Mobile robotics
Neuron chip sets
Quantum computing
Internet of Things

Each of these items will shape the contours of our future, and each owes its potential to those historical efforts and research discoveries of the past years. Further, each of these items will have a very profound effect on our lives and on the computer industry and its personnel. Our privacy and security will continue to be challenged by these game-changing discoveries.

1.2 Dark Side of the Computer: Viruses, Trojans, and Attacks

A computer virus is computer code that is designed to insert itself into other software and, when executed, is able to replicate itself and propagate with the host software or file. Viruses can be designed to damage the infected host by corrupting files, stealing hard disk space or CPU time, logging keystrokes to steal passwords, creating embarrassing messages, and other activities all performed without the computer user's approval or knowledge. Early viruses were boot sector viruses and spread by computer users sharing infected floppy disks. Other viruses attached to e-mail or a part of the body of an e-mail, and when the code viruses were executed, a message with the virus embedded was sent to other mail clients. In some cases, the code could be designed to provide the scripts access to the user's address book and could, in turn, propagate and use those addresses to further propagate the virus-infected message. Other viruses were designed to be attached to data files such as word documents or spreadsheets. These scripts are visual basic code that can execute when the file is loaded, and once the virus has attached itself to an application, the code in the virus will run every time the application runs.[12]

Eugene H. Spafford notes that the first use of the term *virus* as referring to unwanted computer code was offered by Gregory Benford, a research physicist at the Lawrence Livermore Radiation Laboratory, who noticed that "bad code" could self-reproduce among laboratory computers and eventually got into the ARPANET.[13] However, John Von Newmann actually developed the theory of self-replicating programs in 1949. In 1983, Fred Cohen formally defined the term *computer virus*, and he created an example of the self-reproducing code and named it as a computer virus to describe a program that is created to affect other computer programs by modifying them to include a copy of itself in the program.

1.2.1 Development of Computer Viruses

1981—Elk Cloner virus
1986—The Brain virus
1999—Melissa virus
2000—I Love You virus
2001—Code Red virus
2002—Nimda virus
2003—Slammer virus
2004—My Doom virus

The Elk Cloner virus was written for Apple DOS 3.3 and spread via floppy disks; it displayed a short poem and was activated on its 50th use. The Elk Cloner virus was the first PC virus.

The Brain virus was the first worldwide virus to also spread by floppy disks, and the two brothers in Pakistan who wrote the virus did not intend for it to be a destructive virus, yet despite their intentions, it materialized into one.

The Melissa virus was based on a Microsoft Word Macro and was designed to infect e-mail messages by sending infected word documents to the first 50 people in a user's outlook list. The Melissa virus was reported to cause more than $50 million in damages to other computer users and businesses.

The I Love You virus infected millions of computers in a single day simply because the attachment stated "I Love You" and people's curiosity caused them to open the infected attachment, which, when opened, would copy itself in different files on the user's hard drive and also download a file that stole passwords from the victim.

The Code Red virus was directed to attack the U.S. White House as a distributed denial-of-service attack, but it was stopped before it could effect the attack. However, this virus did infect thousands of computers and caused over $1 billion dollars in damages. A second version, Code Red II, attacked Windows 2000 and Windows NT systems.

The Nimda virus was one of the fastest propagating viruses to enter the Internet, and its targets were Internet servers; it really worked as a worm and caused significant damage to many users.

The Slammer virus in 2003 was a Web server virus that also roamed through the Internet at incredible speed. Many corporations in both the financial services and airline industries suffered significant losses estimated in the range of several billion dollars.

The My Doom virus used a denial-of-service attack script and sent search engine requests for e-mail addresses, causing companies such as Google to receive millions of requests and severely slow down services and, in some cases, to close down companies.

Worms do not change other programs, but a worm is a computer program that has the ability to replicate itself from computer to computer and to cross over to network connections. It is important to stress that while worms do not change other programs, they may carry other code that does change programs, such as a true virus.[14]

In 2007, the "Storm" worm used social media approaches to fool computer users into situations where they loaded botnets into their computers, and Bruce Schneier reported that millions of computers were infected by this worm, which carried virus code as well.

A Trojan horse is a program that masquerades as a legitimate application while also performing a covert function. Trojan horse programs do not propagate on their own, so they rely on users to accept the executables from untrusted sources. Consequently, this becomes a major social engineering problem.[15]

1.2.2 Contemporary Threat Landscape

The previously discussed boot sector viruses, file viruses, and macro viruses were some of the earliest targets for virus designers. However, as we move to describe contemporary threat targets, we should also include multipartite viruses, stealth viruses, and polymorphic viruses. In addition to these very difficult viruses, we will also discuss toolkits for distribution of malware and other cyber attack modalities.

Multipartite viruses are a hybrid that can infect files in both the boot sector as well as program files. After the boot sector is infected, and when the system is booted, the multipartite viruses load into the memory and begin the process of infecting other files. As a result of their movement, these multipartite viruses are difficult to remove. If the multipartite virus is both dangerous and difficult to remove, the Stealth viruses are even more difficult to both identify and remove since they are designed to use specific methods to hide themselves from detection. Ankit Fadia describes their method as follows:

> ...They sometimes remove themselves from the memory temporarily to avoid detection and hide from virus scanners. Some can also redirect the disk head to read another sector instead of the sector in which they reside. Some Stealth viruses such as the Whale virus conceal the increase in the length of the infected file and display the original length by reducing the size by the same amount as that of the increase, so as to avoid detection from scanners. For example, the Whale virus adds 9216 bytes to an infected file and then the virus subtracts the same number of bytes, that is 9216, from the size given in the directory.[16]

Polymorphic viruses are the most difficult virus to identify because they are designed to mutate or change the viral code known as the signature each time they spread or infect files. Since antivirus software is created on the basis of the signature of the virus, it becomes almost impossible to be protected against the Polymorphic virus unless the antivirus software vendor has provided a new "patch" to guard against it.[17]

1.2.3 Threat Attacks

Spear-phishing
APT's-RSA SecurID attack
Zero-day vulnerabilities; Operation Aurora-Zero Day Malware Attack
Rootkit-Stuxnet; toolkits
Malware—Flame

Mobile malware
Botnets—DDoS; spam; click fraud
Bots—cyber crime applications

Spear-phishing attacks are more focused than the typical phishing attacks since the typical phishing attack is sent to thousands of people and usually displays a fake logo of an individual's bank asking for them to provide some information as to their log-in or to go to the site and change their password. On the other hand, spear-phishing attacks are more focused on specific individuals, usually at an executive level. Since Web pages provide so much information on companies and their personnel, it is available for those who wish to penetrate the corporate structure by studying and doing in-depth research on the potential target employee. Upon acquiring information as to the potential targets interests, hobbies, etc., the attacker begins to formulate an attack methodology so as to acquire the target employee's interest and confidence. For example, if the target employee is an avid sports car or football enthusiast, the attacker would design information that could be incorporated within an attachment that the target might be interested in obtaining further information about, under the expectation that by opening the file or attachment, the information would be provided. This attachment or link, when opened, would then install malware on the target employee's computer. The malware then installed on the host would await instructions from the command and control (C&C) server owned by the attacker. The attacker could take action immediately or could wait for another time, meanwhile having greater access to the entire corporation through the executive level employee. This spear-phishing attack is also useful to acquire information from government or military employees who could be vulnerable to the same type of attack.

APT attacks, or Advanced Persistent Threats, are sophisticated network attacks in which the attacker seeks to gain information and remain undetected for a substantial period of time, thus acquiring a great deal of information and knowledge on the target. It is certainly possible that a spear-phishing attack might provide the attacker this presence and opportunity. APT attacks are not designed to do damage, but to acquire information or modify data.

Zero-day vulnerabilities that may, at some point, become a zero-day attack are operationalized and successful when the attack is targeted against a software or hardware system's unknown vulnerability. Since the vulnerability is not recognized, a software patch or hardware fix has not yet been offered. The attacker seeks to discover the potential vulnerability, and if discovered, the attacker will keep this program vulnerability private until the time for the attack is determined to be most provident. In short, this search for an exploitable opportunity is to locate something new and totally unknown and to keep it secret until a future attack or decision to sell this information to other cyber criminals.

Rootkit is a set of tools that enable root- or administrator-level access to a computer system. The term *rootkit* has become synonymous with malware and is used to describe malware with rootkit capabilities. However, rootkit can be used for legitimate purposes as well as for malicious purposes. If rootkit is coded with malware to gain root access and take complete control of the computer's operating system and its attached hardware, and then to hide its presence in the system, we then have a very complex toolkit. The Stuxnet incident against the Iranian Natanz uranium enrichment facility was accomplished through the use of a rootkit that permitted entrance into the computer system and the planting of a very sophisticated computer worm used in the attack, which clearly fit the definition of an APT attack, since the attacker had to possess expertise in cyber intrusion methodologies and also was capable of designing state-of-the-art exploits and tools.

The RSA SecurID attack was also an Advanced Persistent Attack in 2011 that compromised RSA's two factor authentication token devices. Several Department of Defense contractor corporations were victimized by this attack, and depending on how long the attackers were inside their systems, we have no idea as to the level of data ex-filtration or knowledge that may have been collected by our adversaries responsible for this APT attack. It is generally assumed that Chinese People's Liberation Army authorities were responsible for this action.

Flame was perhaps one of the most serious attacks occurring in 2012, and it utilized C&C channels installed on servers to download very high-tech malware estimated to be 20 megabytes in size or at least 30 times larger than a typical computer virus. This APT attack was launched against the Iranian oil terminals to collect intelligence in preparation for cyber-sabotage programs designed to hamper and impede Iran's ability to develop nuclear weapons.[18]

Toolkits that are emerging as attack toolkits are software programs containing malicious code designed for both the novice and more experienced cyber-criminal to facilitate their ability to launch attacks against networked computers. An example of an attack toolkit that has been most effective in allowing cyber-criminals to steal bank account numbers from small businesses is named ZeuS, and in 2010, one group of cyber-criminals used ZeuS to acquire $70 million from online banking and trading accounts in an 18-month period. These attack toolkits are often sold on a subscription-based model with regular updates that extend both the exploitable capabilities as well as support services for the attack toolkit. The demand for these attack toolkits has increased since 2006, when some kits were sold for $100 or less. In 2010, ZeuS 2.0 was selling for $8000. Symantec's Security Technology and Response Team discovered 310,000 domains that were found to be malicious and resulted in 4.4 million malicious Web pages per month and 61% were attributed to attack toolkits.

The most prevalent attack kits are the following:

- MPack
- Neosploit
- ZeuS
- Nukesploit
- P4ck
- Phoenix

These attack kits are easy to update and are able to tell their cyber-criminal customers they can target potential victims before security vendors can apply the necessary security patches to prevent the attack.[19]

Mobile malware is now one of our most perplexing problems to address, particularly since more smart cell phones were sold in 2012 than computer laptops. The growing number of people using cell phones or tablets has created enormous problems for corporations as the BYOD (bring your own devices) has virtually overcome corporate Chief Information Officers (CIOs) to maintain any semblance of security for their information and data systems. Quite simply, the introduction of mobile malware brought into the corporate environment or government environment is exceedingly easy. It is not only the introduction of malware by these devices that is bringing problems into the Information systems, but it also is too easy to exfiltrate data since most smart devices have Bluetooth capabilities and near field communication (NFC) capabilities that automatically load data into their devices. In fact, Zitmo is the Trojan that can forward text messages with confidential information from a device to other phone numbers.

Zitmo is used by the cyber-criminal in the following manner: the cyber-criminal sends a text message that appears to look official requesting the targeted victim to update their security certificate or other software updates. The attached link that the targeted victim receives actually installs the Zitmo Trojan on to the victim's smartphone. If the victim executes this attached link, the Trojan returns the message to the cyber-criminal, who is now able to access the victim's bank records and possibly initiate transactions to transfer money from the targeted victims account to the cyber-criminal's account.

DroidKungFu is a malware that contains a rootkit permitting the cyber-criminal to have full control of the targeted victim's smart phone or mobile device. This Trojan is specifically targeted for devices using the Android operating system and is difficult to detect due to the rootkit malware that is capable of hiding the Trojan and attached malware. A cell phone virus does exactly what a computer virus can do to computers, and that is to send targeted victims executable files that infect the smart phone or mobile device.

The Symbian Operating System as well as Apple's Mobile Operating System (iOS) and Android have all been targeted by cyber-criminals to send viruses. CABIR was one of the first cell phone viruses, and Common Warrior followed as a more effective virus, but there are numerous viruses being prepared to take advantage of the large base of mobile users who now have interaction with corporate information and data systems.

Another difficulty is that software vendors have only recently begun preparing antivirus software for the smart phone market. The typical smart phone user is ignoring the need to install antivirus software. Shortly corporations, government agencies, and universities will have to address this problem of securing mobile devices that connect to their information and data systems. An approach that could be considered for establishing policies on mobile devices might contain some or all of the following restrictions:

- Devices must have current security patches.
- Devices must be password enabled.
- Two-factor authentication.
- Containerized capability.
- List of unauthorized Apps, such as "Jail Breaking" and "Rooting," and other Apps to be determined.
- Secure wireless access points and networks.
- Review BYOD policies annually and provide employees with copies of the policies.
- Initiate webinars informing employees of recent attacks and safe practices for the use of computer and Information systems.
- Have a recovery plan in place.

A very difficult challenge for CIOs, network managers, and Chief Information Security Officers (CISOs) regarding the number of BYOD brought into their information system environments is they simply do not know what devices are attaching to their network, and they clearly have no idea as to the types of applications that are running many of these BYOD devices. Further, so many of today's BYOD smart phones and tablets have embedded applications that will automatically seek out and transfer data to or from the device without the user even initiating the transfer action.

1.2.4 Botnets and Cyber Crime Applications

A botnet is not necessarily malicious as there are legitimate purposes and uses for automated programs that execute tasks without user intervention. However, botnets have recently gained notoriety for becoming a significant threat to the Internet due to the increasing malicious use of this technology by cyber-criminals. A botnet is a network of compromised computers that can be coordinated remotely by a cyber-criminal or an attacker to achieve an intended and malicious purpose. The malicious goal may range from initiating a distributed denial-of-service attack, spam attack, click fraud attack or simply renting out an attack service to individuals who may want to have some other person or entity attacked. Thus, the botnet is a network of computers already under the control of the individual who will function as the central entity to control and communicate with each machine. The host components are the compromised machines that are under the control of the Bot Master. The malicious agent that enables a compromised computer to be remotely controlled by the Bot Master is called a Bot Agent. A Bot Agent can be a standalone malware component such as an executable or dynamic link library file or code added to the malware code. The Bot Agent's main function is to be the communication link with the botnet network. This permits the Bot Agent to receive and interpret commands from the Bot Master and to send data back to the Bot Master or to execute attacks as a result of the Bot Master's instructions. The C&C channel is the critical online resource of the Bot Master that permits the control of the bots. Without the C&C channel, the Bot Master cannot direct the malicious activity of the bot. Since the strength of the bot resides in the number of compromised computers under the control of the Bot Master, one can appreciate how important computer security is, so that those acting as Bot Masters cannot add more compromised machines to their collection.[20]

Examples of the malicious use of botnets are found in distributed denial-of-service attacks where the compromised machines are all directed to attack a predetermined victim, corporation, or government entity at a specific time and date. The result of such a massive attack in a simultaneous manner will create a buffer overflow problem for the targeted site's servers and take their site and service down. This type of an attack can also be used to send volumes of spam to a designated target hit.

Click fraud is another example of how a Bot Master can direct their bots to specific sites for the purpose of collecting revenue from advertisers who pay to have potential customers click on their website. Since online advertisers pay for each click of the ads they have on websites, this provides an opportunity for the cyber-criminal to make money from this scheme. The following is an example of how the click fraud is executed.

First, the attacker puts up a website that contains only ads. The attacker then signs up with one or more ad affiliation program such as Google, Ad Sense, or Yahoo. Once arrangements between the ad affiliates and the attacker has been completed, the Bot Master then instructs the botnets under his control to click the ads on his website of ads. This action will trigger payments from online advertisers. Since they are ad affiliates, the payment will be coursed through Google or Yahoo.[21]

Another variation of this same theme is when an owner of a website that has legitimate software on their website contacts the Bot Master and requests the Bot Master to direct the bots to download the advertised software product. Since the software firm will pay the website owner for every downloaded installation of their product, this can result in a large profit to the website owner, especially if the Bot Master has thousands of computers under their control. In this situation, the website owner and the Bot Master both make money from the victimized software provider or firm. The Bot Master becomes a deployment agent or provider. As a deployment provider, the Bot Master can direct the bots to also use malicious software to attack an entity that may be requested by another individual who seeks to take revenge or secure some type of end result that can be accomplished by means of an underground agreement, which results in a "computer hit," an interesting variation of organized crime's "hit man."[22] The Bot Master who serves as a deployment provider can rent their services out to interested customers, and such sites do exist both on the Internet as well as "Deep Web" and "Silk Road."

The use of botnets is not limited to individual attackers since nation-states also envision applications and use for distributed denial-of-service attacks and cyber warfare applications. Other cyber offensive operations can include cyber espionage and cyber attacks against a critical infrastructure of a nation.

1.2.5   TOR and the Deep Web

We began this chapter discussing the historical development of the computer industry and the emergence of the Internet by 1997 after substantial research and investment of the federal government dating back to 1969. In 1996, the government was also funding research throughout the U.S. Naval Research Laboratory, which, by 2003, was released as the TOR ("the onion router") network referred to as the "onion router" due to the layers of encryption, which permitted the emergence of what is now referred to as the Deep Web. The Deep Web had a purpose of permitting law enforcement, military, and governmental organizations to use it for conducting their business in a private fashion or for intelligence and covert operations. Ironically, in 2006, the Deep Web was discovered by cyber-criminals and other actors who were using the Deep Web for illegal purposes such as the sale of drugs, the distribution of child pornography, and a variety of other illegal activities. Both illegal activities and the government covert operations were made possible by the levels of encryption that made it unlikely that the user of the Deep Web would be identified. In terms of the users of the Deep Web, it is instructive to note that there are 800,000 daily TOR users, downloading 30–50 million times a year in which TOR can access more than 6500 hidden websites.[23]

The extraordinary advancements in science and the power of technology and the Internet have enabled societies throughout the world to participate and share in this wealth of discoveries. There is, however, a dark side to the power of technology and the Internet, and this "dark side" appears when individuals choose to use it for criminal purposes such as child pornography, illegal drug sale and purchase, extortion, and other illegal acts. There is also a cost to society in terms of the growing loss of privacy and, perhaps worst of all, the distribution and sale of cyber weapons, which introduces a new scale of terrorism vulnerabilities.

1.3 Vulnerabilities, Risk Assessment, and Risk Management

In view of the increasing number of viruses and attack scenarios, it is incumbent on us to better understand the vulnerability and threat landscape. Risk management processes to protect financial assets, information databases, and intellectual property resources suggest that an active risk assessment process should be established to assist in the identification of how best to deploy security measures. Additionally, there exist a number of strategies for establishing risk mitigation processes as well. Both legal and insurance carriers need to be consulted in the creation of a sound and defensible strategy of both immediate and long-term protection of assets.

1.3.1 Mobile Devices and Smart Phones

The incredible growth of mobile devices has created a landscape vulnerability of immense proportion. The sheer number of these devices, the absence of any meaningful security being operationalized on the devices, and the increasing number of viruses designed for mobile apparatus have been extremely disconcerting. As malware continues to be developed and used in conjunction with botnet attacks, mobile devices are an attractive target for cyber-criminals. The expanding number of corporations and governmental agencies that permit mobile devices to enter their networks as part of a BYOD policy further enhances the vulnerability equation.

The NFC capability of many mobile devices is a vulnerability for both credit card users and merchant's point of sale (POS) terminals because the NFC-embedded chip on a card is in an "always on" state, which means that if a user's card is in the field of an active NFC reader, such as those NFC readers in a POS terminal, the credit card automatically transmits the user's credit card number to the receiving NFC reader. In many smart phones, the software or applications are designed to activate the mobile device's NFC chip to emulate the behavior of a POS terminal's NFC reader. Cyber-criminals can use a "Bump and Play" tactic where the attacker physically bumps into an unsuspecting user for the purpose of scanning their credit card to collect account numbers.[24]

1.3.2 Web Applications

Another continuing weakness, we must address centers on Web applications where we see the following vulnerabilities:

- Cross-site scripting
- Structured query language (SQL) injection
- Insufficient transport layer protection
- Security misconfiguration
- Broken authentication and session management
- Information leakage
- Improper error handling
- Insecure cryptograph storage

These and other insights are the result of Hewlett Packard's (HP's) review of thousands of assessments to ascertain the status of Web application security, and they concluded that many companies and individuals assume that their websites are of little interest to attackers, but in the experience of HP security teams, this is clearly not accurate, and they go on to state: "In fact, the lack of secure programming and IT security best practices only serve as an enabler for the proliferation of malware."[25] Notably, Internet security threats against websites have increased, and the volume and vector of website attacks in which multiple attack techniques are being employed to disrupt services on websites to compromise data or steal financial resources continue to grow with greater sophistication.

1.3.3 Social Media

Corporations and numerous other nongovernmental organizations have employees who are engaged in the use of social media tools. Governmental agencies, the military, and universities also have people who become actively engaged in the use of social media and can unknowingly create problems for their organization by mistakes that have very rapidly circulated to enormous numbers of people. Sometimes, problems emerge not only from a mistake but also because of calculated plans to either embarrass the organization or create a set of problems that can culminate in the loss of financial resources or respect and integrity to the impacted organization. The range of risk that social media can expose organizations to is now being carefully analyzed by use of risk assessment strategies. Typically, someone will be assigned responsibilities to develop a risk management program to identify the range of social media risk exposure and to assess the level of the potential risk and its impact on the organization. After determining whether the risk is present and its potential for harming the organization, the risk will have to be mitigated or managed.

The types of social media channels that are being used today have enormous numbers of adherents and followers who utilize the easy-to-use services provided by these social media channels. The channels by themselves are not the problem; it is those who use and take advantage of this social media who create the problems. Currently, the social media channels in use with high subscription numbers are as follows:

- Facebook
- Twitter
- YouTube
- Vimeo
- Flickr
- Picasa
- Foursquare
- Chatter
- Epinions
- LinkedIn

The range of potential risk to organizations as a result of social media channel subscribers either making inadvertent mistakes or making calculated efforts to harm or embarrass others can result in the following:

- Reputational damage
- Release of confidential information
- Loss of intellectual property
- Disclosure of personal information
- Identity theft
- Hijacking another person's identity off a social media channel
- Malware attack
- Reduced employee productivity
- Defamation of character

In an excellent study by the Altimeter Group, they presented a very important risk management process for addressing the issues of social media risk. Their study discussed and outlined the process for identifying risk, assessing the risk, managing the risk, and monitoring risk vulnerabilities in the future. It also illustrated how to create a decision framework and analysis of risks with the pathway for creating a social media team. The need for an organization to establish social media policies and monitor situations that may necessitate when they update or modify the policies is important and is clearly presented in Altimeter Group's study.[26]

1.3.4 Cloud Computing

The term *Back to the Future* can be applied to the development of cloud computing. Some observers believe that cloud computing evokes a perception of accessing and storing both software and data in the cloud as a representation of the Internet or a network and using associated services. Krutz and Vines suggest that it only represents a modernization of the "time-sharing" model of computing that was the model of computing in the 1960s before the advent of lower-cost computing platforms. The time-sharing model was replaced by a "client-server" model and evolved into the PC, which placed large amounts of computing power at the desktop of the computer user and, in effect, eliminated the time-sharing model of computing. Cloud computing has many of the metered elements of the former time-sharing computing model; however, it also has some challenging new features that many regard as a new future computing model.

Peter Mell and Tim Grance of the National Institute of Standards and Technology define cloud computing as follows: "Cloud computing is a model for enabling convenient, on-demand network access to a shared pool of configurable and reliable computing resources (e.g., networks, servers, storage, applications, services) that can be rapidly provisioned and released with minimal consumer management effort or service provider interaction."[27]

Krutz and Vines observe that the cloud model is composed of six essential characteristics, three service models, and four deployment models. They identify the essential characteristics of cloud computing as follows:

- On-demand self-service
- Ubiquitous network access
- Resource pooling
- Location independence
- Measured service
- Rapid elasticity

The service models are described as follows:

SaaS—Cloud software as a service, in which the provider's applications are provided over a network

PaaS—Cloud platform as a service, in which one deploys customer created applications to a cloud

IaaS—Cloud infrastructure as a service, in which one rents processing, storage, network capacity, and other fundamental computing resources

These four deployment models can be either internally or externally implemented as follows:

Private Cloud—enterprise owned or leased
Public Cloud—sold to the public, megascale infrastructure
Hybrid Cloud—composed of two or more clouds
Community Cloud—shared infrastructure for a specific community[28]

The public cloud offers computing services to the general public, accessible via an Internet connection and shared among thousands of customers. Examples of a public cloud would be Amazon Web services, Microsoft Windows, and Rackspace Cloud. On the other hand, private clouds are typically created and hosted by a single organization, usually behind the corporate firewall, and they provide services to employees. Private clouds can also be hosted by third parties, but they remain dedicated to a single customer. Private clouds will cost more than a public cloud, but they offer greater control over the data. The private cloud configuration provides the owner or user full knowledge of the geographic location and, in most cases, the totality of computing resources. The public cloud may well have its geographical location and computing resources anywhere in the world, and the user may not have knowledge of either the location or computing resources unless specified by contractual language.[29]

Security of one's data and intellectual property is a principal concern when entrusting one's data and information to geographically dispersed cloud platforms not under the direct control of your organization. Depending on which cloud model is selected for use, the burden of security may remain with the customer or it could fall on the cloud provider. In any event, carefully prepared contractual language will be necessary to reflect who is responsible for computer security, what level of protection is being provided, and what performance record the cloud provider has against computer security threats. Also, does the cloud provider meet the security standards of confidentiality, integrity and availability, governance, risk management, and compliance?

Despite all the benefits cloud computing provides to its customers and users, it also brings an array of issues that must be addressed around computer security and privacy of information as a result of the size, structure, and geographical dispersion. The potential vulnerabilities are as follows:

- Leakage and unauthorized access of data among virtual machines running on the same server
- Failure of a cloud provider to properly handle and protect sensitive information
- Release of critical and sensitive data to law enforcement and government agencies without the approval or knowledge of the client

- Ability to meet compliance and regulatory requirements
- System crashes and failure that make the cloud service unavailable for extended periods of time
- Hackers breaking into client applications hosted on the cloud and acquiring and distributing sensitive information
- The robustness of the security protections instituted by the cloud provider
- The degree of interoperability available so that a client can easily move applications among different cloud providers and avoid "lock-in provisions"[30]

Cloud computing offers many new opportunities, but it also brings many new disruptive changes to the entire computer industry.

1.3.5 Big Data

The term *big data* actually entails much more than simply the size of data or a database as it encompasses the technologies, hardware, software, and the analytical capabilities to offer judgments and predictions regarding the collection and use of data. Big data and the processes involved address issues such as how one stores data in both its structured and unstructured format and how to process this massive amount of data that is now being created. So the issue becomes one of understanding how and where data are being created and how to store these data since relational database technology cannot absorb and process the unstructured data being generated because these require new database formats. The retrieval of massive amounts of both structured and unstructured data requires computer processing capabilities that are more than a mainframe-based approach, as the requirements for massive data processing require Hadoop cluster computer processing, which is a unified storage and processing environment that is scalable to large and very complex data volumes.

To appreciate the difference between structured and unstructured data, one only has to recall that structured data are data that are contained in spreadsheets or relational databases and adhere to the SQL, which is an international standard for defining and accessing relational databases. This standard provides an accepted process for storing, processing, and accessing data by defining how data will be stored consistently with commonly accepted international standards. On the other hand, unstructured data are data that most will recognize as digital photographs, video, graphical images, sound bites, and any other number of presentations from social media that do not enjoy a common reference point of storage and accessibility based on a common set of standards such as structured data technology. Therefore, unstructured data will require a new format for database processing, as they will not be accommodated by current relational database technology. This is precisely why the emergence of Hadoop technology is so critical to the processing of what is now being categorized as big data.

Big data is generally viewed by three main categories: its volume, velocity, and variety. In fact, Douglas Laney first articulated these categories for big data, and examples of applications within each category provide insight as to the emerging massive shift that is occurring within the computer industry.

1. Volume: many factors contribute to the increase in data volume. The emergence of a digital environment from the previous analog environment created incredible amounts of unstructured data, basically originating from social media and machine to machine data generated by sensors. To place this into perspective Chris Forsyth, notes the following:

   ...A typical passenger jet that generates ten terabytes of information per engine every thirty minutes of a flight, in a single six hour flight from New York to Los Angeles on a twin-engine Boeing 737 the total amount of data generated is a massive 240 terabytes of data. With the total number of commercial flights approaching 30,000 in the U.S. on any given day, a day's worth of sensor data quickly climbs into the petabyte scale. Multiply that by weeks, months, and years and the number is colossal.[31]

   Digital data exist everywhere, especially generated by social media, mobile phones, and networked sensor nodes present in transportation, automobiles, industrial plants, and utility companies using the smart grid. With over 50 million networked sensors in operation and more than 60% of the world's population using mobile phones and interacting with various social media channels, the amount of unstructured data being generated is phenomenal. A recent report by the McKinsey Global Institute states that big data is a growing torrent with over 30 billion pieces of content shared on Facebook every month. Social media sites, smart phones, and other consumer devices including PCs and laptops have allowed billions of individuals around the world to contribute to the amount of big data being produced each day of the year.[32]

   Another perspective on understanding unstructured data and their volume being produced can be appreciated by the number of blogs on social networking sites, geo-location devices in use, the bar codes being read by merchants, x-rays, phone conversations, video, text messages, ads, and numerous other methods in which data are being produced, acquired, and stored.[33]

2. Data velocity refers to the unprecedented speed in which machine-to-machine data are created and move between millions of sensors that are contained in a variety of consumer electronics, home appliances, automobiles, public utility equipment such as the smart grid, and other applications. These data are in constant movement and are, in reality, a digital stream of data that have to be both managed and secured. Another example of how a large volume of data moves with a velocity of speed occurs daily within our stock markets and financial institutions, where high-frequency stock trading algorithms reflect market changes and must be captured within microseconds. A recent report by Symantec noted the following:

...a large credit card company gained a competitive edge with the advanced analytics from Hadoop by reporting they reduced the process time for seventy-three billion transactions amounting to thirty-six terabytes of data, from one month with traditional methods to a mere thirteen minutes.[34]

3. Variety of big data is generated in both formats of structured and unstructured data feeds, so the data are not only just numbers, dates, or strings but also geo-spatial and video must be stored, processed, integrated in both formats, and then analyzed for its best use. Massive databases that may have taken days or hours in the past to complete may now be completed in minutes or seconds.

Big data is really a term that describes a new generation of technologies and architectures that are designed to extract value from very large volumes of a variety of data sources by enabling high-velocity capture, processing, and, ultimately, analysis. The emergence of big data is about more than deploying a new application or software technology such as Hadoop. It really represents a very significant new information technology domain that, over time, will continue to make incredible advancements, which will, in turn, require new system designs and new skill sets of the personnel working within this domain.[35]

In short, big data is ushering in a most transformative range of changes to the computer industry. These changes will be experienced throughout the world in virtually all organizations and will literally impact billions of people.

The Simons Institute for the Theory of Computing at the University of California-Berkeley noted the following with reference to the theoretical foundation of big data analysis:

The Big Data phenomenon presents opportunities and perils. On the optimistic side of the coin, massive data may amplify the inferential power of algorithms that have been shown to be successful on modest-sized data sets. The challenge is to develop the theoretical principles needed to scale inference and learning algorithms to massive, even arbitrary, scale. On the pessimistic side of the coin, massive data may amplify the error rates that are part and parcel of any inferential algorithm. The challenge is to control such errors even in the face of the heterogeneity and uncontrolled sampling processes underlying many massive data sets. Another major issue is that Big Data problems often come with time constraints, where a high-quality answer that is obtained slowly can be less useful than a medium-quality answer that is obtained quickly. Overall we have a problem in which the classical resources of the theory of computation—e.g., time, space and energy—trade off in complex ways with the data resource.[36]

There is another question that demands further research into the big data era and that will focus on research into the security vulnerabilities that massive big data is introducing into our environments. Will it be easier for cyber attackers to design malware and place it into computing systems, since computer security measures will have to respond to big data as a new threat landscape? Also of concern will be the question of privacy. How will big data impact privacy and what research measures will be designed to weigh the benefits and costs of this incredible new system of technologies?

1.4   Emerging Field of Cybersecurity

From the computer's inception, no thought was given to the necessity of creating computer security programs for it. After all, the development of this field was by scientists, engineers, physicists, and mathematicians. Their work was designed to create and usher in new ways to improve the research and scientific communities' trust, and a set of social values and mores were within the very fabric of their cumulative work. It never occurred to them that one day, people would be inclined to abuse their discoveries or to even use them for immoral, illegal, or criminal purposes. The challenges were never anticipated; consequently, computer security was not built into these technologies. However, after the late 1980s, it was apparent to some that computers would need to have security capabilities. Interestingly, the security on most devices was placed in a default mode, and when it became more apparent that security was necessary for this field, changes in hardware have slowly evolved. Hardware was not the sole security vulnerability, as the software also had security problems. Eventually, encryption emerged as a technique that could protect information data stored within our databases.

Because there emerged viruses, worms, and malware, an industry was created to provide software solutions to protect computer users from these viruses and malware. As the virus and malware designers became more sophisticated in products they were making, the industry has always been in a position of reaction and trying to catch up with the malware designs. The irony is centered on how little it costs to design a virus and how incredibly expensive it is to develop antivirus tools to protect against these viruses.

In addition to an industry committed to creating antivirus tools, we have also witnessed the emergence of major corporations developing both computer security functions as well as computer forensic investigation teams. Since computer fraud, abuse, and theft of intellectual property have now reached a level capable of destroying entire companies, there is a national interest in protecting our information assets.

Since 1984, the federal government has been encouraging industries and our corporations to address the issue of securing their assets, data, and intellectual property. The corporate sector has historically pushed back from these government recommendations and urging because they viewed information systems as cost centers, and since American corporation's executives focused more on quarterly profit and loss statements, they were more interested in profit centers not, cost centers. Another area of corporate push back emerged over the concern of the Freedom of Information Act and also the costs involved in litigation.

After 9/11, many American corporations began to take the security of their data more seriously, and slowly, some movement has been made to offer additional security of their information assets and intellectual property. The wholesale loss of incredible amounts of intellectual property attributed to both Chinese and Russian entities has finally alerted our corporate community. Presidents Clinton, George W. Bush, and Obama have consecutively and consistently called on our corporate community to increase their computer and information security, and we are now seeing action to effect some improvements in these areas.

1.4.1 Framework for Improving Critical Infrastructure Cybersecurity

On February 12, 2014, the National Institute of Standards and Technology issued a report to guide our nation in improving our critical infrastructures. This report was issued as a result of President Obama's Executive Order 13636 regarding efforts to improve our nation's critical infrastructure cybersecurity. Because the national and economic security of the United States depends on the reliable functioning of our critical infrastructure, and since cybersecurity threats exploit the increased complexity and connectivity of our critical infrastructure systems, placing our nation's security, economy, public safety, and health at risk, the Executive Order created a new cybersecurity framework. This framework enables organizations, regardless of size or degree of cybersecurity risk, to apply the following framework core elements, which consist of functions that are envisioned as outcomes:

- Identify
- Protect
- Detect
- Respond
- Recover

These five functions are designed to organize basic cybersecurity activities at their most critical levels. A structure is provided that both advises and guides the management of risk while providing an assessment strategy to address and manage cybersecurity threats and incidents.[37] In short, it is hoped that the National Institute of Standards and Technology Framework for Improving Critical Infrastructure Cybersecurity will become a standard across all major industries and corporations to improve their cybersecurity.

1.4.2   Risk and Threat Assessment

The U.S. Department of Homeland Security has adopted the Threat Agent Risk Assessment methodology as designed by the Intel Corporation. Intel's predictive methodology establishes priorities on areas of concern and then targets the most critical exposure to identify and manage the information security risk. As part of the prediction capability, Intel developed a standardized Threat Agent Library that is used to identify the most likely attack vectors. Thus, their Threat Agent Risk Assessment is used to measure current threat risks. Their methodology then quantifies those threat agents that exceed baseline acceptable risks. An analysis is made of the attacker's objectives and then what attack methods might be anticipated. By preestablishing the known areas of exposure, this process then allows the alignment of a strategy to target the most significant exposures and to apply controls in a direct fashion, not simply across the range of all weak points.[38]

1.5   Summary

The challenge confronting professionals in their effort to improve the state of our cybersecurity is an enormous responsibility, and significant research must be performed to move these efforts forward. Clearly, the early industry solutions to computer security problems were not solved by firewalls, virus scans, authentication credentials, intrusion detection programs, encryption, and cryptography. As impressive as these programs and efforts have been, much more remains to be done to offer greater security to the vast number of people who rely on the tools and technologies of our computer industry. From an historical reference point, one can see how the technology of the computer industry has increased in such exponential terms. This has resulted in major improvements to our society and to the health and welfare of so many citizens. At the same time, we can also observe the very sophisticated viruses, malware, and attacks that have occurred on our cyber systems. We must continue to focus our efforts to improve our research and development role in addressing these new and emerging challenges.

Notes and References

1. Hicks Jr., *Information Systems in Business: An Introduction*, Second Edition, @ 1990 South-Western, a part of Cengage Learning Inc. Reproduced by permission. http://www.cengage.com/permissions, 433.
2. Ibid., 434–435.
3. Ibid., 435–436.
4. Ibid., 437.
5. Ibid., 438–439.
6. Ibid., 439–440.
7. Ibid., 447–448.
8. Denning and Denning, *Internet Besieged: Countering Cyberspace Scofflaws*, 15–16.
9. Ibid., 16–17.
10. Ibid., 18–19.
11. Loc. Cit.
12. Cole, Krutz and Conley, *Network Security Bible*, 146.
13. Spafford, "Computer Viruses," in D. Denning and P Denning, *Internet Besieged: Countering Cyberspace Scofflaws*, 74.
14. Ibid., 76.
15. Cole, Krutz and Conley, Ibid., 147.
16. Fadia, *Unofficial Guide to Ethical Hacking*, 434.
17. Loc. Cit.
18. Piper, "Definitive Guide to Next Generation Threat Protection: Winning the War Against the New Breed of Cyber-Attacks," 20.
19. "Symantec's Cyber-Attack Tool Kits Dominate Threat Landscape," 1–3.
20. Elisan, *Malware, Rootkits and Botnets: A Beginner's Guide*, 56–59.
21. Ibid., 66.
22. Ibid., 68.
23. Grossman and Newton-Small, "The Deep Web," in *Time: The Secret Web, Where Drugs, Porn and Murder Hide Online*, 28–31.
24. Hewlett Packard, "White Paper: HP 2012 Cyber Risk Report," 19–20.
25. Ibid., 2–6, 22.
26. Webber, Li and Szymanski, "Guarding the Social Gates: The Imperative for Social Media Risk Management," 4–7, 12–14.
27. Krutz and Vines, *Cloud Security: A Comprehensive Guide to Secure Cloud Computing*, 2.
28. Loc. Cit.

29. Grimes, "Staying Secure in the Cloud," in *Cloud Security: A New Model for the Cloud Era*, 2.
30. Krutz and Vines, op. cit., xxiii–xxiv.
31. Forsyth and Chitor, "For Big Data Analytics There's No Such Thing as Too Big: The Compelling Economics and Technology of Big Data Computing," 19.
32. Manyika, Chui and Brown et al., "Big Data: The Next Frontier for Innovation, Competition and Productivity," 1–2.
33. Forsyth and Chitor, op. cit., 5.
34. Symantec, "Better Backup for Big Data," 1.
35. Borovick and Villars, "The Critical Role of the Network in Big Data Applications," 1–2.
36. Simons Institute for the Theory of Computing, "Theoretical Foundations of Big Data Analysis," 1.
37. National Institute of Standards and Technology, *Framework for Improving Critical Infrastructure Cybersecurity*, 7–9.
38. Rosenquist, "Prioritizing Information Security Risks with Threat Agent Risk Assessment," 1–5.

Bibliography

Borovick, L., and Villars, R. "The Critical Role of the Network in Big Data Applications." White Paper IDC Analyze the Future. Massachusetts: International Data Corporation, February 2012.

Cole, E., Krutz, R., and Conley, J. W. *Network Security Bible*. Indiana: Wiley Publishing, Inc., 2005.

Denning, D. E., and Denning, P. J. *Internet Besieged: Countering Cyberspace Scofflaws*. New York: Addison-Wesley, ACM Press, 1998.

Elisan, C. C. *Malware, Rootkits and Botnets: A Beginners Guide*. New York: McGraw Hill, 2013.

Fadia, A. *Unofficial Guide to Ethical Hacking*. MacMillan India, Ltd.: Premier Press, 2001.

Forsyth, C., and Chitor, R. "For Big Data Analytics There's No Such Thing as Too Big: The Competing Economics and Technology of Big Data Computing." White Paper. San Jose, CA: Forsyth Communications, March 2012.

Grimes, R. "Staying Secure in the Cloud." In *Cloud Security: A New Model for the Cloud Era*. San Francisco: InfoWorld Deep Dive Series, 2013.

Grossman, L., and Newton-Small, J. "The Deep Web." In *Time: The Secret Web, Where Drugs, Porn and Murder Hide Online*, November 11, 2013.

Hewlett Packard, "White Paper: HP 2012 Cyber Risk Report." Contributors: Haddix, J., Hein, B., Hill, P., Hils, A., Jaydale, P., Lancaster, J., Muthurajan, S. S., Painter, M., Pril, J., Sechman, J., Strecker, R., and Timpe, J., Informationweek.com; UBM Tech: San Francisco, 2013.

Hicks, J. O., Jr. *Information Systems in Business: An Introduction*, Second Edition. South-Western, a part of Cengage Learning Inc., Farmington Hills, MI, 1990. Reproduced by permission. Available at http://www.cengage.com/permissions.

Krutz, R. L., and Vines, R. D. *Cloud Security: A Comprehensive Guide to Secure Cloud Computing*. Indiana: Wiley Publishing Company, 2010.

Manyika, J., Chui, M., Brown, B., Bughin, J., Dobbs, R., Roxburgh, C., and Byers, A. H. "Big Data: The New Frontier for Innovation, Competition and Productivity." New York: McKinsey Global Institute, May 2011.

National Institute of Standards and Technology. "Framework for Improving Critical Infrastructure Cybersecurity, Version 1.0." Washington, DC: US Government Printing Office, February 12, 2014.

Piper, S. "Definitive Guide to Next Generation Threat Protection: Winning the War Against the New Breed of Cyber-Attacks." Maryland: Cyberedge Group, LLC, 2013.

Rosenquist, M. "Prioritizing Information Security Risks with Threat Agent Risk Assessment." IT@Intel, White Paper. Santa Clara, CA: Intel Corporation, December 2009.

Security Technology and Response Organization. "Symantec's Cyber-Attack Tool Kits Dominate Threat Landscape." California: Symantec Corporation, 2011.

Simons Institute for the Theory of Computing. "Theoretical Foundations of Big Data Analysis." Berkeley, CA: University of California–Berkeley, December 2013.

Spafford, E. H. "Computer Viruses," in Denning, D. E., and Denning, P. J. eds., *Internet Besieged: Countering Cyberspace Scofflaws*. New York: Addison-Wesley, ACM Press, 1998.

Symantec. "Better Backup for Big Data." California: Symantec World Headquarters, 2012.

Webber, A., Li, C., and Szymanski, J. "Guarding the Social Gates: The Imperative for Social Media Risk Management." California: Altimeter Group, 2012.

Critical Infrastructures, Key Assets
A Target-Rich Environment

2

THOMAS A. JOHNSON

Contents

2.1 Introduction

Our nation's 16 critical infrastructures have made us a world power, yet as much wealth and power as we have derived from these infrastructures, we must also recognize our vulnerabilities should they become the target of an attack. Clearly, not every one of our 16 infrastructures is vulnerable to a cyber attack; however, those critical infrastructures that are vulnerable to a cyber attack contain some of our nation's most critical assets and resources. The phenomenal advances made in digital electronics are creating opportunities for both scientific advancements as well as dysfunctional consequences, as a result of dual-use capabilities. On one hand, these advances in our digital electronics can enhance productivity, introduce new scientific inventions, and improve the quality of life. On the other hand, these same advancements and discoveries in digital electronics could be weaponized and used to target individuals, infrastructures, and nations.

Our nation's military strength and power have virtually eliminated any other nation or world power from successfully attacking us with their military assets. This was the prevailing view, along with the assessment that our nation was more vulnerable to an asymmetric attack, an attack not on our military but on our critical infrastructure. Today, we still confront the vulnerability of an asymmetric attack on any one of our critical infrastructures, and because of the advancements made in digital electronics, we now must contemplate an attack by a cyber weapon. Cyber weapons can today be part of another nation's military capabilities and assets, and most disturbingly, cyber weapons can also be a part of an individual or group of individuals who now have a capability of launching unbelievable attacks on other individuals or nations. These cyber attacks can also be initiated as though they were launched through another country, thus making both defense mechanisms and counterattack strategies extremely difficult.

2.1.1 President's Commission on Critical Infrastructure Protection (Executive Order 13010)—President Clinton

Our nation's first concerns regarding the vulnerability of our critical infrastructures becoming targeted by terrorists occurred in 1996, when President Clinton issued an Executive Order (EO) that resulted in the establishment of the President's Commission on Critical Infrastructure Protection. EO 13010 stated that "certain national infrastructures are so vital that their incapacity or destruction would have a debilitating impact on the defense or economic security of the United States." EO 13010 listed those infrastructures considered to be the most critical as follows:

- Telecommunications
- Electrical power systems
- Gas and oil storage and transportation

- Banking and finance
- Transportation
- Water supply systems
- Emergency services (including medical, police, and fire)
- Continuity of government[1]

2.1.2 Presidential Decision Directive-63—President Clinton

As a result of this important EO and in response to the President's Commission on Critical Infrastructure Protection's final report, President Clinton signed Presidential Decision Directive-63 (PDD-63) on May 22, 1998. The significance of PDD-63 was to establish a national capability within five years to protect our "critical" infrastructure from intentional disruption. Most importantly, this Directive included, for the first time, not only physical systems but also cyber-based systems essential to the minimum operations of the economy and government.[2]

2.1.3 Office of Homeland Security (EO 13228)— President George W. Bush

Three years after President Clinton enacted PDD-63 to identify and strengthen our nation's critical infrastructures, our nation experienced the 9/11 attack. After this terror attack, President Bush signed a new EO relating to critical infrastructure protection. This new EO 13228, signed on October 8, 2001, established, for the first time, the Office of Homeland Security, and among the many duties assigned to the Office of Homeland Security, it was to coordinate efforts to protect:

- Energy production, transmission, and distribution services and critical facilities;
- Other utilities;
- Telecommunications;
- Facilities that produce, use, store, or dispose of nuclear material;
- Publicly and privately owned information systems;
- Special events of national significance;
- Transportation, including railways, highways, shipping ports, and waterways;
- Airports and civilian aircraft; and
- Livestock, agriculture, and systems for the provision of water and food for human use and consumption.

This list, for the first time, included nuclear sites, special events, and agriculture sectors, which were added from President Clinton's 1998 PDD-63.

Eight days after the October 8, 2001, EO 13228 by President Bush, he issued EO 13231, which established the President's Critical Infrastructure Board and focused its duties almost singularly on our nation's information infrastructure. Most importantly, this EO stressed the importance of information systems as they relate to other critical infrastructures:

- Telecommunications
- Energy
- Financial services
- Manufacturing
- Water
- Transportation
- Health care
- Emergency services[3]

2.1.4   USA Patriot Act (Public Law 107-56)—U.S. Congress

Presidential directives and EOs were critical due to the importance of their implementation. The next major series of acts were initiated by Congress in response to the terror attacks of 9/11. The USA Patriot Act of 2001, known as Public Law 107-56, was enacted to deter and punish terrorist acts not only in the United States but also throughout the world. This act enhanced law enforcement investigative tools and also added the category of "key resources," which were defined as essential to the minimal operations of the economy and government. Following the USA Patriot Act was the July 2002 issuance of the National Strategy for Homeland Security, which expanded on the USA Patriot Act by classifying specific infrastructure sectors as critical and listed the following critical infrastructure sectors:

- Agriculture
- Food
- Water
- Public health
- Emergency services
- Government
- Defense industrial base
- Information and telecommunications
- Energy
- Transportation
- Banking and finance
- Chemical industry
- Postal and shipping

In essence, this listing added to the previous EO 13228 the chemical industry and the postal and shipping services due to their economic importance. Also, most importantly, the national strategy discussed for the first time how our "cyber infrastructure" was clearly connected to, but was distinct from, the physical infrastructure and that the Department of Homeland Security "will place an especially high priority on protecting our cyber infrastructure."[4]

2.1.5 Homeland Security Presidential Directive-7— President George W. Bush

The next major directive addressing our nation's critical infrastructure occurred on December 17, 2003 when President Bush issued HSPD-7, known as the Homeland Security Presidential Directive-7, which clarified executive agency responsibilities for identifying, prioritizing, and protecting the critical infrastructure. This directive ordered the Department of Homeland Security and other federal agencies to collaborate with appropriate private sector entities. HSPD-7 also identified and prepared a list of the lead agencies and their corresponding critical infrastructures, and it also stated that the list could be expanded. The lead agencies and critical infrastructures are presented under the authority of HSPD-7 as follows:

Lead Agency	Critical Infrastructure
Department of Homeland Security	Information technology
	Telecommunications
	Chemicals
	Transportation systems, including mass transit, aviation, maritime, ground/surface, and rail and pipeline systems
	Emergency services
	Postal and shipping services
Department of Agriculture	Agriculture, food (meat, poultry, egg products)
Department of Health and Human Services	Public health, health care, and food (other than meat, poultry, egg products)
Environmental Protection Agency	Drinking water and waste water treatment systems
Department of Energy	Energy, including the production, refining, storage, and distribution of oil and gas, and electric power (except for commercial nuclear power facilities)
Department of the Treasury	Banking and finance
Department of the Interior	National monuments and icons
Department of Defense	Defense industrial base

Homeland Security Presidential Directive-7.[5]

2.1.6 Presidential Policy Directive-21—President Obama

On February 12, 2013, President Obama released Presidential Policy Directive-21 (PPD-21) to enhance and strengthen our national unity of effort to maintain and secure our critical infrastructures. PPD-21 recognized our nation's critical infrastructure as being both diverse and complex, and it includes our distributed networks, different organizational structure, and operating models that function in both the physical space and cyberspace. Our critical infrastructures are both governmental and private, some with multinational ownership. This PPD stated that our critical infrastructures must be secure and able to withstand and rapidly recover from a range of hazards, and as such, we must provide for prevention, protection, mitigation, response, and recovery. In short, our nation's efforts shall have plans and programs to reduce vulnerabilities, minimize consequences, identify and disrupt threats, and increase response and recovery efforts related to our critical infrastructure.[6]

This new PPD-21 Directive identified the Secretary of the Homeland Security Department as both the person and the agency with fixed responsibility to promote national unity of effort and to coordinate the overall federal effort to promote the security and resilience of our nation's critical infrastructures. In addition to the previous responsibilities of the Secretary of Homeland Security, the Secretary is now required to both identify and prioritize physical and cyber threat vulnerabilities and, in coordination with the respective sector agencies, detail the consequences of a threatened attack. Also, the Secretary is to maintain National Critical Infrastructure Centers. This PPD-21 stated that there shall be two National Critical Infrastructure Centers operated by the Department of Homeland Security, one center for physical infrastructure and the second for the cyber infrastructure. Both centers are to function in an integrated manner and serve as focal points for critical infrastructure partners to obtain situational awareness and actionable information to protect the physical and cyber aspects of our critical infrastructure.[7]

Another important federal responsibility centered on the development of the National Cyber Investigative Joint Task Force (NCIJTF) operated by the Federal Bureau of Investigation, in which the NCIJTF serves as a multiagency national focal point for coordinating, integrating, and sharing pertinent information related to cyber threat investigations. The National Cyber Investigative Task Force has representation from the Department of Homeland Security, the intelligence community, the Department of Defense, and other agencies as appropriate. The Attorney General and the Secretary of the Homeland Security Department shall collaborate to carry out their respective critical infrastructure missions.[8]

Another important new responsibility the PPD-21 provided was to address the need for innovation and research and development (R&D), and it stated the following:

The Secretary of Homeland Security, in coordination with the Office of Science and Technology Policy (OSTP), the Sector Specific Agencies (SSAs), Department of Commerce (DOC), and other federal departments and agencies, shall provide input to align those federal and federally-funded research and development (R&D) activities that seek to strengthen the security and resilience of the nation's critical infrastructure, including:

1. Promoting R&D to enable the secure and resilient design and construction of critical infrastructure and more secure accompanying cyber technology;
2. Enhancing modeling capabilities to determine potential impacts on critical infrastructure of an incident or threat scenario, as well as cascading effects on other sectors;
3. Facilitating initiatives to incentivize cybersecurity investments and the adoption of critical infrastructure design features that strengthen all-hazards security and resilience; and
4. Prioritizing efforts to support the strategic guidance issued by the Secretary of Homeland Security.[9]

PPD-21, issued by President Obama, revoked the Homeland Security Presidential Directive HSPD-7, Critical Infrastructure Identification, Prioritization, and Protection EO previously issued on December 17, 2003, by President George W. Bush. However, it was specified that plans developed under HSPD-7 shall remain in effect until specifically revoked or superseded. The new PPD-21 identified the following 16 critical infrastructure sectors and SSAs as follows:

Designated Critical Infrastructure Sectors and SSAs: This directive identifies 16 critical infrastructure sectors and designates associated federal SSAs; in some cases, co-SSAs are designated, where those departments share the roles and responsibilities of the SSA. The Secretary of Homeland Security shall periodically evaluate the need for and approve changes to critical infrastructure sectors and shall consult with the Assistant to the President for Homeland Security and Counterterrorism before changing a critical infrastructure sector or a designated SSA for that sector. The sectors and SSAs are as follows:

Chemical: SSA: Department of Homeland Security
Commercial Facilities: SSA: Department of Homeland Security
Communications: SSA: Department of Homeland Security
Critical Manufacturing: SSA: Department of Homeland Security
Dams: SSA: Department of Homeland Security
Defense Industrial Base: SSA: Department of Defense

Emergency Services: SSA: Department of Homeland Security
Energy: SSA: Department of Energy
Financial Services: SSA: Department of the Treasury
Food and Agriculture: Co-SSAs: U.S. Department of Agriculture and Department of Health and Human Services
Government Facilities: Co-SSAs: Department of Homeland Security and General Services Administration
Health Care and Public Health: SSA: Department of Health and Human Services
Information Technology: SSA: Department of Homeland Security
Nuclear Reactors, Materials, and Waste: SSA: Department of Homeland Security
Transportation Systems: Co-SSAs: Department of Homeland Security and Department of Transportation
Water and Wastewater Systems: SSA: Environmental Protection Agency[10]

2.2   Critical Infrastructure Interdependencies

Pederson, Dudenhoeffer, Hartley, and Permann's important research on critical infrastructure interdependency suggest that most critical infrastructure systems interact through a connectivity that can occur as a result of policies, procedures, or direct proximity. Their research at the Idaho National Laboratory discovered that these interactions create complex relationships, dependencies, and interdependencies that cross infrastructure boundaries. This important research concluded that our ability to provide protection to our critical infrastructure systems is dependent on a more thorough and well-reasoned comprehension of how interdependencies exist between our infrastructure systems. Their research focused on what actually are the infrastructure interdependencies and how they are modeled. Further, their research on modeling the effect that one infrastructure can have on another infrastructure can be assessed by their interdependencies with first-order effects, second-order effects, and third-order effects. For example, in their study of the electrical power infrastructure, they identified the factors and forces that contributed to a recent energy crisis in California. Their analysis followed a model of first-order effects on the gas supply, the oil pipelines, and water. Their study followed the second-order effects into co-generation, refineries, storage terminals, and agriculture. The third-order effects tracked into oil production, road transportation, air transportation, and banking and finance.[11]

This research was extremely important because the individual protection strategy designed for a single critical infrastructure totally ignores the impact of how interdependent all of our 16 critical infrastructures have become. Further, the focus on first-order, second-order, and third-order consequences forces a security strategy to embrace a much more detailed analysis than the previous "silo" approach of protecting a single critical infrastructure, which had been the predominant practice before this research.

2.3 Optimization Models Application to Critical Infrastructures

Brown, Carlyle, Salmeron, and Wood's research project at the Operations Research Department at the Naval Postgraduate School applied bilevel and trilevel optimization models to make critical infrastructures more resilient against terrorist attacks. Their research sought to analyze the vulnerabilities of any critical infrastructure through a set of coordinated terrorist attacks in which they offered informed proposals for reducing the vulnerabilities. This research led to new military and diplomatic planning models for decision support systems. Their research was also instrumental in the business community, focusing on the value of "corporate continuity," a concept since embraced more fully by governmental agencies concerned for governmental continuity. By applying high-fidelity models, they were able to formulate and find data to solve high-fidelity models of critical infrastructure systems. Simpler aggregated models may be more appealing, but unless verified by high-fidelity models, the answers may be suspect and any resulting insights will be forfeited. Also, they discovered that while heuristics are useful, they are not dependable in identifying vulnerability.[12]

The research cited by Brown, Carlyle, Salmeron, and Wood was based on creating three models to analyze four components of an attack against the following:

- The Strategic Petroleum Reserve
- Border Patrol
- Electrical Power Grids

The four components of analysis were (1) criticality, or how essential is the asset; (2) vulnerability and how susceptible the asset is to surveillance or attack; (3) reconstitutability and how hard will it be to recover from inflicted damage; and (4) threat and how probable is an attack on this asset. The models were based on comparison of military to civilian planners and called for decision-making judgments. The research used rather elegant mathematical computations to arrive at their conclusions, and the authors state that their research was based on using high-fidelity models. However, it is important to differentiate between models or simulation, and while this study did use modeling, the real question centers on whether this was more of an Advanced Process Modeling approach, as this approach involves detailed and high-fidelity mathematical models to provide information for decision support and predictive capability. On the other hand, fidelity in simulation has traditionally been defined as the degree to which the simulator replicates reality, and reality was certainly an aspect of their research. Simulation, just like modeling, can also be defined as either "low" or "high" fidelity, and in the case of simulation, it refers to how closely the research represents "real" life. There exists an element of confusion regarding the two types of fidelity, as simulation fidelity is how accurately a simulation represents a real-world function that it purports to capture or represent. Model fidelity is how accurately an individual model represents its portion of the real world.

The high-fidelity mathematical modeling suggests that their optimization models as applied to elements of our nation's critical infrastructure have advanced our knowledge and will better prepare our decision-makers to make important judgments as they perform their duties.

2.4   Internet, Social Media, and Cyber Attacks on Critical Infrastructures

The growth of the Internet and social media has been phenomenal in terms of the vast number of people now living and working in this global interconnected world. It is estimated that in 2014, more than 2.5 billion people are connected to the worldwide network. Another 3 billion people will be utilizing online Internet services within the next five years. To further demonstrate the opportunities, challenges, and risks that await all of us, we are now experiencing the "Internet of Things," where added to this complexity will be literally several billion more machines and devices that will also be available and will interact, guide, and in many cases make decisions apart from human control and judgment. Automation has been developed to provide machine technology that interacts with other vehicles and makes driving judgments to avoid collisions.

> The CISCO Visual Networking Index forecasts that by 2016, there will be 18.9 billion network connections, or almost 2.5 connections for each person on earth, compared with 10.6 billion in 2011. New products and services will be born as more devices are interconnected. Chips and sensors, smaller and more powerful, can be embedded in more products, creating vast amounts of data and linking physical and digital systems. The Internet of Things—cars, ovens, office copiers, electrical grids, medical implants, and other Internet-connected machines that collect data and communicate—could result in 31 billion devices connected to the Internet in 2020.[13]

The increasing number of both people and devices becoming connected in cyberspace will greatly impact specific portions of our nation's critical infrastructure. Those infrastructures most immediately impacted will be the following:

- The electrical grid system
- Transportation
- Telecommunications

Other infrastructure sectors will also be impacted, such as food, water systems, emergency services, and banking and financial services, but the impact on their performance and continuity of service will not be as profound as the former. The salient point is that as societies become so interconnected to both their devices and the critical services they require, this increasing dependency may well increase our vulnerability to disruption of our critical infrastructures.

Escalating attacks on countries, companies and individuals, as well as pervasive criminal activity, threaten the security and safety of the Internet. The number of high-profile, ostensibly state-backed operations continue to rise, and future attacks will become more sophisticated and disruptive. A global digital arms trade has now emerged that sells sophisticated malicious software to the highest bidders including hacker tools and "Zero-Day Exploits" attacks that take advantage of previously unknown vulnerabilities.[14]

Our banking and financial communities have experienced rather sophisticated attacks, as in March 2013, cyber attacks disrupted the banking services of Wells Fargo, J.P. Morgan Chase, Citi Group, U.S. Bancorp, PNC Financial Services, American Express, and Bank of America. Symantec Corporation estimates a cost to consumers of $110 billion globally, and other studies have estimated the cost to be from $25 billion to $500 billion. Another form of disruption and vulnerability that impacts our major corporations is "cyber economic espionage," and General Keith Alexander of our U.S. Cyber Command has termed these attacks as the "greatest transfer of wealth in history" and estimated that American companies have lost over $250 billion in stolen information such as their intellectual property and products as well as decades-long research.[15]

Former Secretary of Defense Leon Panetta has warned of a "cyber Pearl Harbor," in which attacks aimed at our critical infrastructure could cause substantial and widespread destruction as the attacks can be remotely launched against industrial control systems (ICSs) designed to modify or reprogram those ICSs that control pipelines, train tracks, dams, and electrical networks, thus causing both loss of critical services and also damaging important and costly parts of our infrastructure system.

In 2011, the Department of Homeland Security reported a 383% increase in attacks on our critical infrastructure. The Task Force report stated that, over time, future attacks could become even more destructive as cyber weapons and capacities proliferate and as electricity, power, transportation, and communication infrastructures become increasingly dependent on the Internet. The barriers to entry are low on cyber attack tools, unlike nuclear weapons, and individuals with limited experience can quickly become capable of conducting disruptive actions in cyberspace.[16]

2.4.1   Challenge of Protecting Our Nation

An outcome of the 9/11 attack on America has been the creation of the Department of Homeland Security, which has resulted in the transfer of 20 federal agencies and over 190,000 personnel to this new federal department. Our nation's only other example of an effort this broad in scope was the creation of our Department of Defense in 1947. The reassignment of federal agencies and personnel to a new department of Homeland Security is not without major political and personnel problems. In addition to the numerous organizational challenges and, in many cases, conflicts surrounding goals and objectives between various organizational units, we have redefined the fundamental premises of Homeland Security from those of National Security. *National Security* is the responsibility of our federal government, and it is based on the collective and cooperative efforts of our Department of Defense, State Department, and our intelligence community in the defense of our nation as well as protection of our national interests overseas. *Homeland Security* is now defined as protecting our critical infrastructure and key assets with the cooperation of our private sector organizations and with coordinated assistance of our federal agencies.

The critical infrastructures that make America the strongest and wealthiest nation in the world are also our greatest weakness and our Achilles heel. Therefore, it is incumbent on our nation's leaders to fashion both a strategy and appropriate tactical plans to protect the nation. The scope of the·challenge can be measured by the number of infrastructure assets that require our protection. The inventory of assets requiring our vigilance is truly overwhelming, and the national strategy for the physical protection of critical infrastructure and key assets enumerates the challenges as follows:

The Protection Challenge

Agriculture and Food	1,912,000 farms; 87,000 food-processing plants
Water	1800 federal reservoirs; 1600 municipal wastewater facilities

Public Health	5800 registered hospitals
Emergency Services	87,000 U.S. localities
Defense Industrial Base	250,000 firms in 215 distinct industries
Telecommunications	2 billion miles of cable
Energy:	
Electricity	2800 power plants
Oil and Natural Gas	300,000 producing sites
Transportation:	
Aviation	5000 public airports
Passenger Rail & Railroads	120,000 miles of major railroads
Highways, Trucking, and Busing	590,000 highway bridges
Pipelines	2 million miles of pipelines
Maritime	300 inland/coastal ports
Mass Transit	500 major urban public transit operators
Banking and Finance	26,600 FDIC insured institutions
Chemical Industry and Hazardous Materials	66,000 chemical plants
Postal and Shipping	137,000 million delivery sites
<u>**Key Assets**</u>	
National Monuments and Icons	5800 historic buildings
Nuclear Power Plants	104 commercial nuclear power plants
Dams	80,000 dams
Government Facilities	3000 government-owned/operated facilities
Commercial Assets	460 skyscrapers[17]

Each of the aforementioned sectors comprises an important role within our nation's critical infrastructure that contributes to our nation's success, economy, and strength. Since most of these sectors are not governmentally controlled, but in many cases under private ownership, the national strategy requires a rich interface between federal, state, and local governments with private and corporate organizations, thus making the task of designing and managing a national strategy most difficult at best.

In analyzing our nation's critical infrastructure, one of the most inescapable conclusions one can make is the extraordinary problem we as a society have created for ourselves due to deferred maintenance. We simply have not maintained a coherent investment strategy to assure for the maintenance and modernization of the very sectors responsible for our nation's success. Further, since almost 85% of our critical infrastructure is under the direct control of private and corporate organizations, they have equally mismanaged their responsibilities for maintenance and modernization of our infrastructure sectors. As a result, today, we must provide protection of these enormously important resources for both deferred maintenance and modernization.

2.4.2   Three Critical Infrastructures

Three of our nation's most critical infrastructures are selected on the basis of their interdependency impact on all of the remaining 13 critical infrastructures. The three critical infrastructures selected for more detailed analysis are as follows:

1. Energy and the electrical grid system
2. Transportation
3. Telecommunications

Each of these three critical infrastructures can profoundly impact all remaining critical infrastructures, so it is important that we understand their vulnerabilities and risks.

2.4.2.1   *Energy and the Electrical Grid System*

Energy represents our nation's most critical infrastructure, as it is essential to every aspect of life within our nation. Our entire economy is dependent on the energy that is principally produced by our electrical grid system and our oil and gas system. The very quality of life we enjoy in our nation is directly related to the efficient functioning of our energy system. Our health care systems, all aspects of people's employment, as well as our nation's educational systems all rely on our production and use of energy. Our nation's vital national security and defense systems are totally reliant on our energy infrastructure. The energy infrastructure of our nation is fundamentally organized around two principal sectors, electricity and oil and natural gas.

The first sector, which produces electricity, consists of three major components: generation, transmission, and distribution. The generation of electricity occurs through our use of hydroelectric dams, nuclear power plants, and fossil fuel plants. The transmission and distribution systems link into areas of our electrical grid system. The distribution systems manage, control, and distribute the produced electricity into our businesses, government organizations, and our individual homes.[18] The fact that electricity cannot be stored and can be used only at the time it is produced is indicative of how resilient it must be to a terrorist attack. The targeting of this sector can therefore focus on the three principal components of generation plants, transmission lines, and distribution centers and substations. The attack on any one of these three components can create massive problems for our nation.

Thus, contrary to popular belief, it is not only the vulnerability of our nuclear power plants and hydroelectric dams but also the very transmission lines and substations most Americans are not even able to identify as to purpose, type, and function that are also vulnerable.

Most of the electricity produced in the United States is a result of our fossil fuel coal–fired units, which produce over 51% of the power generated, while our nuclear power plants produce 20%, oil and gas produce 18%, and hydropower and other renewable sources produce 11%. These items are representative of our nation's generation of power capabilities. The transmission system includes high-voltage lines, towers, underground cables and transformers, breakers, and relays, while the distribution system consists of lower-voltage distribution lines and cables as well as substations. All together, the greatest types of terrorist threat to our electrical power system centers around both physical attacks by terrorists and cyber and electromagnetic attacks. The physical attacks could focus on any one of the generating stations or transmission and distribution components and either could cause local disruption or, if used in a coordinated fashion with a cyber attack or an electromagnetic attack on our control systems, could result in a serious multistate blackout that could initiate a serious network destabilization outage to our integrated electrical power grid. Theoretically, it is possible to cause our electrical grid system to collapse, with cascading failures in equipment far removed from the point of the attack, thus leading to even longer and more serious blackouts.[19]

In protecting our electrical grid system from cyber attack, we must monitor and be aware of the new advances being made in cyber weapons. We must also better protect our Supervisory Control and Data Acquisition (SCADA) systems with improved security such as firewalls, use of encryption, and more refined measures for detecting cyber intrusion. Intelligent agent-based networks designed to monitor and respond to cyber threats will also be necessary if we hope to better protect our systems. Also, an area where additional R&D is required centers on ways to detect a cyber attack from internal sources such as disgruntled employees.[20]

Our national power grid is made up of three independent electric grids: the Eastern Interconnected System, covering the Eastern two-thirds of the nation and the adjacent Easter Canadian Provinces; the Western Interconnected System, consisting of our Western states West of the Rocky Mountains including the Western Canadian Provinces; and our Texas Interconnected System, covering Texas and part of Mexico. Within this very decentralized system, we have Independent Service Operators, more than 3000 local utilities, more than 15,000 generators of power to produce electricity, 10,000 power plants, and hundreds of thousands of miles of transmission lines and distribution networks, all designed to meet our nation's need for producing and distributing the electricity that we need to run almost every aspect of our society from our businesses, government, schools, and homes.[21] This electricity cannot be stored but must be available on demand, which means our interconnected system must be prepared to distribute electricity from any of the three interconnected systems to these areas requesting to purchase the electricity.

In 1992, the Energy Policy Act was introduced to deregulate the power industry under the assumption that power produced in the Northwest and Southeast at lower cost could be transmitted to those areas where the cost of power was more expensive. The deregulation also required the unbundling of generation transmission and distribution properties, all previously controlled by local governments and local governmental public utilities. Another very critical aspect of this deregulation of the industry occurred in the newly approved legislative authorization of permitting the industry to make campaign contributions to members of Congress. This allowed a perfect alignment of the mutual interests of the industry with members of Congress, all now in a new environment free of regulatory oversight.[22] Thus, in 1992, the potential for abuse was now put into place and needed only a few other conditions to occur in the ensuing years, which would pave the way for the Enron energy scandal. These subsequent conditions occurred in June 1996, with the Financial Accounting Standard Number 125 being issued and permitting Enron to "effectively book all the profit streams expected from a power plant purchase over the next several years in just one year." By buying up plants each quarter and declaring on its balance sheet the profits anticipated over the next several years, it could show quarterly profits, even if the plant failed to produce the profits in succeeding years or even failed entirely.[23]

In March 2000, after four years of litigation, the U.S. Supreme Court upheld the new regulations on transmission lines and the separation of both production and distribution, thus requiring transmission lines to be open to all and, in effect, to increase the value of long distance wheeling on our nation's electrical grid system. Electricity trading increased beyond belief, and for wholesale dealers like Enron, they were able to capitalize on purchasing electricity from the generators at the lowest cost and selling to the distributor at the highest cost. Enron was actually performing in the role of an arbitrage wholesaler, in a totally unregulated market, and these three major conditions cost the rate payers of California over $30 billion and numerous blackouts and brownouts.[24]

Perhaps the irony of our efforts to deal with our nation's most important infrastructure, namely, our electrical grid system, proved to be more vulnerable to those who were entrusted with this system than to the very terrorists we are seeking protection from. In other words, our government officials who carelessly introduced the deregulation environment for our nation's most critical resource and the corporations and executives who exploited this system to enrich their own profits and corporate bonus packages all created an environment in which damages measured between $30 billion to $100 billion to the citizen rate payers of our nation. There is no recorded amount of any terrorist activity that has cost as much or has done as much damage as the damage done by thoughtless Enron corporate executives' and other government officials' careless regulatory performance of duties. Thus, we have learned that our critical infrastructures must be protected not only from terrorists but also from the very people we entrust to regulate and protect our valuable resources.

Our nation's energy infrastructure is dependent also on our ability to manage our oil and natural gas sector. Our economy is dependent on a cost-effective system of oil production, refining, distribution, and transportation of this critical product. Our nation's ability to transport crude oil is based on over 160,000 miles of pipelines, storage terminals, and a refinery system, which includes more than 160 oil refineries that range in the capability of producing between 5000 and 500,000 barrels per day. While our nation has over 600,000 oil wells, we must still import oil to manage the demands from our citizens and corporations. In fact, oil products provide 97% of the energy used in our transportation sector.

The natural gas industry is a vast network of privately owned and operated gas wells, numbering in excess of 275,000 wells, 278,000 miles of natural gas pipelines, and more than 1,119,000 miles of natural gas distribution lines. This system was created to meet market demand and to maintain safety, and while vandalism was taken into account, the system, like so many other parts of our infrastructure, was not designed to withstand a terrorist attack.[25] Since natural gas provides over 25% of residential and industrial energy needs, it is a critical portion of our nation's energy infrastructure.

Altogether, our nation's electrical grid system and our oil and natural gas systems are all critical to the total functioning of almost every aspect of our economy, and any disruption in these services for even a few days could have enormous consequences. The potential range of targets for these systems is enormous, both in terms of geographic issues and the complex interdependencies that require coordinated system-to-system interface. Another important aspect to consider in protecting these systems from terrorist targeting opportunities is to acknowledge how totally dependent each of these industries is on cyber computer systems. Since these industries have not yet experienced sophisticated cyber attacks, they have not fully integrated computer security and intrusion analysis programs to offset and protect themselves from this type of terrorist targeting.

2.4.2.2 Transportation
Our nation's multiple forms of transportation systems have provided not only great convenience to our citizens but also an important and indispensable service to our economic system. Virtually all of our nation's infrastructure

components rely on our transportation systems to provide delivery of either the resources they require or the resources they produce.

Our highway system has been constructed in a pattern of interconnected state and local roads, which include over 4 million miles of paved highway. These roads intersect with over 45,000 miles of interstate highway and toll ways, and included in this system are more than 600,000 bridges. In addition to our highway system, our nation also depends on our railroad network, which extends over 300,000 miles for freight traffic, and a commuter rail system, which covers over 10,000 miles of rail. Another important feature of our nation's transportation system is the 500 commercial service airports and the 14,000 general aviation airports, all providing commercial service to the many components of our nation's infrastructure system.[26]

While our country has invested over $25 billion in protecting our nation's aviation system since the 9/11 attacks, we have not been able to match this investment strategy in other important parts of our infrastructure. For example, Stephen Flynn reports on the 12,000 miles of our inland waterway system, which includes such important rivers as the Mississippi and Ohio River waterways, where barge traffic becomes a very cost-effective form of commercial transportation. A single barge can move the same amount of cargo as 58 trucks at one-tenth the cost, resulting in an annual transportation cost savings to shippers of over $7.8 billion. Of the 257 locks along our inland waterway interstate navigation system, 30 were constructed in the 19th century, and another 92 locks are more than 60 years old on an average planned life span of 50 years. We have over a $600 million backlog in maintenance projects and a need to invest over $5 billion just to keep the system operational.[27]

Our inland waterway system is also critical to the movement of hazardous chemicals, thus providing a safety factor to what would ordinarily travel on our highway system. Also, the nation's power generation plants that require coal and fossil fuel to produce our electricity can be transported in greater volume and at less cost on our waterway system, as opposed to highway traffic, further reducing the cost of electrical power both to residential and commercial users.

Our railroad system, which transports both freight and passengers, also factors into public safety issues and concerns. The railroad freight system carries a large volume of chemicals such as chlorine gas and other materials, which have the potential for being quite hazardous should an accident occur or should they become a terrorist target. Since trains carry more than 40% of all intercity freight, they also remove many of these chemicals that would otherwise be transported over our highway system. When one factors in the movement of 20 million intercity travelers using our railroad system annually and the 45 million passengers who ride our trains and subways operated by local transit authorities, we experience different safety vulnerabilities. Since this volume of passenger traffic cannot be screened for potential weapons as we screen airline passengers, as a nation, we realize a tradeoff in safety for the necessity of managing a system that must move a large volume of passenger traffic at peak travel times while minimizing disruption of boarding and dis-embarking of these rail and subway systems.

Our maritime shipping infrastructure, which includes 361 seaports, as well as our coastal and inland waterway system and the numerous locks, dams, and canals, provides a very complex system to protect, given both the range of cargo ships and the incredible volume of cargo that passes through our ports.

Port security is an especially vulnerable part of our nation's infrastructure with the advent of modern container shipping practices, which are capable of very sophisticated loading of containers on ships in which the speed the containers are both loaded and unloaded leaves little time for the inspection of the cargo loaded within each container. In fact, the number of containers that entered the United States in 2004 exceeded 9 million containers, and 95% of these containers were not inspected. These 40-foot containers have the potential of becoming our "21st century Trojan Horse," as they could be loaded with Weapons of Mass Destruction (WMD) or explosives that could easily pass through our port inspection system without notice. The government's Container Security Initiative, under which cargoes are to be inspected in foreign ports before departing for the United States, is an ideal plan and program; however, it does require a close and very cooperative program with foreign countries to assure for tamper-proof containers. It also will require that the shippers make the appropriate technical modifications so that their containers are tamper proof. The security requirements for providing safety assurance to our U.S. ports will cost over $7.5 billion over the next ten years.[28] It is quite obvious how important our nation's transportation system is to our economy and to our safety. The challenge in protecting our citizens and these transportation systems will require enormous efforts in research to develop new methods of protection.

2.4.2.3 *Telecommunications*

Our nations' telecommunications industry has, over the years, consistently provided reliable, robust, and secure communications that have resulted in our economic prosperity and national security. Our Department of Defense, as well as our federal, state, and local justice agencies, is dependent on the communications capabilities provided by a number of excellent telecommunications firms and companies. Moreover, our nation's economic strength is built on a solid base provided by our telecommunications sector, since all businesses and commercial enterprises rely on our ability to communicate with their customers.

Our telecommunications infrastructure is similar to our energy and electrical grid infrastructure, in that any damage to it would create a cascading impact on other multiple infrastructures because the requirement for fast, secure communication channels and capabilities is implicit in most other infrastructures. As a consequence, the government and the telecommunications industry must often work collaboratively to build and maintain a resilient and secure industry, capable of protecting its widely dispersed critical assets.

> The telecommunications sector provides voice and data service to public and private users through a complex and diverse public-network infrastructure encompassing the Public Switched Telecommunications Network (PSTN), the Internet, and private enterprise networks. The PSTN provides switched circuits for telephone, data, and leased point-to-point services. It consists of physical facilities, including over 20,000 switches, access tandems, and other equipment. These components are connected by nearly two billion miles of fiber and copper cable.[29]

The advances in data network technology accompanied by the incredible demand for data services have resulted in the worldwide proliferation and use of the Internet. While the PSTN remains the backbone of this important infrastructure, the cellular, microwave, and satellite technologies all provide gateways into this very complex system. Because of the convergence of traditional circuit switched networks with the broadband packet-based Internet protocol networks, the telecommunications infrastructure is undergoing a rather significant transformation, which will ultimately lead to the Next Generation Network (NGN). This convergence, along with the growth of the NGN and the emergence of wireless capabilities, continues to provide challenges to our telecommunications industry and to our government. The evolving new infrastructure must remain reliable, robust, and secure.[30]

The telecommunications infrastructure is a very clear target of terrorist organizations. As such, the government has definite responsibility to work with the industry to help ensure its protection. At the same time, the government depends on the cooperation of the industry to obtain electronic evidence of terrorist cell activity. The delicate nature of legally acquiring such evidence is of importance to both the industry, which seeks protection from legal lawsuits and liability, and the government, which seeks legal justification to both continue electronic searching as well as use such material in subsequent litigation against terrorist members and organizations. Because of the realities of both cyber and physical threats to our nation and the telecommunications industry, the government must work with the industry to understand our vulnerabilities and develop countermeasures, and establish policies, plans, and procedures that will result in the mitigation of these risks.

The attack on our World Trade Center and the Pentagon on September 11, 2001, revealed the rather substantial threat that terrorism poses to our telecommunications infrastructure. In both cases, the telecommunications infrastructure demonstrated great resiliency as damage to telecommunications assets at the attack sites was offset by a diverse, redundant, and multifaceted communication capability. Nevertheless, in the future, it is quite apparent that a terrorist attack targeting our telecommunications infrastructure as well as another infrastructure or target in a simultaneous manner would have a most profound impact on our nation. Therefore, we can anticipate that our telecommunications infrastructure will be a more focused target of terrorists in future attempts to attack our nation.

2.4.3   R&D in Support of Our Nation's Critical Infrastructures

On the basis of the government's identification of our nation's critical infrastructure, the Executive Office of the President and the OSTP developed a research plan structured around nine science, engineering, and technology themes that would support the entire critical infrastructure sectors previously enumerated. The nine focused areas to encourage R&D for the critical infrastructure sectors are as follows:

- Detection and sensor systems
- Protection and prevention
- Entry and access portals
- Insider threats
- Analysis and decision support systems
- Response, recovery and reconstitution
- New and emerging threats and vulnerabilities
- Advanced infrastructure architectures and systems design
- Human and social issues[31]

By mapping the long-term overarching goals to five sciences and engineering and technology themes, the following R&D priorities were created:

1. Improve sensor performance
   - Develop technology to detect unexploded ordinance.
   - Develop a real-time global positioning system synchronized for electrical grid monitoring.
   - Improve sensor arrays and improve explosive and radiological detection.
   - Improve sensors for detection of tampering with water systems and building, heating, ventilation and air-conditioning (HVAC) systems.
   - Improve SCADA security for water systems and HVAC systems.

2. Advance risk modeling, simulation, and analysis for decision support
   - Standardize vulnerability analysis and risk analysis of critical infrastructure sectors.
   - Conduct quantitative risk assessments to better quantify terrorism risks to the critical infrastructure sectors.
3. Improve cybersecurity
   - Develop new methods for protection from automated detection of, response to, and recovery from attacks on critical information infrastructure systems.
   - Foster migration to a more secure Internet infrastructure.
4. Address the insider threat
   - Improve technologies such as intent determination and anomalous behavior monitoring for insider threat detection, covering physical and cyber infrastructure.
5. Improve large-scale situational awareness for critical infrastructure
   - Define the communication and computing system architecture needed to create a national common operating picture of the nation's critical infrastructures.[32]

2.5 Cyber Threat Spectrum—Cyberspace Attacks and Weapons

The threat spectrum in which cyberspace attacks may occur can be categorized as follows:

1. Local threats/national threats
   The advent of local threats emerged with the beginning of our computer age and initially took the form of a recreational hacking challenge in which the focus was on whether one could penetrate computer systems. The focus was based on achieving a certain status among the peer group of those first hackers. This hacking community was not confined to a local or national level; we saw this phenomenon occurring in other nations, so it was an international situation as well. At what point did the thrill, challenge, and prestige of such computer hacking give way to obtaining monetary gain for these exploits? Perhaps, it occurred as the recreational hacker fostered the institutional hacker and the emergence of more nefarious hacking began on a worldwide basis.
2. International threats
   International threats occurring within the realm of cyberspace attacks first took the form of organized crime in which the financial

gain was enormous and the ability to operate extortion, pornographic sites, and drug trafficking operations was facilitated by the use of computers and various websites. The factor of anonymity provided a leading edge, especially since law enforcement and prosecutorial capabilities were slow to emerge with any degree of sophistication. Moreover, our legal system was not prepared for the advent of these computer-based activities and lacked the legal authority and legal standing to arrest and prosecute a wide variety of computer-based behavior and ultimately defined criminality.

Industrial espionage emerged as nation-states and certain individuals sought out opportunities to obtain intellectual property and trade secrets and to reap their financial gain either through bribery, extortion, or simply attaining a competitive advantage without having to invest in doing the research.

The opportunity for the terrorist to utilize cyberspace emerged through the use of new software tools and the power to seek political change or aspirations connected with their goods. The ability of the terrorist to threaten to introduce chaos into various governmental systems was clearly present and operationally feasible due to the vast interconnectedness of our telecommunication and network systems. The ability for terrorists to instantly launch their messages gave them an international and worldwide visibility. This in turn provided a unique mechanism for recruiting new members into their organizations. Another facet the terrorist was able to exploit centered on the opportunity to train all new adherents from remote locations.

3. National security threats

National security threats emerged due to the powerful computer systems, software tools capable of exploiting databases, and the total interconnectedness of networks with weak computer security systems in place. From the perspective of national intelligence, the reality of most, if not all, nations' intelligence acquisition processes is that they are designed to acquire information for political and military advantage. In some cases, we have discovered that some nations have permitted their intelligence agencies to access information and data for economic advantage. This has taken the form of disrupting commercial providers of other nations, exploiting and accessing intellectual property, and sharing this property with selected local or national commercial providers for economic benefit.

The information warrior is the category where nations have trained personnel to become sophisticated in the use of computer systems, software tools, and, in some cases, the creation of cyber weapons. The purpose of creating the class of cyber-warrior is based on the need for defensive capabilities so that our enemies are not able to obtain strategic advantage over us from a military point of view. Also, our defensive posture and capabilities are critical to us by minimizing target damage and by maximizing our ability to retain the broadest definition of military decision space totally unimpeded by our opponent's efforts to reduce our military decision space.

2.5.1   Cyber Threat Capability and Cyber Tools

The threat to our nation's critical infrastructure via cyberspace attacks is a direct result of the sophisticated range of digital software tools, the openness of most networks, the interconnectedness of the Internet, and the limited to weak range of cybersecurity programs. The enormous number of lines of code required in creating operating systems and various software applications is astounding. In some cases, it is not uncommon to find that several million lines of software code are necessary to create a program, and the ability of an individual to gain access to this system is a result of specific penetration tools that enable this exploitation. The difficulty in providing cybersecurity to these operational programs is a challenge since cyber attacks can take the form of Zero-Day attacks, in which the attack is a unique, first-time attack with no previous code signature available for defensive purposes. Today, digital attack tools are constantly being developed to penetrate these new defensive countermeasures. In addition, the increasing skills observed in those utilizing computer systems is a direct result of expanding educational programs, and unfortunately, some people choose to use their skills in less than legally or morally acceptable ways.

Thus, cyber threat capability as a result of knowledge, whether acquired in formal educational systems or through informal "hacking community associations," continues to grow and prosper. This capability results in a range of skills as a result of the exchange of knowledge. These factors enable both the use and creation of new digital software tools. These software tools can be applied with the incredible computer equipment that exists today and continue to improve in a continuous flow of productivity based on the increasing power of computer chips, the increasing speed of broadband networks, and the increasing capability to share data well beyond Exabyte capability.

Cyber threat is therefore defined by the capability that one's opponent has in both terms of skills and software or digital tools. However, these tools are based on an array of equipment that must be available along with the knowledge as how to best use tools or skills. Thus, cyber threat equals the capability of the opponent plus the intent to do damage, take action, or simply monitor activities. The manner in which we pursue these cyber threats is based on our legal system, intelligence system, military system, and a range of additional factors.

2.5.2   Cyber Digital Arsenal

The cyber threat spectrum is enhanced by a range of very capable cyber tools and processes. The arsenal of cyber tools includes the following:

1. Trojans
2. Viruses
3. E-mail attacks
4. Distributed denial-of-service attacks
5. Data theft
6. Resource abuse
7. Data modification
8. Web assaults
9. Anonymity
10. Cyber intelligence
11. Zero-Day attacks
12. Threat trends in mobile computing
13. Threat trends in social networks
14. SQL code injection attacks
15. Botnets
16. Phishing
17. Spam
18. Search engine poisoning
19. Web crawlers
20. NFC attacks

Several of these attack processes will be explained and discussed in Chapter 4, "Cyber Intelligence, Cyber Conflicts, and Cyber Warfare." Additionally, several of these computer threats and attacks have been described in Chapter 1.

The evolution of the arsenal of digital cyber threats and cyber weapons is a direct result of expanding criminal activity in which an increasing number of "hacktivist" groups are offering their cyber attack tools for purchase to anyone interested in acquiring their digital attack tools or their cyber services. The items available for sale includes any number of attack strategies from distributed denial-of-service attacks to various malicious malware that they will provide to almost any interested person seeking to use such services or cyber tools.

2.5.3   Rationale of Cyberspace Infrastructure Attacks

Fundamentally, the rational for attacking the critical infrastructure centers on three major points. First is the impact on the national security of the United States by reducing our ability to defend ourselves by limiting the decision space our military maintains in our cyberspace.

Second, the economic strength of the United States could be compromised and fundamentally impacted by attacking only 3 of our 16 critical infrastructures. Our electrical grid system creates interdependencies among all 15 remaining critical infrastructures. The economic cost to our nation as a result of a successful attack on this infrastructure would be devastating. Equally costly to our economy would be successful cyberspace attacks on our transportation and telecommunications infrastructures. Each of these infrastructures also would impact other infrastructures as a result of the nature of interdependencies throughout our nation.

Finally, a successful attack on our infrastructure system would erode public confidence in our nation's ability to maintain both our national security and our economic strength. It is for these reasons that three U.S. presidents have directly addressed this potential problem and have issued EOs to organize our nation to defend against the possible attack either physically or in a cyberspace manner.

2.6   Framework for Improving Critical Infrastructure Cybersecurity

On February 12, 2013, EO 13636, Improving Critical Infrastructure Cybersecurity, was issued by President Obama. This EO followed a period of 15 years of effort by three U.S. presidents to engage both the government and private sector in working to improve both our nations and our corporate and private infrastructure in a cooperative measure of protecting our national and economic security interest. Historically, the private sector has been reluctant to engage as a full cooperative partner in this enterprise. Reasons for their reluctance have centered on the Freedom of Information Act, the potential amount of civil litigation, loss of intellectual property via litigation, civil liabilities, and privacy issues. EO 13636 recognized the need to address the concerns of the private sector, and it did so by issuing an order that tasked the National Institute of Standards and Technology (NIST) with the responsibility to develop with both government and the private sector a "Framework for Improving Critical Infrastructure Cybersecurity."

As a result of increasing cyber intrusions into our critical infrastructure, President Obama acknowledged the need for improving our nation's cybersecurity. The cyber threat to our critical infrastructure continues to grow, and it represents one of the most serious national security challenges we must confront. The national and economic security of the United States depends on the reliable functioning of the nation's critical infrastructure, and through a partnership with the private sector and government, we can improve our information assurance and develop risk-based standards. EO

13636 also established mechanisms for cybersecurity information sharing between the government and the private sector. Cyber threat information was authorized to be shared with the private sector to enable private sector entities to better protect themselves. This EO even reached further by authorizing the Secretary of Defense to expand the enhanced cybersecurity services program to all critical infrastructure sectors and, when warranted, to provide classified cyber threat information from the government to eligible critical infrastructure companies or commercial service providers that offer security services to protect our critical infrastructure.[33]

Perhaps the most important feature of EO 13636 was the assignment for the NIST to guide both commercial and governmental organizations in their efforts to create a framework and improve critical infrastructure cybersecurity. To the credit of the NIST, they issued the Framework as Version 1.0 and labeled it a "living document," which would be improved upon in future versions as information regarding threats, technologies, risk assessment, and business practices continue to improve.

The NIST roadmap for improving critical infrastructure cybersecurity noted their commitment to assisting organizations in both understanding and using the new Framework. For example, they acknowledge that not all organizations have a mature cybersecurity program and the technical expertise to identify, assess, and reduce their cybersecurity risk. The Framework as implemented in practice will assist these companies and sectors in making the improvements to address the increasing number of cyber threats being introduced and used against our critical infrastructures.

The NIST also noted the importance of a cybersecurity workforce and stated the following:

> A skilled cybersecurity workforce is needed to meet the unique cybersecurity needs of critical infrastructure. There is a well-documented shortage of general cybersecurity experts; however, there is a greater shortage of qualified cybersecurity experts who also have an understanding of the unique challenges posed to particular parts of critical infrastructure. As the cybersecurity threat and technology environment evolves, the cybersecurity workforce must continue to adapt to design, develop, implement, maintain and continuously improve the necessary cybersecurity practices within critical infrastructure environments.
>
> Various efforts, including the National Initiative for Cybersecurity Education (NICE), are currently fostering the training of a cybersecurity workforce for the future, establishing an operational, sustainable and continually improving cybersecurity education program to provide a pipeline of skilled workers for the private sector and government. Organizations must understand their current and future cybersecurity workforce needs, and develop hiring, acquisition, and training resources to raise the level of technical competence of those who build, operate, and defend systems delivering critical infrastructure services.

NIST will continue to promote existing and future cybersecurity workforce development activities (including NICE), including coordinating with other government agencies, such as DHS. NIST and its partners will also continue to increase engagement with academia to expand and fill the cybersecurity workforce pipeline.[34]

The new "Framework for Improving Critical Infrastructure Cybersecurity" also addresses the problem of supply chain risk management in which organizations that provide services or products are an essential part of the risk landscape that should be included in organizational risk management programs. Supply chain risk management, especially product and service integrity, is an emerging discipline with fragmented standards and practices. The interdependencies that exist among and between critical infrastructure sectors mandate that greater focus be placed on risk assessment and risk management within these supply chain organizations. Organizations can develop very mature risk processes and risk defense strategies only to become vulnerable to penetration by the weakest links in their supply chain.[35]

The importance of the "Framework for Improving Critical Infrastructure Cybersecurity" resides in the development of a voluntary risk-based cybersecurity framework that is designed on industry standards and best practices designated to assist organizations in managing their cybersecurity risks. The Cybersecurity Framework is a rich collaboration between government and the private sector and is conceived as a "living document" subject to enhancements, improvements, and a level of continuity that will allow increased cooperation by both government and private organizations in the collaborative efforts of more effectively managing risks and protecting our nation's national and economic security.

Critical infrastructure is defined in the Executive Order as "systems and assets, whether physical or virtual, so vital to the United States that the incapacity or destruction of such systems and assets would have a debilitating impact on security, national economic security, national public health or safety, or any combination of those matters." Due to the increasing pressures from external and internal threats, organizations responsible for critical infrastructure need to have a consistent and iterative approach to identifying, assessing, and managing cybersecurity risk. This approach is necessary regardless of an organization's size, threat exposure, or cybersecurity sophistication today.

The critical infrastructure community includes public and private owners and operators, and other entities with a role in securing the nation's infrastructure. Members of each critical infrastructure sector perform functions that are supported by information technology (IT) and industrial control systems (ICS). This reliance on technology, communication, and the interconnectivity of IT and ICS has changed and expanded the potential vulnerabilities and increased potential risk to operations. For example, as ICS and the data produced in ICS operations are increasingly used to deliver critical services and support business decisions, the potential impacts of a cybersecurity incident on an organization's business, assets, health and safety of individuals, and the environment should be considered. To manage cybersecurity risks, a clear understanding of the organization's business drivers and security considerations specific to its use of IT and ICS is required. Because each organization's risk is unique, along with its use of IT and ICS, the tools and methods used to achieve the outcomes described by the Framework will vary.[36]

The Cybersecurity Framework provides a very structured and organized methodology for organizations to

1. Describe their current cybersecurity posture;
2. Describe their target state for cybersecurity;
3. Identify and prioritize opportunities for improvement;
4. Assess progress towards the target state; and
5. Communicate with stake holders about the cybersecurity risk.

More specifically, the Framework is composed of three components: (1) The Framework Core, (2) Framework Implementation Tiers, and (3) The Framework Profile. The NIST's overview of the Framework is explained as follows:

The Framework Core is a set of cybersecurity activities, desired outcomes, and applicable references that are common across critical infrastructure sectors. The Core presents industry standards, guidelines, and practices in a manner that allows for communication of cybersecurity activities and outcomes across the organization from the executive level to the implementation/operations level. The Framework Core consists of five concurrent and continuous Functions— Identify, Protect, Detect, Respond, Recover. When considered together, these Functions provide a high-level, strategic view of the lifecycle of an organization's management of cybersecurity risk. The Framework Core then identifies underlying key Categories and Subcategories for each Function, and matches them with example Informative References such as existing standards, guidelines, and practices for each Subcategory.

Framework Implementation Tiers ("Tiers") provide context on how an organization views cybersecurity risk and the processes in place to manage that risk. Tiers describe the degree to which an organization's cybersecurity risk management practices exhibit the characteristics defined in the Framework (e.g., risk and threat aware, repeatable, and adaptive). The Tiers characterize an organization's practices over a range, from Partial (Tier 1) to Adaptive (Tier 4). These Tiers reflect a progression from information, reactive responses to approaches that are agile and risk-informed. During the Tier selection process, an organization should consider its current risk-management practices, threat environment, legal and regulatory requirements, business/mission objectives, and organizational constraints.

A Framework Profile ("Profile") represents the outcomes based on business needs that an organization has selected from the Framework Categories and Subcategories. The Profile can be characterized as the alignment of standards, guidelines, and practices to the Framework Core in a particular implementation scenario. Profiles can be used to identify opportunities for improving cybersecurity posture by comparing a "Current" Profile (the "as is" state) with a "Target" Profile (the "to be" state). To develop a Profile, an organization can review all of the Categories and Subcategories and, based on business drivers and a risk assessment, determine which are most important; they can add Categories and Subcategories as needed to address the organization's risks. The Current Profile can then be used to support prioritization and measurement of progress toward the Target Profile, while factoring in other business needs including cost-effectiveness and innovation. Profiles can be used to conduct self-assessments and communicate within an organization or between organizations.[37]

The five Framework Core Functions are not intended to form a serial path or result in an end state but are a focal point to assist in an analysis of an operational view of assessing a cybersecurity risk. As such, the Cybersecurity Framework describes each of the five states as follows:

- Identify—Develop the organizational understanding to manage cybersecurity risk to systems, assets, data, and capabilities.
  - The activities in the Identify function are foundational for effective use of the Framework. Understanding the business context, the resources that support critical functions, and the related cybersecurity risks enables an organization to focus and prioritize its efforts, consistent with its risk management strategy and business needs. Examples of outcome Categories within this Function include Asset Management, Business Environment, Governance, Risk Assessment, and Risk Management Strategy.
- Protect—Develop and implement the appropriate safeguards to ensure delivery of critical infrastructure services.
  - The Protect function supports the ability to limit or contain the impact of a potential cybersecurity event. Examples of outcome Categories within this Function include Access Control, Awareness and Training, Data Security, Information Protection Processes and Procedures, Maintenance, and Protective Technology.
- Detect—Develop and implement the appropriate activities to identify the occurrence of a cybersecurity event.
  - The Detect function enables timely discovery of cybersecurity events. Examples of outcome Categories within this Function include Anomalies and Events, Security Continuous Monitoring, and Detection Processes.

- Respond—Develop and implement the appropriate activities to take action regarding a detected cybersecurity event.
  - The Respond function supports the ability to contain the impact of a potential cybersecurity event. Examples of outcome Categories within this Function include Response Planning, Communications, Analysis, Mitigation, and Improvements.
- Recover—Develop and implement the appropriate activities to maintain plans for resilience and to restore any capabilities or services that were impaired due to a cybersecurity event.
  - The Recover function supports timely recovery to normal operations to reduce the impact from a cybersecurity event. Examples of outcome Categories within this Function include Recovery Planning, Improvements, and Communications.[38]

The importance of EO 13636 and the resulting "Framework for Improving Critical Infrastructure Cybersecurity" version 1.0 centers on the establishment of a pathway to connect both government and private organizations in a structured and collaborative partnership in which even classified cyber threats may be shared with sector organizations, all with the intention of enabling improvements in our nation's cybersecurity.

Notes and References

1. Moteff and Parfomak, "Critical Infrastructure and Key Assets: Definition and Identification," 3–4.
2. Loc. Cit.
3. Moteff and Parfomak, 6.
4. Moteff and Parfomak, 7–8.
5. Moteff and Parfomak, 9–10.
6. Presidential Policy Directive/PPD-21, "Presidential Policy Directive—Critical Infrastructure Security and Resilience," 1.
7. Ibid., 2, 4.
8. Ibid., 3.
9. Ibid., 8.
10. Loc. Cit.
11. Pederson, Dudenhoeffer, Hartley and Permann, "Critical Infrastructure Interdependency Modeling: A Survey of U.S. and International Research," iii, 3, 7.
12. Brown, Carlyle, Salmeron and Wood, "Defending Critical Infrastructure," 530, 542–543.
13. Negroponte, Palmisano and Segal, "Defending an Open, Global, Secure, and Resilient Internet," 8.
14. Ibid., 3.
15. Ibid., 17.
16. Ibid., 18–19.

17. "The National Strategy for the Physical Protection of Critical Infrastructures and Key Assets," 9.
18. Committee on Science and Technology for Countering Terrorism, National Research Council of the National Academies, *Making the Nation Safer: The Role of Science and Technology in Countering Terrorism*, 30.
19. Ibid., 180–182.
20. Ibid., 187–190.
21. Perrow, *The Next Catastrophe: Reducing Our Vulnerabilities to Natural, Industrial and Terrorist Disasters*, 215–216.
22. Ibid., 227–228.
23. Ibid., 236.
24. Ibid., 232–233.
25. Committee on Science and Technology for Countering Terrorism, National Research Council of the National Academies, *Making the Nation Safer: The Role of Science and Technology in Countering Terrorism*, 196.
26. Ibid., 212.
27. Flynn, *The Edge of Disaster: Rebuilding a Resilient Nation*, 84–85.
28. Benjamin and Simon, *The Next Attack: The Failure of the War on Terror and a Strategy for Getting it Right*, 249–250.
29. National Strategy for the Physical Protection of Critical Infrastructures and Key Assets, op. cit., 42.
30. Ibid., 48.
31. The Executive Office of the President, Office of Science and Technology Policy, The Department of Homeland Security Science and Technology Directorate, "The National Plan for Research and Development in Support of Critical Infrastructure Protection," vii.
32. Ibid., vii–xi.
33. Executive Office of the President, "Presidential Document—Improving Critical Infrastructure Cybersecurity, Executive Order 13636," 2.
34. National Institute of Standards and Technology, "NIST Roadmap for Improving Critical Infrastructure Cybersecurity," 5.
35. Ibid., 8.
36. National Institute of Standards and Technology, "Framework for Improving Critical Infrastructure Cybersecurity," 3.
37. Ibid., 4–5.
38. Ibid., 8–9.

Bibliography

Benjamin, D., and Simon, S. *The Next Attack: The Failure of the War on Terrorism and a Strategy for Getting it Right*. New York: Times Books, Henry Holt and Company, 2005.

Brown, G., Carlyle, M., Salmeron, J., and Wood, K. "Defending Critical Infrastructure." *Interfaces*, vol. 36, no. 6, 530, 542–543, 2006.

Committee on Science Technology for Countering Terrorism, National Research Council of the National Academies. *Making the Nation Safer: The Role of Science and Technology in Countering Terrorism*. Washington, DC: The National Academies Press, 2003.

Flynn, S. *The Edge of Disaster: Rebuilding a Resilient Nation*. New York: Random House, in cooperation with the Council on Foreign Relations, 2007.

Moteff, J., and Parfomak, P. "Critical Infrastructure and Key Assets: Definition and Identification." Resources Science and Industry Division, CRS Report for Congress, Congressional Research Service, The Library of Congress, Washington, DC, October 1, 2004.

National Institute of Standards and Technology. "Framework for Improving Critical Infrastructure Cybersecurity, Version 1.0," Washington, DC: NIST, February 12, 2014.

National Institute of Standards and Technology. "NIST Roadmap for Improving Critical Infrastructure Cybersecurity," February 12, 2014. Available at http://www.nist.gov/cyberframework/upload/roadmap-021214.pdf.

Negroponte, J. D., Palmisano, S. J., and Segal, A. "Defending an Open Global, Secure, and Resilient Internet." Independent Task Force Report No. 70. New York: Council on Foreign Relations, 2013.

Pederson, P., Dudenhoeffer, D., Hartley, S., and Permann, M. "Critical Infrastructure Interdependency Modeling: A Survey of U.S. and International Research." Technical Support Working Group Agreement 05734, Under Department of Energy Idaho Operations Office, Contract DE-11C07-051D1457. Idaho: Idaho National Laboratory, August 2006.

Perrow, C. *The Next Catastrophe: Reducing our Vulnerabilities to Natural, Industrial and Terrorist Disasters*. New Jersey: Princeton University Press, 2007.

The Executive Office of the President, Office of Science and Technology Policy, the Department of Homeland Security, Science and Technology Directorate. "The National Plan for Research and Development in Support of Critical Infrastructure Protection." Washington, DC: White House, 2004.

The Federal Register. "The Daily Journal of the United States Government, Presidential Document—Improving Critical Infrastructure Cybersecurity." Executive Order 13636. Executive Office of the President, February 12, 2013.

"The National Strategy for the Physical Protection of Critical Infrastructures and Key Assets." Washington, DC: White House, US Department of Homeland Security, 2003.

The White House, Office of the Press Secretary. "Presidential Policy Directive—Critical Infrastructure Security and Resilience." Presidential Policy Directive/PPD-21, February 12, 2013.

Protection and Engineering Design Issues in Critical Infrastructures

3

FRED COHEN

Contents

3.1   Introduction

For thousands of years, financial systems, roads, water systems, and continuity of government were the critical infrastructures of societies. As the dawn of the industrial age occurred, and with the introduction of mass production through machine-based automation, it was only a short time before critical infrastructures would be introduced to society. This dawn was brought about by scientific breakthroughs in many areas in the 1800s. These included increased understanding of mechanical systems and machines of all types and improved understanding of materials and in the area of mining, fostered largely by the invention of dynamite; breakthroughs in transportation associated with railroads; increased understanding of power generation through fossil fuels, such as coal in steam engines and, eventually, other petroleum-based sources; and the introduction of mathematics associated with optimization and motion studies.

The rapid advancement of science and mathematics, combined with improved education in these areas to select portions of the population, produced a global change that increased specialization and the ability of a small number of people to produce far more output with far less resource. This created more specialists in new fields who became very deep and narrow in their innovations but who produced greater value for society by combining forces to form still more infrastructures that ended up shared and became more critical as fewer people could get along without them. So we created more and more critical elements of infrastructure. With the infrastructure improvements came more movement and sharing of goods, services, resources, and expertise, which in turn decreased the time to innovate, increased the combinations of knowledge applied to understanding, and brought about more scientific discovery and engineering advancements.

Telephony became increasingly important and took over from telegraphy, and people innovated, and as they became able to communicate more rapidly, they adapted to it and caused it to be a necessity to compete effectively. Pretty soon, both land and radio telecommunications became critical to rapid communications that were increasingly necessary to deal with the rate at which you had to operate to compete. As things moved faster and speed became a critical element to success, these infrastructures became critical. The more critical they became, the more important they were to make better, faster, and cheaper, so the people made the vital improvements, one after the other. As the systems became more and more reliable, more people started using them and more applications developed. More education was required to work in these industries and more training was required to use the technologies, and the educational system advanced and started to produce more graduates with higher levels of education. Fewer and fewer people were needed to plow the fields to generate food to eat and more and more moved into cities, leading to increased needs for water and power in those cities, which led to water projects on an enormous scale and more mining for more power generation and so the cycle spun.

In war, innovation is often the difference between life and death, so when the winds of World War II showed their bluster, innovations took off in droves, from the increased use of radio communications to radar to nuclear weapons and eventually nuclear power, to penicillin and breakthroughs in medicine, to advances in operations research and the mathematics of efficiency and optimization. The ability to cure new diseases made medical care more critical than it was before, and even though more than 40 million people were killed in World War II, one net effect was ultimately an increased valuation of lives of individuals in many Western societies. Thus, the saving of each individual's life meant that health care and public health gained increasing emphasis, and ultimately, health care moved from small individual practitioners to highly specialized experts working on narrow problems in great depth as a group to save more lives. Health care and public health were increasingly a critical element of our national infrastructures and evolved into this role over a period of more than a hundred years with World War II, as a critical developmental point. Bombing was increasingly important, and the first sea battle where ships never saw each other took place over Midway Island in the Pacific. Air power led to innovations in building planes and rockets and other similar vehicles, and as that became more stabilized as an engineering discipline in the late 20th century, air transportation became a critical infrastructure in much the same way as telephony.

The pattern that has emerged seems to be rather clear. New scientific or mathematical innovation leads to changes in the way societies can operate, and the niche advantages taken by leaders force competition to adopt similar changes. These changes drive innovations from curiosities to competitive advantages to near necessities to necessities and move systems to become infrastructures that thereby become critical. As these developments advance, the need for supplies, expertise, engineering, operations, and governance becomes important; thus, more and more critical infrastructures emerge as a result of and to meet the needs of specialization. The Internet is an example, as is the emergence of biological knowledge as well as the emergence of materials knowledge in which scientific advancements will be forthcoming for years into the future.

As we create more and more critical infrastructures, we consume more and more resources servicing these infrastructures: more education, more and more complex interdependencies, more trust, and more parties, piling each infrastructure on top of other infrastructures and creating ever-greater potentials for the management of these infrastructures. But this is only the beginning of the challenges.

In the United States today, something like $1 trillion of work is needed just to bring critical infrastructure repairs up to the level they are supposed to normally operate. This reflects a breaking of the social contract by the government and those running the infrastructures. While many people are starting to worry about malicious attacks on critical infrastructure, protection also has its mundane aspects. Bridges fall down, roads collapse, water pipes leak, gas pipes explode, and on and on, when inadequate maintenance is done, and malicious attackers wishing to commit sabotage need only make a minor change to a crumbling infrastructure element to destroy it.

3.2   Basics of Critical Infrastructure Protection

Protection fields have some common themes that form the basis that underpins all protection efforts. The details of each aspect of critical infrastructure protection and the common themes that address the cohesion of the process and the design and utility of infrastructures will be presented and discussed.

3.2.1   Design and Utility of Infrastructures

Protection is something that is done to components and composites of components, which we will more often call systems. Infrastructures are almost always systems of systems, with the subsystems controlled by different individuals and groups and with predefined interfaces. For example, the US highway system is composed of state highway systems and the interstate highway system. These highways are connected to local road and street systems.

Each locality controls the local streets, states control state highways, and the country is in charge of the interstate system as a whole. The interfaces are the points where these streets and highways contact each other and where other supporting components of the infrastructure contact each other. For example, most highways have electric lighting at night, and these contact the power infrastructures; most have emergency call booths that contact some communications system; many have rest stops with fresh and waste water facilities; and so forth.

Each component has a physical makeup based on the physics of devices, and engineering is done to create components with properties, combine them to composites with properties, and combine those into larger and larger systems, each with its own properties. The infrastructure as a whole has some basic properties as well, and the engineering designs of the components and the way they fit together create those properties. For example, water systems have incoming water supplies, purification systems, piping of various sorts, pumps and holding stations, pressure controllers, and so forth. Each of these has properties, such as the strength of the pipe and the resulting water pressure it can hold, the maximum flow rate of a pump, the maximum slew rate of a valve, and so forth. The overall water system has properties that emerge from these components, such as the water pressure under normal loads, the total amount of water that it can purify per unit time, the maximum holding tank capacities, and so forth. Engineering takes the properties of the materials and the construction capabilities of the society along with cost and time and other constraints and produces and ultimately builds the overall system.

Infrastructures are operated by operators of different sorts. For example, in California, the Independent System Operator (ISO) operates the power grid as a whole, while each of the power providers and consumers operate their facilities. The price for power is controlled by the local power companies, who are, in turn, controlled by the public utilities commission, and they have to buy from the ISO based on the California energy market, which is an exchange sort of like the New York Stock Exchange, only with very different rules on bidding, buying, and selling.

The different parties have various obligations for their operations; however, each makes its own trade-offs associated with costs and quality of service subject to the regulatory and competitive environments they operate within. Operators literally turn things on and off, repair things that break, charge customers for services, and do the day-to-day operations of components and overall infrastructures.

Many aspects of operations today in advanced infrastructure systems are controlled by automated systems. These automated control systems are called Supervisory Control and Data Acquisition (SCADA) systems. They do things like detecting changes in measurable phenomena and altering actuators to adjust the systems to produce proper measured results. Oil pipelines, as an example, run under pressure so that the oil, which is rather thick compared with water, flows at an adequate rate to meet the need. Too much pressure and the pipes break; too little pressure and the oil stops flowing. As demand changes, the amount of oil flowing out the end changes, so the pumping and valve stations along the way need to adapt to keep the pressure within range. While a person sitting at a control valve 24 hours a day can do some of this sort of work, automated control valves are far less expensive and more reliable at making small adjustments in a timely fashion than people are. The SCADA systems communicate information about pressures and flows so that valves can be systematically controlled to keep the overall system properly balanced and so that it can adapt to changing conditions, like a breakdown or a pressure surge.

Management of the operations is done by operators using their management structure and people, while management of operators takes place through a combination of governmental and privately generated external requirements, including those of shareholders, boards of directors, owners, and a wide range of legal and governmental frameworks. When infrastructures interface at, or cross borders, they are referred to as being international. These exist in the social framework of the societies and the world as a whole. For example, the Internet is a rapidly expanding global infrastructure that is composed of a wide range of highly compatible technology at the level of network packets.

There are common languages that are widely compatible and allow the distribution of content. The World Wide Web that runs over the Internet is best known, and it is based largely on a fairly simple language with embedded graphics. This environment, as most of the IT environment, has a great many interdependencies. The diagram provided here is one that we use to characterize the underlying infrastructures used to gain business utility from these sorts of IT. At the top, we have business utility, which depends on people, including administrators, users, and support personnel, and on applications, which include computer programs, data, files that store the content and software, and input and output devices. These in turn depend on systems infrastructure, which includes operating systems, libraries, and configurations. The applications tend to depend on sets of infrastructure systems like the domain name service that maps host names (like all.net) into Internet protocol (IP) addresses, the identity management systems that control identification and authentication, back-end services and servers that support functions like doing financial transactions and looking up stored content, and protocols that are the common communications methods. There has to be a physical infrastructure underlying all of these, like the physical computers, the networks, whether wired or wireless, the wires, routing of communications, and accessibility of different components from different places. These require a broader range of large-scale critical infrastructures like electrical power, heating and cooling, air in usable condition, communications technologies, government structures and stability, the financial system that allows people to get rewarded for their efforts and use those rewards to support their lives, the environmental conditions necessary for people and systems to operate, supplies to support these systems and people, the people themselves, including the whole societies that they need and work in, and of course the safety and health of the people and their families that are necessary to get them to do their jobs.

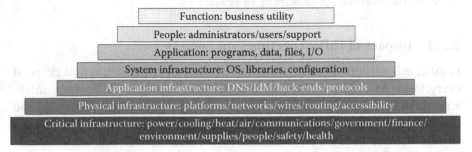

This sort of interdependency picture exists at a high level for all infrastructures and systems that depend on infrastructures. While each infrastructure in each country or region is different, as a general rule, they all have similar sorts of interdependencies, and at a high level, they all look pretty much the same.

3.2.2 Evolution of Infrastructures

Infrastructure components change over time. As a result, some elements of infrastructures are likely to be around for a long time. Even in the most modern of infrastructures, the Internet, some elements are already very hard to change. The Internet became popular at the time when the IP was in version 4 (IPv4). As a result, most of the Internet today runs IPv4. Version 6 has many advantages and is used in many places, but it is highly likely that IPv4 will continue to exist for at least the next 20 years and more likely for the next 50 years or longer. As a result, compatibility means that IPv4 has to be supported and that applications that are likely to be successful have to work within that context. As infrastructures change with time, backward compatibility drives a lot of efficiencies.

Because of the long time frames for infrastructures as a whole, their designs as a whole need to be stable and able to operate over long periods of time with a wide range of equipment replaced over time in incremental steps.

Infrastructures are not built instantly or designed uniformly, even if they are originally created that way. They evolve over time with use.

Infrastructures also wear and, if inadequately maintained, collapse. While elements of the Appian Way are still in place and operating, most of it is long gone. Everything falls apart over time and has to be maintained. While roads often last hundreds of years, they have to be maintained on a regular basis. Bridges rarely last more than 100 years, and those that do have extensive maintenance and refit cycles. Most last more like 50 years before they are replaced. The repair cycle is commonly used for upgrades and the replacement cycle for redesigns. Since these things tend to happen over extended time frames, compatibility with older infrastructure elements often has to be maintained for hundreds of years.

3.2.3   Impact of Infrastructures on Society

Finally, infrastructures change the worlds they operate within and do so at every level. At the level of the individual who uses specific content, infrastructures like the Internet both provide content and communication and change the way people do what they do as well as the things that they do. Infrastructures become ends in and of themselves, driving whole industries and individual innovation. Hundreds of millions of people communicate daily using electronic mail, something few of them ever did before the Internet. The time frames of these communications change many things about how they work, what they say, and the language and expressions they use every day. But this is only the beginning. In the latter part of the 20th century, automated teller machines revolutionized the way people dealt with cash needs. Whereas people previously had to deal with getting cash only on weekdays between 9 a.m. and 5 p.m. at a bank, today, people can get cash almost anywhere almost any time in many cities and towns in much of the world. This revolutionized the carrying of cash, eliminated many robberies and thefts, and created tracking capabilities for governments over individuals. It meant that instead of being tied to the local bank, people could get the amount of money they needed wherever they were, whenever they needed it. It changed the way people thought about money and the way they spent it.

The highway system changed the nature of travel and work in that people no longer had to live right next to where they worked and goods could be transported point to point rather than running through the rail system, which itself revolutionized transportation before the emergence of trucks and cars. This enabled different models of commerce, people who lived their lives moving from place to place became far more common, and communities changed forever. All of these things also changed the consumption patterns of whole societies and altered the environments in which they lived. Moving from place to place also changed the nature of food and how it was delivered. With the advent of refrigeration and the electrical power grid, food could be preserved over time, allowing far wider distribution of the food and its packaging. Smaller groups eating more quickly led to fast-food and snack food and altered eating habits while producing far more waste from food and its packaging, consuming more power and more resources, and changing family farming while creating the huge corporate farms that currently dominate. Water systems changed the face of irrigation but also decimated much of the wildlife and habitat in regions that used to have a lot of available water. Waste management did wonders for the people living near the oceans, but for quite a long time, much of the waste was dumped into the oceans, causing major changes in the oceanic environment. Mining produced the materials needed for energy and manufacturing, but strip mining destroyed large areas of land and destroyed much of the capacity of that land to be used for other purposes. Oil production resulted in oil spills that killed off wildlife and poisoned portions of the oceans.

The list goes on and on. These so-called unanticipated consequences of modern society are intimately tied to the infrastructures created by people to support their lifestyles. The complexity of the overall feedback system is beyond the human capacity to model today, but not beyond the capacity of humanity if we decide to model it. These complex feedback systems that drive extinctions and destruction must be managed if human infrastructures are to thrive while humans survive. For most of the people living in advanced societies, there is no choice but to find ways to understand and engineer critical infrastructures so that they provide sustainable continuity in the face of these realities. From the way the power grids get their power to the way societies treat their resources, these critical infrastructures will largely determine the future of those societies and humanity.

3.3   Random Nature of Faults, Failures, and Engineering

Engineering would be simple in the ideal world, and mathematics associated with much of engineering is based on idealizations because of the need to simplify calculations. Rules of thumb are often used to shortcut complex analysis, engineered systems once analyzed are reproduced in large numbers to avoid reengineering, and many assumptions are made in the use of components when forming composites from them. History and extensive analysis create these rules of thumb, and where the assumptions are violated, recalculation is commonly undertaken. A good example is in digital circuit design, where fan-in and fan-out simplify the analysis of how many outputs can be connected to how many inputs within a given technology. If the same technology is used between inputs, and outputs and other factors such as temperature, humidity, and the electromagnetic environment remain within specified ranges, no additional calculation is needed. One output can connect to a certain number of inputs and everything will continue to work properly. However, if these assumptions are no longer true, either as a result of natural changes in the operating environment or of malicious attacks by outside actors, then the assumptions are no longer true. While most engineered solutions are designed for specific environments, design changes in the field can be very expensive, and if the environment changes and these assumptions do not hold, then infrastructures that depend on these assumptions fail.

A great example is the power infrastructure near Livermore, California, where in the summer of 2006, record temperatures of 115 were sustained for several days in a row. At these temperature levels, the transformers in many neighborhoods failed and had to be replaced, leaving thousands of people without power or air conditioning for several days.

The transformers were replaced with newer transformers, presumably with higher temperature ranges to cover the span of temperatures now anticipated. If temperatures rise around the globe, power and air conditioning systems, water storage areas, and many other infrastructure elements will have increased failure rates because they were designed for different conditions. Another great example of a failure because of a different temperature-related incident was a road collapse in one of the busiest roads in the world, a part of the intersection called "The Maze" that is at the intersection of major roads leading to the Bay Bridge in San Francisco as well as Interstate 80 and several other highways. In this case, a truck loaded with fuel had an accident that resulted in the fuel catching fire, which was hot enough to cause structural failures in the steel beams holding the concrete bridge up, which then fell onto another roadway, disrupting traffic on that section of the highway as well. No normal surface overpass is designed to handle this sort of thing, nor could it reasonably be designed to do so, and this is a truly amazing story because this section of the overpass was completely replaced in less than 30 days under a contract that rewarded rapid performance and punished late performance. A lot of assumptions were not true in this case, including the assumptions that led to the failure and the repair.

3.3.1   Resilience

Similar examples happen in all areas of infrastructure. They fail here and there as components or composites fail, unless adequate redundancy is in place to ensure continuity in the presence of faults in components. The glory of infrastructures that are properly designed and operated is that when one component or composite fails, the infrastructure as a whole continues to operate, making it resilient to failures in components and composites. Or at least that is true if they are properly designed and operated. When they are not designed and operated with adequate redundancy and designed to be resilient to failures, we see cascade failures such as those that have brought down major portions of the U.S. and European Union power grids over the past ten years. A typical failure of the infrastructure may occur as follows:

1. The power grid is operating at or near maximum load during hot days in the summer because of the heavy use of air conditioning.
2. The heat produced by the high power usage added to the high outside temperature causes wires in the power grid to expand, lowering them until they come near to trees or other natural or artificial phenomena.
3. As one power line shorts out from the contact, it has to go off line, and the power it was supplying is replaced by power from other sources.
4. The increased loads on those other sources causes them to heat up and some of them hit trees, causing them to shut down.
5. Continue item 4 until there is not enough power supply to meet demand or until all of the redundant power lines into areas fail and you have major outages.
6. Pretty soon, all of the changing loads create power fluctuations that start to damage equipment and vast parts of the power grid collapse.

This is not just a fantasy scenario. It has happened several times, and this resulted in the collapse of power in the Western states of the United States in one instance. There are many other similar scenarios that are related to running the power grid at too close to its maximum capacity and suffering from a failure somewhere that cascades throughout the rest of the system, and every few years, we see a major outage that spreads over a wide area. Recovery times may last from a few hours to a few days, and there are often broken components that take days or weeks to be repaired.

It has to be noted that the reason for these large-scale outages is that power is shared across vast areas to increase efficiency. Energy is sent from Canada to the United States in summer and from the United States to Canada in winter. This saves building more power plants in both countries, each of which would run more or less a portion of its capacity at different parts of the year. Sharing means that more resources can be brought to bear to meet demands at heavy usage times or during emergency periods, but it also means that interconnections have to be managed and that local effects can spread to far wider areas.

Similar effects in all infrastructures exist, and each is more or less resilient to faults and interdependencies depending on how they are designed, implemented, and operated. By the nature of an infrastructure, it will eventually have faults in components, have components replaced, and be modified for one reason or another. Whether the city grows and needs more water or there is massive inflation and we need to handle more digits in our financial computers, or a new technology comes along and we need to add electric trains to the existing tracks, changes and faults will produce failures within small portions of infrastructures. The challenge of critical infrastructure design is to ensure that these happen rarely, for short times, and that their effects are reasonably limited. The way we do this is by making them fail less often, fail less severely or in safer ways, recover more quickly, and tolerate many faults that don't need to cause failures.

3.3.2   Fault Intolerance and Fault Tolerance

Failures are caused by faults that are exercised and not covered by redundancy. For faults in components that are used all of the time and not covered by any redundancy, failures occur as soon as the faults appear. For example, computers typically have clocks that cause the components to operate in synchronization. If there is a single clock in the computer and it stops working, the computer will stop working. For faults that are not exercised all of the time but do not have redundancy, the fault may occur long before a failure results and the failure may never occur if the fault is never exercised. A good example of this is a bad emergency break cable in a manual transmission car that is never used in hilly areas. Even though the cable would not work, the car may never roll down a slope because the emergency brake is never exercised.

The other example of a fault without a failure is the case where there are redundant components covering the situations so that even though faults are exercised, the failures that they could produce are never seen because of redundancy in the system. A good example is a baseball bat with a minor crack in it. There is natural redundancy in the structure of the wood, so that a crack that goes only part way into the bat will not cause the bat to split. Even though every hit exercises the fault, the bat does not fail, but like a bat with a partial crack in it, if there is a fault that is exercised and the redundancy fails, a failure will occur, just as a solid hit in the wrong way will split the bat.

There are three very different ways to reduce the failure rate of a composite. One way, called fault intolerance, is to make the components higher quality so that they fail less often. For example, since computer clocks are so important to the operation of computers, we can make them out of better components than the rest of the computer to ensure that they do not cause the failure. Similarly, we can make the baseball bat out of metal that is not subject to cracking like wood bats. The second way to reduce failure rates in composites is called fault tolerance, and it is based on adding more and more redundancy so that when components fail, the composite continues to operate. For example, we can make a pair of clocks in the computer so that when one fails, the other can take over. In automatic transmission cars, there is usually a "park" setting on the transmission that sets a pin into the power train, causing wheels to be unable to turn. Finally, there is the approach of designing the composite so that it has fewer components to fail. The more complicated a composite is, the more things there are to go wrong. If it can be made simpler with components that are just as reliable, then the simpler design will likely fail less often. All of these notions can be codified in mathematical terms.

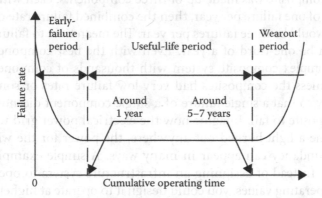

The mathematical characterization starts with the experimental data on component failures, which, for most types of components, fits with the "bathtub curve."[1] At the beginning of their lives, most components have an infant mortality rate. Some significant percentage of them fail very soon after they are created. This is generally thought to be the result of manufacturing errors or imperfections. Those that survive this initial period then go into their normal life cycles, during which they operate at a more or less fixed failure rate until some end-of-life period, during which their failure rate again increases. Hence, the curve looks like a bathtub. The infant mortality portion of the curve can be eliminated by an initial test period, typically called burn-in, during which the components are run at normal operational modes for a period to eliminate those with manufacturing defects. The end-of-life period can be eliminated by systematically replacing components that attain a particular age, commonly called retirement. These mitigations, burn-in and retirement, are fault intolerance techniques that result in a nearly constant failure rate over the normal operating life of components and they are commonly used. Other fault intolerant techniques include building with better manufacturing processes to reduce the failure rates over the life cycles of components; building to tighter tolerances to eliminate many of the microscopic causes of failures; engineering to higher tolerances of temperature, stress, strain, and other similar parameters; and longer burn-in and earlier retirement periods. Better components usually cost more, and there is therefore an engineering tradeoff between quality and cost. Based on the engineering decisions made, the resulting components are usually assumed to then have a fixed rate of failure over an expected lifetime. Fault intolerance makes those failure rates lower.

Fault tolerance is based on the notion that, when assembling a composite out of components, the failure rate of the composite can be controlled through the use of redundancy and maintenance. As a simple example, if every component had to operate properly for a composite to operate properly, and if the composite was made up of three components, each with the same failure rate of one failure per year, then the combined failure rate of the overall system would be three failures per year. The mean time to failure (MTTF) would then be one-third of a year. Even with the best components everywhere, a complex composite system with thousands of components would fail a lot unless the composites had very low failure rates or some form of redundancy so that a single failure of a single component did not cause the entire composite to fail. Imagine how the electrical power grid would work if every time a light burned out anywhere, the power for the whole world failed. Redundancy can appear in many ways. A simple example is called overdesign. Instead of designing an infrastructure system to operate at the expected operating values, you could design it to operate at higher loads, but overdesigning it; the likelihood is that it will never reach its absolute maximum load, the point at which it would break down. The sort of redundancy in this case is at the very lowest level of each component. For example, the steel girders used to build the bridge may be a little bit heavier and larger than needed; thus, it has some redundant metal in the girders to tolerate microscopic faults. This could also be thought of as fault intolerance in that it is designed to decrease the individual failure rate of components. Suppose that instead of building each girder to be a bit stronger than needed, we systematically built in some extra girders so that, under normal load, even if you cut one of the girders out of the bridge, the bridge would still work normally? Forgetting the details of how this is done, if it can be done, then the bridge as a whole will readily survive the loss of any one girder. Of course, since there are more girders, the aggregate failure rate of the components of the bridge goes up. There will be more failures of components, but the MTTF for the composite of the whole bridge will increase because it will require two girders to fail before the bridge collapses. If the composite described earlier had four components, its failure rate would be four per year instead of three, but if anyone could fail and the composite still operate properly, then the MTTF would be half a year. This is likely an improvement over the one-third of a year MTTF of the original design, but it would cost more, about 4/3 as much. The original design cost three girders for two-sixths of a year of operation, while the new design gains one-sixth of a year by paying for one more girder.

That is two-sixth years for three girders, or 1.5 girders per sixth of a year for the original design, and three-sixth years for four girders, or 1.33 girders per sixth of a year for the fault tolerant design. This fault tolerant design is therefore more cost effective in terms of girders per operating year, but there is more!

In the original design, the failure of one girder will make the bridge collapse. In the fault tolerant design, there is the potential for detecting the failure of one girder and repairing or replacing it before the second catastrophic failure takes place. If we can do this, then the bridge can keep operating indefinitely, until such time as a second girder fails before we can detect and repair the first failure. As long as the detection and repair costs every quarter are less than the cost of building a new bridge three times per year, the fault tolerant approach is a winner and we do not have to keep having bridge collapses along the way. The notion of the time to detect and repair from a fault is typically characterized as the mean time to repair (MTTR). Given that everything works on a random basis, a measure called availability results from the combination of the MTTF and MTTR and is characteristic of the percentage of time that the bridge will be available for use, assuming it is out of use during repairs. The resulting average availability equation for a bridge with no redundancy is given as the MTTF (up time) divided by the MTTF plus the MTTR (up time plus down time): MTTF/(MTTR+MTTF). If there is redundancy in place, the equation gets more complicated, but in essence, if the overall rate of repair is faster than the overall rate of failure, the availability will be stable at some rate higher than the nonredundant availability rate, while if the MTTF is less than the MTTR, failures will occur at a rate that will ultimately overwhelm the repair capability. This analysis turns out to be very similar to the analysis for infectious diseases, but that is a different part of the infrastructure.

Of course, this analysis is pretty simplistic. For example, girders do not really fail at a constant rate of one girder per four months. On a heavily loaded day in high winds at rapidly changing temperatures, all of the girders are under more strain than on other days, making the likelihood of simultaneous or nearly simultaneous failures higher. This is an example of what is known as a common mode failure.

The same cause induces similar or identical failures in many components. Another example is interdependencies. Some components of most complex composites are more critical to ongoing operation than other components are because more components depend on them. For example, if there is one large reservoir in a major metropolitan water system, its total failure will likely take the whole system down, while it may have many pipes going from it in many different directions, and any one of those pipes will only cause a relatively smaller outage. In actual designs, combinations of fault tolerance and fault intolerance are combined; for example, the reservoir would likely be designed to be more intolerant, while the piping is typically designed to be more fault tolerant.

Another important thing to understand about common mode failures in infrastructures is that critical infrastructures often involve right of ways that permit other infrastructures taking the same routes to avoid having to dig, buy, and otherwise alter land and uses to achieve delivery of services and goods. The right of way and the bridging of obstacles lead to the combined use of proximate space for multiple infrastructures. For example, a dam might control water flows, secure a lake for fish farming, water plants in other farms, carry vehicular traffic across a gorge, generate electricity, host radio towers, and include oil, gas, and telecommunication lines. An attack on or collapse of the dam would then have far broader consequences. These common mode failures can be very important.

3.3.3   Fail-Safe

A different notion underlying the design of composites that fail less spectacularly is the notion of fail-safe. The idea of fail-safe is to design composites so that they tend to fail in a safe mode when enough components fail and cause the composite to fail. Fail-safe modes apply to almost any sort of system, but they are far more important in cases where the consequences of failure are higher. For example, in nuclear power plants, safe failure modes are a key driver, while in most water systems, fail-safes are only relatively limited parts of the design.

Still, they have some fail-safe methodologies in common. For example, both depend on gravity to operate as a safety mechanism. In nuclear reactors, control-rod control failures produce high core temperatures that melt mechanisms that hold control rods up, so the rods drop by gravity to control the reaction, making for a relatively safe shut-down. Water systems use gravity so that if a pump fails, the water system will continue to provide water for a time because the water supply is higher than the demand, and gravity keeps the water flowing.

Another common example is the use of limiters on programmable logic controllers (PLC) that operate many of the control mechanisms of water systems, nuclear plants, and many other similar control systems. These PLCs typically limit certain mechanical or electrical processes to prevent the system from exceeding design limits. In a water system, there might be limiters on how quickly a slues gate can be opened or closed to prevent rapid changes in water pressure from breaking components. Similar limiters are in place in nuclear power plants to prevent very rapid changes in control settings from breaking parts of the plant. These limiters act as fail-safe mechanisms in many cases by making certain that if a failure in the control system creates a wrong setting, the consequences will be limited so as to, for example, not break the overall plant.

In similar cases, automatic shut-off valves prevent overloads from cascading through systems. A good example is the use of automatic shut-offs on generators and other components of power grids that prevent back voltages resulting from other component failures from cascading throughout the system. Consider a water-turned generator being used to generate power. In normal operation, the water is pushing hard against a turbine of some sort to force the generator to turn, producing torque on the turbine shaft, with resistance coming from the electrical system impeding the movement of a magnet through a loop because of inductance. As more power is used on the electrical side, more torque is produced on the mechanical side. Now suppose this is connected to a major feed into a power grid and another part of the power grid fails. At the speed of light in the wire, an electrical voltage and current change races down the wire toward the generator.

If unchecked, when it hits the generator, it will immediately create an amount of force equal to the change in demand that will push back on the turbine shaft. Since water is an incompressible fluid and it is flowing under the force of gravity, typically at high speed and in high volume, it will not give substantially. That means that all of the force caused by the differential in power has to be absorbed by the turbine blades and the torque on the turbine shaft. If the change in power demand is high enough, the shaft will quite literally twist itself like a pretzel, resulting in physical failure of the turbine and of course a loss of power that feeds back into the rest of the power grid, causing yet more cascading effects on the next turbine, and so forth. The solution comes in the form of limiters of various sorts that prevent changes of a magnitude exceeding the capability of the components. These cause portions of the overall system to fail in safer modes, thus reducing dramatically the MTTR. In the case of the generator, an electrical limiter could prevent the change in power from exceeding a threshold, thereby tripping the generator off line (which removes torque from the drive shaft, which does not cause it to twist up like a pretzel), or perhaps a physical limiter on the drive shaft itself so that it snaps out of gear. In most cases, both sorts of limiters and perhaps others as well will be used so that in case one fail-safe component fails, the composite remains relatively safe.

3.4 In the Presence of Attackers

The discussion up to here has been about the design principles for composites made up of components under "natural" failure modes, that is, under modes where failures come at random because of the nature of the world we live in, the manufacturing processes we use, and so forth. There is an implicit assumption that all of these failures are unintended, and that is the assumption we are now going to abandon.

3.4.1 Intentional, Intelligent, and Malicious Attackers

In the presence of intentional, intelligent, malicious attackers, some, but not all, of the assumptions underlying these design principles fall apart. For example, even the most malicious intentional and intelligent attacks cannot realistically change the laws of physics to the point where water ceases to flow downhill for a substantial period of time. On the other hand, because designers build circuits, girders, pipes, and other components to operate over particular operating ranges, an intentional, intelligent, malicious attacker could realistically alter some of these operating conditions at some places at some times so as to cause changes in the failure rates or modes of components, thus causing failures in the composites that they form. As a simple example, to cause a valve to fail, one might pour glue into it. This will most certainly change the conditions for most valves whose designers did not intend them to operate in an environment in which a high-viscosity fluid is bound to the internal parts of the mechanism. While one could order all of the valves to be sealed to prevent this sort of thing, it would increase the price substantially and prevent only a limited subset of the things that an attacker might do to cause a failure. Further, other approaches to designing defenses might be less expensive and more effective for a wider range of attacks. For example, putting all valves in physically secured areas might accomplish this, as well as preventing a wide range of other attacks, but that may not be practical everywhere either.

The glue in the valve attack is only the simplest sort of thing. In fact, nature could almost reproduce this by having a fire that causes tree sap to be extruded and by chance landing on a valve. Attackers can be far cleverer than this. For example, to cause a computer to fail, they might set off fire detection systems that cause the fire suppression system to pour water into the room with the computer. That is an example of an indirect attack. In the case of setting off fire detection systems, a lot of other side effects may be gained along the way. For example, emergency conditions may result in people leaving the building in an unusual exit pattern, leaving doors open momentarily for entrance by the attacker. By dressing as emergency personnel, attackers may enter surreptitiously during a fire alarm and gain additional access to plant surveillance equipment or steal key components or plant explosives or do a wide variety of other things. Again, this is relatively simplistic, even if it is more complex than the trivial one-step attack.

The next level of complexity comes from amplification phenomena. In the case of amplification, a seemingly small action may result in far larger effects. For example, by changing the air temperature in a control room, the workers and systems in the control room will start to have increased failure rates. These failures can lead to other weaknesses and thus allow other simple steps to cause increasingly harmful effects. If limiters were not in place, which they did not used to be, then a few failures in a power grid on a hot day would be able to cause amplification locally to induce larger failures, which would ultimately cascade and perhaps cause a widespread outage lasting a substantial period of time. In the financial markets, amplification is particularly problematic. For example, by buying or selling a substantial block of stock, the price on that stock changes substantially, causing other people to buy or sell, leading to amplification of the change in price, leading to more buyers and sellers, and so forth. When the market is overpriced, this can lead to rapid drops across many stocks in panic selling and buying frenzies. This points out another common feature of successful attacks at large scale. These sorts of conditions are greatly aided by an abundance of potential energy that can be rapidly turned into kinetic energy.

Whether it is a bubble in the stock market, a dam bursting over with water, a phone system on Mother's Day, or a power grid on the hottest day in years within a region, there is a lot of potential for cascade effects when there is a lot of energy in the system that can be unleashed. Whether it is triggered by accident or malice, the effects of a small act can be greatly amplified by such conditions. Consider a close election in which only a few hundred or thousands of votes in a few districts can change the national outcome. An attacker in these conditions can attain enormous leverage by attacking only a few weak points at the right time, and nature and the nature of people will do the rest. An attacker who is highly skilled leverages such conditions where feasible for optimal effect. Whether they induce cascades to their own advantage, for example by shorting stocks before a major attack is planned on a nation-state, or simply waiting to take advantage of natural conditions, for example, shooting out transformers and insulators on very hot days or damaging a key gas pipeline during a major hurricane, intentional, intelligent, malicious attackers can and often do amplify their effects when attacking infrastructures.

Combinations and sequences of attack steps can be applied in almost unlimited complexity to induce potentially serious negative consequences. For example, a typical sequence would start with attackers entering a facility through a back door left open between smoking breaks or by picking a lock with a bump key. Next, they might enter an empty office and plug in a wireless access point, possibly attaching to an existing connection to transparently proxy the legitimate traffic while sniffing it and using its address and credentials to access other parts of the network. The whole process usually takes less than a minute to do. Next, the attackers might leave the building and go to a nearby motel, where they use a planted transmitter outside the target site to communicate with their planted device inside. From there, they might observe network traffic, looking for servers or accounts with unencrypted user IDs and passwords. Or they might scan the network for vulnerable machines or services. Once they find the way in, they might encounter a SCADA system or a workstation that accesses a SCADA system or an entry into a financial system. Along the way, they might drop in remote controls and reentry mechanisms, download other mechanisms from remote sites, and so forth, creating a large number of long-term holes into the network.

Then they might leave the area and sell the capability to someone else to exploit. The buyer may have many such people working for them and build up capabilities surrounding a city or area. As they gain these capabilities, they might begin to exploit them together to, for example, disable some aspect of emergency response while starting fires and shutting down parts of the water supply. They might even use a reflexive control attack in which they create conditions intended to generate responses, such as sending police resources toward a decoy target, to give them more time to attack their real target.

On a larger scale, more serious and well-funded attackers might combine these capabilities with military operations to compound the damage and disrupt nationwide responses to attacks.

The most sophisticated of these attackers will have national infrastructures of their own that they leverage for advantage. For example, they have intelligence forces that regularly track the critical infrastructures of other countries and identify targeting information for possible attacks, computational infrastructures that analyze enemy infrastructures to identify the minimum amount of resources required to disrupt each element of infrastructure, as well as the key set of infrastructures that must be disabled or destroyed to wither enemy military and industrial capability. In many cases, they know just what to hit and where to hit it on a grand scale.

3.4.2   Capabilities and Intents

Having started down this road, it would be a disservice if we failed to mention that real attackers are not infinite in their capacity to attack. They have real limitations associated with their capabilities, and for the most part, they are motivated in some way toward specific intents. This combination of capabilities and intents can be used to characterize attackers so as to understand what they can realistically do. Without this sort of threat basis, defenses would have to be perfect and work against unlimited numbers of colluding attackers to be designed to be effective. However, with a threat basis for designing defenses, the limitations of attackers can be taken into account in the preparation of protection.

Threat capabilities are often considered in terms of things like finances, weaponry, skill level, number of people, knowledge levels, initial access, and things like that. Intents are often characterized in terms of motivating factors, group rewards and punishments, strategies, and tactics. For example, a high-quality confidence artist typically has little money, weaponry, or initial access but has a lot of skill, a small group of people, and perhaps substantial knowledge and is motivated to get money, stay covert, and rarely use violence. However, typical terrorist groups have substantial finances, weaponry similar to a paramilitary group, training and skills in many areas, multiple small teams of people with some specialized knowledge, and no initial access. They are usually motivated by an unshakable belief system, often with a charismatic leader, use military tactics, and are willing to commit suicide in the process of disrupting a target, killing a lot of people, and making a big splash in the media. The protection against one is pretty clearly very different from the protection against the other, even though there may be some common approaches. Without doing the research to determine who the threats are and their capabilities and intents, it is infeasible to design a sensible protection system against them.

Different methods are available to assess attacker capabilities and intents. The simplest method is to simply guess based on experience. The problem is that few of the people running or working in infrastructures have much experience in this arena and the experience they have tends to be highly localized to the specific jobs they have had. More sophisticated defenders may undertake searches of the Internet and publications to develop a library of incidents, characterize them, and understand historical threats across their industry. Some companies get a vendor who has experience in this area to do a study of similar companies and industries and to develop a report or provide a copy of a report they have previously developed in this area. In the presence of specific threats, a high-quality, highly directed threat assessment done by an investigative professional may be called for, but that is rarely done in design because design has to address a spectrum of threats that apply over time. The most reasonable approach used by most infrastructure providers who want good results is a high-quality general threat assessment done by threat assessment professionals and looking at categories of threats studied over time. Finally, intelligence agencies do threat assessments for countries, and portions of these assessments may be made available to select infrastructure providers.

3.4.3   Redundancy Design for System Tolerance

Given that a set of threats exist with reasonably well-understood capabilities and intents, a likely set of faults and failure modes for the infrastructure can be described. For example, if a group that seeks to poison populations is a threat of import and you run a food distribution system, faults might be in the form of putting poison within food stuffs and failures might be the delivery of substantial quantities of poisoned food into a population, resulting in some deaths and a general disruption of some part of the food chain for a period of time.

To achieve protection, in the language of fault tolerant computing, the goal would be to reduce the number of faults and put redundancy in place to tolerate more faults than you would if there was no threat to the food supply. To do this, a variety of approaches might be undertaken, ranging from sterilization of food in the supply chain process to elimination of sequences in which biological contaminants are introduced before the sterilization point, to multiple layers of sealed packaging so that creating a fake repackaged version requires more and more sophisticated capabilities than are available to the threat.

The general notion than is that, just as there are assumptions about failure modes used to design systems to tolerate naturally occurring faults in the absence of intentional malicious, intelligence threats, different fault models are used to design systems to tolerate the faults in the presence of those threats. It turns out that the fault models for higher-grade threats are more complex and the protective measures are more varied than they are for naturally occurring phenomena, but the basic approach is similar. Some set of potentially redundant protective measures are combined with designs that are less susceptible to faults to design composites that are relatively less susceptible to failures out of components that are individually more susceptible to faults. Of course, perfection is unattainable, but that is not the goal. The goal is, ultimately, to reduce cost plus loss to a minimum.

This notion of reducing cost plus loss is the goal of risk management. In essence, the risks are formed from the combination of threats, vulnerabilities to the capabilities and intents of those threats inducing failures, and consequences of those failures. Risk management is a process by which those risks are managed by combining risk avoidance, transfer, reduction, and acceptance with the goal of minimizing cost plus loss. For example, the risk of a nuclear nation launching an intercontinental ballistic missile at your city water plant, thus causing massive faults that are not defended by the fences and guards at the gate to the reservoir and total loss of use of the water system for quite a long time, is a risk that is typically transferred to the national government in its role of providing for the common defense.

The risk of the attack described earlier where someone walks into the back door and plants a wireless access device is likely one that should be reduced (a.k.a. mitigated) until it is hard to accomplish and unlikely to succeed, at which point the residual risk should be accepted. The risk of having someone walk up and pour poisonous gas into the air intake of your air conditioning system at street level should probably be avoided by not placing air intakes at street level. Of course, this is only the beginning of a very long list with a lot of alternatives for the different circumstances, and in reality, things do not fit quite so neatly into an optimization formula. Decisions have to be made with imperfect knowledge.

The complexity of risk management gets more extreme when interdependencies are considered. For example, suppose you implemented a defense based on detecting intruders and alarming a guard force to respond to detected intrusions. While this seems like a reasonable approach at first, the analysis becomes complex when the target is high valued and the threats are high quality. What if the attacker decides to cut electrical power to the entire location as a prelude to their attack? Then the sensor system may not function properly and your response force may not know where to respond to. So to deal with this, the sensor system and the guard force will have to have the ability to respond in the presence of an outage of external electrical power. Suppose you do that by putting an uninterruptible power supply (UPS) in place for operation over a 30-minute period and include a motor generator for supplementary power after the initial few minutes of outage against the event of a long-term external outage. This sort of analysis is necessary for everything you do to defend your capabilities, and the dependency chain may not be that simple. For example, suppose that the mechanism that turns on the UPS is controlled by a computer. High-quality attackers may figure this out through their intelligence process and seek to defeat that computer system as a prelude to the power outage part of their attack. Suppose that the alarm system depends on a computer to prioritize alarms and facilitate initial assessments before devoting a response force and the attackers can gain access to that computer system.

Then in the alarm assessment phase, the actual attack might be seen only as a false alarm, thus suppressing the response for long enough to do the damage. This means that physical security depends on computer security, which depends on the power system, which depends on another computer system. The chain goes on and on, but not without end, if the designers understand these issues and design to reduce or eliminate interdependencies at the cost of slightly different designs than designers without this understanding tend to produce. This is why the security design has to be done along with risk management starting early in the process rather than after the rest of the system is in place. Imagine all the interdependencies that might be present if no attempt was made to reduce them and you will start to see the difference between a well-designed secure operations environment and an ad hoc response to a changing need for and appreciation of security.

3.4.4   Random Stochastic Models

Relating this back to the notions of faults and failures, the presence of threats creates a situation in which there are a lot more faults than nature would normally create, and those faults are of different sorts than the random stochastic models of the bathtub curve produces. They are otherwise highly improbable combinations of faults that occur in specific sequences. Randomness and nature could never produce most of the sequences seen in attacks, except through the indirect results of nature that produces animals that think, learn, and direct themselves toward goals. At the same time, every naturally occurring event is observed by the attackers just as it is observed by those protecting infrastructures. When a bridge fails, attackers notice how it happened and may decide to target bridges that have similar conditions to reduce the effort in attack. Imagine an attacker that decided to attack all of the bridges known to be in poor condition. There are steam, water, and sewage pipes under almost all major cities, and many of them are old and poorly maintained, inadequately alarmed, and unlikely to be well protected. Attackers know this and, if they have a mind to, may target many of them rather than targeting only a few more well-guarded targets.

To provide protection against intentional, intelligent, malicious threats, systems need to tolerate far more and more complex sorts of faults and be hardened against far more vicious, localized, and directed events than nature could throw at them, and defenders must also understand that the death of 1000 pin pricks may be the mode of attack chosen by some threats. That is not to say that nature is not a force to be reckoned with. It remains a threat to critical infrastructures as it always has been, but simply dealing with nature is not enough to mitigate against the threats of human nature.

To succeed against realistic threats, more and more correlated faults must be considered. Common mode failures must be largely eliminated to be effective against human attackers, and faults are certain to be exercised in spurts instead of in random distributions. Step functions in the exposures of faults will occur as attacks expose systems to harsh environments, and any one system will most surely be defeated or destroyed quickly and without notice unless it is covered by another. In the presence of attackers, engineering takes on whole new dimensions, and assumptions are the things that are exploited rather than the things we can depend upon. At the infrastructure level, it may be necessary to allow some targets to suffer harm to protect the infrastructure as a whole against greater harm, particularly when the defenders are resource constrained.

There are many approaches, of course. Alarm systems are often characterized in terms of nuisance alarm rates and likelihood of detection, while medical measurements talk about false-positives and false-negatives, as do many computer security calculation approaches. These metrics are used to try to balance alarms against response capabilities, which have very direct costs. But approaches to risk management that go beyond the simplistic always end up dealing with two critical things. One of them is the nature of the conflict between attackers and defenders in terms of their skill levels and resources. The other is the notion of time and its effects.

3.5 Issues of Time and Sequence

In the power grid, time problems are particularly extreme because response times are particularly short. Many people have suggested that we use computers and the Internet to detect outages at one place in the power grid so that we can then notify other parts of the grid before the resulting power surges hit them. It sounds like a great idea, but it cannot work because the energy disruptions in power grids travel down the power infrastructure at the speed of light in the wires carrying them. While the wires have dips in them as they go from pole to pole, this increases the total distance by only a small percentage. Power tends to run long distances over fairly straight paths. So if the speed of light in the wire is $6 \cdot 10^8$ meters per second and the distance from California to Washington State is 954 miles, that converts to about 1,535,314 meters, or $1.5 \cdot 10^6$. That's 1/400th of a second, or 2.5 milliseconds. Getting an Internet packet from outside of San Francisco, California (about half of the way from Los Angeles to Seattle), to Seattle, Washington, takes something like 35 milliseconds on an Internet connection. That means that if a computer in San Francisco instantly sent notice to a computer in Seattle the moment there was a failure, it would get to the computer in Seattle 32.5 milliseconds too late to do anything about it. Even if the power grid wires went twice as far out of the way as they would in the best of cases, we would still be 30 milliseconds too late, and that assumes that we do no processing whatsoever on either side of the computer connection. Now some may argue that the Internet connection is slow or that our numbers are off by a bit, and they are probably right on both accounts, but that does not change the nature of the speed of light. While it may be possible to get a signal to Seattle via radio or a laser before the power fluctuation in San Francisco makes its way through the power grid, there will not be enough time to do much, and certainly not enough time to alter the large physical machines that generate the power in a significant way. The only thing you could hope to do would be to disconnect a portion of the power grid from the rest of the grid, but then you would lose the power supplied by each part to the other and would ensure an outage.

Thus, safety cutoffs are used for power generation systems and the slow reconstitution of power systems over periods of days or sometimes weeks and months after large-scale cascade failures.

However, not the entire infrastructure works like the power grid. Water flows far more slowly than communications signals do, oil in pipelines flows even more slowly, and government decision making often acts at speed involving multiple legal processes, which are commonly timed in months to years. The issue of time is as fundamental to protection as the notion of threats. It is embedded in every aspect of protection design, as it is in everyday life. Everything takes time, and with the right timing, very small amounts of force and action can defeat any system or any attack.

3.5.1 Attack Graphs

The descriptions of sequences of attacks undertaken by malicious actors can be more generally codified in terms of graphs, which are sets of "nodes" connected together by weighted "links." These graphs typically describe the states of an attack or the paths from place to place. For example, a graph could be made to describe the vandalism threat against the utility shed. That graph might start with a vandal deciding to do some damage. The node links to each of the typical intelligence processes used by vandals, which in turn link to the shed as a target. The time taken in these activities is really unimportant to the defenders in terms of the start of the attack that they can detect; however, in other cases where more intelligence efforts are undertaken, this phase can have important timing and defense issues. Once the shed has been identified as a target, the vandal might show up with spray paint, or pick up a rock from the ground near the shed, or bring a crow bar. Again, each of these may take time in advance of the attack, but unless the vandal visits the site first and gets detected, it does not matter to the defender. The spray paint might be applied to the outside of the shed and the vandalism then ends—a success for the attacker, with identifiable consequence to the defender. Unless the defender can detect the attempted spray painting in time to get response forces to the shed before the consequences are all realized, the defender has failed to mitigate those consequences.

Of course, the consequences may be accrued over long time frames, perhaps months, if the defender does not notice the paint and others view it. The damage accrues over time as people see the vandalism, and that costs a small amount of the reputation of the defender.

Perhaps the vandal decides to use a rock or brick and throws it through a window. If the defender has anticipated this and cleared the immediate area of rocks and bricks, it means that the vandal has to bring their own rock or brick. Most vandals will not bother, so the defender has defeated this attack by this defensive maneuver. In this case, the defender has to act before the vandal does, but any time before the vandal arrives will do the trick. In this case, the attack graph has the attacker arriving at the location (a node in the graph), but the next step is to pick up a rock or brick, and since the defender has removed these from the premises, the attack graph is severed when no link exists between the arrival step and the pick-up brick step. Another way to think of this defense is that it reduces the link between arrival and getting a brick or rock from virtual certainty when bricks and rocks are present to very unlikely when they are not. The link may be completely severed, or more likely, a brick or rock was missed in the cleanup effort, so the link is just reduced and the attacker needs to expend more effort to search the area to find a brick or rock. Perhaps the severing or reduction in magnitude of that link will lead the vandal to return with a brick or rock of their own. If so, that is another set of links to go get a rock and return. If you detect them on site searching for a rock or brick, can you intercept them or do something else to warn them off and sever the attack graph?

Suppose the vandal brings a crow bar. Maybe the vandal has decided to break into the old shed and use it as a clubhouse to store their spray cans for future defacements. Now an alarm such as the ones described before has a chance of detecting the vandal as they open the door, assuming that they do. The attack graph has the vandal starting to pry the door, followed by a possibility of detection at some time later. Now the race begins. As the attacker works the door, the alarm has to be sent to an assessment process to determine whether to respond or not. The attacker may be delayed by the door, depending on door construction, lock strength, and so forth.

If the door is hardened enough, the attacker may give up, so the prevention severed the attack graph. Or the attacker may come back with a sledge hammer and some friends. More nodes and more links form, each with time frames associated with success and failure, each with measures of success. The path continues until the attacker succeeds in realizing the consequences of concern, gives up, or is stopped by the defender, and in the interval, additional costs and consequences result. Eventually, the attack ends and things go back to the preattack state, with possible changes in the defensive posture.

The process described represents what might be drawn up as one part of an attack graph for one vandal attacking one shed. In reality, there are many vandals and other threats and many facilities to defend. They act asynchronously in most cases, but sometimes, they act in concert, such as during a riot or a coordinated attack process. For example, suppose between the time the first vandal broke into the shed and the time the shed was repaired, a second vandal came along. They might, for example, decide to change the setting on the valve or glue it in place. This second failure can be thought of in terms of the MTTF and MTTR equation described earlier. If inadequate redundancy is in place to cover the situation and the second fault occurs, a failure with far higher consequences may occur.

At a higher level of analysis, the design of protective systems has to consider the rate of arrival of attacks just as the failure rate of components has to be considered in fault tolerance analysis. For the design to be effective, it must handle the highest rate of attacks reasonably expected for the threat set at hand. Otherwise, it will be overwhelmed. Of course, the adversaries, being intelligent, malicious, and intentional, will recognize and try to evaluate the defensive capabilities in some cases to determine how much force to apply at what time and whether the target is worth attacking. The appearance of force may deter attack, while the reality of force may react to attack in time to mitigate the consequences. As conflict intensifies, simultaneous situations in which responses and repairs have not been completed before subsequent attacks are not only possible but also specifically designed by the enemy to win battles. The level of intensity of the conflict must also be considered, along with the criticality of the assets being protected and the capacity to generate additional response forces through local law enforcement and other emergency services, regional capabilities, and ultimately, national and international military organizations.

3.5.2 Game Theory Modeling

If this is starting to seem like a game in which there are multiple actors making moves for individual advantage and defenders working in concert to protect themselves, you have understood the issues very well. In fact, the area of game theory is designed to deal with just such strategic situations in which conflicts between actors with different objectives are interacting. Consider, for example, that the purpose of the shed is to protect the valve from being turned, and as such, its use by a vandal is not particularly harmful. In some sense, the vandal wins and so does the infrastructure because they are not in strict competition with each other. An even better example would be a vagrant who decided to take up residence in the shed and acted as an unofficial guard. While this is not particularly desirable for the utility because of liability issues and the inability to detect a real threat, the sides in this conflict in fact have different but not conflicting, or perhaps a more descriptive word would be noncommon, objectives.

Game theory is generally used to model complex situations in which "players" make "moves" and to evaluate "strategies" for how to make those moves. A game like chess is a two-player, zero-sum game. It is zero-sum because a win for one side is a loss for the other. It uses alternating moves in which each player takes a turn and then awaits the other player; therefore, it is also synchronous. However, attack and defense games such as those played out in the competition between infrastructure attackers and defenders are not this way. They are multiplayer, non-zero-sum, and asynchronous, with noncommon objectives in most cases. The defenders have some set of assets they are trying to protect to retain their business utility, while attackers vary from people trying to find a place to sleep to nation-states trying to engage in military actions.

From the attackers' points of view, the goals are of their own making, but from the defender's perspective, the goals are readily made clear by analysis of business utility. The attacker starts somewhere and the defender needs to keep the attacker from getting to somewhere else, whether that somewhere is physical or virtual. The notion of an attacker starting at a source location and moving toward a target location leads to the use of source (s) target (t) graphs, or s-t graphs. From a conservative perspective, a defender should assume that the attacker is trying to get to the target, even if the attacker is not trying to, so that if it happens, the defender will do the right thing. It turns out that s-t graphs have been analyzed in significant detail by those in operations research and related fields and that there are a lot of mathematical results indicating the complexity of analysis of different cases for these graphs. This is helpful in building up analytical results, but even more helpful in creating capabilities to derive optimal solutions to severing graphs of this sort. Severing such graphs at minimum cost, or using the minimum number of defenses placed at the right points, is called "cutting" the graph, or finding a "cut set." A quick Internet search for "s-t graph min cut" will produce more results than most people will be willing to read, including algorithms for finding approximations to minimum cuts in $\log(n)$ time, where n is the number of nodes and links in the graph. Leveraging this sort of analysis leads to the automated analysis of defenses for cost and coverage of attack graphs (e.g., do they cut the graph, are they optimal cuts, what do they cost)?

In the more general sense, since there are many attack sources out there with different capabilities and intents, and since there may be multiple targets that could cause potentially serious negative consequences, the standard mathematical analysis is helpful only in certain cases. Still, it should provide useful guidance and, in many cases, provide upper and lower bounds on the costs (costs are in terms of whatever you wish to measure about the resulting situation) of defense so that a designer knows when to stop trying new approaches to reduce those costs.

More general games have more complex analytical frameworks and fewer closed form solutions. Eventually, as analysis continues, the thoughtful defender will come to the conclusion that there are a very large number of possible attack graphs and that these have to be generated automatically and with limited granularity to allow analysis to proceed with reasonable time and space consumption. For example, just finding cuts to a graph does not detail how the defenses that make those cuts have to be put in place in time to stop the attack sequence or be placed there in advance. That is, there is an implicit assumption of fixed design rather than moves in the s-t graph approach. This ultimately leads to a simulation-based approach to analysis and design.

3.5.3   Model-Based Constraint and Simulations

Simulation is the only technology currently available to generate the sorts of design metrics necessary to understand the operation of a protection system as a whole and with reasonable clarity. While design principles and analysis provide a lot of useful information, taking the results of that effort and putting it into an event-driven simulation system provides the opportunity to examine hundreds of thousands of different scenarios in a relatively short time frame, generating a wide range of results, and yielding a sense of how the overall system will perform under threat. While simulation cannot replace real-world experience, generate creative approaches, or tell you how well your people and mechanisms will perform in the face of the enemy, it can allow you to test out different assumptions about their performance and see how deviations in performance produce different outcomes. By examining statistical results, a sense of how much training and what response times are required can be generated. Many fault scenarios can be played out to see how the system deviates with time. Depending on the simulation environment, workers can be trained and tested on different situations at higher rates than they would normally encounter to help improve their performance by providing far more experience than they could gain from actual incidents that occur on a day-to-day basis. Even long-time experts can learn from simulations, but there are limitations to how well simulations can perform, and simulations can be expensive to build, operate, and use, depending on how accurate and fine grained you want them to be.

Simulations are also somewhat limited in their ability to deal with the complexity of total situations. One good example of this is intelligence processes, in which elicitation might be used to get an insider to reveal information about the security system and processes. This might be combined with externally available data, like advertising from providers claiming that they provide some components, and perhaps with testing of the system, for example, sending someone who appears to be a vagrant to wander into the area of a shed with a valve to see what detection, assessment, and response capabilities are in place and to plant capabilities for future use. Over a period of time, such a complex attack might involve many seemingly unrelated activities that get fused together in the end to produce a highly effective distributed coordinated attack against the infrastructure element. If this seems too far out to consider, it might be worthwhile examining what the United States and its coalition did in the first Gulf War to defeat Iraqi infrastructure. They gathered intelligence on Iraqi infrastructure ranging from getting building plans from those who built portions of the facilities to using satellite and unmanned aerial vehicles to get general and detailed imagery. They modeled the entire set of infrastructures that were critical to the Iraqi war capability, did analysis, and determined what to hit, where, and in what order to defeat what was a highly resilient million soldier army within a whole country designed for resilience in war.

Another important thing to understand about defense and its models is that defense involves all aspects of operations. Training of workers in what to say and what not to say seems out of place for many enterprises, but for critical infrastructures, this forms a key part of operations security. Performing background checks on workers is another area where many executives get concerned about personal privacy, but it is critical to protecting against a wide variety of attacks that are commonly known and widely used. The goal-directed activities of attackers are hard to characterize, the effects of coincidence in creating weaknesses or enhancing defenses are complex and potentially numerous, and interactions between the physical and information spaces are often poorly understood even by well-qualified experts.

While a simulation can run a model repeatedly given enough time, the number of repetitions required to reasonably cover a complex space such as this can get very high. For that reason, modeling is the key aspect of simulation that is required to make it effective for understanding protection. Since every infrastructure element is indeed unique in some ways, this implies that unique models may be required for each one to get effective analysis at the level of granularity desired.

There is also an even more important area of modeling that is ultimately necessary at a larger scale to protect an infrastructure. Given that there are finite resources and a need for action in response to detected and characterized events, the question of how to assess response options and apply the available resources become central to making decisions in real-time. While you can practice some amount of this activity and tell people that specific assets are more important than others, at the end of the day, a smart attacker using a well-thought-out attack will succeed in causing considerable harm by their ability to focus resources on a point of attack while diffusing defender resources or using reflexive control methods to weaken these. Given that it is very difficult to keep track of a large and complex operation at the level of an infrastructure or set of infrastructures, it becomes important for modeling of the overall situation to be applied to assist decision-makers in understanding how far to go and when to back down and accept a small loss to prevent a large one. This then calls for a form of situation awareness and the ability to anticipate possible futures and respond in such a way as to protect the future while still dealing with the present. This sort of approach is called model-based situation anticipation and constraint. It is designed based on the notion that through situation understanding and analysis, future situations can be predicted and constrained by selecting from available choices to prevent large losses and tend to generate wins. The so-called min-max approach is well defined in game theory; however, analysis of minima and maxima over the complex space that defines realistic security is certainly a difficult thing to achieve. It is, in some sense, comparable to identifying the absolute best move in a chess game at every step, except that chess is pretty simple by comparison.

Since it is too complex to play perfect chess and this is far harder, the game goes to the swiftest of thought with the best model. Hence, an arms race in generating models and simulations is likely to result in situations where the intensity continues to increase over time.

3.5.4 Optimization and Risk Management Methods and Standards

From the standpoint of the critical infrastructure designer and operator, the protection-related design goal is to provide appropriate protection for the elements of the infrastructure they control to optimize the cost plus loss of their part of the infrastructure. This is, of course, at odds with the overall goal of the infrastructure of optimizing its overall cost plus loss and at odds with the national or regional goal of optimizing cost plus loss across all infrastructures. For example, a local utility would be better off from an individual standpoint by doing little to protect itself if it could depend on the national government to protect it, especially since most utilities are in monopoly positions. However, large central governments tend to be more brittle and to create systems with common mode failures out of a desire for global efficiency and reduced effort, while local decision-makers tend to come to different decisions about similar questions because of local optimizations.

Infrastructures are, of course, different from other systems in that they may cross most if not all geographical boundaries, they must adapt over time to changes in technology and application, and they tend to evolve over time rather than go through step changes. The notion of rebuilding the Internet from scratch to be more secure is an example of something that is no more likely to happen than rebuilding the entire road system of the world to meet a new standard. So by their nature, infrastructures have and should have a wide range of different technologies and designs and, with those technologies and designs, different fault models and failure modes. This has the pleasant side effect of reducing common mode failures and, as such, is a benefit of infrastructures over fully designed systems with highly structured and unified controls. It also makes management of infrastructures as whole entities rather complex and limited.

To mitigate these issues, the normal operating mode of most infrastructures is defined by interfaces with other infrastructure elements and ignores the internals of how those elements operate.

Infrastructures can be thought of as composites made up of other composites wherein each of the individual composites is separate and different from the others and yet there is enough commonality to allow them to interoperate in the important ways at the interfaces between them. Because each composite is unique and different, there are a wide range of different technologies and operational modes for these infrastructure elements and each has to be independently secured in the sense of having its own security architecture, design, and implementation. This seeming inefficiency is also a great strength because it also means that to attack a large portion of the infrastructures in a region or country, a large number of different attack plans have to be undertaken, and therefore, in practice, it is nearly impossible for any real threat to produce national or regional catastrophic consequences in terms of infrastructure collapse or to sustain substantial outages for extended periods of time. To get a sense of this, the first Gulf War involved the United States and its allies attacking element after element of the Iraqi infrastructures to reduce its capacity and will to fight. It took months of effort to create and coordinate a plan to accomplish this and weeks of bombing at an intensity level far in excess of any previous military operation to accomplish it. Even then, the infrastructures were only partially destroyed and they were reconstituted in fairly short order, even as the fighting went on.

Because each infrastructure element really has to perform its own risk management activities and optimize according to its own infrastructure design decisions, there is a lot of unit-by-unit design that must ultimately go on to secure infrastructure operations against threats to the management-desired levels of surety. Different infrastructure elements and owners apply different sorts of techniques to this end. Risk management decisions are almost universally made by executives when those executives are aware that they have decisions to make and of the implications of their choices. When it comes to security, it is rare to find executives making those decisions based on a deep understanding of the issues. While many executives who run enterprises come from financial or marketing backgrounds, few key decision-makers come from security backgrounds. So while they often make good business decisions based on financial information, they have to rely on those who work for them to provide good information to facilitate their decision-making processes in the security arena. Hence, the chief information security officer comes into play in large enterprises, but most infrastructures are not large enterprises. The vast majority of local infrastructures are run by local utility companies like water districts, perhaps at the state level for parts of power infrastructures; at local banks for much of the financial industries; owners of small bus lines, cab companies, and city or area public transportation systems for most transportation companies; local fire and police for emergency services; local clinics or small hospital chains for health care; small gas station chains and other similar providers for local energy; and so forth. Each of these small to medium-sized organizations has to make its own security decisions even though each is a part of an overall critical infrastructure.

Due diligence approaches are typically based on the idea that since something has happened to you, it would be negligent not to keep it from happening again unless the harm was too small to justify the cost of defense. This is necessary from a liability standpoint according to the most common notions underlying negligence, and it is often as far as infrastructure providers go, although some do not even go this far and end up losing their operating licenses or getting sued. This is typical for cases in which internal experience is the basis for understanding risks. An expanded version of this uses contacts with others in local industry and perhaps professional society memberships as a basis for risk assessment. This approach is not advisable from a standpoint of optimizing the approach to security, but for some of the smallest providers for whom spending even tens of thousands of dollars on thinking about security is excessive, it is an approach that can reasonably be taken. Unfortunately, it is often an approach taken by far larger providers for whom it is a substantial mistake.

Methodologies used to analyze risks to support decision making in design typically start with probabilistic risk assessment (PRA), which works well for random events but is not designed or intended to work against intentional, intelligent, malicious attackers. Nevertheless, PRA is useful and should be used where it applies. PRA consists of assigning probabilities to a set of events that are seen to be feasible and that can induce identifiable consequences. For example, we might have a 20% chance per year of someone guessing the password to the SCADA system that would allow them to change the chlorination of a water system without getting detected right away, with an expected monetized consequence of 100,000 monetary units. Summing the products of probabilities and consequences yields an expected loss, typically measured on an annualized basis as the annual loss expectancy (ALE). Using the same example, password guessing leading to chlorination changes has an ALE of 20,000 units and contributes along with all of the other considered sources of loss to produce the overall ALE. The goal of risk reduction in this methodology is to optimize the selection of defenses to minimize the ALE plus the cost of defense. The next step is typically to assume that all defenses are independent of each other and have a quantifiable effect on reducing the probability of events. For example, suppose using stronger passwords would reduce the probability of the password guessing attack to 10% at a cost of 100 units per year. Then, investing those 100 units would save an average of 10,000 units per year in loss, producing a reduction in cost plus loss of 9900 units. The return on investment (ROI) is then calculated as 9900/100, or 99 to 1. After doing this analysis on each combination of defenses and their effect on each of the identified causes of loss, the defenses can be sorted by ROI, and since they are assumed to be independent, the ROIs can be sorted and defenses undertaken starting with the best ROI and working down toward the ROI that no longer justifies the investment. Alternatively, budgets can be spent from best ROI to worst until it is exhausted and then again spent next year in a similar manner.

Clearly, PRA has some problems in the protection context.

The assumptions that all attacks and defenses are independent of each other or that you could reasonably generate the probability for each, or that you could list all of the event sequences, or that you could compute expected losses accurately, or that things are relatively static over time and justify substantial investments, or that the reduction in attack probability is directly available are all problematic on their own. Indeed, PRA for security situations has been called a guess multiplied by an estimate taken to the power of an expert opinion. And yet, PRA is widely used in some communities, and there are some actuarial statistics available from commercial companies on event types and occurrence rates.

Covering approaches are often used in cases where generating numbers surrounding PRA are considered infeasible or a waste of time and in which the vulnerabilities can be reasonably characterized against identifiable threats. For example, protecting a small building that holds valves within a utility system from vandals typically consists of covering the obvious things that can be done to such a building. There is a door, and it can be opened, so a lock is required. The lock can be picked, so an alarm is needed to generate a response if there is a break-in. There is a window that can be broken and people can crawl through it, so we might put in bars or make the alarm system detect motion or heat inside the room rather than just a door opening. The walls are wood, so it is easy to break through them, which means that again we need an alarm or to strengthen the walls. Someone might set fire to the building, so a fire alarm is needed. As the list of things that are likely to happen gets longer, the analysis of what risk mitigation to put in place grows, and we may need to think about different designs and different sets of defenses. Do we want to harden more or alarm more and respond in time? What kinds of alarms will work in the environment without generating a lot of false-positives? Do we visit the site periodically and do we have that long to notice something going wrong before great harm is done? How do we assess alarms to eliminate false-positives?

The solution to these challenges comes from a covering approach. In a covering approach, you make a list of all of the bad things that you think can happen and the different protective measures you know of that might apply. Then you identify the costs of each defense and its "coverage" of the events of interest. For example, a motion sensor with audio alarm in the building might cover opening the door, entering through the window, or cutting through the walls, while a door lock may only cover opening the door, but the motion sensor with audio alarm might cost more than a door lock, window bars, and reinforced walls. Further, coverage may not be perfect. For example, a door lock might cover the door being opened, but only if the attacker cannot pick the lock or remove the hinges, so it is only partial coverage of opening the door. Once you have all of the coverage estimates and costs, you can use covering analysis to determine the best set of defense selections to reach full coverage at the desired level of redundancy (perhaps you require at least one defense to cover each known weakness) at the minimum cost. For a single cover, the process starts with choosing all defenses that are "necessary" because they are the only defense that covers a particular weakness. Then, all of the weaknesses covered by that defense are eliminated as already covered by it, and the process is repeated until there are no single covers left. At this point, there are choices of combinations of defenses that cover the remaining weaknesses in different ways, and the goal is to minimize total cost while obtaining coverage, so standard optimization techniques from the field of operations research, such as integer programming, can be used.

Protection posture assessments (PPAs) can be thought of as a form of expert facilitated analysis in which experts are brought in to understand the threats, vulnerabilities, and consequences and to devise approaches to defense. Typically, they start by creating a "business" model of the key operational processes that need to be protected and what they depend on for their operation. This drives to the set of capabilities that are critical for ongoing operations and the consequences associated with failures of those capabilities. Once the consequences of failures are understood, threats are identified through a threat assessment process and classes of event sequences that are within the capabilities and intents of the threat sets and that can induce potentially serious negative consequences are identified.

These event sequences induce failures by generating feasible faults. The result is typically a set of partial paths from source to target, where the source is the starting point of the threat and the target is the potentially serious negative consequence to the defender. An example of a partial path approach is to assume that an attacker starting at the outside and trying to reach a target within a building will have to undertake a process of some sort. The first step might be to gather intelligence on the target, for example, finding the facility. This might be done any number of ways, for example, by looking up the facility on the Internet or using satellite maps, but all of them lead to knowing where it is and something about it. The next step might be to get past the outer perimeter defenses. For example, if the building is in the middle of the desert, attackers would have to get there. They might fly, drive, or walk, depending on their capabilities and intents. The sequence continues, but the basic notion is that each major step from a source (s) to a target (t) can be characterized as a set of paths in a graph that ultimately goes from s to t, also known as an s-t graph. Based on the current defenses in place, the PPA then produces, in one form or another, a characterization of the s-t graph that remains after existing defenses are taken into account. PPAs typically compare existing protections to standards and identify differences between current status and process with standards. The result would be reasonably characterized as a gap analysis. Advice is usually given on the most important urgent, tactical, and strategic things that must be done to mitigate the gaps with a notion that some things are more urgent because they are readily attained by identified threats and have high consequences or because they can be readily addressed with minimal cost and effort and have consequences that make the mitigation very worthwhile for the defender in that time frame. The resulting reports are typically road maps for future defenses.

Scenario-based analysis is, in essence, PPAs with greater rigor and taking more effort, which means higher cost. Scenario-based approaches typically use facilitated larger group processes to generate large numbers of scenarios and then analyze each of the scenarios for its constituent parts to generate an s-t graph similar to that of the PPA approach.

While a PPA typically uses a set of experts with industry knowledge and security expertise in discussions with internal experts within the infrastructure company to get to the s-t graph and produce example scenarios from there, scenario-based approaches focus on generating lists of scenarios in larger group brainstorming efforts and break up those scenarios into parts that can then be recombined to create an s-t graph. The goal of the scenario generation is to come up with a lot of ideas that can then be used to generate the attack graphs, while the PPA typically starts with a model of how attackers attack and a library of historically generated capabilities and intents. But no matter which path is taken, the end result is still a set of s-t graphs for different threats. The scenario-based approach also provides a "learning experience" for the participants and, as such, engages decision-makers from the infrastructure provider in starting to think about protection. This is very beneficial, but often hard to do. A more common version of this approach is to have scenario experiences with multiple infrastructure providers in a larger meeting with groups of experts in different fields to generate the underlying models and awareness and then to undertake PPAs for individual providers.

As risks are characterized and options for mitigation and management presented, decision-makers have to make decisions. It is hard to say, as a general rule, how and why decision-makers make the decisions they make regarding security. But there are some commonalities. Most decision-makers have thresholds associated with changing their decisions. There is a sort of hysteresis built into decisions in that most people do not like to think and really do not like to rethink. If forced to think about an issue, decision-makers must be pushed over a threshold to make a decision, but once over that threshold and once the decision is made, it is far more difficult to change than it was to make in the first place. In the security space, most executive decision-makers have little experience, but they see the news and hear about other infrastructures and understand that they do not want to be dragged through the dirt when and if something fails in their infrastructure. They tend to make threshold decisions in which they decide to accept risks below some level, transfer risks whenever they can do so at a reasonable price, avoid risks only when they know that the risks are there and feel that the risks outweigh the rewards, and mitigate risks when they are not transferred, avoided, or acceptable.

While many executives like the idea of optimization, in the security space, optimization is a very tricky problem because of the lack of good metrics for most of the things that would yield sound business decisions. When an executive asks for the ROI for security decisions, there are really only two choices. Either an ROI will be presented with a poor basis in fact or someone will have to explain why the ROI on security is problematic. In the former case, the executive might buy it or might ask probing questions. If the executive buys it and something goes wrong later, the executive is likely to get the person who presented the ROI information fired. If executives ask probing questions, they are likely to find out that there is little real basis for ROI calculations at the level of an overall security program and fire the messenger sooner rather than later or at least underfund the program. Fear drives many decisions, and to be effective, you have to raise a fear and provide a way to quell it. But after a point, people get tired of the fear mongering and feel taken advantage of when their fears are not realized. This leaves explaining the limitations of ROI in the security space to executives.

A common approach to getting around this issue is to talk about standards. For example, when we build buildings, we follow the local building codes. These are community standards, and their technical aspects are based on calculations and decisions made by others. Builders do not do ROI calculations on every wire in a building to determine whether the set of lights connected to a particular wire justify buying a different sized wire or not. They have standard wire sizes for standard circuit voltages and currents, and they use them all the time. In the security space, there are an increasing number and range of standards that can be applied, and if they are followed, most security functions will work reasonably well. If they are ignored and security fails, then the question of due diligence and suitability for purpose come up and liability arises. Most executives like the idea of being able to claim that they do what everybody else does in the areas where they are not claiming to do better than others. It reduces their personal job risks, it is seen as reasonable and prudent, and it is hard to argue against doing at least that much. In infrastructures, standards are used all the time for integration with other parts of the infrastructures, and without them, we would be largely lost. Imagine how financial transactions would work if everyone had their own interchange formats and did not agree on a standard. Every pair of financial institutions would have to program a unique fungible transfer protocol, and there are a lot of financial institutions out there. Detailed technical security standards are increasingly being used and component designers are increasingly providing components that use these standards to interoperate. At the policy and controls levels, standards have emerged as well, leading to general design principles and approaches in covering the totality of the space that is security. However, this does not mean that standards are the end of the story. They are really only the beginning. Standards are generally based on the notion that the owner and operator will create an architecture within which the standards will apply. Applying standards implies designing within sets of flexible design rules. They may tell you the wire to use, but not what fixture will work.

Finally, and at the end of the day, risk management is about human decision-makers making decisions about future events that are highly uncertain. These human decisions are subjective in nature but have a tendency to be better when they are better informed. Luck favors the prepared.

3.6 Economic Impact on Regulation and Duties to Protect

As discussed earlier, it is generally impossible to design and operate an infrastructure to handle all threats that can ever exist for all time without interruption of normal services and it is very expensive to try to do so. In addition, if design and operations were done in this manner, costs would skyrocket and operators who did a poorer job of protection would be more successful, make more money, be able to charge lower prices, and put competitors out of business. For these reasons, the invisible hand of the market, if left unchecked, will produce weak infrastructures that can handle everyday events but that will collapse in more hostile circumstances.

The question arises of how much the invisible hand of the market should be forced through regulation to meet national and global goals and the needs of the citizenry. There is no predefined answer, but it must be said that the decision is one of public policy. The challenge before those who protect these infrastructures is how to best meet the needs of the market in the presence of regulations. These requirements form the duty to protect that must be met by the designers and operators.

Duties to protect generally come from the laws and regulations, the owners of the infrastructure and their representatives, outside audit and review mandates, and top management. Some of these duties are mandatory because they are externally forced, while others are internally generated based on operating philosophy or community standards. Each individual infrastructure type has different legal and regulatory constraints in each jurisdiction, and as such, each infrastructure provider must peruse its own course of analysis to determine what is and is not mandated and permitted. Nevertheless, we will help to get things rolling by covering the basics.

3.6.1 The Market and the Magnitude of Consequences

The market essentially never favors the presence of security controls over their absence unless the rate of incidents and magnitude of consequences are so high that it becomes hard to survive without strong protective measures in place. The reason that the invisible hand of the market does not directly address such things is that luck can lead to success. For example, suppose that there is a 50% chance of a catastrophic attack on some infrastructure element once a year, but that there are 32 companies in direct competition for that market, that security costs increase operating costs by 5%, that margins are 10%, and that four companies pay the price for security. In this simplistic analysis, it ignores items like the time value of money; after the first year, 14 companies fail, two companies that would have failed continue because they had adequate security, and those not attacked continue to operate. Now we have 18 companies in the market, 4 of them with half the profit of the other 14.

1.1.1   First Generation Computers, 1951–1958

Included the UNIVAC-1;
Used vacuum tubes for controlling functions;
Used magnetic drums for primary storage;
First generation software used symbolic language for programming;
  and
Machine language programs were used by the binary forms of zeroes
  and ones.

1.1.2   Second Generation Computers, 1959–1964

The transistor replaced the vacuum tube and made possible the second
  generation of computers;
Magnetic tape was introduced and replaced the need for punched cards;
  and
COBOL and FORTRAN programming languages were introduced.

1.1.3   Third Generation Computers, 1965–1971

Integrated circuits made possible the third generation of computers as incredible numbers of transistors were deposited on a silicon chip, thus introducing
the era of miniaturization and increased speed.

The nanosecond (one billionth of a second) became the new standard for
measuring access and process time.

IBM's System/360 computers and the first minicomputer by Digital
Equipment Corporation were introduced.

Online computers and remote terminals became popular using regular
telephone lines from remote locations.

Business applications increased, especially in the airline reservation systems and real-time inventory control systems.

1.1.4   Fourth Generation Computers, 1971–1990

The introduction of large-scale integrated (LSI) circuits for both memory
and logic made the IBM 370 mainframe possible by LSI circuits.

The movement to the very-LSI circuits made it possible to place a complete central processing unit (CPU) on one very small semiconductor chip.
This resulted in increased computer performance with a phenomenal lowering of the cost of computers. The processing power of mainframe computers
in the 1960s costing millions of dollars was now available for use in personal
computers (PCs) for less than $1000.

In the second year, seven more fail, with the two who happened to have security surviving from the nine attacked.

Now we have 11 companies left, 7 of which have no security and that are more profitable than the 4 that have security by a factor of 20% to 10%, or two to one. In the next year, three more fail, leaving four without security and four with security. The four without security have now made enough money to buy the four with security, and they abandon the security controls, having demonstrated that they are more efficient and generate higher profits. The uncontrolled market will do this again and again for situations in which the markets are moving rapidly, there is a lot of competition and little regulation, and serious incidents are not so high that it is possible to last a few years without being taken out of business. For those who doubt this, look at the software business and the Internet service provider business.

Most physical infrastructures are not this way because they are so critical and because there is rarely a lot of competition. Most cities have few options for getting natural gas, local telephone, electrical, garbage, or sewage services. However, in the banking arena, Internet services, automobile gas, long distance services, and other arenas, there is substantial competition and therefore substantial market pressure in any number of areas. An example where protection becomes a market issue is in the release of credit card data on individuals. Laws, which we will discuss in more detail, have forced disclosures of many such releases, which have started to have real impacts on companies. The replacement of credit cards, for example, costs something on the order of tens of dollars per individual, including all of the time and effort associated with disabling previous versions, sending agreements as to potential frauds, checking credit reports, and so forth. The losses resulting from these thefts of content are also substantial as the information is exploited on a global basis. The effect on the companies from a standpoint of market presence and reputation can be substantial, and attention of regulators and those who determine rights of usage to public facilities is sometimes affected as well.

3.6.2 Legal Requirements and Regulations

Legal and regulatory requirements for public companies and companies that deal with the public are substantially different from those for private companies that deal only with other companies—so-called business to business businesses.

Critical infrastructure providers come in both varieties. While the customer-facing components of critical infrastructures are the apparent parts, much of the back-end of some infrastructures deals only with other organizations and not with the public at large. Examples of back-end organizations include nuclear power producers who produce power and sell to distribution companies, network service providers that provide high-bandwidth backbone services for telecommunications industry and financial services, companies that extract natural resources like gas and oil for sale to refineries, and companies that provide large water pipes to send large volumes of water between water districts. Most of the commercial ventures performing these services are themselves public companies and are therefore subject to regulations associated with public stocks, and of course, many critical infrastructures are government owned and/or operated or government-sanctioned monopolies.

The regulatory environment is extremely complex. It includes, but is not limited to, regulations on people, things, ownership, reporting, decision making, profit margins, sales and marketing practices, employment, civil arrangements, pricing, and just about anything else you can think of, but most of these are the same as they are for other companies that are not in the critical infrastructure business. As a result, the number of special laws tend to be limited to issues like imminent domain; competitive practices; standards for safety, reliability, and security; information exchanges with governments and other businesses; and pricing and competition regulations. Each industry has its own set of regulations within each jurisdiction, and with more than 200 countries in the world and many smaller jurisdictions contained therein, there are an enormous number of these legal mandates that may apply to any given situation. For example, in California, a law titled SB1386 requires that an unauthorized release of personally identified information about a California citizen must produce notice to that individual of the release or notice to the press of the overall release. If you are a water company in California and allow credit cards for payment of water bills, you have to be prepared to deal with this. Similar laws exist in many other states within the United States.

If you are a telecommunications provider, you have similar requirements for multiple states. If you are a global telecommunications provider, you have additional legal requirements about personal information that may bar you from retaining or transmitting it across national boundaries in the European Union while being required to retain it in other countries, and this is just one very narrow branch of one legal requirement. Emerging Internet sites typically provided by universities or industry organizations provide lists of laws related to businesses and they commonly have hundreds of different legal mandates surrounding security issues, but these are only a start. Building codes, which may be localized to the level of the neighborhood, to limits on levels of toxic substances, to fertilizer composition, to temperature controls on storage, are all subject to regulation. Regardless of the business reasons for making protection decisions, these regulatory mandates represent a major portion of the overall protection workload and include many duties that must be identified and resources that must be allocated to carry out these duties.

Contractual obligations are also legal mandates; however, the requirements they produce have different duties and different rewards and punishments for failures to carry them out. Contracts can be, more or less, arbitrary in what they require regarding rewards and punishments. As such, contracts have the potential to vary enormously. However, in practice, they do not stray very far from a few basics. For critical infrastructures, they typically involve the delivery of a service and/or product meeting time and rate schedules, quality levels, and locations, within cost constraints and with payment terms and conditions. For example, food is purchased in bulk from growers with government-inspected grades of quality, at costs set by the market, within expiration dates associated with freshness mandates, at quantities and prices set by contracts. Wholesalers purchase most of the food, which is then either processed into finished goods or sold directly to retailers, with more or less the same sets of constraints. Retailers sell to the general public and are subject to inspections. While the details may vary somewhat, critical infrastructures most commonly have fairly limited ranges of rates for what they provide, and most rates are published and controlled in some way or another by governments. Payment processes use payment systems compatible with the financial infrastructure, and information requirements involve limited confidentiality.

All of these legal constraints are subject to force majeure, in which war, insurrection, nationalization, military or government takeover, or other changes out of the control of the provider or their customers change the rules without much in the way of recourse.

3.6.3   Other Duties to Protect

Other duties to protect exist because of management and ownership decisions and the oft missed obligation to the public. Management and ownership decisions are directly tied to decision making at the highest levels of the enterprise, and the obligation to the public is a far more complex issue. Ownership and management decisions create what are essentially contractual obligations to employees, customers, and suppliers. For example, there are legal definitions of the term "organic" in many jurisdictions, and owners who decide to sell organic food create obligations to the buying public to meet those local requirements. The farmers who sell organic product must follow rules that are specific to the organic label or be subject to legal recourse. Internet providers who assert that they maintain privacy of customer information must do so or induce civil liability. Duty to the public stems from the obligation implied by infrastructure providers to the people they serve. In many cases, critical infrastructure providers have exclusive control over markets in which they operate as monopolies with government sanction. In exchange for exclusivity, they have to meet added government regulations. They could give up the exclusivity in exchange for reductions in regulations, but they choose not to. Many companies in the telecommunications field choose to act as "common carriers," which means that they will carry any communications that customers want to exchange and pay no attention to the content exchanged. In exchange for not limiting or controlling content, they gain the advantage of not being responsible for it or having legal liability for it.

Common carrier laws have not yet been applied to the Internet in most places, creating enormous lists of unnecessary outages and other problems that disrupt its operation, while telephone lines continue to operate without these problems, largely because of common carrier laws and fee structures.

Employee and public safety and health are another area of duty that is implied and often mandated after providers fail to meet their obligations on a large scale. For emerging infrastructures, this takes some time to evolve, but for all established infrastructures, these duties are defined by laws and regulations. Warnings of catastrophic incidents, evacuations, and similar events typically call for interactions between critical infrastructure providers and local or federal governments. In most cases, reporting chains are defined by regulation or other means, but not in all cases. For example, if a nuclear power plant has a failure that has potential public health and safety issues, it always has a national-level contact it makes within a predefined time frame. If a fire causes an outage in a power substation, regulatory notifications may be required, but affected parties find out well before it makes the media because their lights go out. If a gas pipeline is going to be repaired during a scheduled maintenance process, previous notice must be given to affected customers in most cases, and typically the maintenance is scheduled during minimal-usage periods to minimize effects.

Special needs, like power for patients on life support systems, or manufacturing facilities with very high costs associated with certain sorts of outages, or "red tag" lines in some telecommunications systems that have changes locked out for one reason or another, are also obligations created that require special attention and induce special duties to protect. For providers serving special government needs, such as secure communications associated with the U.S. "Emergency Broadcast System" or the "Amber Alert" system, or public safety closed circuit television systems, additional duties to protect are present. The list goes on and on.

Finally, natural resources and their uses include duties to protect in many jurisdictions and, in the case of global treaties, throughout the world. For example, many critical infrastructure providers produce significant waste byproducts that have to be safely disposed of or reprocessed for return to nature or other uses. In these cases, duties may range from simple separation into types for differentiated recycling or disposal to the requirements associated with nuclear waste for processing and storage over hundreds or even thousands of years. Life cycle issues often involve things like dealing with what happens to the contamination caused by chemicals put into the ground near power lines to prevent plant growth because as rain falls, and Earth movement causes contaminants to spread through ground water into nearby areas. While today, only a few critical infrastructure providers have to deal with these protection issues, over time, these life cycle issues will be recognized and become a core part of the critical infrastructure protection programs that all providers must deal with.

3.7 Critical Infrastructure Protection Strategies and Operations

The protection space, as you may have guessed by now, is potentially very complex. It involves a lot of different subspecialties, and each is a complex field, most with thousands of years of history behind them. Rather than summarize the last 10,000 years of history in each of the subspecialties here, an introduction to each will be provided to give a sense of what they are and how they are used in critical infrastructure protection. Needless to say, there is a great deal more to know than will be presented here, and the reader is referred to the many other fine books on these subjects for additional details.

Protect is defined herein as "keep from harm." Others identify specific types of harm, such as "damage" or "attack" or "theft" or "injury." There are all sorts of harm. Keeping critical infrastructures from being harmed has an underlying motivation in keeping people from being harmed, both over the short run and over the long run. At the end of the day, if we have to disable a power or water system to save peoples' lives, we should do so. As a result, somewhere along the line, the focus has to point to the people served by the critical infrastructure.

Now this is a very people-focused view of the world, and as many will likely note, protection of the environment is very important. The focus on people is not one of selfishness; rather, it is one of expediency. Since harm to the environment will ultimately harm people in the long run, environmental protection is linked to people protection. While it would be a fine idea to focus on the greater good of the world or, perhaps, by implication, the universe, protecting the world might be best served by eliminating all humans from it. This will not likely get past the reviewers, so we will focus on the assumption that keeping the critical infrastructures from being harmed serves the goal of keeping people from being harmed, even though we know it is not always so. At the same time, we will keep in mind that, at the strategic level, things are heavily intertwined, and the interdependencies drive an overall need to protect people (because they are the ones the infrastructures were built to serve) and the implied strategic need to protect the world that those people depend upon.

Most of the subspecialties of the protection field have been historically titled under "security" of one sort or another. Military parlance includes things like Trans-Sec, Op-Sec, Pers-Sec, Info-Sec, Intel, and things like that. Each is more or less an abbreviation for a subspecialty. We will not use the full military spectrum of security types, and lots of variations are included here, but the reader should be aware that parlance differs from infrastructure to infrastructure, from company to company, and from field to field.

The intent of the specialties involved in the protection field is to consolidate a body of knowledge earned at the cost of lives and fortunes into a discipline that, if well applied, reduces the number and severity of incidents in exchange for vigilance and cost. Less vigilance or less cost will, over time, produce more severe and more frequent incidents; however, it is more or less impossible to predict the direct relationship between a protective measure and a specific incident that does not occur because of it. As a result, many have characterized the field and the subspecialties as something ranging from witchcraft to paranoia. We will not argue the point. Most of those who make these characterizations have lived their lives under the protection of these methods and are simply and blissfully unaware of them.

Protection is not a science today despite a strong desire by some in the field to make it into one. This is because of many issues ranging from a lack of respect to a lack of funding. Many attempts to turn subspecialties into science have been successful—the best known example being the field of operations research that arose from efforts during World War II to use mathematics to optimize attack and defense techniques. However, in a field this large, and with the changes in science and technology so rampant, it will take a few more millennia to get there.

3.7.1 Physical Security

Without physical security, no assurances can be provided that anything will be as it is desired. All critical infrastructures have physicality. Protecting that physicality is a necessary but not sufficient condition of providing services and goods and to protection of all sorts. At the same time, perfect physical security is impossible to attain because there is always something with more force than can be defended against in the physical space. Nuclear weapons and forces of nature such as earthquakes and volcanoes cannot be stopped by current defenses in any useful way, but each is limited in physical scope. Asteroids of large enough size and massive nuclear strikes will likely put an end to human life if they come to pass in the foreseeable future, and protection against them is certainly beyond the scope of the critical infrastructure provider. Similarly, the fall of governments, insurrections, and the chaos that inevitably follows make continuity of critical infrastructures very difficult, and delivery of products and services will be disrupted to one extent or another. However, many other forces of nature and malicious human acts may be successfully protected against and must be protected to a reasonable extent to afford stability to critical infrastructures.

Physical security for critical infrastructures generally involves facility security for central and distributed offices and other structures containing personnel and equipment, distribution system security for the means of attaining natural resources and delivering finished goods or services, and a range of other physical security measures associated with the other business operations necessary to sustain the infrastructure and its workers.

As an example, an oil pipeline typically involves a supply that comes from an oil pumping station of some sort that connects to underground storage and supply, a long pipe that may go under and over ground, a set of pressure control valves along the way, and a set of delivery locations where the oil is delivered to the demand. The valves and pumps have to be controlled and are typically controlled remotely through SCADA systems with local overrides. Supply has to be purchased and demand paid for, resulting in a financial system interface. The pipeline has to be maintained so there are people who access it and machines that might work it from the inside during maintenance periods.

For anything that does not move, physical security involves understanding and analyzing the physicality of the location it resides in. The analysis typically starts from a "safe" distance and moves in toward the protected items, covering everything from the center of the Earth up to outer space. In the case of sabotage, for example, the analysis has to start only at the attacker starting location and reach a distance from which the damage can be done with the attacker's capabilities and intents. This series of envelopes around the protected items also has to be analyzed in reverse in the case of a desire to prevent physical acts once the protected items are reached, such as theft, which involves getting the protected items out of the location to somewhere else. Each enveloped area may contain natural and/or artificial mechanisms to deter, prevent, or detect and react to attacks, and the overall system is adapted over time.

Returning to the pipeline example, a pipeline running through Alaska is at quite a distance from most potential threats for most of its length, so the protection mechanisms for most of the pipeline are likely based on natural barriers such as distance that has to be traveled over the frozen tundra, the time it takes to go that distance, and the limits on what you can carry over that distance in that environment without being easily detected in time for a forceful reaction in defense. For underground attack, things are only worse for the malicious human attacker in that circumstance; however, for air attack, it does not take very long to get a decent sized plane or missile to the pipeline and there is no realistic physical barrier to be placed in the airspace above the pipeline. So detection and reaction are the only reasonable defense against the air attack.

Different energy pipelines, for example, the ones delivering natural gas to homes throughout the world, have very different protection requirements and characteristics. These pipelines have many end points that are exposed to the open air and have essentially no physical protection. They run through streets and sewers and are readily reachable by almost anyone. However, the implications of a cut are far less because the total volume of gas flowing through them and the number of people affected are far smaller, even if the effects on the end demand are more immediate. As these pipes come from larger supplies, the need for physical security increases with the volumes flowing and the number of people affected.

The risks increase because of the higher consequences both to end demand and of damage to the infrastructure. A major gas pipe explosion can kill a lot of people, start a lot of fires, and take a lot of time to fix. At the head end, it can cripple portions of a city, and during winter, it can cost many lives.

An excellent book on facilities security is *The Design and Evaluation of Physical Protection Systems* by Mary Lynn Garcia (Elsevier, 2001). This book focuses primarily on the detailed aspects of protecting the highest valued items within facilities and as such represents the extreme in what can reasonably be done when the risks are very high, as they often are for critical infrastructures. For physical security of fixed transportation assets, this book is less useful, even if the concepts remain useful.

The problem with protecting long-distance fixed infrastructure transportation components is that electrical power infrastructure, other energy pipelines, and ground-based telecommunications transport media must traverse large distances. The cost of effective preventative protection all along the way is too high to bear for the consequences experienced in most societies today. Even in war zones, where sabotage is common, every inch of these distribution systems cannot be protected directly.

Rather, there are typically zones of protection into which limited human access is permitted, sensors and distances are put in place to delay attack, and detection of attack along with rapid response makes the price of successful attack high in human terms. There are only so many suicide bombers out there at any given time, and the total number is not so large that it is worth putting perimeter fencing with sensors and rapid response guards next to every inch of infrastructure.

For things that move, the facilities approach is somewhat problematic. A truck carrying a package of import cannot be protected from the center of the Earth to outer space, and except in the rarest of circumstances, guards and protective enclosures will not be present or substantial. Consider package delivery services as an example. Package supply comes from just about any endpoint in the world and is delivered to demand at any other endpoint in the world. Tens of millions of packages a day traverse any substantial portion of the transportation infrastructure, making detailed inspection of every package for every sort of issue infeasible with current or anticipated technology at any reasonable cost. Packages move from trucks to routing and distribution centers, and from those to other trucks, trains, boats, or aircraft. From there, they may go to other transportation centers or be delivered to the demand destination. While the distribution centers are fixed facilities that can be protected using physical protective methods identified earlier, the transportation portion of the effort cannot.

Various approaches to protecting materials in transit exist, including but not limited to, route timing and selection, guards and convoys, packaging, deception, marking, shielding, surveillance technologies, and tracking for detection and response. Insurance helps transfer risk and applies for almost any normal value level, while high valued shipments require additional protection as well as additional insurance.

Obviously, gold bar and large cash shipments tend to use armored cars and armed guards, while most normal packages go in cardboard boxes on unguarded panel vans driven by employees.

For the highest criticality shipments, like nuclear fuels and waste, protection levels tend to be very high, including concealment of when and where shipments come from and go to; the use of false convoys, unmarked convoys, special packaging, military escorts, surveillance from above, sensors on packaging, and limited times of day with little traffic; control of routes to ensure minimal interaction with other traffic and maximum protective capabilities; inspections, sealing, and guarding of areas at end points and along route; emergency plans for contingencies; special forces troops along route and with the transport; air cover; and so forth. The same transportation infrastructures (roads, rails, and bridges) are used for long-haul shipment even of the most critical goods, but they are used in specific manners. Air Force 1 is the designation for the aircraft carrying the president of the United States, and again, special precautions are used for this transport, and the air traffic control system adjusts the normal operation of the air traffic infrastructure to ensure added protection for the president. But most passengers using the same transportation infrastructures have less protection, largely because they are under less of a threat, but also because they are viewed as less consequential from a national security standpoint and the protection is provided by national security resources of the affected nations.

Just as perimeters are used in facility controls, they are used in transportation controls, but they are used quite differently because of the moving perimeter surrounding the transport vehicle. Within the vehicle, perimeters work more or less as they do within any other facility, except that because of weight, noise, movement, and other similar properties that tend to change in transit but not at a fixed location, the available technologies that are insensitive to these conditions and still effective for their protective roles are far fewer and tend to be more expensive. While we might be able to protect a facility from a gas attack, protecting a truck driver from things put into the air is nearly impossible because the driver has to breathe that outside air and the cost of not doing this is very high indeed.

On the other hand, increasingly, packages in transit and the vehicles used for transit are closely tracked and continuously surveyed.

Radiofrequency identification tags are augmenting bar codes and are used on individual packages and items to allow them to be tracked as they pass entries and exits of facilities and vehicles. Video surveillance is in place to watch goods being stored and moved, and the vehicles themselves are tracked in real-time via satellite. These sorts of active defenses allow rapid detection of theft, rerouting, stoppages, delays, and other events and allow rapid response to these events to limit damage. The infrastructure that vehicles travel on also have protective measures such as safety standards; real-time detection of traffic blockages, police, fire, and other emergency response forces for incident handling; sensors and video surveillance for detection of various passing loads; and other similar capabilities that augment physical protection of material in transit, typically from a detection and response standpoint.

Finally, but certainly not least important, physical security for people is critical to the operation of any critical infrastructure because it is the people who operate the infrastructures, and over time, they will all fail without people. People have to be physically protected from harm for critical infrastructures to operate properly, but people tend to move and are not willing or able to be strictly controlled like packages or material or facilities. Keeping people safe at the physical level runs the gamut from public protection of governmental dignitaries, who are part of the government's critical infrastructure, to protection of engineers, designers, operators, testers, and maintenance personnel who are also critical to all infrastructures.

While we may be able to guard the president, prime minister, premier, or dictator all day and night, it is not feasible or rational to do the same for everyone else. In critical infrastructure protection, the people who most need to be protected are not usually the executives, but rather the workers who touch the infrastructures. They tend to be people with lower pay rates who work in the same work environment (whether it be anywhere near power poles for a lineman or in front of the same desk for control system operators) day after day, and their jobs tend to be highly repetitive—except when it is especially important they do their jobs well—during emergencies.

The pilot's saying goes "hours and hours of boredom followed by a few seconds of terror." A power control station during normal operation is a very quiet and sedate place with constant whirring noises and perhaps a few people coming and going per hour, all quietly doing their jobs. However, during an emergency, it tends to be a bit livelier as people scurry to handle the emergency issues correctly according to procedure and in time frames necessary to limit the damage. You can fall asleep driving a truck because it is boring, but when a car shows up in front of you going in the opposite direction while you are going around an almost blind curve, you need to react fast and react right. If the pilot, driver, and operator are not properly trained, rested, and safe, they cannot react properly and the emergency will turn into a disaster.

For those who wish to attack critical infrastructures, these workers tend to be targets because they are not very well paid compared to executives, and they have the direct ability to do harm. The cost of protecting mobile workers such as drivers and maintenance personnel outside of fixed facilities is usually too high to justify strong protections. While armored truck drivers are better protected than linemen at work, none of them are protected outside of the normal work environment, such as at home or when on vacation, and work protection does not extend to their families like it does to some executives. More on the issues this brings will be discussed under personnel security; however, there is also a bit more to say about physical security for workers at work.

Fire and police workers are great examples of critical infrastructure workers who are in danger because of their work and for whom special protection is provided. They have special equipment and training designed to provide the maximum amount of safety attainable while still doing their jobs efficiently and cost effectively. They work in teams, which allows them to help each other and call for additional help when a need arises. They have special clothing and equipment: bullet-resistant clothing for police and fire-resistant clothing for fire fighters. Police have guns and handcuffs, while firefighters have air tanks, masks, and axes. These pieces of equipment and training encompass both safety and security and they are largely inseparable.

Back at the fire house, protections are far lower for firefighters because they tend to be supported and not attacked by their communities. Police stations require far greater protection, including the presence of special security holding areas for criminals, interrogation rooms, and other similar areas with special protection. Guns and ammunition have to be protected as well as computers with access to criminal databases and investigative and personnel records. Hospitals and other medical facilities, on the other hand, have very different protection profiles to protect the health and safety of their workers. Protection of workers is highly dependent on the nature of the infrastructure, the locations where the workers are present, and the nature of the work they need to do in those locations. Along with equipment and facility protective measures, training and awareness come into play for workers, and depending on the specifics, systems and processes may even be designed to ensure that individual workers cannot do serious harm alone and that lone workers are not exposed to undue hazards.

3.7.2   Personnel Security

When we talk about personnel security, we are generally talking about things we do to protect the critical infrastructures from malicious human actors who are authorized to act, rather than protecting those humans from being harmed or protection from personnel not authorized to act. This includes methods intended to gain and retain people who are reliable, trustworthy, and honest, making provisions to limit the potential negative effects of individuals and groups of individuals on the infrastructures, deterrence, surveillance, and combinations of rewards and punishments associated with proper and improper behaviors.

The personnel life cycle typically starts for the critical infrastructure provider with a job application. At that point, applicants undergo a background investigation to check on what they said about themselves and its veracity, to verify their identity, and to gain an understanding of their history as an indicator of future performance and behavior. Not all providers do these activities, and those that do not are far more likely to have problem employees and problem infrastructures.

Depending on the type of check undertaken, the background can reveal previous criminal acts, lies on the application (which are very common today), foreign intelligence ties, a false identity, high debt levels or other financial difficulty, or any number of other things that might affect employment. For many positions of high trust, clearances by government may be required. Obviously, police would be hesitant to hire people with criminal records, firefighters would hesitate to hire arsonists, and financial industries would hesitate to hire financial criminals or those with high debt, but any of these are potentially problematic for all of these positions and many more.

After a background check and clearance process is undertaken, protection limits the assignment of personnel to tasks. For example, foreign nationals might be barred from certain sensitive jobs involving infrastructures that provide services to government agencies and military installations, people with inadequate experience or expertise might not be assigned to jobs requiring high skill levels in specialty areas, and people without government clearances would be barred from work at certain facilities.

In the work environment, all workers must be authenticated to a level appropriate to the clearance they have, and the authentication and authorization levels for certain facilities may be higher than others. Over the period of work, some workers may not be granted access to some systems or capabilities unless and until they have worked at the provider for a certain length of time, under the notion that trust grows with time. Periodic reinvestigation of workers might be undertaken to see if they are somehow getting rich when they are not highly paid or have large debts that are growing, making them susceptible to blackmail. For highly sensitive positions, workers may have to notify their employer of arrests, travel to certain locations, marriages and divorces, and even relationships outside of marriage. Obviously, this information can be quite sensitive and should be carefully protected as well, but that is covered under information protection below.

Human reliability studies have been performed on a wide array of people and for many factors, and in particularly sensitive jobs, these sorts of efforts can be used as a differentiator.

Behaviors are often identified after the fact for workers who have violated trust, but on a predictive basis, such indicators are poor at identifying people who will betray trust. People who appear very loyal may in fact just be good at deception or trained to gain insider access. Insiders who might normally be worthy of trust may be put under duress and, at the risk of having family members killed or infidelity exposed, may violate trusts. Again, the personnel security issues are very complex.

3.7.3 Operational Security

Operations security has to do with specific processes (operations) undertaken. It tends to be in effect for a finite period of time and be defined in terms of specific objectives. Threats are identified relative to the operation, vulnerabilities are associated with the capabilities and intents of the specific threats to the operation, and defensive measures are undertaken to defeat those threats for the duration of the operation. These defenses tend to be temporary, one-time, unstructured, and individualized.

Operations consist of special purpose efforts, typically to meet a crisis or unusual one-off situation. The trans-Alaska pipeline creation was an operation requiring operations security, but its normal use requires operational security. The bridge that collapsed in Oakland, California, due to a fuel truck fire was repaired in a matter of a few weeks, and this is clearly an exceptional case, an operation requiring operations security. However, the normal process of building and repairing roads is an operational security issue.

For operations, security is a one-off affair, thus, it is typically less systematic and thoughtful in its design, and it tends not to seek optimization as much as a workable one-off solution and costs are not controlled in the same way because there are no long-term life cycle costs typically considered. Decisions to accept risks are far more common, largely because they are being taken once instead of many times, so people can be far more attuned and diligent in their efforts than will happen day after day when the same things are repeated. In some cases, operations security is more intensive than operational security because it is a one-off affair, so more expensive and specialized people and things can be applied.

Also, there is little, if any, history to base decisions on because each instance is unique, even if a broader historical perspective may be present for experienced operations workers.

Operational security is a term we use for the security we need around normal and exceptional business processes. This type of operational security tends to continue indefinitely and be repeated, readily and not focused on a specific time frame or target. In other words, these business processes are the day-to-day things done to make critical infrastructures work. Protection of normal operations tends to be highly structured and routine, revisited periodically, externally reviewed, and evolutionary.

An example of operations is the maintenance process surrounding outages of power, which are commonplace. While these activities are each unique in some sense, they are all fairly common and use repeatable processes. Every transformer or wire in the electrical power grid is expected to fail at some time, and the process for repair or replacement is well understood by all concerned. They do more or less the same thing every day. They have storms, floods, earth movement, and so forth again and again and they are used to it in the sense of having a well-developed set of security issues that are addressed in a standard and evolving way over time.

Operational security is largely about defining and refining processes over time. Consider, for example, the air traffic system. Over a period of more than 50 years, stepwise improvements in all aspects of air operations have produced a system that is the safest form of human transportation per passenger mile by far. Even the simultaneous hijacking of several planes and intentional driving of them into buildings did not significantly change the overall safety statistics, but the focus on never allowing a similar accident to recur is symptomatic of how air traffic safety is done. The operational security of the system called for increased inspections, but these inspections were not one-off. They are carried out across the world millions of times per day, and as flaws are found over time, they are mitigated to eliminate one after the other with the ultimate goal of perfection, never achieved, but hoped to be reached asymptotically.

3.7.4   Information Protection

Information protection addresses ensuring the utility of content. Content can be in many forms, as can its utility. For example, names and addresses of customers and their current amounts due are useful for billing and service provisioning, but if that is the sole purpose of their presence, they lose utility when applied to other uses, such as being stolen for use in frauds or sold for advertising purposes. Since utility is in context of the infrastructure, there is no predefined utility, so information systems must be designed to maximize utility specific to each infrastructure provider or they will not optimize the utility of content. The cost of custom systems is high, so most information systems in most critical infrastructures are general purpose and thus leave a high potential for abuse.

In addition to the common uses of content such as billing, advertising, and so forth, critical infrastructures and their protective mechanisms depend on information for controlling their operational behaviors. For example, SCADA systems are used to control the purification of water, the voltage and frequency of power distribution, the flow rates of pipelines, the amount of storage in use in storage facilities, the alarm and response systems of facilities, and many similar mechanisms, without the proper operation of which, these infrastructures will not continue to operate. These controls are critical to operation and if not properly operating can result in loss of service; temporary or long-term loss of utility for the infrastructure; the inability to properly secure the infrastructure; damage to other devices, systems, and capabilities attached to the infrastructure; or, in some cases, interinfrastructure collapse through the interdependency of one infrastructure on another. For example, an improperly working SCADA system controlling stored water levels in a water tower could empty all of the storage tanks, thus leaving inadequate supply for a period of time. As the potential for negative consequences of lost information utility increases, so should the certainty with which that utility is ensured.

For example, most water towers are controlled by systems of pumps and drains that are controlled by SCADA systems with built-in controls, limiting how they can be operated. If the water level gets too low, they will try to automatically turn on pumps and will do so unless these pumps are manually overridden on site or are nonfunctional, or if the SCADA system is disconnected from those pumps or not operating properly. More certainty comes at the price of more limited functionality and higher cost; thus, information protection trades cost for surety. A less expensive SCADA system can be used at the cost of less reliable operation, particularly when under attack. A centralized system may save costs, but it exposes the connections used to do remote control to attacks that would not be present in a distributed system with local SCADA controls. Most SCADA systems have local PLCs with operational settings and limits configured by central systems through controlled telecommunications infrastructure and physically local overrides of safety and operational limits.

Information is subject to regulatory requirements, contractual obligations, owner- and management-defined controls, and decisions made by executives. Many aspects of information and its protection are subject to audit and other sorts of reviews. As such, a set of duties to protect are defined and there is typically a governance structure in place to ensure that controls are properly defined, documented, implemented, and verified to fulfill those duties. Duties are codified in documentation that is subject to audit, review, and approval and that defines a legal contract for carrying out protective measures and meeting operational needs. Typically, we see policy, control standards, and procedures as the documentation elements defining what is to be done, by whom, how, when, and where. As tasks are performed, these tasks are documented and their performance reviewed with sign-offs in logbooks or other similar mechanisms. These operational logs are then used to verify from a management perspective that the processes as defined were performed and to detect and correct deviations from policy.

The definition of controls is typically required to be done through an approved risk management process intended to match surety to risk to keep costs controlled while providing adequate protection to ensure the utility of the content in the context of its uses.

This typically involves identifying consequences based on a business model defining the context of its use within the architecture of the infrastructure, the threats and their capabilities and intents for harming the infrastructure, and the architecture and its protective features and lack thereof. Threats, vulnerabilities, and consequences must be analyzed in light of the set of potentially complex interdependencies associated with both direct and indirect linkages. Risks can then be accepted, transferred, avoided, or mitigated to levels appropriate to the situation.

In large organizations, information protection is controlled by a chief information security officer or some similarly titled position. However, most critical infrastructure providers are small local utilities that have only a few tens of workers in total and almost certainly do not have a full-time information technology (IT) staff. If information protection is controlled at all, it is controlled by the local IT worker. As in physical protection, deterrence, prevention, detection and response, and adaptation are used for protection. However, in smaller infrastructure providers, design for prevention is predominantly used as the means of control because detection and response are too complex and expensive for small organizations to handle and adaptation is too expensive in its redesigns. While small organizations try to deter attacks, they are typically less of a target because of the more limited effects attainable by attacking them.

As is the case for physical security, information protection tends to be thought of in terms of layers of protection encircling the content and its utility; however, most information in use today gains much of its utility through its mobility. Just as in transportation, this limits uses of protective measures based on situational specifics. To be of use, information must be processed in some manner, taking information as input and producing finished goods in the form of information useful for other purposes at the other end of each step of its production. Information must be protected at rest, in motion, and in use to ensure its utility.

Control of the information protection system is typically more complex than that of other systems because information systems tend to be interconnected and remotely addressable to a greater degree than other systems.

While a pipeline has to be physically reached to do harm, a SCADA system controlling that pipeline can potentially be reached from around the world by using the interconnectedness of systems whose transitive closure reaches the SCADA system. While physically partitioning SCADA and related control systems from the rest of the world is highly desirable, it is not the trend today. Indeed, regulatory bodies have forced the interconnection of SCADA systems to the Internet in the attempt to make more information more available in real-time. Further, for larger and interconnected infrastructures such as power and communications systems, there is little choice but to have long-distance connectivity to allow shared sourcing and distribution over long distances. Increasingly complex and hard-to-understand and manage security barriers are being put in place to allow the mandated communication while limiting the potential for exploitation. In addition, some efficiency can be gained by collaboration between SCADA systems, and this efficiency translates into a lot of money, exchanged for an unquantified amount of reduction in security. SCADA systems are only part of the overall control system that functions within an infrastructure for protection. Less time-critical control systems exist at every level, from the financial system within a nonfinancial enterprise to the governance system in which people are controlled by other people. All of these, including the paper system, are information systems.

All control systems are based on a set of sensors, a control function, and a set of actuators. These must operate as a system within limits or the system will fail. Limits are highly dependent on the specifics of the situation, and as a result, engineering design and analysis are typically required to define the limits of control systems. These limits are then coded into systems with surety levels and mechanisms appropriate to the risks. Most severe failures come about when limits are improperly set or the surety of the settings or controls limiting those settings being applied is inadequate to the situation at hand. For example, the slew rate of a water valve might have to be controlled to prevent pipe damage.

If the PLC controlling that valve is improperly set or the setting can be changed or the control does not operate as designed, the control can fail, the slew rate exceeds limits, and the pipe bursts.

To be effective, the sensors must reflect the reality to the level of accuracy and granularity and with the timeliness required for effective control to keep the overall system operating properly within limits. For example, in the pipe-burst case, faulty sensor data might lead to the controller identifying that slew rates are too slow and thus cause the controller to increase the slew rate control signal to a level where the pipe bursts. Redundancy is typically used to prevent sensor faults from causing such system failures. However, additional slew rate controls might limit actuator rates so that even if a sensor is bad, the maximum control signal cannot cause a slew rate on a properly functioning valve to exceed pipe burst limits.

Actuators must carry out the actions given them by control systems in a timely, accurate, and precise enough fashion to meet the control requirements of the system as well. For example, in the pipe-burst case, even if the PLC and communications operate properly, the actuator that turns the valve or the valve itself may fail, leading to the same sort of failure. While all possible failure modes may not be controllable, a proper control system will use sensor data to recognize errors in the valve operation and allow the control system to try to limit the movement of the actuator until a repair can be undertaken.

The control limits identified for fault conditions imply that the control system must properly translate the current situation and sensor inputs into actuator outputs, compensating appropriately for variations in timeliness, accuracy, and precision to keep the overall system operating within limits. In more complex situations, simultaneous failures of sensors and valves might lead to system failures in even the best planned control system. That is why fail-safe modes are typically created for such systems to increase surety still further, and in severe cases, physical limitations are used to ensure that the fail-safes are indeed safe failure modes.

This implies security mandates that ensure that proper operation is underway and that variances from normalcy are detected and reacted to either within or outside of the normal control system and within the normal or emergency operating limits. Thus, the security system is also a control system charged with ensuring the utility of content for other systems.

Physical security alarm and response systems, surveillance systems, and emergency communications all depend on the information protection function operating properly. Over longer time frames, information protection is key to financial payment and purchasing systems, emergency services, external support functions, and so forth. In other words, information protection supports and depends on a wide variety of other infrastructure elements.

In other infrastructures, such as financial systems, control systems may be far more complex, and it may not be possible to completely separate them from the Internet and the rest of the world. For example, electronic payment systems today operate largely over the Internet, and individuals as well as infrastructure providers can directly access banking and other financial information and make transfers or payments from anywhere. In such an infrastructure, a far more complex control system with many more actuators and sensors is required, and a far greater management structure is going to be needed.

In voting systems, to do a good job of ensuring that all legitimate votes are properly cast and counted, a paper trail or similar unforgeable, obvious, and hard-to-dispute record has to be apparent to the voted and the counters. The recent debacles in voting associated with electronic voting have clearly demonstrated the folly of such trust in information systems when the risks are so high, the systems so disbursed, and the operators so untrained, untrusted, and inexperienced. These systems have largely been out of control and therefore untrustworthy for the use.

Ongoing operations of infrastructures require change control, and in the information domain, change controls are particularly problematic.

For engineered systems, change controls and configuration management are part of an engineering function. The designers and engineers who put devices in place have to analyze and set limits on their settings and changes in settings and create the controls that limit changes and force authorities into making changes beyond preset limits. Such changes also involve additional engineering to ensure that the proper analysis has been done to allow those changes to take place without causing the system to fail. These and all such changes have to go through a security process to ensure that only the authorized parties have made such changes as part of an authorized change process. Otherwise, an attacker could exploit the lack of change controls to alter the control system and alter the infrastructure to cause harm.

The more one looks at these complexities, the more one is reminded of songs like "There's a Hole in My Bucket." In this song, to fix the hole in the bucket, they need straw that has to be cut by a knife that is dull and needs to be sharpened by a sharpening stone that gets too hot unless it is cooled by water, which cannot be fetched because there is a hole in the bucket. The question comes of how deeply these issues have to be examined to ensure continuity of operations, and the answer is, unfortunately, all the way to the end. Despite the desire to believe that attackers could never be so clever as to do all of that, real attackers do all of that and more to defeat high-valued systems, and critical parts of critical infrastructures are called critical because they are high valued and worth targeting and seriously attacking. Because of the high level of entanglement of information technologies and systems into critical infrastructures, where present, a great deal of in-depth understanding and analysis is necessary to avoid very indirect effects from long distances. Because of the lack of a long history of information engineering, inadequate knowledge and technical results are present in this field for high-surety implementations to be engineered on large scales. Because of the level of change within the industry and the unsettled nature of these technologies today, there are no history and tradition of engineering and a body of engineering knowledge that allow true clarity around these issues for simple and easily defined solutions to be readily put in place.

For more detailed coverage of information protection issues, the reader is referred to *The CISO Tool Kit—Governance Guidebook* by Fred Cohen, which gives a high-level summary of the field as it exists today and provides guidance on the different things required to provide information protection in enterprises of all sizes and sorts.

3.7.5   Intelligence and Counterintelligence Exploitation

Understanding threats and the current situation involves an effort to gain intelligence, while defeating attempts to characterize the infrastructure for exploitation is called counterintelligence because it is intended to counter the adversary intelligence process. In the simplest case, a threat against an infrastructure might have a declared intent to cause failures for whatever reason. This threat is characterized regarding capabilities and intents to identify if there are any weaknesses in the infrastructure that have not properly addressed the threat. If there are, then temporary and/or permanent changes may be made to the infrastructure or its protective systems to address the new threat. Depending on the urgency and severity, immediate action may be required, and of course threats may be sought out and arrested by interactions by law enforcement, destroyed or disabled by military action through government, and so forth.

Based on the set of identified and anticipated threats and threat types, those threats are likely to undertake efforts to gain information about the infrastructure to attack it. The counterintelligence effort focuses on denying these threats the information they need for successful attack and exploiting their attempts to gain intelligence to defeat their attempts to attack. It is essentially impossible to discuss intelligence and counterintelligence separately because they are two sides of the same coin. To do either well, you need to understand the other and understand that they are directly competitive.

A simple defeat approach might be something like refusing them the information they need by identifying it as confidential, but this will not likely stop any serious threat from trying other means to gain that information.

For example, if one wants to attack a power infrastructure, an attacker can simply start anywhere that has power and trace back the physical power lines to get to bigger and bigger power transmission facilities, control and switching centers, and eventually power sources. Trying to stop an attacker by not publishing the power line maps will not be very effective, and in the Internet and satellite imagery era, attackers can literally follow the wires using overhead imagery to create their own map. Clearly, little can be done about this particular intelligence effort, but perhaps a defender can conceal the details of how these infrastructures are controlled or other such things to make some of the attacker's jobs harder. To get a sense of the nature of this game, a table sometimes works for looking at intelligence and counterintelligence measures. Here is an example of what to expect using A for attacker and D for defender:

Intelligence	Counterintelligence
A seeks to identify facilities, devices, locations, and security measures in place at facilities as well as in intervening infrastructure elements.	D tries to prevent publication of details of anything about facilities, locations, or defenses in use.
A looks in public records to find submissions required for building plans, inspections, and other reporting and regulatory compliance records.	D understands what is in these records and tries to reduce their utility to A by removing things like room names, facility use, and details.
A looks for suppliers to identify equipment in use, including calling all suppliers of certain types and claiming to be a large customer and looking for references to other users and use cases.	D uses contracts and awareness programs with suppliers to limit knowledge revealed and limits what supplier sales people know to reduce things they are able to tell others.
A calls claiming to be a supplier of a particular sort of part and asking about the maintenance program in use and offering discounts.	D trains employees in procedures for dealing with vendors to ensure that they can be authenticated as legitimate before answering questions.

Of course, this cat-and-mouse game goes on and on, and a systematic approach must ultimately be used to attain success in the counterintelligence arena. A more detailed accounting of intelligence and counterintelligence methods associated with elicitation is included in *Frauds, Spies, and Lies, and How to Defeat Them* (Fred Cohen, ASP Press, 2005).

Clearly, the intelligence field can be quite complex and deeply involved, and for some threats, it can be very severe. Part of the threat characterization used in risk management is the identification of the intelligence capabilities of adversaries along with the systems about which such information would help the attacker gain an advantage. For a local water system, the threats are unlikely to be as severe as they are for a global financial system, and the threat types are likely to be very different. The amount and type of effort that a national government may go through to disrupt power supply to military bases are likely to be very different from the amount and type of effort an Internet attacker working for organized crime may go through to take credit cards. To get a sense of just how far things may go, it may be helpful to read *The Ultimate Spy Book* (Keith Melton and DK Publishing). This book includes pictures and stories of actual intelligence and counterintelligence operations carried out by national governments as authenticated by former Central Intelligence Agency and Komitet Gosudarstvenno Bezopasnosti (KGB; Komitet, Committee of State Security) heads.

Critical infrastructures have to deal with real intelligence attacks from serious threats. For example, power control systems, telecommunications systems, network systems, and banking systems have had planted software codes put into SCADA and other similar control systems during outsourced upgrade. In one case, a critical infrastructure provider found that an employee for a contractor who had worked for them for years was not who they claimed to be and had all of the behaviors associated with a foreign intelligence operative. Network intelligence probes take place in an ongoing fashion from other nations, and their intelligence operatives regularly carry out operations to get information and gain access to controls of critical infrastructures.

This ongoing gathering of intelligence against critical infrastructures of all countries is part and parcel of attaining and sustaining military offensive and defensive capabilities against the possibility of war or attempts to force or influence situations of competitors and enemies, and since today's friends may be tomorrow's enemies, no country or infrastructure is exempt.

However, it is not just nation-states that use these techniques. The lowest level Internet-based attacker, organized crime, competitive bidders on projects, professional thieves, government agents and law enforcement, private investigators, reporters, and many others are seeking intelligence on critical infrastructure providers all the time, whether it is to gain a competitive advantage in a sales process or any of a thousand other nefarious purposes. Critical infrastructure providers are targets of intelligence attacks and must act to defend themselves and their workers, suppliers, customers, and others against these efforts.

Of course, part of the effort to defend against these sorts of attacks involves identifying weaknesses and countermeasures, and that implies the ability to do intelligence attacks against your own people, systems, facilities, and methods. While many companies do these sorts of activities from time to time, this brings up even more complexity because by sanctioning such activities, in addition to defenders finding weaknesses, so do those performing the intelligence efforts. Modeling threats is worthy, but the defender also has to define the limits of safe efforts and identify what is worth protecting as well. All of this is part of the overall intelligence and counterintelligence effort that should be undertaken by all critical infrastructure providers.

3.7.6   Life Cycle Protection Issues

As the previous discussion shows, protection issues in critical infrastructures apply across life cycles. Life cycle issues are commonly missed, and yet they are obvious once identified.

From the previously cited *CISO Tool Kit—Governance Guidebook*, life cycles for people, systems, data, and businesses have to be considered, and for the more general case, life cycles for all resources consumed and outputs and waste generated have to be considered. That means modeling the entire process of all infrastructure elements "from the womb to the tomb"—and beyond.

Consider the ecological infrastructure of a locality, even ignoring regional and global issues. As natural resources are pulled from the Earth to supply the infrastructure, they are no longer available for future use, the location they were taken from may be altered and permanently scarred, other life forms living there may be unable to survive, the relationship of those resources to their surroundings may alter the larger scale ecology, and over longer time frames, these effects may outweigh the benefits of the resources themselves. Suppose the resource is coal burned to supply power. The extraction may produce sink holes that disrupt other infrastructures like gas lines or the water table, or it may create problems for roads or future uses.

The coal, once removed, typically has to be transported, using a different infrastructure, to the power plant. If this is at a distance, more energy is used in transportation, there is interdependency on that infrastructure for the power infrastructure, and the transportation is part of the life cycle that can be attacked and may have to be defended. Since the coal depends on the transportation infrastructure, the security of that infrastructure is necessary for the coal to go where it is going and the security systems may have to interact, requiring coordination. For example, if the fuel was nuclear rather than coal, different transportation security needs would be present, and if the power plant is running low and previous attacks have caused transportation to be more expensive, these attacks may have to be protected against as well.

The steps go on and on throughout the interacting life cycles of different things, people, systems, and businesses, and all of these life cycle steps and interactions have to be accounted for to understand the protective needs for the individual and overall infrastructures.

Regardless of the details involved in each infrastructure element, the nature of life cycles is that there are many complex interacting elements involved in them and they are best managed by the creation of models that allow them to be dealt with systematically and analyzed in conjunction with other models of other life cycles.

From a protection standpoint, these models allow the analyst to cover things more thoroughly and with more certainty than they otherwise would likely be able to do, and as events in the world show weaknesses in the models, the models can be updated as part of their life cycles to improve with age and experience. This not only allows the protection analyst to improve with time but also provides the basis for the creation of policies, control standards, and procedures designed to meet all of the modeled elements of the life cycles of all infrastructure components. Thus, the models form the basis for understanding the protective needs and the life cycles help form the basis for the models. These life cycle models can also be thought of as process models; however, they are described and discussed this way to ensure that the processes cover all aspects of all interacting components from before they are created until after they are consumed. The model of life cycles is one that itself helps ensure that protection coverage is complete.

Finally, it is important to note that while all infrastructure components have finite life cycles, the totality of infrastructures is intended to have an infinite life cycle. Life cycles that are usually noticed are at the inception of the idea of having the infrastructure, the creation of the components and composites, and their ultimate destruction. However, the widely ignored and absolutely critical elements of maintenance and operation, upgrades, and postdestruction clean-up and restoration of surrounding environment are often ignored by the public at large, even though they are the hard part that has to be done day to day.

3.7.7 Change Management

Change happens whether we like it and plan for it or not. If we fail to manage it, it will cause critical infrastructures to fail, while if we manage it reasonably well, the infrastructures will change with the rest of the world and continue to operate and facilitate our lifestyles and the advancement of humanity and society.

While those who wish to tear down societies may wish to induce changes that are disruptive, change management is part of the protective process that is intended to help ensure that this does not happen.

Changes can be malicious, accidental, or intended to be beneficial, but when changes occur and protection is not considered, they will almost certainly produce weaknesses that are exploitable or result in accidental failures. In a sense, change management belongs under the heading of life cycles and yet they are typically handled separately because they are typically considered within each part of life cycles and most commonly within the normal operating portion of the overall life cycle of any component of interest.

Returning to the coal-fired power plant example, the power plant itself has changes made to it to reflect technology updates, such as cleaner operation. Such changes may involve the introduction of additional technologies, such as smoke stack scrubbers. These scrubbers may introduce new life cycles involving the replacement of component parts, and attackers may see the introduction of scrubbers as an opportunity to add a mechanism that will allow them to disable the power plant on command. Perhaps they have the capability to add some materials to the scrubber assembly that can weaken its operation or cause an explosion under certain operating conditions. Maybe they can get into the supply chain for replacement parts and add in substandard components that cause disruptions. Or perhaps they are able to have their specialists involved in maintenance to gain access to the plant and use that access to implant other devices or capabilities for subsequent exploitation. Maybe the scrubbers involve computer controls that grant network access, and that access changes the security level of the network as a whole by introducing a path to alter operations or deny services based on scrubber changes.

It seems clear from this example that any change can have rippling effects on everything that change related to and everything that the related things relate to, and so forth. That is exactly why change management must be in place. All of the interdependencies involved in an infrastructure may be involved in the side effects of any change.

The change management process must allow for a systematic understanding of the direct and indirect implications of all changes and the ability to limit the effects of a change on one thing relative to changes in other things. Otherwise, every change will require potential redesign or at least reanalysis of all infrastructures. The change management process must allow analysis to determine how far to look to ensure that a component change does not cause operation of the composite to exceed limits that form the basis for its inclusion in other composites. Additionally, if a component change alters the composite to a level resulting in changes to those external interfaces, then the larger composite must be reviewed in the same manner to identify the limits of the scope of a change.

In doing this analysis, interdependencies will be examined and the true cost of change will be understood. As a result of such analysis, seemingly inexpensive and trivial changes may be found to have very high potential risks and costs, while seemingly expensive solutions to simple problems may in fact be far more cost-effective in the overall analysis. Hence, change management is key to protection and key to making sound decisions about the life cycles of infrastructures.

3.7.8   Strategic Critical Infrastructure Protection

Strategic critical infrastructure protection is about the overall long-term protection of the totality of critical infrastructure and humanity as a whole. As such, it is less about the protection of any given infrastructure element and more about the protection of the evolving overall community of support systems that support human life and society on Earth and, eventually, as humanity expands through space, to other places.

As a starter, it must be recognized that all resources are finite and that the notion that "the solution to pollution is dilution" cannot stand. The notion of sustainability, however, must be balanced for some time with the notion of progress, because if humanity is to survive the ultimate end of the sun or even the next major asteroid hit, we will need to improve our technology. This then means that we need to expend our limited nonrenewable (at least for a long time to come they are not renewable) resources wisely to advance ourselves to the level where we can exist on renewable resources alone. Coal will run out soon, but oil will run out sooner, at least here on Earth, with current consumption patterns. In the time frame of infrastructures, coal is not yet a serious problem, but oil is because it is now at or about at its peak production for all time and production will start to decline and never again return to its previous levels. Going to coal means more pollution and has many other implications, and that means that protection of the power and energy infrastructure implies research and development in that arena with plans for transition and change management starting now rather than at the last minute.

In shorter time frames, there is the notion that protection extends beyond the immediate. While in most businesses, time frames of months to a few years are the common approach to optimization, in critical infrastructures, time frames of at least tens of years and more often scores to hundreds of years are more realistic. This changes the nature of investment and, as a result, the investment in protection. While a local music store might buy some stock with the intent of only one turn every few months, infrastructure providers typically think in terms of changing out components over periods of many years and composites over at least tens of years and doing so in an evolutionary manner.

For example, when telephone lines in a neighborhood get to the point where they need to be reworked, they can be reworked with the existing technology and used in that technology for the next 30–50 years or reworked with a new technology for that same time frame. Twisted pair wires or fiber optics to the curb is the question being answered today in the United States and Europe, and with the introduction of cable infrastructure and the increasing demands for bandwidth, the competitive landscape would seem to favor fiber. However, twisted pair is much less expensive and has very well-understood properties and easier installation and maintenance, and bandwidth is increasing because of new coding methods. These are strategic decisions that, in 10 to 20 years, may make or break competing infrastructures. While this may seem like simple economics, it is more than that.

The protection mechanisms and costs of protection can be quite different for different technologies. Fiber is less susceptible to exploitation in many ways, but it is more susceptible to fracture under bending and Earth movement. Availability is very important for infrastructures, and delays in installation may be very advantageous given that technologies are changing all the time. When fiber is removed, it has little of any value, but old copper wires are increasing in material value with time and are recyclable for reuse. The cable is a shared medium, while fiber telephone infrastructure may or may not be shared, depending on the implementation. With fiber to the curb, electronic devices are required at the curb, leading to potential increased cost of theft and potential for abuse, and there are complex interactions with other infrastructure elements. For example, wires carry their own power to the end points while fiber cannot, leading to increased interdependency and surety needs.

If sustainability over time is to be attained, standards must be applied, and these standards must stand the test of time because the evolutionary nature of infrastructure implies that they will be here for a long time to come. Power in Europe and much of the rest of the world is different in terms of voltage from that in the United States. This means that equipment is often incompatible. While this can work for power, which is relatively geographically limited, it cannot work very well for information and telecommunications, which have to interact on a global basis. At a minimum, some sorts of translation capabilities are required. Standards are also critical within infrastructures. For example, if different frequencies are used, radios cannot communicate, and if different pipe sizes and pressures are used, pipes may burst or have to be refitted.

Critical infrastructures are strategic assets that have profound implications on economics, quality of life, and survival of populations, and as such, they need to be protected for the well-being of the people whose government, industry, and effort create and sustain them. In times of war, critical infrastructures are vital to military operations and are the first targets of hostile operations. In times of competition, those infrastructures are the key to health, wealth, and prosperity.

Who can seriously doubt the impact of the Interstate highway system in the United States for creating the conditions that allowed it to survive and prosper in the second half of the 20th century? Who can doubt the value of the Appian Way to Rome? Water infrastructure ended the massive flooding and droughts in Egypt and is moving toward doing the same in China today. Telecommunications is increasingly changing the Third World by bringing information infrastructure, knowledge of the world, and education to small towns and villages. In short, the strategic value of critical infrastructures is fundamental to the life cycles of societies and the protection of those societies equates to a large extent to the protection of those critical infrastructures.

Understanding the strategic value of infrastructures also helps to understand the true nature of the risk management surrounding them. To understand the consequences of infrastructure failures, the modeling must go beyond the individual business that comprises each element of the infrastructure to the value of that infrastructure to the society as a whole and the implications of its failure to that society. Further, individual infrastructure elements may have relatively direct small effects, but in the aggregate, when many of them fail because of common modes of failure or interdependencies, a domino effect can take place, collapsing an entire society. Thus, the overall critical infrastructures of a society must be addressed by the society as a whole or the society as a whole will suffer the consequences of local optimization.

Nowhere is this clearer today than in the power industry in the United States. The deregulation surrounding power has led to a wide range of systemic vulnerabilities in order to create local optimizations. The society as a whole is now paying more for power, has had more and larger power outages since deregulation than it had before deregulation, has less excess capacity both in power generation and in distribution, and has seen more and larger frauds than ever took place before deregulation. Large-scale long-term investment is down because of the need to meet short-term profit goals, and as supply dwindles, prices go up. This is similar to the situation in the oil and gas industry in the United States, which has not built refinery capacity, reduced cost, and simultaneously increased profit by decreasing the supply and increasing price. The invisible hand of the market has not stepped in because, in gas sales, as everyone slowly increases prices, all gain additional profits. Since there is little excess capacity and the business is mature in terms of gas stations, market share is largely fixed. Nobody can gain substantial market share by small price differences, and the small owners who own the stations cannot reduce price because they have very small margins and limited supply. The effect is a drag on the economy, concentration of wealth, and more brittle energy supply.

3.7.9 Technology and Process Options

There are a lot of different technologies and processes that are used to implement protection. A comprehensive list would be infeasible to present without an encyclopedic volume, and the list changes all the time, but we would be remiss if all of the details were left out. The lists of such things, being so extensive, are far more amenable to computerization than printing in books. Rather than add a few hundred pages of lists of different things at different places, we have chosen to provide the information within a software package that provides, what amounts to, checklists of the different sorts of technologies that go in different places. To give a sense of the sorts of things typically included in such lists, here are some extracts.

In the general physical arena, we include perimeters, access controls, concealments, response forces, property location and geology, property topology and natural barriers, property perimeter artificial barriers, signs, alarms, and responses, facility features and paths, facility detection, response, and supply, facility time and distance issues, facility location and attack graph issues, entry and exit controls, mantraps, and emergency modes, surveillance and sensor systems, response time, force levels, and observe, orient, decide, and act (OODA) loops, perception controls, and locking mechanisms. Within locking mechanisms, for example, we include selection of lock types, electrical lock-out controls, mechanical lock-out controls, fluid lock-out controls, and gas lock-out controls, time-based access controls, location-based access controls, event sequence-based access controls, situation-based access controls, lock fail-safe features, lock default settings, and lock tamper-evidence.

Similar sorts of lists exist in other arenas. For example, in technical information security, under network firewalls, we list outer router, routing controls, and limitations on ports, gateway machines, demilitarized zones (DMZs), proxies, virtual private networks (VPNs), identity-based access controls, hardware acceleration, appliance or hardware devices, inbound filtering, and outbound filtering. Each of these has variations as well. Under Operations Security, which is essentially a process methodology with some technologies in all areas of security that support it, we list time frame of operation, scope of operation, threats to the operation, secrets that must be protected, indicators of those secrets, capabilities of the threats, intents of the threats, observable indicators present, vulnerabilities, seriousness of the risk, and countermeasures identified and applied. In the analysis of intelligence indicators, we typically carry out or estimate the effects of these activities that are common to many threats:

- Review widely available literature;
- Send intelligence operatives into adversary countries, businesses, or facilities;
- Plant surveillance devices (bugs) in computers, buildings, cars, offices, and elsewhere;
- Take inside and outside pictures on building tours;
- Send e-mails in to ask questions;
- Call telephone numbers to determine who works where, and to get other related information;
- Look for or build up a telephone directory;
- Build an organizational chart;
- Cull through thousands of Internet postings;
- Do Google and other similar searches;
- Target individuals for elicitation;
- Track the movement of people and things;
- Track customers, suppliers, consultants, vendors, service contracts, and other business relationships;
- Do credit checks on individual targets of interest;
- Use commercial databases to get background information;
- Access history of individuals including airline reservations and when they go where;
- Research businesses people have worked for and people they know;
- Find out where they went to school and chat with friends they knew from way back;

- Talk to neighbors, former employers, and bartenders;
- Read the annual report; and
- Send people in for job interviews, some of whom get jobs.

It rapidly becomes apparent that (1) the number of alternatives is enormous for both malicious attacker and accidental events, (2) the number of options for protection is enormous and many options often have to be applied, and (3) no individual can attain all of the skills and knowledge required to perform all of the tasks in all of the necessary areas to define and design the protective system of an infrastructure. Even if an individual had all of the requisite knowledge, they could not possibly have the time to carry out the necessary activities for a critical infrastructure of substantial size. Critical infrastructure protection is a team effort requiring a team of experts.

3.8   Protection Design Goals and Duties to Protect

In a sense, the goal of protection may be stated as a reduction in negative consequences, but in real systems, more specific goals have to be clarified. There is a need to define the duties to protect if those duties are going to be fulfilled by an organization. The obvious duty that should be identified by people working on critical infrastructure protection is the duty to prevent serious negative consequences from occurring, but as obvious as this is, it is often forgotten in favor of some other sort of duty, like making money for the shareholders regardless of the implications to society as a whole.

A structured approach to defining duties to protect uses a hierarchical process starting with the top-level definition of duties associated with laws, owners, directors, auditors, and top management. Laws and regulations are typically researched by a legal team and defined for internal use. Owners and directors define their requirements through the setting of policies and explicit directives.

Auditors are responsible for identifying applicable standards against which verification will be performed and the enterprise measured. Top executives identify day-to-day duties and manage process.

Duties should be identified through processes put in place by those responsible; however, if this is not done, the protection program should seek out this guidance as one of its duties to be diligent in its efforts. Identified duties should be codified in writing and be made explicit, but if this is not done by those responsible, it is again incumbent on the protection program to codify them in documentation and properly manage that documentation. There is often resistance to any process in which those who operate the protection program seek to clarify or formalize enterprise-level decisions. As an alternative to creating formal documents or forcing the issue unduly, the protection executive might take the tactic of identifying the duties that are clarified in writing and identifying that no other duties have been stipulated as part of the documentation provided for the design of their protection program.

While it may be for the good of the public and society to have these clarified, it is often risky to the protection designer to force such issues. This is the heart of the most fundamental ethical challenge faced by protection professionals. The refusal of higher-level decision-makers to fulfill their duties to the public puts the ethical professional in a bind. The code of ethics of most protection professionals does not codify the protection of the public well-being, but the code of ethics of most of the engineering professions do. Engineers, particularly professional engineers who are certified or licensed by government, have some leverage in asserting professional responsibility and are rarely overruled by management on technical issues such as the strength of a load bearing wall or the proper gage of wire for a building. When they are, they are faced with an ethical choice that often involves peoples' lives, and many, if not most, will refuse to compromise safety. Replacing the engineer will only get more refusals and whistle blowing, but in the protection profession, there are few, if any, mandated standards for critical infrastructure protection, there are no government-approved professional certification or licensing programs except for internal government programs, and protection professionals who refuse to yield are typically fired and replaced by someone—anyone—who will do what management wants.

The task of the protection executive is to find a way to influence management to properly specify the duties to protect and, based on these duties, to fund the protection efforts. Depending on the size of the infrastructure provider, the individual tasked with protection may be the same person who implements it and has other tasks, and this individual may report directly to the chief operating officer or board or may work for a director within a department in a division in a business unit and never encounter any executive high enough to even communicate directly with anyone who sets policy. The further from top management, the harder it is to influence or identify duties to protect, and the more skilled the individual has to be to succeed.

Many approaches may be taken to defining duties to protect. It is fairly common to use outside experts to do this because of their potential to be viewed as independent experts, the potential that they could take the heat while the insiders can leverage their work for gaining internal consensus, and because they may have more specific expertise in this area than internal protection specialists do. The insider can also do extensive research in the various aspects of duties to protect, find internal support for this activity, and try to get others to define these duties. Several good books have been published that discuss this issue along with other issues, and specific duties are defined by specific authors of books in each of the specialist fields involved in the protection function. For example, physical security specialists know that there are safety and health requirements from a legal standpoint, and part of their duty to protect is to not introduce unnecessary hazards into the environment through the introduction of protective measures. Fire exits must not be disabled to prevent someone from leaving a secure facility. Other approaches must be taken.

3.8.1   Operating Environment

The operating environment has to be characterized to gain clarity around the context of protection. Just as a bridge designer has to know the loads that are expected for the bridge, the length of the span, the likely range of weather conditions, and other similar factors to design the bridge properly, the protection designer has to know enough about the operating environment to design the protection system to operate in the anticipated operating conditions. The specific parameters are highly specific to the infrastructure type and protection area. For example, physical security of long-distance telecommunications lines has different operating environment parameters than do personnel security in a mining facility.

Security-related operating environment issues tend to augment normal engineering issues because they include the potential actions of malicious actors in the context of the engineering environment. While engineers design bridges to handle natural hazards, the protection specialist must find ways to protect those same bridges when they are attacked in an attempt to intentionally push them beyond design specifications. The protection designer has to understand what the assumptions are and how these can be violated by intentional attackers, and this forms the operating environment of the protection designer.

Typical elements of the environment include the people and processes in place, the facilities that these processes and people operate within, the surroundings, the threats in effect and their typical actions, the normal and abnormal uses of the infrastructure and all of its components, the interfaces between other infrastructures and their components, the critical success and failure points and criteria, the duties to protect discussed earlier, and the organizational context. If this sounds like it is a lot more than what is required for simple design of infrastructure components and composites, it sounds like it should. The protection environment is far more complex than the operational design environment, and yet far less time, money, and effort are typically spent on the protection design and execution than on the operational design and execution. Such is the nature of the protection challenge.

3.8.2   Design Methodology

A systematic approach to design is vital to success in devising protection approaches. Without some sort of method to the madness, the complexity of all of the possible protection designs is instantly overwhelming. There are a variety of design methodologies. There are many complaints in the literature about the waterfall process in which specifications are developed, designs undertaken, evaluations of alternatives completed, and selections made, with a loop for feedback into the previous elements of the process. However, despite the complaints, this process is still commonly embraced by those who are serious about arriving at viable solutions to security design challenges. In fact, this process has been well studied and leads to many positive results, but there are many alternative approaches to protection design.

As an overall approach, one of the more meaningful alternative approaches is to identify the surety level of the desired outcome for the overall system and its component parts. Surety levels can be thought of in fairly simple terms, low, medium, and high, for example. For low surety, a different process is undertaken because the consequences are too low to justify serious design effort. For medium consequences, a systematic approach is taken, but not pushed to the limit of human capability for design and analysis. For high consequences, the most certain techniques available are used and the price is paid regardless of the costs. Of course, realistic designers know that there is no unlimited cost project, that there are tradeoffs at all levels, and that such selection is only preliminary, and this sort of iterative approach to reducing the space of possibilities helps to focus the design process.

While at some level, the designs of a beam, or a wall, or a wire do not have mathematically ideal solutions, walls, nor beams, nor wires come in every size for a reasonable price. Designers in every field know the limitations on parts and create design rules to help those select parts that they can actually attain. Just as this is far more pressing for one-off designs than for designs in which millions of duplicate components are being made, in the protection arena, unless you are making large numbers of custom parts and components, the composite will be made up of existing components that are integrated into the composite through a systems integration process. While simple projects may be completely specified at the start, almost no protection systems are completely specified before the implementation starts.

The protection design process generally starts with a list of goals, perhaps derived from the combination of the duty to protect and the characteristics of the operating environment. Typical designers are systematic but not automatic. Rather, they understand the nature of the problem first and then analyze it and suggest a variety of alternative approaches. A set of architectural pictures are presented in which options for overall structure and delegation of protective duties are described for each major design option. The architect then thinks through the implications of each of the selections and seeks to find how they break down and where they have limitations that will be overcome by threats. Operational problems are considered in light of experience, and potentials for work-around are identified. Redundancy requirements are analyzed briefly to determine how much redundancy is required to prevent the system from being brittle in different ways. A set of architectural selections are made and some preliminary ideas are typically put forth. These ideas are then run past the various parties that design, operate, and work in the operating environment, and potential objections or limitations are identified. Alterations are made to suit the need, and a second round of selection is done in which the architect has answered most of the questions. From this feedback process, a proposed design or small set of proposed alternatives are presented that are far more detailed in terms of how they operate, what will be needed, and how they will address the operational needs while still providing protection. After discussions and feedback are undertaken, one or two of the options are selected and more detailed design begins.

In the more detailed design phase, specifics are put on all of the component parts of the architecture. Specific parts or manufacturers may not be specified at this point, but the operating characteristics are selected, at least within ranges, and things like fence heights and types, camera types and coverage requirements, ranges of distances, likely lighting requirements, network topologies, response time ranges, likely force levels, and other similar items are identified and assumed to be attainable based on experience. Cost estimates are made, and after some rounds of feedback and interaction are undertaken, the design is solidified and more specific parts are detailed and specified.

3.9   Process, Policy, Management, and Organizational Approaches

This is very similar to other engineering disciplines, and rightly so. Protection system design is an engineering exercise, but it is also a process definition exercise in that along with all of the things that are created, there are operational procedures and process requirements that allow the components to operate properly together to form the composite. Protection is a process, not a product. The protection system, and the infrastructure as a whole, has to function and evolve over time frames, and in the case of the protection system, it has to be able to react in very short time frames as well as adapt in far longer time frames. As a result, the process definitions and the roles and actions of the parties have to be defined as part of the design process, in much the same way as the control processes of a power station or water system require that people and process be defined while the plant is designed. Except that in the case of infrastructures like power plants and water systems, the people in these specialty fields and their management typically already know what to expect. In protection, they do not.

The problem of inadequate knowledge at the management and operational level relating to protection will solve itself over time, but today, it is rather serious. The technology has changed in recent years, and the changes in the threat environment have produced serious management challenges to Western societies, but in places like the former Soviet Union and in oppressive societies with internal distrust, these systems are well understood and have been in place for a long time. The challenge is getting a proper mix of serious attention to protection and reasonable levels of trust based on reasonable assumptions.

A management process must be put in place in order to ensure that whatever duties are identified and policies mandated, they are managed so that they get executed, the execution is measured and verified, and failures in execution are mitigated in a timely fashion. The protection designer must be able to integrate the technical aspects of the protection system into the management aspects of the infrastructure provider to create a viable system that allows the active components of the protection system to operate within specifications or the overall protective system will fail. This has to take into account the failures in the components of the active system, which include not only technology but also people, business process, management failures, and active attempts to induce failures. For example, an inadequate training program for incident evaluation will yield responses that cause inadequate resources to be available where and when needed, leading to reflexive control attack weaknesses in the protection system.

These sorts of processes have to be deeply embedded into the management structure of the enterprise to be effective. Otherwise, management decisions about seemingly irrelevant matters will result in successful attacks. A typical example is the common decision to put content about the infrastructure on the Internet for external use with business partners. Once the information is on the Internet, it is available on a more or less permanent basis to attackers, many of whom constantly seek out and collect permanent records of all information on potential future targets. It is common for job descriptions to include details of operating environments in place, which leads attackers to in-depth internal knowledge of the systems in use. Because there are a limited number of systems used within many infrastructure industries, a few hints rapidly yield a great deal of knowledge that is exploitable in attacks. In one case, a listing of vendors was used to identify lock types, and a vulnerability testing group was then able to get copies of the specific lock types in use, practice picking those locks, and bring special pick equipment to the site for attacks. This reduced the time to penetrate barriers significantly. When combined with a floor plan that was gleaned from public records associated with a recent renovation, the entry and exit plan for covert access to control systems was devised, practiced, and executed. If management at all levels does not understand these issues and make day-to-day operational decisions with this in mind, the result will be the defeat of protective systems.

The recognition that mistakes will be made is also fundamental to the development of processes. It is not only necessary to devise processes associated with the proper operation of the protective system and all of the related information and systems. In addition, the processes in place have to deal with compensation for failures in the normal operational modes of these systems so that small failures do not become large failures. In a mature infrastructure process, there will not be heroic individual efforts necessary for the protective system to work under stress. It will degrade gracefully to the extent feasible given the circumstance, according to the plan in place.

Policy is typically missing or wrong when infrastructure protection work is started, and it is not always fixed when the work is done. It is hard to get top management to make policy changes, and all the harder in larger providers. Policies have to be followed and have legal standing within companies, while other sorts of internal decisions do not have the same standing. As a result, management is often hesitant to create policy. In addition, policy gives leverage to the protection function, which is another reason that the management in place may not want to make such changes. Since security is usually not treated as a function that operates at top management levels, there is typically nobody at that level to champion the cause of security, and it gets short shrift. Nevertheless, it is incumbent on the protection architects and designers to find ways to get policies in place that allow leverage to be used to gain and retain an appropriate level of assurance associated with their function.

At a minimum, there are generally accepted principles that apply to protection-related issues, including, most importantly, separation of duties. There are a wide range of standards used at the policy and process level, and they include any number of different principles, like proportionality so that protection is proportional to need, risk management so that decision making is rationalized, adequate knowledge to perform the assigned tasks so that competent work is done, and assignment of explicit responsibilities so that the "blame game" cannot be played *ad infinitum* without progress being made. Separation of duties is, in most cases, the most important of all because it asserts that the people specifying and verifying that protection is done and done properly are not the same people who implement protection. Without this, the foxes are watching the hen house, so to speak.

This then brings up the issue of organizational structure. Many executives are highly offended by the notion that the protection program should have any effect on their management decisions about the structure of their organization. Time and again, we see organizations placing information security within the IT department; physical security within the facilities department, operational security within the operations department; personnel security within the human resources department; and so forth. While this seems to make logical sense to management, the security functions of an organization need to be recognized as a separate function, and that function has to be independent of the management chains that it affects. By analogy, if the auditors work for the chief financial officer, they cannot carry out their duties to assure the management and shareholders that the books are not fraudulent, but at the same time, the auditors cannot directly alter the financial information. Security functions have the same general requirements associated with separation of duties, and the infrastructure protection function must be independent of the operational aspects of the business if it is to be effective.

3.9.1   Analysis Framework

Given that there are specified business and operational needs, specified duties to protect, and a reasonably well-defined operating environment, proposed architectures and designs, along with all of the processes, management, and other things that form the protection program and plan, need to be evaluated to determine whether protection is inadequate, adequate or excessive, reasonably priced, and performing for what is being gained and to allow alternatives to be compared.

Unlike engineering, finance, and many other fields of expertise that exist in the world, the protection arena does not have well-defined and universally applied analysis frameworks. Any electrical engineer should be able to compute the necessary voltages, currents, component values, and other things required to design and implement a circuit to perform a function in a defined environment. Any accountant can determine a reasonable placement of entries within the double entry bookkeeping system. However, if the same security engineering problem is given to a range of protection specialists, there are likely to be highly divergent answers.

One of the many reasons for the lack of general agreement in the security space is that there is a vast array of knowledge necessary to understand the entire space and those who work in the space range over a vast range of expertise. Another challenge is that many government studies on the details of things like fence height, distances between things, and so forth, are sensitive because if the details are known, they may be more systematically defeated, but on the whole, the deeper problem seems to stem from a lack of a coherent profession.

There are many protection-related standards, and to the extent that these standards are embraced and followed, they lead to more uniform solutions with a baseline of protection. For example, health and safety standards mandate a wide range of controls over materials, building codes ensure that certain protective fences do not fall over in the wind or accidentally electrocute passersby, standards for fire safety ensure that specific temperatures are not reached within the protected area for a period of time in defined external conditions, standards for electromagnetic emanations limit the readability of signals at a distance, and shredding standards make it very hard to reassemble most shredded documents when the standards are met. While there are a small number of specialized experts who know how to analyze these specific items in detail, protection designers normally just follow the standards to stay out of trouble—or at least they are supposed to.

Unfortunately, most of the people who work designing and implementing protective systems are unaware of most of these standards, and if they are unaware, they most certainly do not know whether they are following these standards and cannot specify them as requirements or meet them in implementation.

From a pure analysis standpoint, there are a wide range of scientific and engineering elements involved in protection, and all of them come to bear in the overall design of protective systems for infrastructures. However, the holy grail of protection comes in the form of risk management: the systematic approach to measuring risk and making sound decisions about risk based on those measurements. The problem with this starts with the inability to define risk in a really meaningful way, followed by the inability to measure the components in most definitions, the high cost of accurate measurements, the difficulty in analyzing the effect of protective measures on risk reduction, and the step functions in results associated with minor changes in parameters.

Nevertheless, despite the enormous complexity in the protection field, there are actually only a limited number of techniques available, and for the most part, they do not allow for linear scaling in selection and quantity of implementation. For example, you either have a fence to keep people out or not. You can control the height in steps of about 12 inches and put different sorts of things on the fence, and put it almost anywhere you want it, but if you do not use a fence, the next step up is a wall, and the next step down is nothing. Fence, wall, moat, there are not that many options, and you cannot have a fence that is almost like a moat. You can have either, both, or neither. The number of incremental variations available in technology selection is very limited in protection, and as a side effect, regardless of the ability to vary risk calculations to a large number of decimal points, after you finish all of the calculations and computations, you still have to choose between a fairly small number of options for each sort of protective mechanism. The accuracy of risk management really only has to be good enough to make a good choice. This calls for design rules and heuristics rather than continuous mathematical techniques that lead to exact calculated answers.

Almost no protection design will ever call for a one-foot fence, a quarter inch perimeter, or a wall that is 500 feet tall. The list of real solutions tends to be finite and bounded, and the useful analysis framework focuses on the selection and placement of protective measures from this fairly small set.

In fact, there are, strictly speaking, two different sorts of design frameworks present. There is the underlying science of protection that is almost nonexistent in many areas and highly subjective in most other areas, and there is the rule-based approach that uses common design rules to make common decisions. The design-rule approach is just emerging and is increasingly applied under names such as "best practice," which is a misnomer for minimally acceptable practice and other similar names. The protection science approach is one that is sporadically developed in select areas and underdeveloped in most areas. The design rule approach is often extended to organizations in the form of standard design approaches.

3.9.2   Standard Design Approaches

The standard design approaches are based on the notion that in-depth protection science and/or engineering can be applied to define a design that meets the essential criteria that work for a wide range of situations. By defining the situations for which each design applies, an organization can reduce or eliminate design and analysis time by simply replicating a known design where the situation meets the design specification criteria. Thus, a standard fence for protecting highways from people throwing objects off of overpasses can be applied to every overpass that meets the standard design criteria, and "the paralysis of analysis" can be avoided.

The fiats that have to be watched carefully in these situations are that (1) the implementations do indeed meet the design criteria, (2) the design actually does what it was intended to do, and (3) the criteria are static enough to allow for a common design to be reproduced in place after place. It turns out that, to a close approximation, this works well at several levels. It works for individual design components, for certain types of composites, and for architectural level approaches.

By using such approaches, analysis, approval processes, and many other aspects of protection design and implementation are reduced in complexity and cost, and if done on a large scale, the cost of components can go down because of mass production and competition. However, mass production has its drawbacks. For example, the commonly used mass production lock and key systems used on most doors are almost uniformly susceptible to the bump-key attack. As the sunk cost of a defense technology increases and it becomes so standard that it is almost universal, attackers will start to define and create attack methods that are also readily reproducible and lower the cost and time of attack. Standardization leads to common mode failures.

The cure to this comes in the combinations of protective measures put in place. The so-called defense-in-depth is intended to mitigate individual failures, and if applied systematically with variations of combinations forming the overall defense, then each facility will have a different sequence of skill requirements for attack and the cost to the attackers will increase while their uncertainty increases as well. They have to bring more and more expensive things to increase their chances of success unless they can gather intelligence adequate to give away the specific sequences required, and they have to have more skills, train longer, and learn more to be effective against a larger set of targets. This reduces the threats that are effective to those with more capabilities and largely eliminates most of the low-level attackers (the so-called ankle biters) that consume much of the resources in less well-designed approaches.

As it turns out, there is also a negative side effect to effective protection against low-level attacks. As fewer and fewer attackers show up, management will find less and less justification for defenses. As a result, budgets will be cut and defenses will start to decay until they fail altogether in a rather spectacular way. This is why bridges fall down and power systems collapse and water pipes burst in most cases. They become so inexpensive to operate and work so well that maintenance is reduced to the point where it is inadequate. It works for a while and then fails spectacularly.

Subsequently, in a case where businesses run infrastructures and short-term profits are rewarded over long-term surety, management is highly motivated and rewarded by shirking maintenance and protection and leaving success to luck in these areas.

So we seem to have come full circle. Standard designs are good for being more effective with less money, but as you squeeze out the redundancy and the costs, you soon get to common mode failures and brittleness that cause collapses at some future point in time. So along with standard designs, you need standard maintenance and operational processes that have most of the same problems, unless rewards are aligned with reliability and long-term effectiveness. Proper feedback, then, has to become part of the metrics program for the protection program.

3.9.3   Design Automation and Optimization

For protection fields, there is only sporadic design automation and optimization, and the tools that exist are largely proprietary and not sold widely on the open market. Unlike circuit design, building design, and other similar fields, there has not been a long-term academic investigation of most areas of protection involving intentional threats that has moved to mature the field. While there are many engineering tools for the disciplines involved in protection, most of these tools do not address malicious actions. The user can attempt to use these to model such acts, but these tools are not designed to do so and there are no widely available common libraries to support the process.

In the risk management area, as a general field, there are tools for evaluating certain classes of risks and producing aggregated risk figures, but these are rudimentary in nature, require a great deal of input that is hard to quantify properly, and produce relatively little output that has a material effect on design or implementation. There are reliability-related tools associated with carrying out the formulas involved in fault tolerant computing and redundancy, and these can be quite helpful in determining maintenance periods and other similar things, but again, they tend to ignore malicious threats and their capacity to intentionally induce faults.

For each of the engineering fields associated with critical infrastructures, there are also design automation tools, and these are widely used, but again, these tools typically deal with the design issue, ignoring the protective issues associated with anything other than nature.

There are also some tools for working through issues associated with attack graphs. For example, there are several companies with network security simulation tools that use these tools to model sources of security-related weaknesses in computer networks and provide advice on what to mitigate to what extent and in what order. However, these tools are problematic because they require a lot of expertise to apply effectively for an infrastructure. There are also special-purpose tools that perform similar analysis for physical security issues. These tools allow a facility to be characterized and calculations to be performed with regard to times so that different protective and response options can be evaluated and simulated in terms of effectiveness under attack. These are typically only available to limited audiences, and many of the details such as time values and difficulty levels are kept as either trade secrets or classified by governments. Special-purpose tools are occasionally developed by governments for devising protective schemes for special types of facilities. For example, there are specific risk management and design assistance tools for nuclear power facilities, certain types of chemical plants, and certain types of military installations. While such tools are certainly useful and can be applied, they are rarely applied in practice today.

3.9.4   Control Systems

Control systems represent a different sort of IT than most designers and auditors are used to. Unlike the more common general-purpose computer systems in widespread use, these control systems are critical for the moment-to-moment functioning of mechanisms that, in many cases, can cause serious negative physical consequences. Generally, these systems can be broken down into sensors, actuators, and PLCs themselves controlled by SCADA systems.

They control the moment-to-moment operations of motors, valves, generators, flow limiters, transformers, chemical and power plants, switching systems, floor systems at manufacturing facilities, and any number of other real-time mechanisms that are part of the interface between information technologies and the physical world. When they fail or fail to operate properly, regardless of the cause, the consequences can range from a reduction in product quality to the deaths of tens of thousands of people, and beyond, and this is not just theory, it is the reality of incidents like the chemical plant release that killed about 40,000 people in a matter of an hour or so in Bhopal India and the Bellingham Washington SCADA failure of the Olympic Pipeline Company that, combined with other problems in the pipeline infrastructure at the time, resulted in the deaths of about 15 people and put the pipeline company out of business.

3.9.5 Control Systems Variations and Differences

Control systems are quite a bit different from general-purpose computer systems in several ways. These systems differences in turn make a big difference in how they must be properly controlled and audited and, in many cases, make it impossible to do a proper audit on the live system. Some of the key differences to consider include, without limit, the following:

- They are usually real-time systems. Denial of services or communications for periods of thousandths of a second or less can sometimes cause catastrophic failure of physical systems, which in turn can sometimes cause other systems to fail in a cascading manner. This means that real-time performance of all necessary functions within the operating environment must be designed and verified to ensure that such failures will not happen. It also means that they must not be disrupted or interfered with except in well controlled ways during testing or audits. It also means that they should be as independent as possible of external systems and influences.
- They tend to operate at a very low level of interaction, exchanging data like register settings and histories of data values that reflect the state or rate of change of physical devices such as actuators or sensors.
- That means that any of the valid values for settings might be reasonable depending on the overall situation of the plant they operate within and that it is hard to tell whether a data value is valid without a model of the plant in operation to compare the value to.
- They tend to operate in place for tens of years before being replaced and they tend to exist as they were originally implemented. They do not get updated very often, do not run antivirus scanners, and, in many cases, do not even have general-purpose operating systems. This means that the technology of 30 years ago has to be integrated into new technologies and that designers have to consider the implications over that time frame to be prudent. Initial cost is far less

important than life cycle costs and consequences of failure tend to far outweigh any of the system costs.

- For the most part, they do not run the same protocols as other systems, relying on things like distributed network protocol (DNP), perhaps within intercontrol center communications (ICCP), or Modbus and OLE process control (OPC). These often get executed over serial ports and are often limited to 300 to 1200 baud modem speeds, and have memory on the order of a few thousand bytes.
- Most of these systems are designed to operate in a closed environment with no connection outside of the control environment. However, they are increasingly being connected to the Internet, wireless access mechanisms, and other remote and distant mechanisms running over intervening infrastructure. Such connections are extremely dangerous, and commonly used protective mechanisms like firewalls and proxy servers are rarely effective in protecting control systems to the level of surety appropriate to the consequences of failure.
- Current intrusion and anomaly detection systems largely fail to understand the protocols that control systems use and, even if they did, do not have plant models that allow them to differentiate between legitimate and illegitimate commands in context.
- Even if they could do this, the response times for control systems is often too short to allow any such intervention, and stopping the flow of control signals is sometimes more dangerous than allowing potentially wrong signals to flow.
- Control systems typically have no audit trails of commands executed or sent to them; have no identification, authentication, or authorization mechanisms; and execute whatever command is sent to them immediately unless it has a bad format. They have only limited error detection capabilities, and in most cases, erroneous values are reflected in physical events in the mechanisms under control rather than error returns.
- When penetration testing is undertaken, it very often demonstrates that these systems are highly susceptible to attack. However, this is quite dangerous because as soon as a wrong command is sent to such a system or the system slows down during such a test, the risk is run of doing catastrophic damage to the plant. For that reason, actual systems in operation are virtually never tested and should not be tested in this manner.

In control systems, integrity, availability, and use control are the most important objectives for operational needs, while accountability is vital to forensic analysis, but confidentiality is rarely of import from an operational standpoint at the level of individual control mechanisms. The design and review process should be clear in its prioritization. This is not to say that confidentiality is not important. In fact, there are examples such as reflexive control attacks and gaming attacks against the financial system in which control system data have been exploited, but given the option of having the system operate safely or leaking information about its state, safe operation should be given precedence.

3.10 Questions to Probe

Finally, while each specific control system has to be individually considered in context, there are some basic questions that should be asked with regard to any control system and a set of issues to be considered relative to those questions.

3.10.1 Question 1: What Is the Consequence of Failure and Who Accepts the Risk?

The first question that should always be asked with regard to control systems is the consequences associated with control system failures, followed by the surety level applied to implement and protect those control systems. If the consequences are higher, then the surety of the implementation should be higher. The consequence levels associated with the worst-case failure, ignoring protective measures in place, indicate the level at which risks have to be reviewed and accepted. If lives are at stake, likely the chief executive officer (CEO) has to accept residual risks. If significant impacts on the valuation of the enterprise are possible, the CEO and chief finance officer (CFO) have to sign off.

In most manufacturing, chemical processing, energy, environment, and other similar operations, the consequences of a control system failure are high enough to require top management involvement and sign-off. Executives must read the audit summaries and the chief scientist of the enterprise should understand the risks and describe these to the CEO and CFO before sign-off. If this is not done, who is making these decisions should be determined and an audit team should report this result to the board as a high priority item to be mitigated.

3.10.2 Question 2: What Are the Duties to Protect?

Along with the responsibility for control systems comes civil and possibly criminal liability for failure to do the job well enough and for the decision to accept a risk rather than mitigate it. In most cases, such systems end up being safety systems, having potential environmental impacts, and possibly endangering surrounding populations.

Duties to protect include, without limit, legal and regulatory mandates, industry-specific standards, contractual obligations, company policies, and possibly other duties. All of these duties must be identified and met for control systems, and for most high-valued control systems, there are additional mandates and special requirements. For example, in the automotive industry, safety mechanisms in cars that are not properly operating because of a control system failure in the manufacturing process might produce massive recalls, and there may be a duty to have records of inspections associated with the requirements for recalls that are unmet within some control systems. Of course, designers should know the industry they operate in, as should auditors, and without such knowledge, items such as these may be missed.

3.10.3   Question 3: What Controls Are Needed, and Are They in Place?

Control systems in use today were largely created at a time when the Internet was not widely connected. As a result, they were designed to operate in an environment where connectivity was very limited. To the extent that they have remote control mechanisms, those mechanisms are usually direct command interfaces to control settings. At the time they were designed, the systems were protected by limiting physical access to equipment and limiting remote access to dedicated telephone lines or wires that run with the infrastructure elements under control. When this is changed to a nondedicated circuit, when the telephone switching system no longer uses physical controls over dedicated lines, when the telephone link is connected via a modem to a computer network connected to the Internet, or when a direct IP connection to the device is added, the design assumptions of isolation that made the system relatively safe are no longer valid.

Few designers of 25 years ago were knowledgeable of modern threats, and none knew that the Internet would connect their control system to foreign military information warfare experts and saboteurs. Memory and processing were precious and expensive and used carefully to get the desired functionality out of them. They designed for the realities of the day. Today's designers are often unaware of the risks of updated technologies and the extent to which these technologies are prone to failures. Modern control systems may have embedded systems that run operating systems with many millions of lines of code that do things ranging from periodic checks for external updates to running flight simulators from within spreadsheet programs. Almost none of this unnecessary functionality is known to the designers who use these systems, and the resulting unpredictability of these systems means that increased vigilance must be used to make certain that they do what they are supposed to and nothing else.

When connecting these systems to the Internet, such connections are typically made without the necessary knowledge to do them safely. Given the lack of clarity in this area, it is probably important to not make such connections without having the best experts consider the safety of those changes. This sort of technology change is one of the key things that make control systems susceptible to attack, and most of the technology fixes put in place with the idea of compensating for those changes do not make those systems safe. Here are some examples of things we have consistently seen in reviews of such systems:

- The claim of an "air gap" or "direct line" or "dedicated line" between a communications network used to control distant systems and the rest of the telephone network is almost never true, no matter how many people may claim it. The only way to verify this is to walk from place to place and follow the actual wires, and every time we have done it, we have found these claims to be untrue.
- The claim that "nobody could ever figure that out" seems to be a universal form of denial. Unfortunately, people do figure these things out and exploit them all the time, and of course, our teams have figured them out to present them to the people who operate the control systems, demonstrating that they can be figured out.
- Remote control mechanisms are almost always vulnerable, less so between the SCADA and the things it controls when the connections are fairly direct, but almost always for mobile control devices, any mechanisms using wireless, any system with unprotected wiring, any system with a way to check on or manage from afar, and anything connected either directly or indirectly to the Internet.
- Encryption, VPN mechanisms, firewalls, intrusion detection sensors, and other similar security mechanisms designed to protect normal networks from standard attacks are rarely effective in protecting control systems connected to or through these devices from attacks that they face, and many of these techniques are too slow, cause delays, or are otherwise problematic for control systems. Failures may not appear during testing or for years, but when they do appear, they can be catastrophic.
- Insider threats are almost always ignored, and typical control systems are powerless against them. However, many of the attack mechanisms depend on a multistep process that starts with changing a limiter setting and is followed by exceeding normal limits of operation. If detection of these limit-setting changes were done in a timely fashion, many of the resulting failures could be avoided.

- Change management in control systems is often not able to differentiate between safety interlocks and operational control settings. Higher standards of care should be applied to changes of interlocks than changes in data values because the interlocks are the things that force the data values to within reasonable ranges. As an example, interlocks are often bypassed by maintenance processes and sometimes not verified after the maintenance is completed. Standard operating procedure should mandate safety checks including verification of all interlocks and limiters against known good values and external review should keep old copies and verify changes against them.
- If accountability is to be attained, it must be done by an additional audit device that receives signals through a diode or similar mechanism that prevents the audit mechanism from affecting the system. This device must itself be well protected to keep forensically sound information required for investigation. However, since there is usually poor or no identification, authentication, or authorization mechanism within the control system itself, attribution is problematic unless explicitly designed into the overall control system. Alarms should be in place to detect loss of accountability information, and such loss should be immediately investigated. A proper audit system should be able to collect all of the control signals in a complex control environment for periods of many years without running out of space or becoming overwhelmed.
- If information from the control system is needed for some other purpose, it should run through a digital diode for use. If remote control is really needed, that control should be severely limited and implemented only through a custom interface using a finite state machine mechanism with syntax checks in context, strict accountability, strong auditing, and specially designed controls for the specific controls on the specific systems. It should fail into a safe mode and be carefully reviewed and should not allow any safety interlocks or other similar changes to be made from afar.
- To the extent that distant communication is used, it should be encrypted at the line level where feasible; however, because of timing constraints, this may be of only limited value. To the extent that remote control is used at the level of human controls, all traffic should be encrypted and the remote control devices should be protected to the same level of surety as local control devices. That means, for example, that if you are using a laptop to remotely control such a mechanism, it should not be used for other purposes, such as e-mail, Web browsing, or any other nonessential function of the control system.

- Nothing should ever be run on a control system other than the control system itself. It needs to have dedicated hardware, infrastructure, connectivity, bandwidth, controls, and so forth. The corporate LAN should not be shared with the control system, no matter how much there are supposed to be guarantees of quality of service. If voice over IP replaces plain old telephone service (POTS) throughout the enterprise, make sure it is not replaced in the control systems. Fight the temptation to share an Ethernet between more than two devices, to go through a switch or other similar device, or to use wireless, unless there is no other way. Just remember that the entire chain of control for all of these infrastructure elements may cause the control system to fail and induce the worst case consequences.
- Finally, experience shows that people believe a lot of things that are not true. This is more so in the security arena than in most other fields and more critical in control systems than in most other enterprise systems. When in doubt, do not believe them. Trust, but verify.

Perhaps more dangerous than older systems that we know have no built-in controls are modern systems that run complex operating systems and are regularly updated. Modern operating platforms that run control systems often slow down when updates are underway or at different times of day or during different processes. These slowdowns sometimes cause control systems to slow unnecessarily. If an antivirus update causes a critical piece of software to be detected in a false-positive, the control system could crash, and if a virus can enter the control system, the control system is not secure enough to handle medium- or high-consequence control functions. Many modern systems have built-in security mechanisms that are supposed to protect them, but the protection is usually not designed to ensure availability, integrity, and use control, but rather to protect confidentiality. As such, they aim at the wrong target, and even if they should hit what they aim at, it will not meet the need.

Note and Reference

1. Yang and Sun, "A Comprehensive Review of Hard-Disk Reliability."

Bibliography

Yang, J., and Sun, F.-B. "A Comprehensive Review of Hard-Disk Drive Reliability." In *Proceedings of the Annual Reliability and Maintainability Symposium*, 1999.

Cyber Intelligence, Cyber Conflicts, and Cyber Warfare

4

THOMAS A. JOHNSON

Contents

4.1 Introduction

One of the most comprehensive books on information warfare was authored by Dorothy E. Denning, and her exceptional analysis presented a comprehensive account of both offensive and defensive information warfare targets, methods, technologies, and policies. Denning's interest was in operations that exploit or target information sources to gain advantage over an adversary. Her study assessed computer intrusions, intelligence operations, telecommunication eavesdropping, and electronic warfare, all with the purpose of describing information warfare technologies and their limitations, as well as the limitations of defensive technologies.[1]

4.2   Information Warfare Theory and Application

One of our nation's first major information warfare challenges occurred in 1990 and 1991, when five hackers from the Netherlands penetrated computer systems at 34 military sites through use of the Internet. Information was gathered from sites that also supported our military planning for Operation Desert Storm and ultimately provided information as to the exact locations of troops, weapons, and movement of warships in the Gulf region. Reports after the Gulf War concluded that the information was offered to Iraq but was declined by Iraq on the basis that Iraq authorities considered this information as false and part of an elaborate deceptive operation, which was not the case.[2] While the United States was victimized in this operation, it became apparent to authorities within the military, including the White House, that our defensive operations had to be improved and refined. Our nation's efforts in refining offensive technologies and our military's capabilities and use of these offensive technologies far outdistanced our focus on defensive technologies.

An example of the offensive technologies applied in the very beginning of the Iraq War was demonstrated when coalition forces neutralized or destroyed key Iraqi information systems with electronic and physical weapons and included the following situation: virus-loaded computer chips on printers assembled in France and shipped to Iraq via Jordan were designed to disable Windows and mainframe computers in Iraq. While this operation actually preceded the invasion by a number of weeks, it was later determined that this effort resulted in taking half their displays and printers out of commission. Activities such as these were followed by specific electronic attacks at the very start of the invasion.

During the first moments of Operation Desert Storm, clouds of anti-radiation weapons fired from helicopters and aircraft disabled the Iraqi air defense network. Ribbons of carbon fibers, dispensed from Tomahawk missiles over Iraqi electrical power switching systems, caused short circuits, temporary disruptions, and massive shutdowns in power systems. An Air Force F-117 Stealth fighter directed a precision-guided bomb straight down the air-conditioning shaft of the Iraqi telephone system in downtown Baghdad, taking out the entire underground coaxial cable system, which tied the Iraqi high command to their subordinate elements. This eliminated the primary method of communications between the command center in Baghdad and subordinates in the field. Once the command and control centers were out of action, the coalition went after Iraq's radar systems, taking away their ability to "see" the battle space. Blind and deaf, Iraq had little chance of victory.[3]

As the Iraqi War ended, Soviet General S. Boganov, Chief of the General Staff Center for Operational and Strategic Studies, said: "Iraq lost the war before it even began. This was a war of intelligence, electronic warfare, command and control and counter intelligence…modern war can be won by 'informatika' and that is now vital."[4] Russia and China both took note of the new capabilities in information warfare and clearly have responded by preparing their militaries with both defensive and offensive strategies and capabilities.

While offensive information warfare strategies can be launched from virtually any corner of the world, and by any nation-state so inclined, the necessity for creating sound defensive strategies is clear. However, it is much more difficult to design, prepare, and implement defensive strategies that include prevention, deterrence, intrusion warnings, and detection and counteroffensive attack defense mechanisms.

4.2.1 Cyberspace

Cyberspace can be defined as the space in which information circulates from one medium to another and where it is processed, duplicated, and stored. It is also the space in which tools communicate, where information technology becomes ubiquitous. So in effect, cyberspace consists of communication systems, computers, networks, satellites, and communication infrastructure that all use information in its digital format. This includes sound, voice, text, and image data that can be controlled remotely via a network, which include technologies and communication tools such as the following:

- Wi-Fi
- Laser
- Modems
- Satellites
- Local networks
- Cell phones
- Fiber optic
- Computers
- Storage devices
- Fixed or mobile equipment[5]

As we obtain our information through cyberspace and as all aspects of society become more dependent on acquisition of their information, one can easily surmise why this will become a theater for information warfare. Since our nation's 16 critical infrastructures are so dependent on their operations through the area we define as cyberspace, it is only understandable that cyberspace will eventually become a vehicle for launching cyber attacks, and there is a need for creating defensive strategies and operations to prevent this from happening.

Bruce Schneier relates that in the 21st century, war will inevitably include cyber war as war moved into space with the development of satellites and ballistic missiles, and war will move into cyberspace with the development of specialized weapons, software, electronics, tactics, and defenses. Schneier discusses the properties of cyber war in terms of network hardware and software and notes the fundamental tension between cyber attacks and cyber defenses. Regarding cyber attacks, one of our concerns should center on the ability of an attacker to launch an attack against us, and since cyber attacks do not have an obvious origin, unlike other forms of warfare, there is something very terrifying not knowing your adversary—or thinking you know who your adversary is only to be wrong. As Schneier states, "imagine if after Pearl Harbor, we did not know who attacked us?"[6] Many people experienced this very fear after the 9/11 attacks in the United States, which involved physical plane attacks. One can only imagine the terror if the attack was a total cyber electronic attack alone by an unknown source.

It should be quite obvious that as a result of the rapid development of technologies, the digital environment has ushered in an era where most nations will have to begin to plan for cyber warfare. It would be unreasonable for militaries to ignore the threat of cyber attack and not invest in defensive strategies.

John Arquilla of the Naval Postgraduate School and David Ronfeldt of the Rand Corporation introduced the concept of "cyber war" for the purpose of contemplating knowledge-related conflict at the military level as a means to conduct military operations according to information-related principles. It meant to disrupt, if not destroy, information and communication systems that an adversary relies upon.[7] Of course, if the information and communication systems can be used to gather information on the adversary, these systems would be most useful from an intelligence point of view and would continue to be used to acquire further intelligence.

Martin Libicki, from the National Defense University, identified seven forms of information warfare and categorized these as follows:

- Command and control warfare
- Intelligence-based warfare
- Electronic warfare
- Psychological warfare
- Hacker warfare
- Economic information warfare
- Cyber warfare[8]

Dorothy Denning suggests several possible futures for war and military conflict, and as a result of the Gulf War, she sees that future wars may well be a continuation of the Gulf War, wherein future operations will exploit new developments in technology, particularly sensors and precision-guided weapons, but will be accompanied by military force on the ground, sea, and air. A second future scenario is one in which operations take place almost exclusively in cyberspace. Under this scenario, wars will be fought without any armed forces. Instead, trained military cyber-warriors will break into the enemy's critical infrastructures, remotely disabling communication command and control systems that support both military and government operations. Additional attacks will be targeted toward the critical infrastructures such as banking, telecommunications, transportation systems, and the electrical power grid of the adversary.[9]

4.2.2 Cyber Battle Space

Cyber battle space is the information space of focus during wartime, and it consists of everything in both the physical environment as well as the cyberspace environment. Each side seeks to maximize its own knowledge of battle space while preventing its adversary from access to the information space.[10] Battle space will be defined by both offensive and defensive operations conducted by the militaries of the future. As technologies experience scientific enrichment, nations will apply these discoveries for both offensive and defensive purposes. Some nations will be guided by collateral damage potential and may well place limitations on the development of cyber weapons, while other nations will ignore the potential hazards of collateral damage to civilian populations.

4.2.3 Offensive Operations

As Ed Skoudis has so accurately reported, there are literally thousands of computer and network attack tools available, as well as tens of thousands of different exploit techniques. Even more alarming is there are hundreds of methods available that permit the attackers to conceal their presence on the machine by modifying the operating system and using rootkit tools. Also noteworthy is the fact that once an adversary has gained access to your computer system, the process of manipulation will begin so that they will remain undiscovered by hiding their tracks.[11] In Advanced Persistent Threat (APT) attacks, we know that adversaries will create tunnels and encrypt the data they are interested in exfiltrating from the target's databases.

The methodology used by cyber-warriors to attack or gain access to a computer system varies from network mapping to port-scanning, but in its simplest terms, the adversary will focus on using reconnaissance in which they will study the selected target. This will include use of Whois database searching for domain names and Internet protocol (IP) address assignments.

In addition, if the target has a website, a search of the website and useful information will be further researched for intelligence gathering purposes. Social media sites will also be analyzed, looking for additional contact information on friends, family, and associates. Sites such as Facebook and LinkedIn are examples of sites with a great deal of information on the targeted individuals.

There exist numerous ways for an attacker to gain access to computer systems by employing operating system attacks, which will include buffer overflow exploits, password attacks, Web application attacks, and structured query language injection attacks. Cyber attacks can also provide access through the use of network attacks in which sniffing tools will be used, as well as IP address spoofing, session hijacking, and Netcat tools. Once access is gained by cyber attackers, they will use rootkits and kernel-mode rootkits to maintain their access. Their next step will be to hide their presence on the target's computer system by altering event logs or creating hidden files and hiding evidence on network covert channels and tunneling operations.[12]

Of course, there are also a number of classified cyber weapons that have been created by various militaries. The United States focuses on evaluating our cyber weapons for collateral damage assessment and evaluation before approval for inclusion in our nation's inventory of weapon systems.

4.2.4 Defensive Operations

Effective defensive operations begin with an understanding of the value of the information system and the databases within the total information system. What is the value placed on the system both by the attacker and the potential target? This implies that the operational use of the system has definite value in a number of ways, from financial measures to a range of criticality factors. The sensitivity of the data and how the users of the system gain access to the system are important to understand and protect. So the process of protecting computer-based information systems implies that a rather sophisticated threat modeling process will be required in which the network is mapped and the physical and logical layout of the network is fully documented. Once the network is fully mapped, the range of possible attacks can be simulated so that infection vectors might be identified. The possible computer attacks can be assessed on a threat level based on severity and both the impact and cost to the targeted system. Based upon this threat modeling and assessment, it is feasible to select appropriate defensive operational solutions. The range of defensive security solutions available for targeted offensive cyber attacks varies depending on the cyber attack motifs and objectives. Defensive solutions have to be available not only for a range of attacks but also for those times before an infection by a cyber attack and during the attack. After a cyber attack, remediation and recovery measures have to be in place.[13]

It is incumbent on all defensive operations to have an Incident Response Plan that permits the detection of a cyber attack threat. This, of course, implies detecting anomalies or unusual patterns of behavior that do not conform to or significantly deviate from the established baseline of computer activity. Detecting network anomalies implies log analysis so that, ultimately, it is possible to isolate the source of the anomaly. Computer forensics can assist in determining the timeline of an attack and should answer what occurred and when it happened by the following:

- When the infection vector reached the target
- When the malware was installed
- When the malware first reached out to the attacker
- When the malware first attempted to spread
- When the malware first executed its directive
- When the malware destroyed itself, if this was the type of malware designed to do so[14]

Threat mitigation is an important part of cyber defensive operations as it focuses on minimizing the impact of the threat on the targeted information system. When an alert for a possible threat has been raised, the first step for an incident responder is to isolate those computer systems from the network. Containment has to occur quite rapidly to avoid a network-wide infection. Network and host anomaly detection systems will provide the alert for the Incident Response Team to contain those computers vulnerable to the cyber attack. Once the containment has been accomplished, the compromised systems are then subject to verification and integration processes. After the containment systems have verified that a cyber attack did indeed occur, the threat has to be detected and must be classified so that the malware may be removed and the compromised systems can be remediated and restored.[15] This process of classification will also assist in the establishment of preventive measures.

Defensive operations also have to prepare for attacks by insiders, as not all attacks are from the outside. The recent removal of volumes of classified national security data by Edward Snowden from the National Security Agency (NSA) is an excellent example of a threat from insiders. The insider threat is one of the most difficult threats to detect and prevent, since an insider threat is from someone who already has access to the organization's network. Further, there is an assumption of the individual as being a trusted colleague and employee. The following are points that serve as a starting basis in mitigating an insider threat:

- Full background investigation of employee
- Have a policy for enforcement against inside threat employees

- Employee restricted to least privileged access
- Detailed auditing of user sessions
- Anomaly detection tuned to detect insider threat
- Elimination of shared credentials
- Network access control to limit devices
- Effective employee supervision
- Data leakage policies[16]

Skoudis and Liston have provided a number of defense strategies to offensive attacks in their excellent book, *Counter Hack Reloaded: A Step-by-Step Guide to Computer Attacks and Effective Defenses*, and these are contained within the following categories:

- Reconnaissance
  - Defenses against search engine and web based reconnaissance
  - Defenses against Whois searches
  - Defenses against domain name system (DNS)-based reconnaissance
- Scanning
  - Defenses against war dialing
  - Defenses against network mapping
  - Defenses against port scanning
  - Vulnerability-scanning defenses
  - Intrusion Detection System (IDS) and Intrusion Prevention System (IPS) evasion defenses
- Operating System Attacks
  - Buffer overflow attack defenses
  - Defenses against password-cracking attacks
  - Defending against browser exploits
- Network Attacks
  - Sniffing defenses
  - IPS spoofing defenses
  - Session hijacking defenses
  - Netcat defenses
- Denial-of-Service Attacks
  - Distributed denial-of-service (DDoS) defenses
- Trojans, Backdoors, and Rootkits
  - Defenses against application level Trojans, backdoors, bots, and spyware
  - Defending against user-mode rootkits
  - Defending against kernel-mode rootkits
- Hidden Files
  - Defenses from hidden files
  - Defenses against covert channels[17]

Skoudis and Liston's comprehensive description of defenses is an outstanding resource and provides a well-reasoned approach for analyzing defensive operations.

4.3 Cyber Intelligence and Counter Intelligence

The digital transformation that has impacted all aspects of our life in terms of business, education, medicine, agriculture, and our critical infrastructure has also had a profound effect on our national security and those agencies responsible for our nation's defense and security. Our nation's 16 intelligence agencies are also making transformational changes in the manner in how their collection, processing, and exploitation of data are acquired and how the analysis and dissemination of the information are presented.

After the 9/11 attack on our nation, a National Commission was appointed to review the work and performance of our intelligence community, and this resulted in major modifications of the intelligence agencies, but most importantly, it resulted in the creation of the Office of the Director of National Intelligence. The Director of National Intelligence is charged with providing greater cooperation and information sharing between each of our intelligence agencies and to oversee the $50 billion dollar budget allocated to our nation's intelligence community.

Our nation's intelligence community is distributed in three major pathways as follows:

Office of the Director of National Intelligence
1. Principal National Intelligence Programs
    a. Central Intelligence Agency
    b. Defense Intelligence Agency
    c. National Geospatial-Intelligence Agency
    d. National Reconnaissance Office
    e. National Security Agency
    f. FBI-National Security Branch
2. Armed Forces—Military Intelligence
    a. Air Force Intelligence
    b. Naval Intelligence
    c. Army Intelligence
    d. Marine Corp Intelligence
    e. Coast Guard Intelligence
3. National-Government Department Intelligence Operations
    a. Department of Homeland Security—Office of Intelligence & Analysis

    b. Department of Energy—Office of Intelligence & Counter Intelligence
    c. Treasury Department—Office of Intelligence & Analysis
    d. State Department—Bureau of Intelligence & Research
    e. Drug Enforcement Agency—Office of National Security Intelligence

James Clapper, Director of the Office of National Intelligence, identified the core function of his office as the integration of intelligence with the requirement for a global information technology infrastructure through which the intelligence community can rapidly and reliably share information.

This infrastructure is much more than hardware, software, data, and networks. It also encompasses the policies, procedures, and strategies that drive responsible and secure information sharing. Ultimately, mission success depends on our diverse workforce bringing forth and implementing innovative ideas that are linked to the National Intelligence Strategy and the Intelligence Communities Information Technology Enterprise Strategy. In doing so, we enable our mission partners, war fighters, and decision-makers to have secure and timely information that helps them meet mission needs and keep our nation secure.[18]

If the core function of the integration of intelligence is to be achieved, the creation of the Intelligence Community Information Technology Enterprise Strategy was an exceptional achievement. The strategic goals of the Information Technology Enterprise Strategy center on defining, developing, implementing, and sustaining a single, standards-based interoperable, secure, and survivable intelligence community Information Technology Enterprise Architecture. This architecture has to deliver user-focused capabilities that are to be provided as a seamless, secure solution for trusted collaboration on a basis of people to people, people to data, and data to data that will enhance mission success while ensuring protection of intelligence assets and information.[19] Not only is this Information Technology Enterprise Architecture Program fundamental to creating a mechanism for intelligence agencies to work more cooperatively, but it also has enabled the intelligence community to be better prepared for the digital transformation in their basic collection, processing, and analysis functions.

4.3.1　Cyberspace and Cyber Intelligence

In 1995, the Central Intelligence Agency (CIA) realized that advances in technology were outdistancing their internal capabilities, and the Agency was simply not prepared to seize the collection and analysis opportunities that would become available through the high-tech environment that was emerging outside the Agency. As a result, the Agency created the Office of

Clandestine Information Technology, and its work was designed to prepare for the espionage operations in cyberspace. Within four years, by 1999, most of the technical operations in the CIA's Counter Terrorism Center were based in cyberspace. The result was in the production of terabytes of intelligence data. However, as former CIA Agent Henry Crumpton notes, "...these monumental advances in technology have not made collection easier...in some ways technical collection is much harder, because of the massive amounts of data, new requisite skills, diverse operational risks, organizational challenges and bureaucratic competition."[20] By 2000, these changes would usher in an era of new collection platforms; namely, the Predator and this unmanned aerial vehicle (UAV) would, in less than ten years, transform how wars would be fought not only to this day as well as into the future.

The National Security Council directed the CIA to find a means to locate, identify, and document Osama bin Laden, and the only feasible way to achieve this task was through the use of advanced technology. Two of our nation's most extraordinary CIA Agents, Cofer Black, of the Counter Terrorism Center, and Henry Crumpton were responsible with other Agents Rich and Alec in the development of the Predator platform, which joined a UAV with an unmanned aerial system (UAS) utilizing a command control link via a satellite with the purpose of collecting data and mapping the Afghanistan areas where al-Qaeda and Osama bin Laden were working and hiding. The photos collected convinced the Agents that this new instrument of technology collection was going to be an effective instrument, and indeed, there was an identification of Osama bin Laden, and this information was immediately reported to the Clinton White House, but the targeting of this site by a cruise missile launched from a U.S. Navy ship in the Indian Ocean would have taken six hours, and unless assurance could have been given that the group would remain there for six hours, no authorization for use of the cruise missile was given. Eventually, the realization that the Predator would have to be armed with a weapon system was acknowledged, and the munition of choice was a Hellfire missile. Ironically, the CIA agents had attached an Army weapon to an Air Force platform under the command of the CIA, and this created a major bureaucratic argument as the Department of Defense (DoD) viewed this as an instrument of war and believed that, as an instrument of war, it belonged under the purview of the DoD. The CIA countered that the DoD refused to put military on the ground to locate Osama bin Laden, and as a result, the National Security Council directed the CIA to locate Osama bin Laden. Eventually, 15 governmental agencies were involved, and the final authority was designated to the CIA for this operation.[21]

In the decade to follow, UASs would proliferate as a collection tool and often as a weapon platform. By 2011, some pundits, in a vigorous defense of President Obama's employment of armed Predators, noted that drone attacks have become a centerpiece of national security policy. Some experts would proclaim the armed Predator the most accurate weapon in the history of war. In 2001, we had no idea that would be the case. We just wanted verification of our Human Intelligence, a way to employ our intelligence and to eliminate Osama bin Laden.[22]

4.3.2 New Drone Wars

The advantage of using drones not only for collection of intelligence but also for using weapon systems armed to the drone removes pilots and ground forces from risk of being captured or killed, and accordingly, it has lowered the threshold for the use of force. Predator and Reaper drones can hover over a target for over 14 hours at altitudes in excess of 25,000 feet, and to date, the United States has launched armed drone attacks in Afghanistan, Libya, Iraq, Pakistan, Philippines, Somalia, and Yemen. Moreover, the United States has conducted more than 1000 drone strikes since 2008 in Afghanistan; 48 drone strikes in Iraq from 2008 to 2012; and in 2011, it launched 145 drone strikes in Libya, 400 drone strikes in Pakistan, 100 drone strikes in Yemen, 18 drone strikes in Somalia, and 1 strike in the Philippines.[23]

Israel and the United Kingdom have used armed drones, and as of 2013, the British military launched 299 drone attacks in Afghanistan, and Israel conducted 42 missions in 2008–2009 in the Gaza conflict. To date, there are 76 nations that have developed drone capabilities, but only China and Iran have joined the United States, United Kingdom, and Israel with the ability to arm their drones with weapons. While the balance of the nations has the ability to deploy drones for surveillance missions, it will only be a matter of time until they can also weaponize their drone systems.[24]

The use of drones requires technical capabilities and also may entail bilateral treaties that permit the right to base drones on the ground, as well as to permit overflight operations in the air space of the host or nearby nations.

Daniel Byman observes that drones have done their job remarkably well by killing key terrorist leaders and by denying terrorists sanctuaries in Pakistan and Yemen and at little financial cost and no risk to U.S. forces and with fewer civilian casualties than if other weapon systems were used. Since President Obama has used drone strikes, an estimated 3300 al-Qaeda, Taliban, and other Jihadist terrorists have been killed.[25] Nevertheless, the United States does need to be aware of how the ease of use of drones may also raise concerns in other nations.

Audrey Kurth Cronin observes that after more than a decade of war, the U.S. citizens have articulated to governmental leadership that they are tired of the wars, the financial cost, and the injuries and deaths to the U.S. military members, and if there still exists a need to fight against terrorists, the most acceptable choice of weapon is the drone. However, the problem for our leadership is that the drone program has taken on a life of its own, to the point where tactics are driving strategy rather than the other way around. Cronin also is concerned as to whether drones are undermining U.S. strategic goals as much as they are advancing them. Another concern focuses on the opportunity cost of devoting a large percentage of U.S. military and intelligence resources to the drone campaign. For example, she states the following:

> The U.S. Air Force trained 350 drone pilots in 2011, compared with only 250 conventional fighter and bomber pilots trained that year. There are sixteen drone operating and training sites across the U.S. and a 17th is being planned. There are also twelve U.S. drone bases stationed abroad, often in politically sensitive areas.[26]

The new drone war strategy clearly minimizes injury and death to U.S. military and is not as expensive in terms of alternative weapon systems that might be used. Also, the collateral damage and loss of life to civilians in the targeted war area are significantly reduced. Nevertheless, some citizens of the United States as well as other nations are questioning the extensive use of this new drone strategy. So the process of intelligence and military operations will be questioned, and the responsibility of our intelligence, military, and civilian governmental leadership will, by necessity, have to provide clear and understandable responses.

In a democracy such as ours, which places a high value on civil liberties and privacy, it is inevitable for tension to begin over intelligence practices and military strategies and operations. After the 9/11 attacks and the review of our intelligence agencies, many expressions of failure were voiced by citizens as well as governmental leaders. Most recently, Edward Snowden's release of the NSA's programs has also raised serious questions as to the nature, role, and propriety of intelligence operations and programs.

4.3.3 Intelligence Paradox

The fundamental intelligence paradox centers on the need to reconcile intelligence programs, practices, and operations while preserving the public trust, within the democracy we live and serve.

Jennifer Sims and Burton Gerber provide the most incisive assessment of the intelligence paradox by their analysis of intelligence requirements and the protection of civil liberties, where they observe the following:

> In democracies the state's interest in maximizing power for national security purpose must be balanced with its interest in preserving the public trust. In the U.S. case, this trust requires protection of constitutional freedoms and the American way of life. History tells us that intelligence practices unsuited either to the temperament of American political culture or to the new threats embedded in the international system will probably trigger more failure, and

all too swiftly. Thus, national security decision-makers face a conundrum: the best intelligence systems, when turned inward to address foreign threats to vital domestic interests, can threaten the very institutions of democracy and representative government that they were set up to protect in the first place.[27]

The nature of how our nation addresses our intelligence policy includes governmental leaders, in Congress as well as the White House and also our judicial system. All three branches of our government are intimately involved in the creation, oversight, and interpretation of our nation's intelligence community's collection policy operations and analytical production of work products. So the question of how to manage the conundrums involved in gathering and maintaining secrets must by, its very nature, include those significant branches of our government. How the intelligence community earns the trust and cooperation of the American people in its domestic fight against transnational threats while simultaneously expanding intrusive domestic surveillance is an issue that goes beyond the decision-makers of the intelligence community, as it requires the engagement of the full panoply of our nation's intelligence leaders who have, all too frequently, found their role similar to an iceberg, in which two-thirds of the body is hidden from its participation in the very policies they have tangentially been involved in creating. For example, as intelligence programs and policies are created, all participants have to address some of the most difficult issues confronting intelligence programs in a democracy, such as whether, when, and how the government may consort with criminals, influence elections, listen in on private conversations, eliminate adversaries, withhold information from the public, what kind of cover may be used by intelligence officers, and how covert action proposals are vetted within the government. These are all programs that have been used in the past and with the approval of our nation's highest elected officials. So in effect, intelligence policy is not the exclusive domain of the intelligence agency professionals. In essence, decisions about intelligence policy, who formulates the policy, and who will be responsible for the policies determine how a given set of intelligence institutions and the democratic system it serves can productively coexist.[28] Clearly, a challenge confronting both our government and the intelligence community is the realization that substantial numbers of American citizens are uncomfortable with the intelligence communities use of clandestine operations, deception, or the collection of telephone and Internet metadata.

The incredible advancements in technology and the accompanying digital revolution have irreversibly altered the collection and analysis of intelligence data. The global reliance on information technology throughout all nations and their intelligence agencies has so fundamentally changed not only the intelligence process but also military warfare. Today, the challenges are not only in the use of offensive cyber weapons by nation-states, but also, the ability of individuals to design software attacks, exfiltrate intellectual property, and compromise databases is a challenge confronting our nation's intelligence community. Each of our 16 intelligence agencies is focused on the development of programs that will produce information in a timely fashion that will answer the question which is foremost in the mind of our nation's leadership and that is central to the "warning" question. Will there be another terrorist attack within or against the United States, by whom, and in what manner? Since our nation experienced the 9/11 attacks, we as a society are acutely aware of our vulnerabilities, and we want to be protected from such terrorist activity. So we depend on our intelligence community to provide actionable information to our governmental leaders so their decision making will result in well-developed policies premised upon well-researched and analyzed fact patterns. On some occasions, especially in controversial areas, the dialogue over the appropriateness of collection methods may be viewed by some as a deviation from the norms, mores, and sensitivities of the general public. Our nation's public is disengaged from the difficulties of operating intelligence programs and the sincere efforts of our intelligence professionals to work within a structure that permits our coexistence of democratic principles. The value of providing the information that will protect our citizens on the safety and freedom they wish to enjoy is a core principle of our intelligence professionals. As a nation, we have had little public dialogue on the conundrums facing our intelligence community. The intelligence paradox will take careful and thoughtful dialogue from all parties as those who work within our intelligence community seek to protect our citizens and to protect and uphold the democratic values of our society.

4.3.4   TOR, the Silk Road, and the Dark Net

The intelligence community paradox focuses on operations in our society that have challenged our democratic principles and freedoms guaranteed by our constitution. Another point of view that must be considered in assessing this paradox focuses on the freedoms we enjoy in our society, which is supported and assured by our security and intelligence forces, as their mission is to protect the lives, liberties, and sanctity of our people and our society. In the performance of this role, we observe additional paradoxes, and in the case of freedom of speech and freedom of the press, how should one assess these freedoms when organizations and entities, in their desire to inform the public of various intelligence activities, actually disclose information that can be harmful to others? The release of information at both a sensitive and classified level by Bradley Manning to the WikiLeaks organization resulted in many individuals' safety and lives being placed in danger. Bradley Manning was convicted of his furnishing of classified information to WikiLeaks. However, WikiLeaks claimed status as a news agency and stated that their purpose of publishing this information was only to inform the public, and they have sought protection under the First Amendment to the U.S. Constitution. Another example is John Young's Cryptome, which, in the past 15 years, has published the names of 2619 CIA sources, 276 British Intelligence Agents, and 600 Japanese Intelligence Agents and has also published on his cryptome.org website numerous databases of aerial photography including detailed maps of former Vice President Richard Cheney's secret bunker in March of 2005.[29] The function of Cryptome, WikiLeaks, Black Net, and several others of similar nature is to publish and make available material they receive from others, which they maintain is to provide information to the general public to maintain democracy and freedom by publishing material they assess is important for the public to be aware of and totally informed.

TOR, or "the onion router," is considered an almost unbreakable secure anonymity program that permits users to hide their IP address and to enjoy an incredible amount of secrecy. The Defense Advanced Research Projects Agency and the U.S. Naval Research Laboratory were responsible for the creation of TOR. The irony of this was instead of solely allowing the government to function in secrecy, TOR eventually became the "machine that would ultimately hemorrhage the governments secrets," as Bradley Manning used TOR to provide WikiLeaks with a vast amount of data files and e-mail transmissions. In fact, Julian Assange relied on TOR as its core tool for protecting the anonymity of its sensitive sources who submitted material to WikiLeaks.[30]

TOR personifies the intelligence paradox, since, on the one hand, both the intelligence community and the military used TOR to collect military strategy, secrets, and information and could do so without the awareness or knowledge of their adversaries. Conversely, TOR can also be used by adversaries, pornographers, child exploiters, or foreign intelligence agencies against the U.S. government's agencies. The onion router or TOR has a "Hidden Service," and if a website activates this feature, it can mask its location and permit users to find it in cyberspace without anyone being able to locate where the site is physically hosted. To access a TOR Hidden Service, the user has to run TOR, and both the user's physical location as well as the site will be masked or hidden. Andy Greenberg reports the following regarding TOR:

> ...TOR is used by child pornographers and black hat hackers. Seconds after installing the program a user can untraceably access sites like Silk Road, an online bazaar for hard drugs and weapons, or one of several sites that claim to offer untraceable contract killings, but TOR is also used by the FBI to infiltrate those law breakers ranks without being detected.[31]

By 2006, the value of TOR became apparent to the world computing community because both Iran and China began using TOR to filter their Internet and monitor and spy on Iranian and Chinese government opposition groups.[32]

TOR's ability to use triple encryption is the feature that provides its incredible security and anonymity, and it is quite obvious that any group or individual who uses TOR can take advantage of its masking capabilities and can then use it as intelligence agencies will or as those wishing to expose secrets and intelligence operations. The third group ranges from criminals, to child exploiters, and to nation-states seeking to weaken the U.S.

TOR not only allows users to surf the Web anonymously, but it is also the portal to the Deep Web and to numerous sites such as Silk Road, WHMX, and many more dark sites. These sites have provided access to users who are interested in acquiring drugs such as heroin, LSD, ecstasy, cocaine, and crystal meth; counterfeit currency; fake identities; and United Kingdom passports. Lev Grossman and Jay Newton-Small's research on the Deep Web puts into perspective how large and hidden this environment is, as the Web most people are aware of consists of 19 terabytes, whereas everything else is 7500 terabytes, and that is without content being indexed by search engines, including illegal commerce sites, password-protected sites, databases, and old websites. In fact, their research by November 2013 suggested that TOR is downloaded 30 to 50 million times a year, with 800,000 daily TOR users, in which it is possible to access 6500 hidden websites. TOR's privacy for all its users enables both illegal activity as well as permits privacy for law enforcement, intelligence, and military communication.[33]

4.4 DoD—The U.S. Cyber Command

In his periodic report to Congress, James Clapper, Director of National Intelligence, stated that as a result of the worldwide threat assessment compiled by the 16 intelligence agencies under his direction, the most critical concerns are related to cyber threats and the potential for cyber attacks, which use cyber weapons and can be difficult to defend against. The growing concern for cyber attacks against our critical infrastructure as well as the penetration of corporate networks and the loss of intellectual property continues to be a problem that is growing and requires action by the U.S. government.

Jason Healey observed that the DoD began to organize around cyber and information warfare just after the first Gulf War of 1991. The Air Force Information Warfare Center was created in 1993, and both offense and defense operations were combined in the 609th Information Warfare Squadron. Since this unit was an Air Force unit, it was not able to assume responsibility for all cyber defense operations that existed outside of its domain. The Pentagon, in an effort to more thoroughly address the problem of cyber activities, established the Joint Task Force-Computer Network Defense in 1998. By 2000, this Joint Task Force was given responsibilities for both offense as well as defense. By 2004, responsibilities for offensive and defensive operations were again separated, and the NSA was given the offensive mission space, and the Defense Information Systems Agency was assigned the defensive mission responsibility. Once again, this strategy lasted only until 2010, when both missions of offense and defense were combined within the U.S. Cyber Command, under the leadership of General Keith Alexander, who was also the director of the NSA. The DoD determined that as a result of the cyber capability of both the NSA and the U.S. Cyber Command, it was quite appropriate to have a four-star general lead both Commands.[34]

Major General John A. Davis, Senior Military Advisor for Cyber to the Under Secretary of Defense (Policy) and former Director of Current Operations, U.S. Cyber Command, Fort Meade, commenting on recent activities in refining the cyber strategy for the DoD, stated the following:

- DoD has established service cyber components under the U.S. Cyber Command;
- Established Joint Cyber Centers at each Combatant Command;
- Implemented a Military-Orders process to handle cyber action as it is handled in other operational domains;
- Established an interim command-and-control framework for cyberspace operations across joint service and defense agency operations;
- Developed a Force Structure Model for Cyber Force organizations;
- Established a Plan and developed orders to transition to a new Network Architecture called the Joint Information Environment or JIE;
- DoD's mission is to defend the nation in all domains, but in cyberspace the DoD shares its role with other members of the Federal Cybersecurity Team, including the Department of Justice and the FBI, the lead for investigation and law enforcement;
- Other Team Members are the Department of Homeland Security—the lead for protecting critical infrastructure and government systems outside the military—and the intelligence community which is responsible for threat intelligence and attribution;
- DoD has defined three main cyber missions and three kinds of Cyber Forces which will operate around the clock to conduct these missions:
  - National Mission Forces to counter adversary cyber attacks;
  - Combat Mission Forces to support combatant commanders as they execute military missions;
  - Cyber Protection Forces will operate and defend the networks that support military operations worldwide.[35]

The Pentagon, responding to the growing threat of cyber activities in cyberspace, expanded the force of the U.S. Cyber Command from 900 personnel to include 4900 military and civilian personnel. The three types of forces under the U.S. Cyber Command are (1) National Mission Forces, with the responsibility to protect computer systems critical to the national and economic security such as our electrical grid system, power plants, and other critical infrastructures; (2) Combat Mission Forces to assist commanders in planning and executing attacks or other offensive operations; and (3) Cyber Protection Forces to fortify and protect the DoD's worldwide networks.[36]

General Keith Alexander, U.S. Cyber Command, informed Congress that the potential for an attack against the nation's electrical grid system and other critical infrastructure systems is real, and more aggressive steps need to be taken by both the federal government and the private sector to improve our digital defenses. Offensive weapons are increasing, and it is only a matter of time before these weapons might wind up in the control of extremist groups or nation-states that could cause significant harm to the United States. In the meantime, the U.S. Cyber Command has formed 40 Cyber Teams; 13 teams are assigned the mission of guarding the nation in cyberspace, and their principal role is offensive in nature. Another 27 Cyber Teams will support the military's war fighting commands, while others will protect the Defense Department's computer systems and data. General Alexander also notified Congress that we still need a definition of what constitutes an act of war in cyberspace. Alexander stated that he does not consider cyber espionage and the theft of a corporation's intellectual property as acts of war, but he did state that "you have crossed the line" if the intent is to disrupt or destroy U.S. infrastructure.[37]

The question raised by General Alexander as to what constitutes an act of war in cyberspace is an important question, yet it is not easily answered due to the complexity of issues it raises.

4.4.1   Rules of Engagement and Cyber Weapons

Another critical aspect of formulating a strategy of cyber war centers on the creation of formal rules of engagement. A framework to standardize all cyber-related structures and relationships within not only the respective military services but also other federal agencies must be in place. After the framework is in place and cyber weapons have passed all military tests for inclusion in the DoD weapons inventory, the rules of engagement must be developed with the assistance of appropriate military legal officers, the U.S. State Department, and of course, the White House and Executive Branch of government.

Even upon the approval of rules of engagement for the use of cyber weapons, James Lewis of the Center for Strategic and International Studies has provided insight into the range of dilemmas that cyber weapons create, for example: Who authorizes use? What uses are authorized and at what level? Is it a Combatant Commander, U.S. Cyber Command Commander in Chief, or down the rank structure? The President? What sort of action against the United States justifies engagement and use of a cyber weapon?[38]

In addition, cyber warfare may not be able to embrace the established norms for armed conflict. The well-established principles of proportionality and not targeting civilian populations are clearly present in those conflicts with traditional physical arms and most military weapons. However, the creation and application of cyber weapons make it extremely difficult to both design and apply cyber weapons consistent with these traditional rules of engagement. Nevertheless, the Stuxnet worm that impacted the Iranian Nuclear program in 2010, which is believed to have damaged 1000 gas centrifuges at the Natanz Uranium Enrichment facility, was created to attack only specific targets and in effect minimized any civilian damage.[39] So this was an example of a sophisticated cyber weapon within the boundaries of rules of engagement.

Martin Libicki's excellent report on "Brandishing Cyber Attack Capabilities" for the Rand National Defense Research Institute and prepared for the Secretary of Defense explored ways in which cyber attack capabilities can be "brandished" as a manner in which a deterrence effect might be realized if the adversary has knowledge of the cyber weapon capabilities. The difficult challenge is how to demonstrate cyber war capabilities. If one hacks into an adversary's system, he or she will recognize your cyber weapon's capabilities, but typically, this attack can be used only once, as the enemy will reengineer the attack mechanism. Also, the ability to penetrate an enemy's system does not prove the capacity for breaking the system or inducing a system to fail and keep on failing. The difference between penetration of a system and actually causing system failure may be interpreted differently by the adversary's leaders. It is possible that one may have a deterrence effect, while the latter may actually permit the adversary to improve their system or to provoke them into a counterattack mode. On the other hand, demonstrating a cyberattack capability can accomplish three objectives: (1) declare the possession of a cyber attack weapon; (2) suggest the intent to use the cyber weapon in the event of the adversary's continuing animosity, belligerence, and other special circumstances; and (3) indicate the profound consequences that the cyber attack weapon will induce on the enemy.[40]

Perhaps the Stuxnet worm that was directed to Iran's Natanz Uranium Enrichment Facility was an example of brandishing a cyber weapon to cause Iran to stop its program from developing a nuclear weapon capability. Clearly, the virus was targeted to focus on industrial control system architecture capabilities. To this degree, the brandishing of Stuxnet as a cyber attack weapon clearly indicated possession of such capability. Second, the targeting of Iran's nuclear enrichment facility also demonstrated intent to use such cyber weapons to encourage Iran's leadership to reassess their nuclear weapons program. Finally, the Stuxnet worm also demonstrated the profound consequences that a similar or different cyber weapon might induce.

In any event, as the report noted:

> The credibility of the cyber attack threat will depend on a state's track record in cyberspace coupled with its general reputation at military technology and the likelihood that it would use such capabilities when called on.[41]

The importance of establishing rules of engagement to guide any nation in responding to a cyber attack by another nation-state can be demonstrated by a number of recent cyber attacks:

2003 Titan Rain Targets U.S.: Highly skilled hackers allegedly working out of the Chinese province of Guangdong access systems and steal sensitive but unclassified records from numerous U.S. military bases, defense contractors, and aerospace companies.

2007 Cyber Attacks Hit Estonian Websites: DDoS attacks cripple websites for the Estonian government, news media, and banks. The attacks, presumably carried out by Russian-affiliated actors, follow a dispute between the two countries over Estonia's removal of a Soviet-era war memorial in Tallinn.

2008 Cyber Strike Precedes Invasion of Georgia: Denial-of-service attacks of unconfirmed origin take down Georgian government servers and hamper the country's ability to communicate with its citizens and other countries when Russian military forces invade.

2010 Stuxnet Undermines Iran's Nuclear Program: The Stuxnet worm is planted in Iranian computer networks, eventually finding its way to and disrupting industrial control equipment used in the country's controversial uranium enrichment program. The United States and Israel are believed to be behind the attack.

2011 RSA Breach Jeopardizes U.S. Defense Contractors: Hackers steal data about security tokens from RSA and use it to gain access to at least two U.S. defense contractors that use the security vendor's products.[42]

On the basis of numerous reports, the Pentagon believes that Unit 61398 of China's People's Liberation Army (PLA) has accessed data from over 40 DoD weapons programs and 30 other defense technologies. In addition, the intellectual property from numerous American corporations has also been exfiltrated. The Pentagon also has been hacked by Russia with malicious viruses that have penetrated our nation's defense systems. The Pentagon likewise notes Iran's attack and destruction of more than 30,000 computers at Saudi Arabia's state-owned oil company Saudi Aramco. Iran has also been credited with attacks on J.P. Morgan Chase and Bank of America.[43]

Documents leaked by Edward Snowden suggested that the cyber offensive operations of the United States resulted in 231 operations in 2011 against

Iran, China, Russia, and North Korea. It is clear that there exists a very vigorous program of cyber offensive actions that are being implemented by many nation-states, and this has resulted in President Obama issuing the Presidential Policy Directive Number 20, which ordered our intelligence community to identify a list of cyber offensive operations and capabilities we may need to protect our nation and advance U.S. national objectives.[44]

It would be worth noting that Thomas Rid's observation on most cyber operations that are viewed as cyber offensive actually amount to intelligence collection activities and are not designed to sabotage critical infrastructure settings.[45] However, with advances in both cyber weapons and technology, this may be a situation that varies from nation to nation.

Another aspect of cyber weapons and cyber attacks that causes great concern was U.S. Secretary of State John Kerry's comment that cyber attacks today are a 21st century nuclear weapons equivalent. Even more alarming is that those wishing to attack the United States can be inside our network in minutes, if not seconds. As a result of these concerns, Presidential Policy Number 20 established principles and processes for the use of cyber operations, including the offensive use of computer-attacks. Presidential authorization is required for those cyber operations outside of a war zone, and even self-defense of our nation involving cyber operations outside of military networks requires presidential authorization. Portions of Presidential Policy 20 remain classified and address issues such as preemptive and covert use of cyber capabilities.[46]

In discussing rules of engagement and cyber weapons, one should take note that as Harold Koh, our former U.S. State Department Legal Advisor, said, "established principles of international law do apply in cyberspace, and cyberspace is not a 'law free zone' where anyone can conduct hostile activities without rules or restraint."[47] We must also realize that Article 51 of the United Nations Charter authorizes self-defense in response to an armed attack, but to date, this has not included cyber attacks or cyber weapons and cyber offensive operations, but these are all clearly events that will force clarification and consensus to formulate the policies, rules, and laws to govern cyber operations.

4.5 Nation-State Cyber Conflicts

One of the major difficulties in determining the course of cyber attacks is finding proof of the actual perpetrator and the location from where the attack was launched. Since computer attacks involve massive numbers of botnets, which can be configured into a DDoS attack, it is not unusual for botnets to be directed to the attack target from nations throughout the world. The Bot Master's servers controlling the botnets can be located in nations throughout the five continents. Further, IP sites can be spoofed to make it appear an attack is coming from a site when in reality it is being routed through other attack servers. Another difficulty centers on determining the source of the attack: was it by a governmental or military operation? Was it a criminal operation? Was it a group of hactivists? Was it youthful hackers? Was it an intelligence espionage operation? Was it a number of groups working under the direction of a government purchasing the services of any of these groups or additional contractors selling their services to anyone who would purchase their skill sets?

The importance of the identification of the true attackers is only one part of the equation, as it is also imperative to identify the actual source sponsoring the attack. Since we now are living in an era where cyber attacks can easily be elevated to cyber warfare, we must not only know whom to defend against but also not respond with a counter cyber attack to a source or nation-state that had no role or responsibility in the original attack. An example is the case of the "Solar Sunrise" attack, in which the networks of the U.S. DoD were penetrated and which was initially thought to be an attack by Russia, when in fact it turned out to be an attack by two teenagers from California in 1998.

Within two years, the "Moonlight Maze" attack occurred, and this time, over two million computers were affected in agencies such as the Pentagon, the U.S. Department of Energy, the Command Center of Space and Naval War Systems (SPAWAR), several private research laboratories, and other sites as well. Upon investigation, Russia and the Moscow Science Academy were accused of involvement.[48] However, what is the range of appropriate responses open to the United States? Activities such as these occurring in 2000 are substantially different from the range of activities occurring in 2014, and the measures of redress today can be more severe than in previous years. Today, actions such as these could conceivably be defined as acts of war and open a range of counter attacks.

4.5.1 Cyber War I—2007 Estonia Cyber Attacks

Many observers now point to the 2007 Estonia Russian Conflict as the first real cyber war, due to the massive DDoS attack on Estonia, which lasted for an extended period of time. The reason for many claiming this event as the first cyber war centered on the actual engagement of the North Atlantic Treaty Organization (NATO) in establishing a Cyber Defense Center by 2008 in Tallinn, Estonia. Another reason for calling this the first cyber war centered on the fact this was the largest DDoS attack ever seen, with over a million computers targeting all aspects of Estonia's financial, commerce, and communications nationwide. In short, Estonian citizens were not able to use their credit cards, do their banking, or receive news and communicate with their officials through normal communication channels. Further, most DDoS attacks last no more than a few days, but this attack lasted several weeks and forced Estonia to view this as an act of war, and as a member state of NATO, they requested the North Atlantic Council of the NATO Military Alliance to come to their aid. NATO's establishment of a Cyber Defense Center in Tallinn was the first time NATO took this action, and cybersecurity experts traced cyber activity back to machines that Estonia claimed were under the control of Russia. However, Russia denied any activity and stated their sites were spoofed.

The source of the conflict between Estonia and Russia dates back to when the Soviet Army liberated Estonia from the Nazis in World War II. Russia claimed its innocence and stated that this was action by hactivists and others who spoofed their attacks as coming from Russia. Estonia rejected this notion and claimed that this was Russian activity and was much more than a wave of cyber crime that Russia claimed it represented, because the DDoS attacks were launched against Estonia's information systems and the targets were government, banks, and private company websites.

In the first days of the attack, websites usually receiving 1000 visits per day were now receiving 2000 requests per second. The botnets represented over a million computers worldwide, and computers from the United States, Canada, Brazil, and Vietnam were used in parts of the DDoS attack. The Estonian Minister of Defense stated that they discovered instructions in Russian on how to attack websites in Estonia, which were circulated over the Internet. Estonia stated that the attacks were a terrorist act, regardless of who the terrorists were, and Estonia requested the help of the international community. NATO became involved, and immediately, the discussion was no longer about delinquent individuals or criminal activity as the focus was on defining the responsibilities of a government, thus opening a new discussion involving diplomatic relationships and regional issues involving cyber attacks.[49]

To retain a balanced perspective, we must also make note of the request that Russia made to the international community in its fight against cyber criminals. Interior Minister Rashid Nurgailiyev called for the world to combine forces to fight against criminal groups operating over the Internet, and he made this request in April 2006, one full year before the Estonian conflict. The Interior Minister stated to an international conference in Moscow that cyber criminals can cause as much damage as weapons of mass destruction.[50]

The finding of definitive proof in this Estonian–Russian cyber conflict has been difficult because Russia has denied its involvement and stated that the actions were by others who spoofed their network sites, and Estonia rejected their argument; however, to date, there has been no definitive proof either way due to the complexities involved in these cyber attacks.

4.5.2 China—PLA Colonel's Transformational Report

China has made a significant transformational change in its military as a result of two very major points. The first point was their observation and reaction to the performance of the U.S. military operations in the first two

Gulf Wars. China recognized that their military capabilities were out of touch with the realities of modern warfare. Even before both Gulf Wars, Chinese political leaders were stunned when actions between the People's Republic of China (PRC) and Taiwan reached a point where the United States decided that it would not tolerate any more missiles being launched by the PLA into Taiwan and two U.S. aircraft carrier groups were dispatched into the South China Sea. China's recognition that their Navy could not respond to this event set into motion substantial changes in planning to develop a naval capability for the PRC. Additionally, the second point of major transformational change was the PLA Colonel's Report in a volume translated as "unrestricted warfare" in which this report set the stage for major reforms in the Chinese doctrine of information warfare.

Colonel Qiao Liang and Colonel Wang Xiansui observed that the 1991 Gulf War represented a major gap between the Chinese and the American military. The Iraqi army was equipped with Soviet and Chinese weapons systems similar to the Chinese Army, but Iraq was defeated in 42 days due to the advanced technology and information warfare strategy of the U.S. Both Colonel's collaborated to produce a book that has become a Chinese standard reference on a new form of warfare in which new weapons; namely, computers, would play a pivotal role in warfare. Traditional warfare would be changed forever due to the use of information systems and advanced technology and the integration of these two systems would become fundamental to the changes and advancements required for a new modern Chinese military.[51]

Sims and Gerber noted that the new doctrine of PLA warfare would focus the PLA's offensive capabilities aimed at the enemy's infrastructure such as banking infrastructure, power grid systems, and other critical infrastructures.[52] The important point centered on the use and application of a strategy designed around asymmetric warfare where weaker nations might attack stronger nations by using tactics and plans that fall outside the traditional military on military battle engagements. The PLA's articulated strategy of asymmetric warfare focused on those aspects of a society's source of power, which inevitably are the economic systems and critical infrastructure. The strategy of attacking these critical infrastructures weakens a nation to the point that direct military-to-military engagements would not be necessary.

Our governmental leaders have criticized Chinese authorities for the massive amount of theft of intellectual property from our corporations, research laboratories, defense contractors, and our military. China has routinely dismissed these allegations and termed them without foundation. However, the release of the Mandiant Group Report APT 1, exposing one of China's cyber espionage units, would change the tone of the Chinese response to a statement of "without foundation" to that of "it is unprofessional to accuse the Chinese military of launching cyber attacks without any conclusive evidence."

The evidence to challenge the Chinese position was acquired by Mandiant Group, a private security firm that tracks computer security breaches throughout the world. Mandiant Group specializes in investigation of APT attacks, and in their 2010 "M-Trends Report," they stated their research showed substantial APT attacks from China, but they could not determine the extent of the Chinese government's involvement. By 2013, Mandiant Group had secured the evidence to permit a change in their assessment in which their position is that the Chinese government is aware of these APT attacks. In explaining their position, Mandiant Group released a full report of their review of APT-1, which is a group of more than 20 APT groups performing cyber espionage. The APT-1 group has performed computer intrusions in 150 victim organizations since 2006 and has operated four large networks in Shanghai and in the Pudong district. The research revealed that the PLA's Unit 61398 is similar in its mission, capabilities, and resources to the APT-1 group. Moreover, the nature of Unit 61398's work is considered by China to be a state secret. Research has revealed that the APT-1 group has systematically stolen hundreds of terabytes of data from 141 organizations and companies involving 20 major industries. As stated previously in this book, APT attacks focus not on doing damage but on exfiltration of data and remaining hidden within the target organization's information system for as long a period of time as possible. In the case of the APT-1 group's average time within an organization, it averaged to 356 days, with the longest period of time being over four years. In one case, the APT-1 group was observed stealing 6.5 terabytes of compressed data from one organization in a 10-month period and over 937 command and control servers that were hosted on 849 separate IP addresses in 13 countries, of which 709 were registered in China and 109 were registered in the United States with an attack infrastructure of over 1000 servers.[53] Despite numerous Chinese claims of denial of any inappropriate cyber espionage activities, the evidence collected by the Mandiant Group and other agencies was sufficient in May 2014 to allow the U.S. Department of Justice to indict five major Chinese individuals and charge them with multiple counts of illegal cyber espionage. Immediately after the announcement of these indictments, Chinese cyber activity slowed to a virtual crawl; however, at this writing, the PLA cyber activity is again on the increase.

The Communist Party of China has assigned the task of cyber espionage and data theft against organizations around the world to the PLA Unit 61398. The APT-1 group, which is located within the same building as PLA Unit 61398, has targeted four of the seven strategic emerging industries that China has identified in its 12th Five-Year Plan. The attack lifecycle used to acquire this information is a classic APT attack where initial entry to the targets system is made through a spear-phishing attack or setting up a link to a malicious website. After the initial compromise, the next phase of the attack is to establish a presence within the system by accessing one or more computers within the targeted organization. "Ghostrat" and "Poison Ivy" are examples of backdoors found in hacker websites that establish outbound connections from the targeted victim to the computer controlled by attackers. In most sophisticated attacks, the attacker will create a tunnel and encrypt the plain text so the target organization will not see the exfiltration of data, while in the target system, the attacker will attempt to escalate their privileges to gain access to public key infrastructure certificates, privileged computers, and other resources. Since the main goal of the APT attack is to acquire data and exfiltrate as much intellectual property as possible, the attacker will remain in the victim's organization for as long as possible.[54]

In a special report on understanding the Chinese Intelligence Agencies' cyber capabilities, the Australian Strategic Policy Institute reported the following international cyber attacks attributed to the Chinese government intelligence operatives:

Date	Target	Industry
June 2007	U.S. Pentagon	Government
March 2009	BAE Systems	Defense Contractor

Cyber attacks attributed to the PLA Third Department are the following:

Date	Target	Industry
March 2011	RSA	Security firm
April 2011	L-3 Communications	Defense contractor
May 2011	Lockheed Martin	Defense contractor
May 2011	Northrop Grumman	Defense contractor
January 2013	New York Times	Media

These cyber attacks identified by the Australian Strategic Policy Institute are consistent with the Mandiant Group report and also are a reflection of the importance the PLA Lieutenant General Qi Jianguo attaches to seizing and maintaining superiority in cyberspace as he believes seizing cyberspace is more important than seizing command of sea and air during World War II.[55]

The Washington Post reported on the public version of the Pentagon report that disclosed some of the compromised weapons designs that have been obtained by Chinese cyber espionage activities and listed the following:

- Designs for the Advanced Patriot Missile System—Pac-3
- Terminal High Altitude Defense for shooting down missiles
- Navy's Aegis Ballistic-missile defense system
- F/A-18 Fighter Jet

- V-22 Osprey
- Black Hawk helicopter
- Navy's new Littoral combat ship
- F-35 Joint Strike Fighter

The illegal obtaining of these weapons systems designs represents billions of dollars of combat advantages for China and a savings for them of at least 25 years of research development. Further, this incredible amount of cyber theft from U.S. defense contractors creates three major problems. First, access to advanced U.S. weapons systems designs provides an immediate operational advantage to China. Second, it accelerates China's ability to use our designs to develop their military systems on our dollar and saves them billions of dollars of investment. Third, by understanding our weapons systems designs, China's military will be in a position to penetrate our systems and put our personnel at risk.[56]

Cyber espionage by China is not the only manner in which they obtain important weapons designs information, as the 2013 Annual Report to Congress by the Office of the Secretary of Defense on Military and Security Developments Involving the PRC reported the following:

In March 2012, Hui Sheng Shen and Huan Ling Chang, both from Taiwan, were charged with conspiracy to violate the U.S. Arms Export Control Act after allegedly intending to acquire and pass sensitive U.S. defense technology to China. The pair planned to photograph the technology, delete the images, bring the memory cards back to China, and have a Chinese contact recover the images.

In June 2012, Pratt & Whitney Canada (PWC), a subsidiary of U.S. aerospace firm and defense contractor United Technologies Corporation (UTC), pleaded guilty to illegally providing military software used in the development of China's Z-10 military attack helicopter.

UTC and two subsidiaries agreed to pay $75 million and were debarred from license privileges as part of a settlement with the U.S. Department of Justice and State Department.

PWC "knowingly and willfully" caused six versions of military electronic engine control software to be "illegally exported" from Hamilton Sundstrand in the United States to PWC in Canada and then to China for the Z-10, and made false and belated disclosures about these illegal exports.

In September 2012, Sixing Liu, aka "Steve Liu," was convicted of violating the U.S. Arms Export Control Act and the International Traffic in Arms Regulations (ITAR) and possessing stolen trade secrets. Liu, a Chinese citizen, returned to China with electronic files containing details on the performance and design of guidance systems for missiles, rockets, target locators, and unmanned aerial vehicles. Liu developed critical military technology for a U.S. defense contractor and stole the documents to position himself for employment in China.[57]

There can be no doubt about the rapid success of the development of the Chinese military apparatus being directly attributable to the incredible amount of weapons systems designs documents they have stolen from our nation's defense contractors. The PLA's use of APT attacks has been, in large measure, responsible for the acquisition of terabytes worth of classified documents. At the same time, our nation's defense contractor's inadequate computer security defense systems reveals an appalling scenario of their inability to secure their systems and costing our nation an incredible amount of money, but more importantly placing the lives of our military personnel at risk.

4.5.3   America—The NSA

The NSA is one of America's 16 Intelligence Agencies, and its principal responsibility is to protect the national security interests of the U.S. The NSA is responsible for cryptology, signals intelligence, computer network operations, and information assurance.

For years, few Americans took note or were even aware of this organization; however, in June 2013, events unfolded that positioned the NSA into a worldwide discussion over the appropriateness of cyber espionage. The person who catapulted the NSA into the focus of the entire world community was Edward Snowden. Snowden was working as a contract employee for Booz Allen Hamilton, a firm that had a contract with the NSA, and in this capacity, Snowden had access to the NSA's databases. Before his employment at Booz Allen Hamilton, Snowden was employed at Dell Computer, Inc., where he also had access to the NSA's databases. Evidently, Snowden decided to collect data while working at Dell, and he took a position at Booz Allen Hamilton to acquire additional data all for the express purpose of releasing the information to call attention to the activities of the NSA. The release of the information and classified security documents has resulted in a terrible loss to our nation. In addition to informing our adversaries as to our collection methods and revealing very complex security programs, it has also created a financial burden on our government. U.S. corporations providing the NSA with data, even though under the legal court orders by virtue of the Foreign Intelligence Surveillance Act (FISA), still experienced major public relations problems as citizens were concerned over their possible loss of privacy. The international community reacted by reducing business with major U.S. corporations, and some nations even considered total rejection of further business with some U.S. corporations. The irony is that China's PLA 61398 activities were in fact designed for the cyber espionage of intellectual property from a vast number of corporations throughout the world, whereas the National Security cyber espionage activities never focused in that domain and was consistently focused on the security of our nation, and NSA activities were directed to identifying terrorist or other security threats to our country.

Snowden has released through the *Guardian* newspaper an extraordinary amount of classified information he had no legal right to release. Snowden expressed his concern for the loss of privacy of Americans as a result of several NSA programs. Perhaps, the release of data that were erroneously characterized as the NSA's listing of telephone conversations drew the most attention and concern. This story has been retold in media accounts, and it is totally incorrect, as the NSA's authority for the capture of telephone contacts between intelligence targets is limited to a specific and detailed process, which is outlined as part of the NSA's charter.

However, to fully appreciate the reason for the bulk collection of telephone metadata, we must return to the 9/11 terrorist attack against the World Trade Center in New York. The aftermath of this attack and the report of the Congressional Review Committee on the failure of our intelligence community for not being able to "connect the dots" resulted in the George W. Bush Administration authorizing new programs to rectify this inability. With the passage of the USA Patriot Act, new programs were established, and with these new programs came additional oversight from both the Congress and the FISA Court. The following case from the 9/11 attack on the World Trade Center highlights why the intelligence community was not able to track telephone contacts to other terrorists, and why the new programs introduced would remedy that inability.

After the al-Qa'ida attacks on the World Trade Center and the Pentagon, the 9/11 Commission found that the U.S. Government had failed to identify and connect the many "dots" of information that would have uncovered the planning and preparation for those attacks. We now know that 9/11 hijacker Khalid al-Midhar, who was on board American Airlines flight 77 that crashed into the Pentagon, resided in California for the first six months of 2000. While NSA had intercepted some of Midhar's conversations with persons in an al-Qa'ida safe house in Yemen during that period, NSA did not have the U.S. phone number or any indication that the phone Midhar was using was located in San Diego. NSA did not have the tools or the database to search to identify these connections and share them with the FBI. Several programs were developed to address the U.S. government's need to connect the dots of information available to the intelligence community and to strengthen the coordination between foreign intelligence and domestic law enforcement agencies.[58]

To more fully appreciate the operations of the NSA, it is appropriate to describe their mission and the authorization documents that permit the NSA's operations. Specific focus will be placed on the authorizing Executive Order 12333, FISA Section 702 and Business Records FISA, Section 215, as these are controlling authorities and most germane to Snowden's release of classified information.

NSA Mission Legal Authorities

NSA Mission

NSA's mission is to help protect national security by providing policy makers and military commanders with the intelligence information they need to do their jobs. NSA's priorities are driven by externally developed and validated intelligence requirements, provided to NSA by the President, his national security team, and their staffs through the National Intelligence Priorities Framework.

NSA Collection Authorities

NSA's collection authorities stem from two key sources: Executive Order 12333 and the Foreign Intelligence Surveillance Act of 1978 (FISA).

Executive Order 12333

Executive Order 12333 is the foundational authority by which NSA collects, retains, analyzes, and disseminates foreign signals intelligence information. The principal application of this authority is the collection of communications by foreign persons that occur wholly outside the United States. To the extent a person located outside the United States communicates with someone inside the United States or someone inside the United States communicates with a person located outside the United States those communications could also be collected. Collection pursuant to EO 12333 is conducted through various means around the globe, largely from outside the United States, which is not otherwise regulated by FISA. Intelligence activities conducted under this authority are carried out in accordance with minimization procedures established by the Secretary of Defense and approved by the Attorney General.

To undertake collections authorized by EO 12333, NSA uses a variety of methodologies. Regardless of the specific authority or collection source, NSA applies the process described as follows:

1. NSA identifies foreign entities (persons or organizations) that have information responsive to an identified foreign intelligence requirement. For instance, NSA works to identify individuals who may belong to a terrorist network.

2. NSA develops the "network" with which that person or organization's information is shared or the command and control structure through which it flows. In other words, if NSA is tracking a specific terrorist, NSA will endeavor to determine who that person is in contact with, and who he is taking direction from.

3. NSA identifies how the foreign entities communicate (radio, email, telephony, etc.).
4. NSA then identifies the telecommunications infrastructure used to transmit those communications.
5. NSA identifies vulnerabilities in the methods of communication used to transmit them.
6. NSA matches its collection to those vulnerabilities, or develops new capabilities to acquire communications of interest if needed.

This process will often involve the collection of communications metadata—data that helps NSA understand where to find valid foreign intelligence information needed to protect U.S. national security interests in a large and complicated global network. For instance, the collection of overseas communications metadata associated with telephone calls—such as the telephone numbers, and time and duration of calls—allows NSA to map communications between terrorists and their associates. This strategy helps ensure that NSA's collection of communications content is more precisely focused on only those targets necessary to respond to identified foreign intelligence requirements.

NSA uses EO 12333 authority to collect foreign intelligence from communications systems around the world. Due to the fragility of these sources, providing any significant detail outside of classified channels is damaging to national security. Nonetheless, every type of collection undergoes a strict oversight and compliance process internal to NSA that is conducted by entities within NSA other than those responsible for the actual collection.

FISA Collection

FISA regulates certain types of foreign intelligence collection including certain collection that occurs with compelled assistance from U.S. telecommunications companies. Given the techniques that NSA must employ when conducting NSA's foreign intelligence mission, NSA quite properly relies on FISA authorizations to acquire significant foreign intelligence information and will work with the FBI and other agencies to connect the dots between foreign-based actors and their activities in the U.S. The FISA Court plays an important role in helping to ensure that signals intelligence collection governed by FISA is conducted in conformity with the requirements of the statute. All three branches of the U.S. government have responsibilities for programs conducted under FISA, and a key role of the FISA Court is to ensure that activities conducted pursuant to FISA authorizations are consistent with the statute, as well as the U.S. Constitution, including the Fourth Amendment.

FISA Section 702

Under Section 702 of the FISA, NSA is authorized to target <u>non-U.S. persons</u> who are reasonably believed to be located <u>outside</u> the United States. The principal application of this authority is in the collection of communications by foreign persons that utilize U.S. communications service providers. The United States is a principal hub in the world's telecommunications system and FISA is designed to allow the U.S. Government to acquire foreign intelligence while protecting the civil liberties and privacy of Americans. In general, Section 702 authorizes the Attorney General and Director of National Intelligence to make and submit to the FISA Court written certifications for the purpose of acquiring foreign intelligence information. Upon the issuance of an order by the FISA Court approving such a certification and the use of targeting and minimization procedure, the Attorney General and Director of National Intelligence may jointly authorize for up to one year the targeting of non-United States persons reasonably believed to be located overseas to acquire foreign intelligence information. The collection is acquired through compelled assistance from relevant electronic communications service providers.

NSA provides specific identifiers (for example, email addresses, telephone numbers) used by non-U.S. persons overseas who the government believes possess, communicate, or are likely to receive foreign intelligence information authorized for collection under an approved certification. Once approved, those identifiers are used to select communications for acquisition. Service providers are compelled to assist NSA in acquiring the communications associated with those identifiers.

For a variety of reasons, including technical ones, the communications of U.S. persons are sometimes incidentally acquired in targeting the foreign entities. For example, a U.S. person might be courtesy copied on an email to or from a legitimate foreign target, or a person in the U.S. might be in contact with a known terrorist target. In those cases, minimization procedures adopted by the Attorney General in consultation with the Director of National Intelligence and approved by the Foreign Intelligence Surveillance Court are used to protect the privacy of the U.S. person. These minimization procedures control the acquisition, retention, and dissemination of any U.S. person information incidentally acquired during operations conducted pursuant to Section 702.

The collection under FAA Section 702 is the most significant tool in the NSA collection arsenal for the detection, identification, and disruption of terrorist threats to the U.S. and around the world. One notable example is the Najibullah Zazi case. In early September 2009, while monitoring the activities of al Qaeda terrorists in Pakistan, NSA noted contact from an individual in the U.S. that the FBI subsequently identified as Colorado-based Najibullah Zazi. The U.S. Intelligence Community, including the FBI and NSA, worked in concert to determine his relationship with al Qaeda, as well as identify any foreign or domestic terrorist links. The FBI tracked Zazi as he traveled to New York to meet with co-conspirators, where they were planning to conduct a terrorist attack. Zazi and his co-conspirators were subsequently arrested. Zazi pled guilty to conspiring to bomb the New York City subway system. The FAA Section 702 collection against foreign terrorists was critical to the discovery and disruption of this threat to the U.S.

FISA (Title I)

NSA relies on Title I of FISA to conduct electronic surveillance of foreign powers or their agents, to include members of international terrorist organizations. Except for certain narrow exceptions specified in FISA, a specific court order from the Foreign Intelligence Surveillance Court based on a showing of probable cause is required for this type of collection.

Collection of U.S. Person Data

There are three additional FISA authorities that NSA relies on, after gaining court approval, that involve the acquisition of communications, or information about communications, of U.S. persons for foreign intelligence purposes on which additional focus is appropriate. These are the Business Records FISA provision in Section 501 (also known by its section numbering within the Patriot Act as Section 215) and Sections 704 and 705(b) of the FISA.

Business Records FISA, Section 215

Under NSA's Business Records FISA program (or BR FISA), first approved by the Foreign Intelligence Surveillance Court (FISC) in 2006 and subsequently reauthorized during two different Administrations, four different Congresses, and by fourteen federal judges, specified U.S. telecommunications providers are compelled by court order to provide NSA with information about telephone calls to, from, or within the U.S. The information is known as metadata, and consists of information such as the called and calling telephone numbers and the date, time, and duration of the call—but no user identification, content, or cell site locational data. The purpose of this particular collection is to identify the U.S. nexus of a foreign terrorist threat to the homeland.

The government cannot conduct substantive queries of the bulk records for any purpose other than counterterrorism. Under the FISC orders authorizing the collection, authorized queries may only begin with an "identifier," such as a telephone number, that is associated with one of the foreign terrorist organizations that were previously identified to and approved by the Court. An identifier used to commence a query of the data is referred to as a "seed." Specifically, under Court-approved rules applicable to the program, there must be a "reasonable, articulable suspicion" that a seed identifier used to query the data for foreign intelligence purposes is associated with a particular foreign terrorist organization. When the seed identifier is reasonably believed to be used by a U.S. person, the suspicion of an association with a particular foreign terrorist organization cannot be based solely on activities protected by the First Amendment. The "reasonable, articulable suspicion" requirement protects against the indiscriminate querying of the collected data. Technical controls preclude NSA analysts from seeing any metadata unless it is the result of a query using an approved identifier.[59]

It is obvious that this detailed accounting of the NSA's authorities and oversight would not easily capture the media attention, so the continuing public scrutiny of the NSA was bereft without all important aspects to help those interested place the operations into a context for clearer understanding. Of course, this does not imply total acceptance of these activities and operations, but it does provide additional information for the public's consideration.

Another point that should be made is references from several congressmen and public figures that the NSA's cyber operations were of little value and did not prevent any acts or near-acts of terrorism. This is refuted by 50 of the 54 cases provided to several of the Congressional committees. General Keith Alexander, Director of the NSA and Commander, U.S. Cyber Command, also stated that these cyber operations enabled the disruption of terrorist plots in the United States and in over 20 countries throughout the world. He went on to further explain the 54 cases as follows:

Of the fifty-four cases, forty-two involved disruptive plots—disrupted plots. Twelve involved cases of material support to terrorism. Fifty of the fifty-four cases led to arrests or detentions. Our allies benefited, too. Twenty-five of these events occurred in Europe, eleven in Asia and five in Africa. Thirteen events had a homeland nexus. In twelve of those events, Section 215 contributed to our overall understanding and help to the FBI—twelve of the thirteen. That's only with a business record FICA can play. In fifty-three out of fifty-four events, Section 702 data played a role, and in many of these cases, provided the initial tip that helped unravel the threat stream. A significant portion, almost half of our counterterror reporting, comes from Section 702.[60]

The Congressional Research Service, which prepares reports for Congress, its members, and committees, prepared the Report on "NSA Surveillance Leaks: Background Issues for Congress" and the following is a summary of their Report:

Recent attention concerning NSA surveillance pertains to unauthorized disclosures of two different intelligence collection programs. Since these programs were publicly disclosed over the course of two days in June, there has been confusion about what information is being collected and what authorities the NSA is acting under. This report clarifies the differences between the two programs and identifies potential issues that may help members of Congress assess legislative proposals pertaining to NSA surveillance authorities.

One program collects in bulk the phone records—specifically the number that was dialed from, the number that was dialed to, and the date and duration of the call—of customers of Verizon Wireless and possibly other U.S. telephone service providers. It does not collect the content of the calls or the identity of callers. The data are collected pursuant to Section 215 of the USA Patriot Act, which amended the FISA of 1978. Section 215 allows the FBI, in this case on behalf of the NSA, to apply to the FISC for an order compelling a person to produce "any tangible thing," including records held by a telecommunications provider concerning the number and length of communications, but not the contents of those communications. The FBI must provide a statement of facts showing that there are "reasonable grounds to believe" that the tangible things sought are "relevant to an authorized investigation." Some commentators have expressed skepticism regarding how there could be "reasonable grounds to believe" that such a broad amount of data could be said to be "relevant to an authorized investigation," as required by the statute.

The other program collects the electronic communications, including content, of foreign targets overseas whose communications flow through American networks. The Director of National Intelligence has acknowledged that data are collected pursuant to Section 702 of FISA. As described, the program may not intentionally target any person known at the time of acquisition to be located in the United States, which is prohibited by Section 702. Beyond that, the scope of the intelligence collection, the type of information collected and companies involved, and the way in which it is collected remain unclear. Section 702 was added by the FISA Amendments Act of 2008. Before the enactment of Section 702, FISA only permitted sustained domestic electronic surveillance or access to domestic electronically stored communications after the issuance of an FISC order that was specific to the target.

The Obama Administration has argued that these surveillance activities, in addition to being subject to oversight by all three branches of government, are important to national security and have helped disrupt terror plots. These arguments have not always distinguished between the two programs, and some critics, while acknowledging the value of information collected using Section 702 authorities, are skeptical of the value of the phone records held in bulk at NSA. Thus, recent legislative proposals have focused primarily on modifying Section 215 to preclude the breadth of phone record collection currently taking place. They have also emphasized requiring greater public disclosure of FISC opinions, including the opinion(s) allowing for the collection of phone records in bulk.

This report discusses the specifics of these two NSA collection programs. It does not address other questions that have been raised in the aftermath of these leaks, such as the potential harm to national security caused by the leaks or the intelligence community's reliance on contractors.

According to intelligence officials, the two programs have "helped prevent over fifty potential terrorist events," which appear to encompass both active terror plots targeting the U.S. homeland and terrorism facilitation activity not tied directly to terrorist attacks at home or abroad. Of these, over 90% somehow involved collection pursuant to Section 702. Of the 50, at least 10 cases included homeland-based threats, and a majority of those cases somehow utilized the phone records held by NSA. The Administration has provided four examples:

- *Najibullah Zazi*: NSA, using 702 authorities, intercepted an e-mail between an extremist in Pakistan and an individual in the United States. NSA provided this e-mail to the FBI, which identified and began to surveil Colorado-based Najibulla Zazi. NSA then received Zazi's phone number from the FBI, checked it against phone records procured using 215 authorities, and identified one of Zazi's accomplices, an individual named Adis Medunjanin. Zazi and Medunjanin were both subsequently arrested and convicted of planning to bomb the New York City subway.
- *Khalid Ouazzani*: NSA, using 702 authorities, intercepted communication between an extremist in Yemen and an individual in the United States named Khalid Quazzani. Ouazzani was later convicted of providing material support to al-Qaeda and admitted to swearing allegiance to the group. The FBI has claimed that Ouazzani was involved in the early stages of a plot to bomb the New York Stock Exchange.

- *David Headley*: According to intelligence officials, the FBI received information indicating that Headley, a U.S. citizen living in Chicago, was involved in the 2008 attack in Mumbai that took the lives of 160 people. NSA, using 702 authorities, also became aware of Headley's involvement in a plot to bomb a Danish newspaper. It is unclear from public statements how Headley first came to the FBI's attention. He pled guilty to terrorism charges and admitted to involvement in both the Mumbai attack and Danish newspaper plot.
- *Basally Saeed Moalin*: NSA, using phone records pursuant to 215 authorities, provided the FBI with a phone number for an individual in San Diego who had indirect contacts with extremists overseas. The FBI identified the individual as Basally Saeed Moalin and determined that he was involved in financing extremist activity in Somalia. In 2013, Moalin was convicted of providing material support to al-Shabaab, the Somalia-based al-Qaeda affiliate.[61]

The *Washington Post*, reviewing a series of disclosures of classified intelligence material provided by Edward Snowden, discovered that U.S. intelligence services participated in 231 offensive cyber operations in 2011. Additionally, they reported on operations that placed "covert implants" and sophisticated malware in computers, routers, and firewalls on tens of thousands of machines every year. Of the 231 offensive operations, 75% of these cyber operations were directed to top priority targets, which included Iran, Russia, China, and North Korea. The DoD stated that they do engage in computer network exploitation, but they do not engage in any economic espionage.[62] This is probably the major difference between China and America.

As a matter of fact, the number of nations that are engaged in cyber operations is increasing every year. Also, as advances in technology continue to increase, nations will apply these technologies to become more effective at the exploitation of their adversaries. The next level will be the development of cyber weapons on a scale that will displace the need for kinetic forces. To control these developments, the international community will have to engage diplomats as well as the respective leadership of the principal nations possessing these cyber weapons to formulate plans, programs, and guidelines that will ultimately protect all nations.

4.6   Cyber Warfare and the *Tallinn Manual* on International Law

After the cyber attacks on Estonia and at the request of the Estonian government to seek assistance from NATO to be defended against further attacks,

NATO responded by establishing in 2009 the NATO Cooperative Cyber Defense Center of Excellence. This Center of cyber defense brought forth a group of international legal practitioners and scholars to examine how current legal norms may be applicable to this new form of cyber warfare. The goal of this group of legal scholars was to produce a nonbinding document applying existing law to cyber warfare, and while their work product, titled the *Tallinn Manual*, is not an official document, it is a very important document as it highlights the nature of cyberspace and the potential for cyber conflicts, which could progress to cyber warfare. The *Tallinn Manual* also now serves as a bedrock document to assist nations throughout the world in reviewing their respective laws, policies, and cyber operation programs.

The *Tallinn Manual* is not a manual on cybersecurity, nor is it focused on cyber espionage, theft of intellectual property, or criminal activities in cyberspace. The overriding purpose of the *Tallinn Manual* is to focus on cyber warfare. Therefore, as a general matter, the focus of the manual is on how international law governs the resort to force by states as an instrument of their national policy, as well as the international law that regulates the conduct of armed conflict or the law of war.[63]

The *Tallinn Manual* is organized around the current international cybersecurity law, in which it examines states and cyberspace looking at issues of state responsibility and also the use of force. Within the *Tallinn Manual* are 95 rules that represent consensus of the working group of legal scholars, and while these rules have no constitutional or treaty authority, they do express a level of consensus on important aspects one should consider in making judgments regarding cyber warfare. The second part of the *Tallinn Manual* addresses the current body of international laws that focuses on the law of armed conflict and directs attention on the conduct of hostilities.

Those interested in further research may wish to examine some of the 95 rules of this manual, and it may be of interest to review the following rules:

Rule 5—Control of Cyber Infrastructure
Rule 7—Cyber Operations Launched from Governmental Cyber Infrastructure
Rule 8—Cyber Operations Routed Through a State
Rule 9—Countermeasures
Rule 24—Criminal Responsibility of Commanders and Superiors
Rule 30—Definition of a Cyber Attack
Rule 32—Prohibition on Attacking Civilians
Rule 44—Cyber Booby Traps
Rule 66—Cyber Espionage
Rule 91—Protection of Neutral Cyber Infrastructure
Rule 92—Cyber Operations in Neutral Territory[64]

Harold Koh, a Legal Advisor at the U.S. Department of State, also has been interested in how the United States will respond to the new challenges of operating in cyberspace. In particular, how do we apply old laws of war to new cyber circumstances while also anticipating new advances in technology? In the analysis of international law in cyberspace, the United States has concluded that established principles of law do apply in cyberspace, and as such, cyberspace is not a law-free zone where anything goes. The position of the United States is guided by the application of both domestic and international laws.[65]

Despite the growing body of international law being focused on the activities in cyberspace, and given the enormous number of cyber attacks and cyber espionage cases, the United States has articulated its role for international strategy for cyberspace as follows:

> When warranted, the United States will respond to hostile acts in cyberspace as we would to any other threat to our country. All states possess an inherent right to self-defense, and we recognize that certain hostile acts conducted through cyberspace could compel actions under the commitments we have with our military treaty partners. We reserve the right to use all necessary means—diplomatic, informational, military, and economic—as appropriate and consistent with applicable international law, in order to defend our nation, our allies, our partners, and our interests. In so doing, we will exhaust all options before military force whenever we can; will carefully weigh the costs and risks of action against the costs of inaction; and will act in a way that reflects our values and strengthens our legitimacy, seeking broad international support whenever possible.[66]

As nations adopt cyber operations, whether they are cyber espionage or range into the next level of cyber offensive weapons, we will need to develop a body of law to regulate activities and protect all nations and their citizens. The potential harm that could be unleashed by a cyber weapon is simply staggering. In addition, those nation-states that develop cyber offensive weapon capabilities will have to provide assurance for their security so that they do not become available to terrorists or individuals attempting to hold nations to a "blackmail" strategy by seeking financial exchange for not exploiting the use of the cyber weapon.

The need for international cooperation in addressing the area of cyberspace is critical, and it will continue to be a challenging problem until the leading nations can formulate a strategy of mutual safety for one another. Time is of the essence, as unaddressed, we will see hostilities continue to increase until that point in which it becomes difficult, if not impossible, to effect appropriate action to control the use of cyber weapons.

Notes and References

1. Denning, *Information Warfare and Security*, xiii–xiv.
2. Ibid., 3–4.
3. Ibid., 5.
4. Ibid., 7.
5. Ventre, *Information Warfare*, 23.
6. Schneier, *Schneier on Security*, 222–223.
7. Denning, op. cit., 67.
8. Denning, op. cit., 36.
9. Denning, op. cit., 65.
10. Ibid., 23.
11. Skoudis and Liston, *Counter Hack Reloaded: A Step-by-Step Guide to Computer Attacks and Effective Defenses*, 2nd Edition, 2006. Printed and electronically reproduced by permission of Pearson Education, Inc., Saddle River, New Jersey, 5–6.
12. Ibid., 20–23.
13. Elisan, *Malware, Rootkits and Botnets: A Beginners Guide*, 216–242.
14. Ibid., 258–264.
15. Ibid., 275–279.
16. Ibid., 290–293.
17. Skoudis and Liston, op. cit., xiii–xviii.
18. Office of the Intelligence Community Chief Information Officer, "Intelligence Community Information Technology Enterprise Strategy," ii.
19. Ibid., 4.
20. Crumpton, *The Art of Intelligence: Lessons from a Life in the CIA's Clandestine Service*, 78–81.
21. The reader is directed to the section on the "Predator," 148–160, in Crumpton's *The Art of Intelligence*, as this is the first-person account of the emergence of what has become a transformation of warfare. The details of Crumpton's account are fascinating and representative of emerging technology and its impact on organizations.
22. Crumpton, Ibid., 158.
23. Kreps and Zenko, "The Next Drone Wars: Preparing for Proliferation," 68–71.
24. Ibid., 72.
25. Byman, "Why Drones Work: The Case for Washington's Weapon of Choice," 32–33, 42.
26. Cronin, "Why Drones Fail: When Tactics Drive Strategy," 44, 53.
27. Sims and Gerber, Editors, *Transforming U.S. Intelligence*, xi.
28. Ibid., xii.
29. Greenberg, *This Machine Kills Secrets: How WikiLeakers, Cypher Punks and Hacktivists Aim to Free the Worlds Information*, 100–102.
30. Ibid., 135–136, 139, 157.
31. Ibid., 140.
32. Ibid., 149.
33. Grossman and Newton-Small, "The Secret Web: Where Drugs, Porn and Murder Hide Online," 29–31.
34. Healey, "The Future of U.S. Cyber Command," 1.

35. Pellerin, "DOD at Work on New Cyber Strategy, Senior Military Advisor Says," 1.
36. Nakashima, "The Pentagon to Boost Cyber Security Force," 1.
37. Lardner, "Pentagon Forming Cyber Teams to Prevent Attacks," 2.
38. Corrin, "Cyber Warfare: New Battlefield, New Rules," 2.
39. Ibid., 3.
40. Libicki, *Brandishing Cyber-Attack Capabilities*, vii–viii, xi.
41. Ibid., 3.
42. Corrin, op. cit., 5.
43. Koepp and Fine, Editors, *America's Secret Agencies: Inside the Covert World of the CIA, NSA, FBI and Special OPS*, 53.
44. Ibid., 54.
45. Limnell, "Is Cyber War Real?: Gauging the Threats," 166–168.
46. Negroponte, Palmisano and Segal, *Defending an Open, Global, Secure and Resilient Internet*, 23, 28, 35–36.
47. Koepp and Fine, Editors, op. cit., 55.
48. Ventre, op. cit., 173.
49. Ventre, op. cit., 156–157.
50. Ibid., 158.
51. Ibid., 58–61.
52. Sims and Gerber, Editors, op. cit., 201.
53. Mandiant Group, "Apt-1 Exposing One of China's Cyber Espionage Units," 2–5.
54. Ibid., 7, 24, 27.
55. Feakin, "Enter the Cyber Dragon: Understanding Chinese Intelligence Agencies Cyber Capabilities," 2, 6.
56. Nakashima, "Confidential Report Lists U.S. Weapons Systems Designs Compromised by Chinese Cyber Spies," 1–3.
57. Office of the Secretary of Defense, "Annual Report to Congress: Military and Security Developments Involving the People's Republic of China," 12–13.
58. Obama, National Security Address to the National Defense University, 1.
59. National Security Agency, "Charter, Mission, Authorities, Annotated Comments."
60. Alexander, *National Security Agency Speech at AFCEA's Conference*, 2–3.
61. Erwin and Liu, "NSA Surveillance Leaks: Background and Issues for Congress," 10–11.
62. Gellman and Nakashima, "U.S. Spy Agencies Mounted 231 Offensive Cyber-Operations in 2011, Documents Show," 1–3.
63. Schmitt, Editor, *Tallinn Manual on the International Law Applicable to Cyber Warfare*, 4.
64. Ibid., v–ix.
65. Koh, "Koh's Remarks on International Law in Cyberspace," 1–2.
66. Johnson, Editor, *Power, National Security, and Transformational Global Events: Challenges Confronting America, China and Iran*, 311.

Bibliography

Alexander, K. *National Security Agency Speech at AFCEA's Conference, Maryland.* Washington, DC: Transcript by Federal News Service, 2013.

Byman, D. "Why Drones Work: The Case for Washington's Weapon of Choice." In *Foreign Affairs*, vol. 92, no. 4, pp. 32–33, 42. New York, 2013.

Corrin, A. "Cyber Warfare: New Battlefield, New Rules." Virginia: FCW: 1105 Government Information Group, 2012.

Cronin, A. K. "Why Drones Fail: When Tactics Drive Strategy." In *Foreign Affairs*, vol. 92, no. 4, pp. 44, 53. New York, 2013.

Crumpton, H. *The Art of Intelligence: Lessons from a Life in the CIA's Clandestine Service*. New York: The Penguin Press, 2012.

Denning, D. E. *Information Warfare and Security*. Massachusetts: Addison-Wesley, 1999.

Elisan, C. C. *Malware, Rootkits and Botnets: A Beginners Guide*. New York: McGraw Hill, 2013.

Erwin, M. C., and Liu, E. C. "NSA Surveillance Leaks: Background and Issues for Congress." Washington, DC: Congressional Research Service, 2013.

Feakin, T. "Enter the Cyber Dragon: Understanding Chinese Intelligence Agencies Cyber Capabilities." Special Report. Australia: Australian Strategic Policy Institute, 2013.

Gellman, B., and Nakashima, E. "U.S. Spy Agencies Mounted 231 Offensive Cyber Operations in 2011, Documents Show." In *The Washington Post*. Washington, DC, 2013.

Greenberg, A. *This Machine Kills Secrets: How WikiLeakers, Cypher Punks and Hacktivists Aim to Free the Worlds Information*. New York: Dutton, Published by the Penguin Group, 2012.

Grossman, L., and Newton-Small, J. "The Secret Web: Where Drugs, Porn and Murder Hide Online." In *Time*, 2013.

Healey, J. "The Future of U.S. Cyber Command." In *The National Interest*. Washington, DC, 2013.

Johnson, T. A., Editor. *Power, National Security, and Transformational Global Events: Challenges Confronting America, China and Iran*. Florida: CRC Press, Taylor and Francis Group, 2012.

Koepp, S., and Fine, N., Editors. *America's Secret Agencies: Inside the Covert World of the CIA, NSA, FBI and Special OPS*. New York: Time Books, 2013.

Koh, H. H. "Koh's Remarks on International Law in Cyberspace." In *Council on Foreign Relations*. New York, 2012.

Kreps, S., and Zenko, M. "The Next Drone Wars: Preparing for Proliferation." In *Foreign Affairs*, vol. 93, no. 2, pp. 68–71. New York, 2014.

Lardner, R. "Pentagon Forming Cyber Teams to Prevent Attacks." In *The Big Story*. New Jersey: Associated Press, 2013. Available at NorthJersey.com.

Libicki, M. C. *Brandishing Cyber-Attack Capabilities*. California: Rand National Defense Research Institute, 2013.

Limnell, J., and Rid, T. "Is Cyber War Real?: Gauging the Threats." In *Foreign Affairs*, vol. 93, no. 2, pp. 166–168. New York, 2014.

Mandiant Group. "APT-1 Exposing One of China's Cyber Espionage Units," 2013. Available at www.mandiant.com.

Nakashima, E. "Confidential Report Lists U.S. Weapons Systems Designs Compromised by Chinese Cyber Spies." In *The Washington Post*. Washington, DC, May 27, 2013.

Nakashima, E. "The Pentagon to Boost Cyber Security Force." In *The Washington Post*. Washington, DC, January 27, 2013.

National Security Agency. "Charter, Mission, Authorities, Annotated Comments." Washington, DC: National Defense University, 2013.

Negroponte, J. D., Palmisano, S. J., and Segal, A. "Defending an Open, Global, Secure, and Resilient Internet." Independent Task Force Report No. 70. New York: Council on Foreign Relations, 2013.

Obama, B. National Security Address to the National Defense University, 2013.

Office of the Intelligence Community Chief Information Officer. "Intelligence Community Information Technology, Enterprise Strategy 2012–2017." Washington, DC: Office of the Director of National Intelligence, Reports and Publications, 2012.

Office of the Secretary of Defense. "Annual Report to Congress: Military and Security Developments Involving the People's Republic of China," 2013.

Pellerin, C. "DOD at Work on New Cyber Strategy, Senior Military Advisor Says." Washington, DC: Armed Forces Press Service, 2013.

Schmitt, M. N., Editor. *Tallinn Manual on the International Law Applicable to Cyber Warfare*. United Kingdom: Cambridge University Press, 2013.

Schneier, B. *Schneier on Security*. Indiana: Wiley Publishing Company, 2008.

Sims, J. E., and Gerber, B., Editors. *Transforming U.S. Intelligence*. Washington, DC: Georgetown University Press, 2005.

Skoudis, E., and Liston, T. *Counter Hack Reloaded: A Step-by-Step Guide to Computer Attacks and Effective Defenses*, 2nd Edition. Saddle River, New Jersey: Printed and Electronically reproduced by permission of Pearson Education, Inc., 2006.

Ventre, D. *Information Warfare*. New Jersey: John Wiley and Sons, 2009.

Cybersecurity
A Primer of U.S. and International Legal Aspects

5

JULIE LOWRIE

Contents

5.1   Introduction

Cyberspace, like a virtual battleground, has become a place for confrontation: appropriation of personal data, espionage of the scientific, economic and commercial assets of companies which fall victim to competitors or foreign powers, disruption of services necessary for the proper functioning of the economy and daily life, compromise of information related to our sovereignty and even, in certain circumstances, loss of human lives are nowadays the potential or actual consequences of the overlap between the digital world and human activity.[1]

This "virtual battleground" in cyberspace has only continued to increase global awareness of security and impact global political stability exponentially, cutting a wide swath across physical geographical boundaries, impacting the security of individuals, commercial enterprises, economies, and the sovereignty and stability of global nations. Many of the international commerce and business development operations in developed and developing nations are integrally connected to the Internet. For example, Canada's entire economy is tied to digital technology, with 87% of Canada's commercial enterprises using the Internet to effectively conduct its business in 2012.[2]

For those world citizens whose freedom of speech is restricted or prohibited, the Internet provides a nearly anonymous avenue where individuals can associate without government restriction and intervention, can use the Internet to mobilize and inform others about contemporaneous political activities or events affecting those in a specific community, can operate individual water systems for rural farmers, and can provide and mobilize assistance to those affected by natural disasters. However, those same benefits can be accessed and used by mal-intentioned individuals and factions that wish to destabilize or overthrow governments or engage in acts of terrorism.

In recent news, shortly before local elections were scheduled to take place on March 30, 2014, Turkish Prime Minister Recep Tayyip Erdoğan became the target of electronic eavesdropping where phone conversations between Erdoğan and his son were surreptitiously recorded, purportedly disclosing Erdoğan's requests to his son to get rid of large sums of money; these recordings were then posted online.[3] After these disclosures, high-level Turkish security meetings attended by Erdoğan were surreptitiously recorded and then released on the Internet via YouTube.[4] As a result, Erdoğan then immediately banned YouTube, having banned Twitter before the most recent leak.[5] Erdoğan directed blame for the digital breaches to his opponents in the upcoming elections in Turkey.[6] Because of Erdoğan's ban of YouTube and Twitter, a feminist activist group, FEMEN, staged demonstrations against Erdoğan at local election polls on March 30, 2014.[7]

The leakers' use of social media to expose potential political corruption and the subsequent reactive responses in Turkey raise a series of important questions. What legal authority does Erdoğan have to ban social media websites in Turkey? Will his actions create such public outcry and protest that will undermine and contribute to internal political instability? By banning social media sites, is he violating other international laws or norms of conduct? Is he violating Turkey's own internal cybersecurity policies? What are the global implications for Turkey, as a member of any international organization? Could the leakers' conduct be considered to be an armed attack? If so, what international treaties or agreements are triggered? If triggered, does that create an international "domino effect" among other nations? Lastly, how does a sovereign nation like Turkey make the distinction that conduct in cyberspace was negligent or a mistake, based on deficiencies in software or hardware, or was intentional conduct, which may trigger an armed conflict? These questions, among others, have appeared repeatedly as the developing and developed world nations recognize and acknowledge their global interconnectivity through the Internet and begin to grapple with the universal need to establish norms and standards of conduct, protect business innovation, and safeguard individual privacy and free speech among the world's citizenry.

5.2   What Is Cybersecurity?

The legal playing field where the U.S. local, state, and federal authorities and international bodies and member states of the European Union (EU) aim their legal bat to regulate, govern, and protect their identified tangible and intangible assets from cybercrime, espionage, and attack puts kindred terminology into play, which, at first blush, seem to be identical because the players wear the same uniforms when whizzing around the bases. But upon closer inspection, those players have simply adopted a specific term without ever ascribing a precise definition to that word, while others have adopted a specific definition that fails to correlate to any scientific or existing statutory framework. Either way, failing to develop and establish uniform and standardized definitions consistent with an overall strategy, legal structure, and scientific basis will ultimately impact the ability of all players to identify their strengths and weaknesses, create sound gaming statistics, and develop an easy-to-understand rule book that can be seamlessly adopted and fluidly applied in practice with other global players.

The development and adoption of precise definitions for the primary terms of art dealing with the security of various informational systems and their physical and virtual devices, interconnected through the Internet, have been identified as a required component if and when cybersecurity is launched as an actual science. Such a development would put the study of cybersecurity under the rigorous scrutiny of the scientific method, which requires the repeatability of experiments based on precise definitions and conditions. "Precise definitions matter. Until there is a precise set of objects that can be examined carefully and clearly, it will not be possible to increase the level of rigor."[8]

In analyzing data and security breaches, and the relevant legal framework throughout the EU, the Directorate General for Internal Policies Policy Department A: Economic and Scientific Policy, Industry, Research and Energy of the European Parliament (the "Directorate") concluded in September 2013 that "consistent and unambiguous definitions across legislative instruments are often lacking."[9] The Directorate's report further outlines the level of impact that the lack of standardized terms for defining data and security breaches can have on identifying, reporting, and reacting to such breaches. The lack of standardized terms has resulted in an inability to globally match "apples to apples" and affects the accuracy in reporting the actual number, nature, and type of breaches that have occurred over a given period of time. Lastly, in one of the most deadly and critical aspects of identifying specific events by standardized terms, an international group of experts found that the same lack of agreed-upon definitions impacts the application of international cyber warfare.

> State practice is only beginning to clarify the application to cyber operations of the *jus ad bellum*, the body of international law that governs a State's resort to force as an instrument of its national policy. In particular, the lack of agreed-upon definitions, criteria, and thresholds for application, creates uncertainty when applying the *jus ad bellum* in the cyber context.[10]

Acknowledging that standardized and globally accepted definitions for significant and repeating terms of art affecting cybersecurity do not presently exist among global nation-state, business, and individual stakeholders, an overview of the relevant U.S. and international legal environment must identify, at a minimum, what has been identified as a definition, or the lack thereof, for the word *cybersecurity*. What exactly does the word *cybersecurity* mean, and is that definition expansive enough to be borderless? And if so, is that definition universally accepted throughout the world, or is that definition finite, limited, and restricted only to certain nation-states? The word *cybersecurity* seems to be used interchangeably, like the ubiquitous use of the word *glue*. As we all know, not all glues are created equal, meaning that the ingredients found in specific types of glue will make the difference between glue that sticks and one that just does not or, even worse, will actually muck things up, generating more problems than solutions. The same analogy can be made about definitions.

A definition of cybersecurity must adequately contemplate and address the physical and virtual nature of the assets to be protected, in addition to the breadth and scope of coverage because

> Cybersecurity is a complex problem with many different facets, and that legal and legislative analyses of cybersecurity issues must distinguish not only among different cyber threat actors, such as nation-states, terrorists, criminals, and malicious hackers, but also among different types of cyber threats. Such cyber threats include threats to critical infrastructure, which could lead to loss of life or significant damage to our economy; and threats to intellectual property, which could affect our nation's long-term competitiveness.[11]

Without a clear, concise, and descriptive definition of cybersecurity, how can a nation-state promulgate an overarching statutory scheme designed to create a strong and effective national strategy that will encompass and protect all its physical and virtual assets affected, impacted, connected to, operated through, or touched, directly or indirectly, by digital technology from external and internal threats? If cybersecurity is not clearly defined, how will a nation-state be able to regulate the conduct of its economic business stakeholders without overregulating them into extinction? Take the example of the United States, one of the largest nation-states globally, which arguably should easily be able to articulate a clear and concise definition for the word *cybersecurity*, yet it does not.[12] In fact, the Department of Homeland Security (DHS) uses the word *cybersecurity* in its publications without ever defining precisely what aspects it does and does not cover,[13] and even the defunct Cybersecurity Act of 2012 used the word *cybersecurity* without ever providing a definition. The proposed bill at least provided a definition for what it termed *cybersecurity services*:

> (4) CYBERSECURITY SERVICES—the term "cybersecurity services" means products, goods, or services used to detect or prevent activity intended to result in a cybersecurity threat.[14]

This definition does not stand independently and must be reviewed within the context of a "cybersecurity threat," which is defined as follows:

> (5) CYBERSECURITY THREAT—the term "cybersecurity threat" means any action that will result in unauthorized access to, exfiltration of, manipulation of, or impairment to the integrity, confidentiality, or availability of an information system or information that is stored on, processed by, or transiting an information system."[15]

In its June 2013 seminal report for the Congress on federal laws relating to cybersecurity, the Congressional Report Service highlighted the lack of a uniform, universally accepted definition for cybersecurity:

> The term *information systems* is defined in 44 U.S.C. § 3502 as "a discrete set of information resources organized for the collection, processing, maintenance, use, sharing, dissemination, or disposition of information," where information resources is "information and related resources, such as personnel, equipment, funds, and information technology."

Thus, cybersecurity, a broad and arguably somewhat fuzzy concept for which there is no consensus definition, might best be described as measures intended to protect information systems—including technology (such as devices, networks, and software), information, and associated personnel—from various forms of attack. The concept has, however, been characterized in various ways. For example, the interagency Committee on National Security Systems has defined it as "the ability to protect or defend the use of cyberspace from cyber attacks," where cyberspace is defined as a global domain within the information environment consisting of the interdependent network of information systems infrastructures including the Internet, telecommunications networks, computer systems, and embedded processors and controllers[16] (Committee on National Security Systems, National Information Assurance [IA] Glossary, April 2010, http://www.cnss .gov/Assets/pdf/cnssi_4009.pdf).

On the other hand, the International Telecommunications Union (ITU), the United Nations' specialized agency for information and communications technology, adopted the following definition of cybersecurity in its April 2008 recommendations on network, data, and telecommunications security:

> Cybersecurity is the collection of tools, policies, security concepts, security safeguards, guidelines, risk management approaches, actions, training, best practices, assurance and technologies that can be used to protect the cyber environment and organization and user's assets. Organization and user's assets include connected computing devices, personnel, infrastructure, applications, services, telecommunication systems, and the totality of transmitted and/or stored information in the cyber environment. Cybersecurity strives to ensure the attainment and maintenance of the security properties of the organization and user's assets against relevant security risks in the cyber environment. The general security objectives comprise the following: Availability; Integrity, which may include authenticity and non-repudiation; Confidentiality.[17]

While the ITU definition of cybersecurity does not clearly define what would be the contemplated cyber environment, this definition is far more inclusive than the aforementioned cobbled-together definition presented in current U.S. cybersecurity legislation. The ITU definition encompasses the individual, enterprise, and governmental information systems, identifying, in general, the physical and virtual assets it seeks to protect. While a finite, discreet definition of cybersecurity may create a uniform standard in the application of the panoply of the overarching legal regulatory schemes currently in place, does having an inflexible, agreed-upon definition create the right solution to a 21st century issue? David Satola and Henry Judy posit that the current domestic and international legal architecture is outdated, is not geared to adjust quickly to the dynamic cyber environment, and is not a 21st century response to the new digital landscape.[18] According to the authors, the current legal architecture does not adequately address "the lack of consensus on the fundamental and related issues of jurisdiction and sovereignty," which makes "it difficult to effectively cross borders to address international cybersecurity incidents," while contract law is generally the only remedy available when cybersecurity issues arise from unintentional coding errors or negligently written software.[19] Lastly, the authors note that the concept of cybersecurity "varies depending on the physical, educational, and economic resources available in different jurisdictions. It differs depending on the sensitivity of the data to be protected and needs to reflect different cultural expectations and priorities, among many other factors."[20] Instead of adopting a specific definition for cybersecurity, this chapter attempts to incorporate Satola and Judy's suggested modular approach by identifying an overview of the U.S. federal and international laws that currently comprise the legal framework that attempts to address and regulate the changing cybersecurity landscape.

5.3   Current U.S. Comprehensive National Cybersecurity Strategy

In general, current U.S. and various state laws involving cybersecurity, either directly or indirectly, have developed in reaction to abuses and malicious activity occurring in specific economic sectors. In his discussion paper "Cyber Norm Emergence at the United Nations—An Analysis of the Activities at the UN Regarding Cybersecurity," Tim Maurer postulated that "cybersecurity can be divided into four major threats: espionage, crime, cyber war, and cyber terrorism."[21] Maurer credits Harvard Professor Joseph Nye for identifying the underlying sources for these present-day threats: (1) flaws in the design of the Internet, (2) flaws in the hardware and software, and (3) the move to put more and more critical systems online.[22] In the United States, the government controls or manages only a small portion of the cyber environment, while the private sector designs, markets, installs, and operates much of the software and hardware that are utilized in the technological operation of power grids, water sanitation and delivery, transportation, communications, and financial systems nationwide. As a result, the United States can only control cyber threats to the vulnerabilities evident in these private systems by creating additional legislation allowing oversight, regulation, and monitoring based on potential impacts to national security.

While there have been a recent spate of legislative bills proposed to create a standardized overarching U.S. federal cybersecurity legal scheme seeking to cover both government and private computer and network systems, none of them have successfully been enacted into law.[23] In 2003, the White House initiated its inaugural national cybersecurity strategy when the White House, through then President George W. Bush, released The National Strategy to Secure Cyberspace in February 2003.[24] Bush identified, proposed, and emphasized the importance of, and participation of, a public–private partnership to implement the national strategy to secure cyberspace.[25]

Bush's strategy prioritized five concerns: (1) creating a national cyberspace security team, (2) a cyberspace threat and vulnerability reduction program, (3) a cyberspace security awareness program, (4) a plan to secure the federal cyberspace, and (5) national and international cooperation for cyberspace security.[26]

While these five strategic priorities did not translate into the passage of any meaningful legislation, the Comprehensive National Cybersecurity Initiative (CNCI) originated as a classified offshoot of Bush's National Strategy.[27] In December 2008, an appointed Commission on Cybersecurity for the 44th Presidency ("Commission") from the Center for Strategic and International Studies (CSIS) issued a report that presented three fundamental findings: "(1) cybersecurity is now a major national security problem for the United States, (2) decisions and actions must respect privacy and civil liberties, and (3) only a comprehensive national security strategy that embraces both the domestic and international aspects of cybersecurity will make us more secure."[28]

Following up on the CSIS Commission's recommendations, President Barack Obama issued a revised and updated CNCI as National Security Presidential Directive 54 released on March 2, 2010,[29] which primarily addressed cybersecurity in the federal systems, both classified and civilian; mandated the use of EINSTEIN 2, an intrusion detection system, across all federal systems; and reduced federal external network access points to the Internet to only those trusted providers contracted with the government.[30] The 2010 CNCI mandated information sharing across various federal agencies in an effort to develop a more robust cyber defense system,[31] to support initiatives to create a more cyber-savvy federal employee base, to develop future leading technology for cybersecurity, to develop a multiprong approach to global chain risk assessment, and to define the federal role for extending cybersecurity into critical infrastructure domains.[32] Following Obama's issuance of the 2010 CNCI, the Congress considered a variety of bills involving cybersecurity; however, none of them were successfully passed.

In the absence of a legislated cybersecurity legal standard, on February 12, 2013, the Obama White House issued Executive Order (EO) 13636, Improving Critical Infrastructure Security, which sets out a national policy on cyber intrusions, identifies the nature and scope of the U.S. national policy on the security of critical infrastructures, creates a process for information sharing and coordination with private entities to enhance and better protect critical infrastructure assets, defines critical infrastructures and critical infrastructure sectors, and directs the development of standards and a framework for improved cybersecurity of critical infrastructures. The EO contemporaneously directs the Secretary of the DHS to uphold the individual privacy and civil rights of individuals and to ensure their inclusion in the execution and implementation of the Order's mandates, adopting the Fair

Information Practice Principles and other relevant "privacy and civil rights policies, principles and frameworks."[33]

While the EO cites "repeated cyber intrusions of critical infrastructures" as one of the most important national security issues presently facing the United States, the EO creates a federal partnership with U.S. businesses as the best way "to improve cybersecurity information sharing and collaboratively develop and implement risk-based standards."[34] The EO tasks the Secretary of Commerce to direct the director of the National Institute of Standards and Technology (NIST) with developing a framework for improving the cybersecurity of critical infrastructures.

The EO directs the DHS to initiate and establish a collaborative partnership between government and the private sector in an effort to better assess cyber threat risks, identify evolving cyber threats, and proactively protect the nation's critical infrastructure against such cyber risks. It further tasks government agencies, including the DHS, to create a voluntary process between the government and private entities to rapidly share unclassified data relating to cyber threat risks and incidents[35] and extends voluntary participation to select owners and operators of identified critical infrastructures for classified information sharing in the Enhanced Cybersecurity Services (ECS) program.[36] The Presidential Policy Directive-21 (PPD-21), issued contemporaneous with the EO, creates a procedural mechanism and federal oversight to develop collaborative partnerships with public and private stakeholders. PPD-21 imbues the DHS, in general, with the responsibility to oversee, monitor, coordinate, and provide guidance and program strategy to affected government, private entities, and owners and operators of critical infrastructures.[37]

While EO 13636 broadly defines critical infrastructures as those "systems and assets, whether physical or virtual, so vital to the United States that the incapacity or destruction of such systems and assets would have a debilitating impact on security, national economic security, national public health or safety, or any combination of those matters,"[38] PPD-21 defined the term *critical infrastructure* to comport with

> the meaning provided in section 1016(e) of the USA Patriot Act of 2001 (42 U.S.C. 5195c (e)), namely systems and assets, whether physical or virtual, so vital to the United States that the incapacity or destruction of such systems and assets would have a debilitating impact on security, national economic security, national public health or safety, or any combination of those matters.[39]

As part of its designated responsibilities under PPD-21, the DHS is tasked with developing processes and best practices for risk assessment of cyber threats and the development of overall risk assessment reports for critical infrastructure sectors. PPD-21 broadly identified 16 general critical infrastructure sectors domiciled in the United States and assigned specific-sector agencies to each sector.[40] Refer to Chapter 2, Section 2.1.5, in this text for a complete listing of the lead agencies and critical infrastructures under the authority of Homeland Security Presidential Directive-7.

By opening participation in the ECS program to critical infrastructure entities, the EO expanded ECS coverage to a broader base of stakeholders. Participation in ECS is voluntary and permits the sharing of classified information involving indicators of malicious cyber activity between DHS and qualified public and private entities involved in the operation of critical infrastructure assets.

> ECS is a voluntary information sharing program that assists critical infrastructure owners and operators as they improve the protection of their systems from unauthorized access, exploitation, or data exfiltration. DHS works with cybersecurity organizations from across the federal government to gain access to a broad range of sensitive and classified cyber threat information. DHS develops indicators based on this information and shares them with qualified Commercial Service Providers (CSPs), thus enabling them to better protect their customers who are critical infrastructure entities. ECS augments, but does not replace, an entities' existing cybersecurity capabilities.[41]

ECS deploys EINSTEIN 3-Accelerated (E³A), a real-time network intrusion detection and prevention system that performs deep packet inspection to identify, prevent, and block malicious activity from entering federal civilian agency networks.[42] E³A has been operationalized for every (.gov) website as part of the government's efforts to reduce cyber threat risk to the system networks utilized by all federal civilian agencies, in furtherance of the EO's mandate to improve the security of federal systems. E³A is operated with E³A sensors placed at network Internet access points where incoming and outgoing network traffic is then monitored for cyber indicators in real-time. According to the DHS, "A cyber indicator (indicator) can be defined as human-readable cyber data used to identify some form of malicious cyber activity and are data related to:

1. IP addresses;
2. Domains;
3. E-mail headers;
4. Files; and
5. Strings."[43]

E³A matches detected cyber indicators against its database of known malicious signatures from both classified and unclassified sources to detect potential or actual threats, which are logged in real time and shared with the U.S. Computer Emergency Readiness Team (CERT), the DHS division responsible for coordinating defenses against and responses to cyber incidents across the United States.[44]

Since E³A was initially designed and developed by the National Security Agency (NSA)[45,46] and has the capability to read electronic content, its use in federal civilian systems continues to raise significant privacy concerns[47,48] despite DHS's description of the privacy protection processes it has implemented to protect individual privacy from abuse, misuse, and inadvertent disclosure, which it outlined in detail in its Privacy Impact Assessment Report issued in April 2013.[49]

An important milestone produced by the EO's mandate was completed on February 12, 2014, when NIST issued a Framework for Improving Critical Infrastructure Cybersecurity (NIST Framework).[50] The NIST Framework is based on three separate categories that are interrelated and provide a basic roadmap for an organization to conduct a self-assessment of its enterprise information protection plan. The NIST Framework consists of Framework Core, Framework Profile, and Framework Implementation Tiers.[51] "The Framework Core is a set of cybersecurity activities, outcomes, and informative references that are common across critical infrastructure sectors,"[52] which provides the organization with the detailed guidance for developing its own individual organizational risk profile. The Framework Profile represents outcomes based on business needs, which can be adjusted based on the categories selected under the Framework Core and Tiers. The Framework Implementation Tiers "provide context on how an organization views cybersecurity risk and the processes in place to manage that risk."[53] While not mandatory, the NIST Framework provides a benchmark that organizations can use to gauge where their cybersecurity activities fall within the NIST Framework, as the minimum standard of care for risk-based cybersecurity. The NIST Framework provides references for each category and activity to other more detailed standards issued by professional industry organizations.

5.4   Current U.S. Federal Laws Involving Cybersecurity

To protect the physical, intangible, or virtual assets in those affected specific sectors, including those critical infrastructure sectors, federal legislators passed laws earmarked to address those perceived abuses which, at the time, affected those identified sectors. The reader is referred to Table 5.1. It was adapted from the Congressional Research Services and identifies over 50 statutes that directly or indirectly address some aspect of cybersecurity.[54]

Table 5.1 Laws Identified as Having Relevant Cybersecurity Provisions

Year	Popular Name	Law	Stat.	U.S.C.	Applicability and Notes	CRC Reports
June 18, 1878	Posse Comitatus Act	Ch. 263	20 Stat. 152	18 U.S.C. § 1385	Restricts the use of military forces in civilian law enforcement within the United States. May prevent assistance to civil agencies that lack DoD expertise and capabilities.	RS20590
July 2, 1890, and later	Antitrust Laws (p. 22): Sherman Antitrust Act Wilson Tariff Act Clayton Act § 5 of the Federal Trade Commission (FTC) Act	Ch. 647 Ch. 349, § 73 P.L. 63-212 Ch, 311, § 5	26 Stat. 209 28 Stat. 570 38 Stat. 730 38 Stat. 719	15 U.S.C. §§ 1–7 15 U.S.C. §§ 8–11 15 U.S.C. §§ 12–27 15 U.S.C. § 45(a)	"Antitrust laws" generally means the three laws listed in 15 U.S.C. § 12(a) and § 5 of the FTC Act, which forbids combinations or agreements that unreasonably restrain trade. May create barriers to sharing of information or collaboration to enhance cybersecurity among private sector entities.	
Mar. 3, 1901	National Institute of Standards and Technology (NIST) Act	Ch. 872	31 Stat. 1449	15 U.S.C. § 271 et seq.	The original act gave the agency responsibilities relating to technical standards. Later amendments established a computer standards program and specified research topics, among them computer and telecommunication systems, including information security and control systems.	
Aug. 13, 1912	Radio Act of 1912	Ch. 287	37 Stat. 302		Established a radio licensing regime and regulated private radio communications, creating a precedent for wireless regulation. Repealed by the Radio Act of 1927.	

Date	Name	Ch.	Stat.	U.S.C.	Description	Report
June 10, 1920	Federal Power Act	Ch. 285	41 Stat. 1063	16 U.S.C. § 791a et seq., § 824 et seq.	Established the Federal Energy Regulatory Commission (FERC) and gave it regulatory authority over interstate sale and transmission of electric power. The move toward a national smart grid is raising concerns about vulnerability to cyber attack.	R41886
Feb. 23, 1927	Radio Act of 1927	Ch. 169	44 Stat. 1162		Created the Federal Radio Commission as an independent agency (predecessor of the Federal Communications Commission [FCC]) and outlawed interception and divulging private radio messages. Repealed by the Communications Act of 1934.	
June 19, 1934	Communications Act of 1934	Ch. 652	48 Stat. 1064	47 U.S.C. § 151 et seq.	Established the FCC and gave it regulatory authority over both domestic and international commercial wired and wireless communications. Provides the president with emergency powers over communications stations and devices. Governs protection by cable operators of information about subscribers.	RL32589 RL34693

(Continued)

Table 5.1 (Continued) Laws Identified as Having Relevant Cybersecurity Provisions

Year	Popular Name	Law	Stat.	U.S.C.	Applicability and Notes	CRC Reports
July 26, 1947	National Security Act of 1947	Ch. 343	61 Stat. 495	50 U.S.C. § 401 et seq.	Provided the basis for the modern organization of U.S. defense and national security by reorganizing military and intelligence functions in the federal government. Created the National Security Council, the Central Intelligence Agency, and the position of Secretary of Defense. Established procedures for access to classified information.	
Jan. 27, 1948	U.S. Information and Educational Exchange Act of 1948 (Smith-Mundt Act)	Ch. 36	62 Stat. 6	22 U.S.C. § 1431 et seq.	Restricts the State Department from disseminating public diplomacy information domestically and limits its authority to communicate with the American public in general. Has been interpreted by some to prohibit the military from conducting cyberspace information operations, some of which could be considered propaganda that could reach U.S. citizens, since the government does not restrict Internet access according to territorial boundaries.	R41674

Sep. 8, 1950	Defense Production Act of 1950	Ch. 932	64 Stat. 798	50 U.S.C. App. § 2061 et seq.	Codifies a robust legal authority given the president to force industry to give priority to national security production and ensure the survival of security-critical domestic production capacities. It is also the statutory underpinning of governmental review of foreign investment in U.S. companies.	RS20587 RL31133
Aug. 1, 1956	State Department Basic Authorities Act of 1956	P.L. 84-885	70 Stat. 890	22 U.S.C. § 2651a	Specifies the organization of the Department of State, including the positions of coordinator for counterterrorism. As the Internet becomes increasingly international, concerns have been raised about the development and coordination of international efforts in cybersecurity by the United States.	R40989
Oct. 30, 1965	Brooks Automatic Data Processing Act	P.L. 89-306	79 Stat. 1127		Gave General Services Administration (GSA) authority over acquisition of automatic data processing equipment by federal agencies and gave NIST responsibilities for developing standards and guidelines relating to automatic data processing and federal computer systems. Repealed by the Clinger-Cohen Act of 1996.	

(Continued)

Table 5.1 (Continued) Laws Identified as Having Relevant Cybersecurity Provisions

Year	Popular Name	Law	Stat.	U.S.C.	Applicability and Notes	CRC Reports
July 4, 1966	Freedom of Information Act (FOIA)	P.L. 89–487	80 Stat. 250	5 U.S.C. § 552	Enables anyone to access agency records except those falling into nine categories of exemption, among them classified documents, those exempted by specific statutes, and trade secrets or other confidential commercial or financial information.	R41406 R41933
June 19, 1968	Omnibus Crime Control and Safe Streets Act of 1968	P.L. 90-351	82 Stat. 197	42 U.S.C. Chapter 46, §§ 3701 to 3797ee-1	Title I established federal grant programs and other forms of assistance to state and local law enforcement. Title III is a comprehensive wiretapping and electronic eavesdropping statute that not only outlawed both activities in general terms but also permitted federal and state law enforcement officers to use them under strict limitations.	
Oct. 15, 1970	Racketeer Influenced and Corrupt Organizations Act (RICO)	P.L. 91-452	84 Stat. 941	18 U.S.C. Chapter 96, §§ 1961–1968	Enlarges the civil and criminal consequences of a list of state and federal crimes when committed in a way characteristic of the conduct of organized crime (racketeering).	96-950

Oct. 6, 1972	Federal Advisory Committee Act	P.L. 92-463	86 Stat 770	5 U.S.C. App., §§ 1–16	Specifies conditions for establishing a federal advisory committee and its responsibilities and limitations. Requires open, public meetings and that records be available for public inspection. Has been criticized as potentially impeding the development of public/private partnerships in cybersecurity, particularly private-sector communications and input on policy.	R40520
Nov. 7, 1973	War Powers Resolution	P.L. 93-148	87 Stat. 555	50 U.S.C. Chapter 33, §§ 1541–1548	Establishes procedures to circumscribe presidential authority to use armed forces in potential or actual hostilities without congressional authorization.	R41199 R41989
Dec. 31, 1974	Privacy Act of 1974	P.L. 93-579	88 Stat. 1896	5 U.S.C. § 552a	Limits the disclosure of personally identifiable information held by federal agencies. Established a code of fair information practices for collection, management, and dissemination of records by agencies, including requirements for security and confidentiality of records.	

(Continued)

Table 5.1 (Continued) Laws Identified as Having Relevant Cybersecurity Provisions

Year	Popular Name	Law	Stat.	U.S.C.	Applicability and Notes	CRC Reports
Oct. 25, 1978	Foreign Intelligence Surveillance Act of 1978 (FISA)	P.L. 95-511	92 Stat. 1783	18 U.S.C. §§ 2511, 2518–9 50 U.S.C. Chapter 36, §§ 1801–1885c	In foreign intelligence investigations, provides a statutory framework for federal agencies to obtain authorization to conduct electronic surveillance, utilize pen registers and trap and trace devices, or access specified records.	98-326 R40138
Oct. 13, 1980	Privacy Protection Act of 1980	P.L. 96-440	94 Stat. 1879	42 U.S.C. Chapter 21A, §§ 2000aa-5 to 2000aa-12	Protects journalists from being required to turn over to law enforcement any work product and documentary materials, including sources, before dissemination to the public.	
Oct. 12, 1984	Counterfeit Access Device and Computer Fraud and Abuse Act of 1984	P.L. 98-473	98 Stat. 2190	18 U.S.C. § 1030	Provided criminal penalties for unauthorized access and use of computers and networks. Part of the Comprehensive Crime Control Act of 1984.	97-1025
Oct. 16, 1986	Computer Fraud and Abuse Act of 1986	P.L. 99-474	100 Stat. 1213	18 U.S.C. § 1030	Expanded the scope of the Counterfeit Access Device and Computer Fraud and Abuse Act of 1984. For government computers, criminalized electronic trespassing, exceeding authorized access, and destroying information; also criminalized trafficking in stolen computer passwords. Created a statutory exemption for intelligence and law enforcement activities.	

Date	Name	P.L.	Stat.	U.S.C.	Description	CRS
Oct. 21, 1986	Electronic Communications Privacy Act of 1986	P.L. 99-508	100 Stat. 1848	18 U.S.C. §§ 2510–2522, 2701–2712, 3121–3126	Attempts to strike a balance between privacy rights and the needs of law enforcement with respect to data shared or stored by electronic and telecommunications services. Unless otherwise provided, prohibits the interception of or access to stored oral or electronic communications, use or disclosure of information so obtained, or possession of electronic eavesdropping equipment.	R41733 R41756 RL34693
Oct. 30, 1986	Department of Defense Appropriations Act 1987	P.L. 99-591	100 Stat. 3341-82, 3341-122	10 U.S.C. § 167	Established unified combatant command for special operations forces, including the U.S. Strategic Command, under which the U.S. Cyber Command was organized.	
Jan. 8, 1988	Computer Security Act of 1987	P.L. 100-235	101 Stat. 1724	15 U.S.C. §§ 272, 278g-3, 278g-4, 278h	Required NIST to develop and the Secretary of Commerce to promulgate security standards and guidelines for federal computer systems except national security systems. Also required agency planning and training in computer security (this provision was superseded by the Federal Information Security Management Act [FISMA]).	

(Continued)

Table 5.1 (Continued) Laws Identified as Having Relevant Cybersecurity Provisions

Year	Popular Name	Law	Stat.	U.S.C.	Applicability and Notes	CRC Reports
Oct. 18, 1988	Computer Matching and Privacy Protection Act of 1988	P.L. 100-503	102 Stat. 2507	5 U.S.C. § 552a	Amended the Privacy Act (see p. 32), establishing procedural safeguards for use of computer matching on records covered by the act.	
Dec. 9, 1991	High Performance Computing Act of 1991	P.L. 102-194	105 Stat. 1594	15 U.S.C. Chapter 81	Established a federal high-performance computing program and requires that it address security needs and provide for interagency coordination.	RL33586
Oct. 25, 1994	Communications Assistance for Law Enforcement Act (CALEA) of 1994	P.L. 103-414	108 Stat. 4279	47 U.S.C. § 1001 et seq.	Requires telecommunications carriers to assist law enforcement in performing electronic surveillance and directs the telecommunications industry to design, develop, and deploy solutions that meet requirements for carriers to support authorized electronic surveillance.	RL30677
May 25, 1995	Paperwork Reduction Act of 1995	P.L. 104-13	109 Stat. 163	44 U.S.C. Chapter 35, §§ 3501–3549	Gave the Office of Management and Budget (OMB) authority to develop information-resource management policies and standards, required consultation with NIST and GSA on information technology (IT), and required agencies to implement processes relating to information security and privacy.	

Date	Name	P.L.	Stat.	U.S.C.	Description	
Feb. 8, 1996	Telecommunications Act of 1996.	P.L. 104-104	110 Stat. 56	See 47 U.S.C. § 609 nt. for affected provisions.	Overhauled telecommunications law, including significant deregulation of U.S. telecommunications markets, eliminating regulatory barriers to competition.	R41499
Feb. 8, 1996	Communications Decency Act of 1996	P.L. 104-104 (Title V)	110 Stat. 133	See 47 U.S.C. §§ 223, 230	Intended to regulate indecency and obscenity on telecommunications systems, including the Internet. Has been interpreted to absolve Internet service providers and certain web-based services of responsibility for third-party content residing on those networks or websites.	
Feb. 10, 1996	Clinger-Cohen Act (Information Technology Management Reform Act) of 1996	P.L. 104-106, (Div. D and E)	110 Stat. 642	40 U.S.C. § 11001 et seq.	Required agencies to ensure adequacy of information-security policies, OMB to oversee major IT acquisitions, and the Secretary of Commerce to promulgate compulsory federal computer standards based on those developed by NIST. Exempted national security systems from most provisions.	
Aug. 21, 1996	Health Insurance Portability and Accountability Act (HIPAA) of 1996	P.L. 104-191	110 Stat. 1936	42 U.S.C. § 1320d et seq.	Required the Secretary of Health and Human Services to establish security standards and regulations for protecting the privacy of individually identifiable health information, and required covered health care entities to protect the security of such information.	RL34120

(Continued)

Table 5.1 (Continued) Laws Identified as Having Relevant Cybersecurity Provisions

Year	Popular Name	Law	Stat.	U.S.C.	Applicability and Notes	CRC Reports
Oct. 11, 1996	Economic Espionage Act of 1996	P.L. 104-294	110 Stat. 3488	18 U.S.C. § 1030, Chapter 90, §§ 1831–1839	Outlaws theft of trade secret information, including electronically stored information, if "reasonable measures" have been taken to keep it secret. Also contains the National Information Infrastructure Protection Act of 1996, amending 18 U.S.C. § 1030 (see the Counterfeit Access Device and Computer Fraud and Abuse Act of 1984), broadening prohibited activities relating to unauthorized access to computers.	
Oct. 30, 1998	Identity Theft and Assumption Deterrence Act of 1998	P.L. 105-318	112 Stat. 3007	18 U.S.C. § 1028	Made identity theft a federal crime. Provides penalties, and directed the FTC to record and refer complaints.	R40599
Oct. 5, 1999	National Defense Authorization Act for Fiscal Year 2000	P.L. 106-65	113 Stat. 512	10 U.S.C. § 2224	Established the Defense Information Assurance Program and required development of a test-bed and coordination with other federal agencies.	
Nov. 12, 1999	Gramm-Leach-Bliley Act of 1999	P.L. 106-102 (Title V)	113 Stat. 1338	15 U.S.C. Chapter 94, §§ 6801–6827	Requires financial institutions to protect the security and confidentiality of customers' personal information; authorized regulations for that purpose.	RL34120 RS20185

Date	Name	Public Law	Statute	U.S.C.	Description	
Oct. 30, 2000	Floyd D. Spence National Defense Authorization Act for Fiscal Year 2001	P.L. 106-398 (Titles IX and X)	114 Stat. 1654A-233; 1654A-266	10 U.S.C. Chapter 112, §§ 2200–2200f	Established the DoD information assurance scholarship program; set cybersecurity requirements for federal systems superseded by FISMA in 2002.	R40980
Oct. 26, 2001	USA PATRIOT Act of 2001	P.L. 107-56	115 Stat. 272	See 18 U.S.C. § 1 nt. and classification tables	Authorized various law enforcement activities relating to computer fraud and abuse.	
July 30, 2002	Sarbanes-Oxley Act of 2002	P.L. 107-204	116 Stat. 745	15 U.S.C. § 7262	Requires annual reporting on internal financial controls of covered firms to the Securities and Exchange Commission. Such controls typically include information security.	
Nov. 25, 2002	Homeland Security Act of 2002	P.L. 107-296 (Titles II and III)	116 Stat. 2135	6 U.S.C. §§ 121–195c, 441–444, and 481–486	Created the Department of Homeland Security and gave it functions relating to the protection of information infrastructure, including providing state and local governments and private entities with threat and vulnerability information, crisis-management support, and technical assistance. Strengthened some criminal penalties relating to cyber crime.	

(Continued)

Table 5.1 (Continued) Laws Identified as Having Relevant Cybersecurity Provisions

Year	Popular Name	Law	Stat.	U.S.C.	Applicability and Notes	CRC Reports
Nov. 25, 2002	Federal Information Security Management Act of 2002 (FISMA)	P.L. 107-296 (Title X) P.L. 107-347 (Title III)	116 Stat. 2259 116 Stat. 2946	44 U.S.C. Chapter 35, Subchapters II and III 40 U.S.C. 11331, 15 U.S.C. 278g-3 and 4	Created a cybersecurity framework for federal information systems, with an emphasis on risk management, and required implementation of agency-wide information security programs. Gave oversight responsibility to OMB, revised the responsibilities of the Secretary of Commerce and NIST for information-system standards, and transferred responsibility for promulgation of those standards from the Secretary of Commerce to OMB.	
Nov. 26, 2002	Terrorism Risk Insurance Act of 2002	P.L. 107-297	116 Stat. 2322	15 U.S.C. § 6701 nt.	Provides federal cost-sharing subsidies for insured losses resulting from acts of terrorism.	
Nov. 27, 2002	Cyber Security Research and Development Act, 2002	P.L. 107-305	116 Stat. 2367	15 U.S.C. §§ 278g, h, 7401 et seq.	Requires the National Science Foundation to award grants for basic research and education to enhance computer security. Required NIST to establish cybersecurity research programs.	

Date	Name	P.L.	Stat.	U.S.C.	Description	Report No.
Dec. 17, 2002	E-Government Act of 2002	P.L. 107-347	116 Stat. 2899	5 U.S.C. Chapter 37; 44 U.S.C. § 3501 nt, Chapter 35, Subchapter 2, and Chapter 36	Serves as the primary legislative vehicle to guide federal IT management and initiatives to make information and services available online. Established the Office of Electronic Government within OMB, the Chief Information Officers (CIO) Council, and a government/private-sector personnel exchange program; includes FISMA; established and contains various other requirements for security and protection of confidential information.	RS20185
Dec. 4, 2003	Fair and Accurate Credit Transactions Act of 2003	P.L. 108-159	117 Stat. 1952	See 15 U.S.C. § 1601 nt. for affected provisions	Required the FTC and other agencies to develop guidelines for identity theft prevention programs in financial institutions, including "red flags" indicating possible identity theft.	
Dec. 16, 2003	Controlling the Assault of Non-Solicited Pornography and Marketing (CANSPAM) Act of 2003	P.L. 108-187	117 Stat. 2699	15 U.S.C. Chapter 103, §§ 7701–7713 18 U.S.C. 1037	Imposed regulations on the transmission of unsolicited commercial e-mail, including prohibitions against predatory and abusive e-mail, and false or misleading transmission of information.	
July 15, 2004	Identity Theft Penalty Enhancement Act 2004	P.L. 108-275	118 Stat. 831	18 U.S.C. §§ 1028, 1028A	Established penalties for aggravated identity theft.	R40599

(Continued)

Table 5.1 (Continued) Laws Identified as Having Relevant Cybersecurity Provisions

Year	Popular Name	Law	Stat.	U.S.C.	Applicability and Notes	CRC Reports
Dec. 17, 2004	Intelligence Reform and Terrorism Prevention Act of 2004	P.L. 108-458	118 Stat. 3638	42 U.S.C. § 2000ee 50 U.S.C. § 403-1 et seq., § 403-3 et seq., § 404o et. seq.	Created the position of Director of National Intelligence (DNI). Established mission responsibilities for some entities in the intelligence, homeland security, and national security communities and established a Privacy and Civil Liberties Board within the Executive Office of the President.	
Aug. 8, 2005	Energy Policy Act of 2005	P.L. 109-58	119 Stat. 594	16 U.S.C. 824o	Requires FERC to certify an Electric Reliability Organization to establish and enforce reliability standards for bulk electric-power system facilities.	R41886
Oct. 4, 2006	Department of Homeland Security Appropriations Act, 2007	P.L. 109-295	120 Stat. 1355	6 U.S.C. § 121 nt.	§ 550 required the Secretary of Homeland Security to issue regulations (6 C.F.R. Part 27) establishing risk-based performance standards for security of chemical facilities; regulations include cybersecurity standards requirement (6 C.F.R. § 27.230(a)(8)).	
Aug. 5, 2007	Protect America Act of 2007	P.L. 110-55	121 Stat. 552	50 U.S.C. § 1801 nt.	Provided authority for the Attorney General and the DNI to gather foreign intelligence information on persons believed to be overseas. The act expired in 2008.	

Date		P.L.	Stat.	U.S.C.		
Dec. 19, 2007	Energy Independence and Security Act of 2007	P.L. 110-140	121 Stat. 1492	42 U.S.C. §§ 17381–17385	Gave NIST primary responsibility for developing interoperability standards for the electric-power "smart grid."	R41886
July 10, 2008	Foreign Intelligence Surveillance Act of 1978 (FISA) Amendments Act of 2008	P.L. 110-261	122 Stat. 2436	See 50 U.S.C. § 1801 nt. for affected provisions	Added additional procedures to FISA for acquisition of communications of persons outside the United States.	98-326
Sep. 26, 2008	Identity Theft Enforcement and Restitution Act of 2008	P.L. 110-326	122 Stat. 356	18 U.S.C. § 1030	Authorized restitution to identity theft victims and modified some of the activities and penalties covered by 18 U.S.C. 1030.	R40599 97-1025
Feb. 17, 2009	Health Information Technology for Economic and Clinical Health Act	P.L. 111-5 (Title XIII of Div. A and Title IV of Div. B)	123 Stat. 226	42 U.S.C. § 17901 et seq.	Expanded privacy and security requirements for protected health information by broadening HIPAA breach disclosure notification and privacy requirements to include business associates of covered entities.	R40546

Source: Various sources, including National Research Council. *Toward a Safer and More Secure Cyberspace.* National Academy Press, Washington, DC, 2007; The White House. Cyberspace Policy Review. May 29, 2009. Available at http://www.whitehouse.gov/assets/documents/Cyberspace_Policy _Review_final.pdf; and CRS, Congressional Research Services.

Note: Prepared by Rita Tehan, Information Research Specialist (rtehan@crs.loc.gov,7-6739) and Eric A. Fischer.

5.5   International Comprehensive Cybersecurity Strategy

While there are a number of international organizations creating alliances among member nations throughout the world,[55] two international bodies whose efforts heighten worldwide awareness about security in the growing cyber environment and increased development and access to Internet connectivity are the United Nations (UN) and the North Atlantic Treaty Organization (NATO). NATO coordinates and complements its efforts in support of its politico-military mission to provide a strategic and unified defense for its European members with the UN.[56]

5.5.1   UN Cybersecurity Policy and Strategy

The UN is an international organization created on October 24, 1945, for the purpose of keeping peace, developing "friendly relations among nations," helping "nations work together to improve the lives of poor people," and coordinating the efforts of nations to "achieve these goals."[57] There are presently 193 nations who are UN members. Since the UN does not wield any authority over its member nations to enforce its global mission, the UN, as an international organization, essentially acts as a "norm entrepreneur"[58] and agent of change to its member nations and the world at large, providing research and suggested models concerning a variety of issues, including cybersecurity and international governance of the Internet. Chapter 3, Article 7, of the UN Charter establishes six principal organs to operate and self-govern: General Assembly, Security Council, Economic and Social Council, Trusteeship Council, International Court of Justice, and a Secretariat.[59] Chapter 4, Article 22, permits the principal organs to establish additional committees or subsidiaries to assist them, as needed, in the performance of their duties.[60] Chapter 9, Article 57,[61] establishes the use of specialized agencies that are governed by interagency agreements from the Economic and Social Council pursuant to Chapter 10, Article 63.[62]

The Internet Governance Forum (IGF) and the ITU are two of the primary international multistakeholder advisory entities operating under the UN umbrella, responsible for researching, collaborating, and advising on global issues involving Internet governance and cybersecurity. While neither the IGF nor the ITU possesses any authority to create or enforce any laws, both IGF and ITU operate as "think-tanks" that collaborate and collect ideas, input, and research from multiple sources, such as academicians, private industry, government officials, general public, advocacy groups, and others, to recommend best industry practices to be cyber safe and keeping the Internet "borderless" and accessible to all global citizens.[63,64]

The IGF operates as an open multistakeholder forum where global public and private individuals and entities can meet to discuss topics and issues of concern that impact Internet governance. The IGF was established in 2006 by the Secretary-General, head of the UN Secretariat, "to support the United Nations Secretary-General in carrying out the mandate from the World Summit on the Information Society (WSIS) with regard to convening a new forum for multi-stakeholder policy dialogue."[65]

Based on its initial mission mandate, IGF provides a multistakeholder advisory forum where global private and public stakeholders can discuss "public policy issues relating to key elements of Internet governance in order to foster the sustainability, robustness, security, stability and development of the Internet,"[66] among other issues, such as emerging concerns affecting everyday users of the Internet and promoting the adoption and implementation of WSIS principles in Internet governance processes. Besides creating a global open discussion forum, IGF provides an outlet for regional and national IGF groups to communicate, publish reports, and discuss issues related to individual regions, as well as supply free training and educational materials relating to e-government and Internet governance policies. In meeting its mandate to the UN Secretary-General, IGF hosts an annual conference where emerging issues and topics relating or impacting Internet governance are presented, which can be attended in person and via online broadcasts.

In contrast to the IGF, the ITU is a direct agency of the UN, and "its membership includes 191 Member States and more than 700 Sector Members and Associates."[67] The ITU represents three core sectors in its role as leading the UN for information and communication technologies: radio communication, standardization, and development.[68] According to Article 1 of the ITU's Constitution, the ITU's mission can be summarized as follows: (1) to promote the use of telecommunications to developing nations, (2) to foster cooperation and participation by member nations to enhance and improve the use of telecommunications, (3) to provide technical assistance and develop efficient technical facilities to create broader access by the public, and (4) to encourage international participation in and adoption of a broader approach in tackling telecommunication issues.[69]

The ITU is headed by a General Secretariat and governed by a Council, which acts on behalf of the Plenipotentiary Conference, the primary governing body whose membership is composed of delegates from member nations and meets only every four years. The ITU is additionally composed of world conferences and three sector boards: radio communication sector, telecommunication standardization sector, and telecommunication development sector.[70] The ITU Constitution empowers the ITU to "undertake studies, make regulations, adopt resolutions, formulate recommendations and opinions, and collect and publish information concerning telecommunication matters"[71] in operationalizing its stated purposes.

In 2012, the ITU took the lead in sponsoring the World Conference on International Telecommunications (WCIT), held in Dubai, where the 1988 International Telecommunications Regulations (ITR) were on the agenda to be reviewed and amended.[72] The ITU believed that the 1988 ITR needed review and revisions to update them to the significant changes resulting from the increased use and ubiquity of wireless communications and interoperability of telecommunications equipment and lines between nations.[73] The 2012 ITR, which were approved by 89 members at the WCIT, contained several provisions that raised serious controversy among developed member states, such as Canada, the United States, and the EU.

Before the adoption of the 2012 proposed ITR, the European Parliament ("Euro Parliament") issued Resolution 2012/2881 encouraging its 27 members to reject the proposed 2012 ITR primarily because the Euro Parliament believed that several revised provisions to the ITR were not in the best interest of a free and open Internet by establishing interconnection charging mechanisms to access data residing extraterritorial, that neither the ITU nor any other centralized entity was the appropriate entity to regulate the Internet, and that based on the nature of the proposals, the ITU could itself regulate the Internet.[74] The United States voiced its disagreement with the proposed ITR early on, particularly because of the proposed interconnection charging mechanisms, which the United States and U.S. Internet corporations, such as Google, Facebook, and others, believed charging access fees would block the free flow of information and communications for Internet users worldwide.

Ultimately, a majority of the Western developed member states refused to sign the proposed treaty, including the United States, "citing an inability to resolve an impasse over the Internet."[75] Refusing to sign the proposed treaty permits those member states to continue to be covered under the 1988 treaty, and therefore, they are not subject to the terms and conditions specified in the new 2012 treaty. For any member state who signed the 2012 treaty working with a member state who did not sign the 2012 treaty, both member states are bound only by the terms of the 1988 treaty, leaving developing nation member states to follow the fortunes of the developed nation member states. Despite the number of nation members who refused to sign, the ITU adopted the 2012 treaty, essentially covering 60% of the world's population under the new agreement.[76]

It is a relatively recent development that a consensus of UN members has rated cyber threats against member constituents and systems as one of the more significant concerns facing the world today.[77] Maurer pins increased UN attention and escalation of cyber threats to the forefront beginning in 1998 because the Russian government first introduced a cyber crime resolution to the General Assembly and an exponential growth explosion in the Internet began in 1998.[78]

5.5.2 NATO Cybersecurity Policy and Strategy

NATO was created as a result of the signing of the North American Treaty ("Treaty") on April 4, 1949, following continued Soviet challenges to the security of newly established nations that were attempting to recover from the devastation of Europe from World War II. Presently, NATO is composed of 28 nations in Europe and North America.[79] Subsequent to its creation, NATO has provided politico-military support, training, education, and peace-keeping to the member nations that have been subject to attack or external conflict. While NATO emphasizes peace first and foremost in resolving potential conflict among nations, the Treaty provides a strong measure of solidarity in the alliance by linking adverse action to all members in the event of attack to one nation member. This important linchpin is reflected in Article 5 of the North American Treaty:

> The Parties agree that an armed attack against one or more of them in Europe or North America shall be considered an attack against them all and consequently they agree that, if such an armed attack occurs, each of them, in exercise of the right of individual or collective self-defence recognised by Article 51 of the Charter of the United Nations, will assist the Party or Parties so attacked by taking forthwith, individually and in concert with the other Parties, such action as it deems necessary, including the use of armed force, to restore and maintain the security of the North Atlantic area.[80]

This solidarity of security to NATO members extends to and may be triggered by cyber attacks, which NATO addresses individually through its members' networks, an articulated cybersecurity strategy,[81] and the NATO Cooperative Cyber Defense Centre of Excellence located in Tallinn, Estonia.[82] On December 27, 2013, the UN has specifically identified that conduct in cyber space is subject to international law,[83] thereby strengthening the impact and current applicability of NATO's Article 5 in the event of nation-sponsored or initiated cyber attacks against NATO members.

5.5.3 EU Data Protection

The EU is an economic and political international body composed of 28 European member states whose representatives democratically govern through various interconnected institutions, the primary ones being the Euro Parliament, Council of European Union ("EU Council"), and the European Commission ("EU Commission"). According to its website,[84] the

Euro Parliament is composed of members who are directly elected by voters of the EU every five years.

> Parliament is one of the EU's main law-making institutions, along with the Council of the European Union ("the Council"). The European Parliament has three main roles:
>
> - Debating and passing European laws, with the Council
> - Scrutinizing other EU institutions, particularly the Commission, to make sure they are working democratically
> - Debating and adopting the EU's budget, with the Council.[85]

The EU Council is the governmental body composed of national ministers from each EU member country who "meet to adopt laws and coordinate policies." The EU Council is charged with approving the annual budget, passing EU laws, coordinating economic policies of member countries, executing agreements between the EU and other nations, developing foreign and defense policies for the EU, and fostering cooperation between prosecutive and law enforcement entities of member nations.[86] The EU Commission operates for the purpose of representing the interests of the EU as a whole.

The legal authority through which the governing bodies of the EU operate is based in two primary treaties, which bestow the authority and power to issue regulations, directives, decisions, recommendations, and opinions. As opposed to a regulation, an issued directive is "a legislative act that sets out a goal that all EU countries must achieve. However, it is up to the individual countries to decide how."[87] Pursuant to former Article 7(a) of the Treaty of the European Union,[88] the Euro Parliament and EU Council issued Directive 95/46/EC (the "Data Protection Directive") on October 24, 1995, on the protection of the personal data of individuals and the free movement of such data through the EU.[89]

Instead of a hodgepodge of statutes enacted to protect personal data as these relate to specific industries, as is the case in the U.S. statutory scheme, the Data Protection Directive establishes a broad, overarching framework for EU member states to adopt or interrelate with their own personal data protection legal scheme. The two primary objectives of the Data Protection Directive were "to protect the fundamental right to data protection and to guarantee the free flow of personal data between Member States."[90] In furtherance of these objectives, the Data Protection Directive offers descriptions of conditions, criteria, responsibilities, and data relevancy relating to the collection, processing, access, retention, and use of personal individual information for EU citizens, and the rights of those individuals over how their personal data are collected, processed, accessed, handled, and retained.[91] The Data Protection Directive sets benchmarks for data protection for its member states to achieve through its own regulatory processes and creates general processes whereby EU citizens can restrict or remove their personal data from the public. Many of the EU member states have already established laws and regulations relating to an individual citizen's right to their personal data and the protection of that data.[92] The Data Protection Directive excludes protection of personal data under Article 13 when there is a specific need to protect public and national security and other limited situations, as described below:

> Member States may adopt legislative measures to restrict the scope of the obligations and rights provided for in Articles 6(1), 10, 11(1), 12 and 21 when such a restriction constitutes a necessary measure to safeguard:
>
> a. National security;
> b. Defence;
> c. Public security;
> d. The prevention, investigation, detection and prosecution of criminal offences, or of breaches of ethics for regulated professions;
> e. An important economic or financial interest of a Member State or of the European Union, including monetary, budgetary and taxation matters;
> f. A monitoring, inspection or regulatory function connected, even occasionally, with the exercise of official authority in cases referred to in (c), (d) and (e);
> g. The protection of the data subject or of the rights and freedoms of others.[93]

Framework Decision 2008/977/JHA ("LE Data Protection") describes the protections that are to be utilized by law enforcement and prosecutorial entities when such entities need to share personal data of EU citizens when cooperating with other law enforcement and prosecutorial entities in conducting criminal investigations and prosecutions.[94]

In furtherance of Article 29 of the Data Protection Directive, the Euro Parliament and EU Council adopted Regulation 45/2001 on December 18, 2000, which established legally enforceable rights for individuals in the protection of their personal data and created data processing obligations over member states and a "supervisory authority responsible for monitoring the processing of personal data."[95] On the same date, the Euro Parliament reaffirmed the importance of an EC citizen's fundamental right to data protection by specifically embodying this right as Article 8 of its Charter of Fundamental Rights of the European Union ("EU Charter"), which states, in pertinent part:

> 1. Everyone has the right to the protection of personal data concerning him or her.
> 2. Such data must be processed fairly for specified purposes and on the basis of the consent of the person concerned or some other legitimate

basis laid down by law. Everyone has the right of access to data which has been collected concerning him or her, and the right to have it rectified.

3. Compliance with these rules shall be subject to control by an independent authority.[96]

In recent years, the Orders of the EU Court of Justice, the highest level of judicial appeal for EU citizens, have interpreted the language of Article 7(f) of the Data Protection Directive with that of Article 8 of the EU Charter to create a distinct and powerful individual right of data protection that precludes laws of member states that seek to release personal data without the consent of the individual even when such data have already been published in the public domain.[97]

As a result of the dynamic nature of the Internet and the constantly changing technological development impacting the collection, use, and distribution of electronic data and the potential erosion of the ability of the Data Protection Directive to protect personal data, on January 25, 2012, the EU Commission released its proposal on the issuance of a regulation that would initiate a new framework for personal data protection. The proposed regulation contains five primary components: (1) territorial scope ensuring a fundamental right to data protection no matter the geophysical location of the business or its servers, (2) international transfers permitted where data protection is ensured, (3) enforcement where significant fines are imposed on foreign businesses failing to comply with EU data protection rights, (4) cloud computing data processors subject to clear rules on obligations and liabilities, and (5) establishment of comprehensive rules for the protection of personal data shared with law enforcement.[98]

After the whistleblower disclosures concerning the intelligence surveillance activities of the U.S. National Security Agency (NSA), on November 27, 2013, the EU Commission set forth a series of steps designed to restore trust in data flows between the United States and EU,[99] with the centerpiece again focusing on a renewed emphasis to pass uniform international data protection reform. The EU Commission proposed that the following actions be taken immediately concerning data sharing between EU and U.S. law enforcement partners:

1. A swift adoption of the EU's data protection reform
2. Making Safe Harbor safe
3. Strengthening data protection safeguards in the law enforcement area
4. Using the existing Mutual Legal Assistance and Sectorial agreements to obtain data

5. Addressing European concerns in the on-going U.S. reform process
6. Promoting privacy standards internationally.[100]

The Safe Harbor Framework "allows for the provision of solutions for transfers of personal data in situations where other tools would not be available or not practical."[101] Galexia, a private specialist management firm, describes the U.S. Safe Harbor as

an agreement between the European Commission and the United States Department of Commerce that enables organisations to join a Safe Harbor List to demonstrate their compliance with the European Union Data Protection Directive. This allows the transfer of personal data to the US in circumstances where the transfer would otherwise not meet the European adequacy test for privacy protection.[102]

Pursuant to the U.S. Safe Harbor, U.S. businesses operating under the U.S. Safe Harbor are required to certify with the U.S. Department of Commerce that those businesses comply with the Safe Harbor Framework. However, in a 2008 report by Galexia, who conducted the limited review of U.S. businesses certifying themselves as Safe Harbor compliant, Galexia identified serious concerns with the administration of the U.S. Safe Harbor, in particular, relating to transparency, adherence to the Framework Principles, and enforcement efforts by the relevant U.S. agencies.[103] After the discovery of the NSA intelligence surveillance activities, the EU Commission issued a communication relating to the functioning of the Safe Harbor where it determined that "EU–U.S. Safe Harbor Framework lacked transparency and effective enforcement, and recommended revising the Framework."[104] As of March 10, 2014, the Euro Parliament has suspended the Safe Harbor Framework, as well as the Terrorist Finance Tracking Program; however, the authority to renegotiate and/or cancel these agreements rests with the EU Commission.[105]

The EU Commission's earlier January 2012 reform proposal introduced a "right to be forgotten" on the Internet as one of the primary changes to the existing framework established under the Data Protection Directive.[106] According to the EU Commission proposal, Article 17 of the proposed regulation requires a data controller to erase individual personal data and to abstain from republishing the data under specific grounds. Such grounds include obsolescence, incompatibility, or changes to the need and purpose for the data; the data subject withdraws consent to the initial basis of processing or the storage period exceeds what was consented to; the data subject objects to data processing on other legal grounds; and the data processing is not compliant under the Regulation.[107] While the Euro Parliament and Council have not issued a regulation as proposed by the

EU Commission, the "right to be forgotten" has created a hot debate globally about the right to information versus the "right to be forgotten" on the Internet.[108,109]

Despite the absence of an EU Regulation, the EU Court of Justice has recently enforced the concept of the "right to be forgotten" based on the current provisions of the Data Protection Directive. On May 13, 2014, the EU Court of Justice ordered Google, Inc., and its global subsidiaries ("Google") doing business with the EU to honor individual EU citizen requests to erase personal data from the Google search engines.[110] A Spanish citizen had requested that Google remove search results that linked his name to a notice in a local newspaper for an auction of real property to pay for debts he owed approximately 16 years earlier.[111]

In essence, the Court held that as a search engine, Google has a greater obligation to create "interference" by removing those links from its search engine results when an individual has requested to have data removed, even though the personal data were in the public domain and could be accessed directly from the newspaper's records. According to the Court, Google, as

the operator of a search engine is obliged to remove from the list of results displayed following a search made on the basis of a person's name links to web pages, published by third parties and containing information relating to that person, also in a case where that name or information is not erased beforehand or simultaneously from those web pages, and even, as the case may be, when its publication in itself on those pages is lawful.[112]

In the case at bar, the Court determined that the interest of the public to information and Google's business interests in the data were trumped by the data subject's "right to be forgotten" because

Those rights override, as a rule, not only the economic interest of the operator of the search engine but also the interest of the general public in having access to that information upon a search relating to the data subject's name. However, that would not be the case if it appeared, for particular reasons, such as the role played by the data subject in public life, that the interference with his fundamental rights is justified by the preponderant interest of the general public in having, on account of its inclusion in the list of results, access to the information in question.[113]

While Google is presently struggling to identify an appropriate business solution whereby it can comply with the Court's order with respect to its EU operations,[114] the holding has far-reaching implications involving the use of the personal data of EU citizens for non-EU technology firms, like Yahoo! and Facebook, and governmental organizations involved in investigating and prosecuting criminal matters.

5.6   Issues Involving Electronic Data Collection for Law Enforcement Purposes

In general, electronic evidence sought by U.S. law enforcement and prosecutorial entities usually falls under some umbrella of protected personal data that are in the possession of government organizations, such as the Social Security Administration, or nongovernmental organizations, such as financial institutions, health care entities, telecommunications carriers, Internet service providers (ISPs), data storage providers, and others, all of which have statutory constraints relating to the access or use of protected personal data. Statutory hurdles and constitutional Fourth Amendment challenges must be overcome by U.S. federal law enforcement and prosecutorial agencies and approved by the Attorney General or court approved, to conduct lawful wiretaps to intercept the content of the subject electronic communications both in criminal and intelligence matters.[115] Once approved by a federal court of competent jurisdiction, failure to comply with the order to produce electronic communications by a "telecommunications carrier, a manufacturer of telecommunications transmission or switching equipment, or a provider of telecommunications support services" subjects the violator to substantial civil penalties.[116] With respect to obtaining electronically stored information, U.S. authorities must follow other Fourth Amendment right to privacy statutory requirements set forth in the federal Stored Communications Act (SCA).[117]

As opposed to the piecemeal U.S. legal framework providing data protection under limited circumstances, the EU has adopted a sweeping fundamental individual right of data privacy, and, as noted earlier, requests to use or share the personal data of EU citizens must fall within the requisite exceptions noted in Article 13 of the Data Protection Directive.[118] If law enforcement and prosecutorial entities satisfy those requirements, then those entities must additionally and adequately comply with the data processing procedures required in the LE Data Protection.[119] Other than specific instances identified in the LE Data Protection, information sharing of personal data for criminal matters among the law enforcement entities of member states is controlled primarily by mutual legal assistance treaties (MLATs). In the case of the U.S. Customs and Border Patrol, a division of DHS, the European Community entered into an agreement with DHS in which DHS agreed to various undertakings in an effort to satisfy the specific data processing procedures required under the Data Protection Directive so that international airlines could transmit personal data involving EU airline passengers to DHS.[120]

The actual geophysical location of the computer server where the electronic data reside has posed potential extraterritorial jurisdictional issues for both U.S. and international law enforcement personnel entities in cases where law enforcement has been authorized to obtain specific electronic evidence. Because there are no geophysical boundaries in cyberspace where electronic data are stored, U.S. and international laws have not yet been adapted to effectively address the extraterritoriality of electronic evidence.

In a recent federal case in New York, Microsoft Corporation petitioned the court to quash a search warrant that had been issued in the Southern District of New York seeking certain electronic communications from the ISP Microsoft. Microsoft asserted that it did not have to produce a client's e-mail communications because those e-mails were stored at their data center in Dublin, Ireland. As such, Microsoft contended that "courts in the United States are not authorized to issue warrants for extraterritorial search and seizure, and that this is such a warrant."[121] The court identified language within the warrant language that related to Microsoft's control and dominion over the stored information as being operative factors in denying Microsoft's request in this case.

> That warrant authorizes the search and seizure of information associated with a specified web-based e-mail account that is 'stored at premises owned, maintained, controlled, or operated by Microsoft Corporation, a company headquartered at One Microsoft Way, Redmond, WA.[122]

After reviewing the statutory language of the SCA, the court analyzed Microsoft's simple argument that the government obtained a search warrant in accordance with the SCA and that "federal courts are without authority to issue warrants for the search and seizure of property outside the territorial limits of the United States"[123] in light of the SCA's structure, legislative history, and the "practical consequences" that would result from Microsoft's argument.[124] According to the court's interpretation of the SCA,

> The SCA created "a set of Fourth Amendment-like privacy protections by statute, regulating the relationship between government investigators and service providers in possession of users' private information." Id. at 1212. Because there were no constitutional limits on an ISP's disclosure of its customer's data, and because the Government could likely obtain such data with a subpoena that did not require a showing of probable cause, Congress placed limitations on the service providers' ability to disclose information and, at the same time, defined the means that the Government could use to obtain it. See id. at 1209-13.[125]

The court reasoned that an SCA warrant is not a conventional search warrant but instead a

> Hybrid: part search warrant and part subpoena. It is obtained like a search warrant when an application is made to a neutral magistrate who issues the

order only upon a showing of probable cause. On the other hand, it is executed like a subpoena in that it is served on the ISP in possession of the information and does not involve government agents entering the premises of the ISP to search its servers and seize the e-mail account in question.[126]

As a result of its hybrid structure, the court postulated that the warrant did not "implicate principles of extraterritoriality"[127] and noted that, historically, case law has held "that a subpoena requires the recipient to produce information in its possession, custody, or control regardless of the location of that information."[128] The court ultimately determined that an SCA warrant does not implicate the "presumption against extraterritorial application of American law"[129] in that the warrant seeks to "obtain account information from domestic service providers who happen to store that information overseas."[130] After the April 25, 2014, order, Microsoft has appealed the order, which had not yet been argued and decided at publication date. The court's ruling and analysis carry potentially significant ramifications for cloud and domestic ISPs whose stored electronic data the government seeks to obtain under the SCA and definitely present an insider's view into how little Fourth Amendment right to privacy protections exist for electronic data stored on domestic or international servers.[131] In citing Orin Kerr's "A User's Guide to the Stored Communications Act" and referencing the article's discussions about the lack of Fourth Amendment privacy protections in communications revealed to third parties, the court incorporated the Third Party Doctrine into its legal reasoning process.[132,133] The Third Party Doctrine

> Provides that when an individual knowingly supplies information to a third party, his expectation of privacy is diminished because that person is assuming the risk that the third party may reveal the information to government authorities. As a result, information imparted to third parties generally falls outside the scope of Fourth Amendment protection and, accordingly, the government can access this information by requesting or subpoenaing it without informing the party under investigation.[134]

Since the search warrant the government sought to enforce was obtained pursuant to the SCA, the court found no need to analyze the impact of the Third Party Doctrine in the case at bar as the SCA, by its very provisions, imbues Fourth Amendment protections to e-mail communications revealed to third parties, which may not have received such protections.

The current U.S. legal view that e-mail communications revealed to third parties, as is the case with big data and cloud computing storage providers and ISPs, are not afforded the same Fourth Amendment privacy protections puts U.S. data storage and ISPs squarely at a distinct disadvantage with their EU-based counterparts, in that U.S. businesses, as presently structured, cannot provide the level of data privacy required by the EU Data Protection

Directive. EU domiciled data storage and ISP businesses, while subject to the EU fundamental individual right to data protection and the "right to be forgotten" on the Internet, are not subject to U.S. court orders, subpoenas, or search warrants. While U.S. domiciled data storage and ISP business may have enjoyed a competitive advantage over their EU counterparts in the past because participation in the U.S. Safe Harbor Framework is not as stringently enforced, that advantage has now vanished.

As discussed earlier, U.S. criminal investigative agencies, such as DHS, must work through MLATs or other EU-approved information sharing agreements that meet the stringent requirements of the legal authority, tenets, and policies of the EU. If upheld on appeal, Judge Francis' holding provides U.S. criminal investigative agencies with a legal basis under the SCA to reach electronic data from U.S. domiciled businesses that are stored on servers geophysically positioned far from the borders of American jurisprudence. The disclosure of intelligence surveillance of U.S. businesses by the NSA, the legal case law supporting the premise of little, if any, expectation of privacy in communications revealed to third parties (essentially affecting all U.S. enterprises doing business in the EU), and the failure of U.S. agencies to effectively administer the provisions of the Safe Harbor Framework have contributed to the EU's lack of trust and confidence in representations made by U.S. officials to the contrary.

Microsoft's decision to appeal Judge Francis' ruling comes on the heels of the ongoing EU–U.S. negotiations relating to an international framework for data protections, referred to as the "Data Protection Umbrella Agreement" (DPUA),[135] all of which have received heightened scrutiny as a result of the NSA surreptitious surveillance activities. Among other data protection requirements, the DPUA seeks to provide EU citizens who do not reside in the United States with the same right of judicial redress as U.S. nationals in the EU receive.[136] In general, a provisional agreement has been reached that does not authorize any data transfer but "include the scope and purpose of the agreement, fundamental principles and oversight mechanisms."[137] The United States reports seeking legislative changes to obtain the changes sought by the EU.

5.7 Whistleblower or Criminal Leaker?

In general, whistleblowers provide a window of transparency into the potential illegal activity occurring within an organization and, by doing so, serves the "public's right to know" about individual or group misconduct occurring within government or nongovernment organizations, misconduct that may be illegal or prohibited. In some cases, employees may be in the unique position of being the only eyewitnesses to gross, unethical, and illegal misconduct within an organization, putting them squarely in the crosshairs of those who hide the truth of their activities, thereby thrusting those employee witnesses into choosing to remain silent to protect their careers or blowing the whistle to protect the public and, in some cases, the organization. So, are whistle-blowers really heroes or villains? Do they serve an important purpose in the realm of cybersecurity, or are they a distraction and nuisance? At first blush, the answer to all of these questions seems to be in the affirmative.

The actions of whistleblowers can, in fact, shine a beacon of light into an otherwise dark, unexposed corner of an organization where inappropriate conduct, misconduct, or criminal activity exists within an entity. Whistleblowers may be employees, contractors, vendors, or consultants who are in a position to have received information of potential wrongdoing by an organization. According to the 2014 Report to the Nations by the Association of Certified Fraud Examiners, tips are the most common way in which occupational fraud schemes are detected, with over 40% of reported cases detected as the result of a tip and over half of those tips reported by employees of the organization.[138] While approximately 14% are anonymous, the remainder of tipster's whistleblowing are known to the organization.[139]

On the flip side of the coin, disgruntled employees, information technology employees, and contractors comprise the most common categories of individual insider threats for the exfiltration of confidential or classified data.[140] The CERT Insider Threat Center states that

> a malicious insider is a current or former employee, contractor, or other business partner who has or had authorized access to an organization's network, system, or data and intentionally exceeded or misused that access in a manner that negatively affected the confidentiality, integrity, or availability of the organization's information or information systems.[141]

In the realm of cybersecurity, an individual may, in fact, be categorized as both a whistleblower and a malicious insider based on the facts and circumstances of the event, characterizations that fit the case of Chelsea Manning (formerly known as Bradley Manning) and Edward Snowden, both of whom exfilitrated large amounts of classified data from protected U.S. computer systems.[142] In the case of Manning, she electronically submitted the removed data to WikiLeaks, a known leaking organization, while in the case of Snowden, he delivered the data to a news media outlet.

Manning was an Army intelligence analyst stationed in Iraq during the Iraq war and had authorized access to the classified defense and diplomatic databases available through the protected U.S. computer networks. From November 2009 through April 2010, Manning exfiltrated from protected U.S. computer networks approximately 250,000 diplomatic cables, over 400,000 records belonging to the Department of Defense, and battle videos, among other classified records, which Manning delivered to WikiLeaks for publication on their Internet website.[143] Manning was convicted in July 2013 of numerous violations of the Uniform Code of Military Justice,[144] which included federal charges of espionage under the Espionage Act of 1917, 18 U.S.C. § 793; fraud and related activities in relation to computers pursuant to Title, 18 U.S.C. § 1030; and theft of government property pursuant to Title, 18 U.S.C. § 641.[145] As a result, Manning was sentenced to serve 35 years and received a dishonorable discharge.[146]

On the other hand, Snowden was at one time an employee of the Central Intelligence Agency and later the NSA before becoming an employee of several intelligence contractors. At the time of his NSA disclosures, Snowden was an employee of Booz Allen Hamilton, a private consulting firm contracted with NSA, and he previously had worked in the same capacity for Dell, another NSA contractor.[147] As a contracted intelligence analyst, Snowden had access to protected U.S. computer systems containing classified data, and from which he exfilitrated confidential and classified data concerning NSA's surveillance activities in the global and domestic bulk warrantless collection of electronic communications. While not yet determined, Snowden then made between 200,000 and 1.7 million classified documents available to media outlets. On June 13, 2013, a federal criminal complaint was issued charging Snowden with similar charges as those Manning faced, that is, two counts of espionage under the 1917 Espionage Act, Title, 18 U.S.C. §§ 793, 798, and theft of government property, in violation of Title, 18 U.S.C. § 641.[148]

Although Manning and Snowden have been criminally charged, they both have asserted that they are whistleblowers, who disclosed classified information to the public believing that the public has a right to know what their government is doing in their name.[149,150] The Military Whistleblower Protection Act (MWPA), Title, 10 U.S.C. § 1038, was available to Manning, but it does not appear that Manning sought its protection before she downloaded confidential and classified documents and released them to WikiLeaks. No whistleblower protections exist for those employees of federal contractors, such as Snowden. As a result of the recent disclosures of classified materials, a flurry of legislative bills have been proposed to reform MWPA and the Whistleblower Protection Enhancement Act of 2012 (WPEA), Title, 5 U.S.C. § 2302(b) (8), which encompasses federal employees but not contractors.[151,152]

Despite the proposed changes, the reporting requirements under both statutes mandate the audience to whom a whistleblower must report in order to receive the protections from retaliation under the statutes. The WPEA provides a broader reporting audience, while the proposed changes to the MWPA would expand the audiences for protected disclosures "to include testimony to congressional and law enforcement staff, courts, grand jury and court martial proceedings."[153] The proposed changes come a little too late to benefit Manning, who had, in fact, defended her actions as a whistleblower during her court martial proceedings in June 2013.[154,155]

Nonetheless, this begs the question as to whether or not an enhanced MWPA or WPEA would have protected Manning and Snowden from facing criminal charges.[156] The simple answer to that question is probably no. No whistleblower antiretaliation provisions can protect a covered reporter when there are perceived potential violations of related statutes implicating state secrecy or the national defense, which has been particularly true with leakers who have been criminally prosecuted during the presidency of Barack Obama. More whistleblowers have been criminally prosecuted during this presidency than in any other. Moreover, there appears to have been greater overreaching by the U.S. government in its efforts to charge whistleblowers with some criminal offense or to investigate them for years with no resulting charges filed.[157,158]

Materials related to the national defense, whether classified or not, that are released without authorization to parties who are not authorized to receive them can potentially subject the individual leaking such materials to criminal sanctions pursuant to a legal framework structured similarly to the hodgepodge design of those statutes related to cybersecurity, with individual statutes addressing the disclosure of certain types of confidential, protected information.

> While there is no one statute that criminalizes the unauthorized disclosure of any classified information, a patchwork of statutes exists to protect information depending upon its nature, the identity of the discloser and of those to whom it was disclosed, and the means by which it was obtained.[159]

As a result, a leaker can be charged under various provisions of the 1917 Espionage Act, Title, 18 U.S.C. §§ 793–798, as fit the pertinent facts and circumstances related to the subject criteria. Violators convicted under the Espionage Act can be subject to a minimum penalty of up to 1 year in prison with a fine to a maximum sentence of the death sentence, depending on the provisions charged.[160] Leakers may also face additional charges, such as Title, 18 U.S.C. § 1030 (a)(1), Excess of authorized access to computer; Title, 18 U.S.C. § 641, Theft or conversion of government property; Title, 50 U.S.C. § 3121, Intelligence Identities Protection Act; Title, 18 U.S.C. § 1924, Unauthorized removal of classified material; Title, 18 U.S.C. § 952, Unauthorized release of diplomatic code; Title, 50 U.S.C. § 783, Unauthorized release of classified information to foreign governments; and Title, 18 U.S.C. § 371, Conspiracy, when more than one individual violator is involved.

As the world advances technologically into a networked global environment, the criminal prosecution of a whistleblower who leaks information to an unauthorized party may result in unintended consequences for the

United States, particularly when facts demonstrate that no action was ever taken to stop the misconduct after the proper officials had been notified and when the leaked information clearly substantiates the misconduct identified by the whistleblower. The government's aggressive pursuit of criminal prosecution against leakers under such circumstances does raise the specter of punishment and retribution and pits the concept of state secrecy based on claims of national defense and security against the public's right to know the truth about its government's activities.[161]

5.8   Concluding Comments

The need and ability to appropriately address the cybersecurity needs of a networked virtual global environment in a manner that comports with domestic and international legal frameworks will escalate as new technology develops and impacts citizenry worldwide. The U.S. legal framework for cybersecurity is complex, is cumbersome to interpret and apply, lacks uniformly accepted concise definitions, and by its static nature, is brittle and inflexible, impeding its ability to grow and develop consistent with the quick growth and rapidly changing technological landscape. The majority of U.S. statutes involving cybersecurity are designed to protect personal data from unauthorized disclosures to unauthorized third parties; however, the application of those statutes is limited to personal data collected only by specific business sectors. In contrast, the EU, through its Charter, has created a fundamental right of individual data protection, which cuts across every business sector, and sets uniform criteria that give EU citizens the ability to remove or correct information. With the continued growth of a networked world, U.S. businesses must satisfy the EU personal data protection requirements, a mandate that will be even more stringently applied as a result of the Snowden disclosures exposing the NSA surveillance activities.

Leaks of classified data during 2010 through 2014 spotlight the disintegration of any identifiable boundaries between the collection of human intelligence to protect national security and that to detect or prevent criminal activity. Snowden's disclosures identifying the massive global surveillance network controlled by the NSA lend credence to the contention that the United States controls worldwide information economics, at least in the domain of global espionage and intelligence gathering, bestowing upon the United States an absolute power based on its "central position in networks."[162] It is this precise type of challenge that the United States and its global neighbors must tackle with wisdom, restraint, respect for individual rights to privacy and balancing transparency of actions against the actual needs to preserve the national defense while simultaneously ensuring the integrity and protection of global cyber assets in a networked world.

Notes and References

1. Excerpted from the foreword by Delon, F. 2008. "French Secretary General for Defence and National Security, to France's Strategy for Cyber Security." Available at http://www.ssi.gouv.fr/IMG/pdf/2011-02-15_Information_system_defence _and_security_-_France_s_strategy.pdf (accessed March 29, 2014).
2. Statistics Reported by Statistics Canada 2012. Available at http://www.statcan .gc.ca/daily-quotidien/130612/dq130612a-eng.htm (accessed March 30, 2014).
3. Moore, J. March 27, 2014. "Turkey YouTube Ban: Full Transcript of Leaked Erdoğan Corruption Call with Son." *International Business Times*. Available at http://www.ibtimes.co.uk/turkey-youtube-bantranscript-leaked-erdogan-corrup tion-call-son-1442150 (accessed March 30, 2014).
4. Boulton, R. and Coskun, O. March 28, 2014. "Turkish Security Breach Exposes Erdoğan in Power Struggle." *Reuters*. Available at http://www.reuters.com/article /2014/03/28/us-turkey-election-idUSBREA2R12X20140328 (accessed March 28, 2014).
5. Moore, J. op. cit.
6. Boulton, R. and Coskun, O. op. cit.
7. The Daily Star. March 30, 2014. "Femen Stages Bare-Breasted Protest Against Turkish PM." *The Daily Star*. Available at http://www.dailystar.com.lb/News /Middle-East/2014/Mar-30/251709-femen-stages-bare-breasted-protest -against-turkish-pm.ashx#axzz2xTVdeiKJ (accessed March 30, 2014).
8. The Mitre Corporation. 2010. "Science of Cyber-Security." JASON Report JSR-10-102, 22. Available at http://www.fas.org/irp/agency/dod/jason/cyber.pdf (accessed January 11, 2014).
9. European Parliament, Directorate General for Internal Policies Policy Department A: Economic and Scientific Policy, Industry, Research and Energy. September 2013. "Data and Security Breaches and Cyber-Security Strategies in the E.U. and Its International Counterparts." IP/A/ITRE/NT/2013-5, PE 507.476, 41. Available at http://www.europarl.euro.eu (accessed January 11, 2014).
10. NATO Cooperative Cyber Defence Center of Excellence. 2013. *Tallinn Manual on the International Law Applicable to Cyber Warfare*, 45. Available at http://issuu .com/nato_ccd_coe/docs/tallinnmanual?e=5903855/1802381# (accessed July 15, 2014).
11. Contreras, J. L., DeNardis, L. and Teplinsky, M. June 2013. "America the Virtual: Security, Privacy, and Interoperability in an Interconnected World: Foreword: Mapping Today's Cybersecurity Landscape." *American University of Law Review*, 48.
12. General Accounting Office. February 2013. "Cybersecurity: National Strategy, Roles and Responsibilities Need to Be Better Defined and More Effectively Implemented." Available at http://www.gao.gov/assets/660/652170.pdf (accessed September 29, 2013).
13. Department of Homeland Security. n.d. *Cybersecurity Results*. Available at http:// www.dhs.gov/cybersecurity-results (accessed January 11, 2014).
14. United States Senate Bill 2105. *The Cybersecurity Act of 2012*, 182–183. Available at https://www.govtrack.us/congress/bills/112/s2105/text (accessed January 13, 2014).
15. Ibid.

16. Committee on National Security Systems. April 2010. "National Information Assurance (IA) Glossary." Available at http://www.cnss.gov/Assets/pdf/cnssi _4009.pdf.

17. For further information concerning the ITU and its recommendations, see http://www.itu.int, International Telecommunications Union. April 2008. "Series X: Data Networks, Open Systems Communications and Security," 2.

18. Satola, D. and Judy, H. September 3, 2010. "Electronic Commerce Law: Towards A Dynamic Approach To Enhancing International Cooperation And Collaboration In Cybersecurity Legal Frameworks: Reflections on the Proceedings of the Workshop on Cybersecurity Legal Issues at the 2010 United Nations Internet Governance Forum." *William Mitchell Law Review*, vol. 37, no. 1745, 141.

19. Satola, D. and Judy, H. loc. cit.

20. Ibid., 139.

21. Maurer, T. September 2011. "Cyber Norm Emergence at the United Nations— An Analysis of the UN's Activities Regarding Cyber-security." Discussion Paper 2011-11. Massachusetts: Belfer Center for Science and International Affairs, Harvard Kennedy School, 8.

22. Ibid., 9.

23. Congressional Research Services. June 2013. "Federal Laws Relating to Cybersecurity: Overview and Discussion of Proposed Revisions." Report 7-5700.

24. White House. February 2003. "The National Strategy to Secure Cyberspace." Available at http://www.us-cert.gov/sites/default/files/publications/cyberspace _strategy.pdf (accessed March 30, 2014).

25. White House. "The National Strategy to Secure Cyberspace." loc. cit.

26. Ibid., x.

27. Center for Strategic and International Studies. December 2008. "Securing Cyberspace for the 44th Presidency A Report of the CSIS Commission on Cybersecurity for the 44th Presidency." Available at http://csis.org/files/media /csis/pubs/081208_securingcyberspace_44.pdf (accessed August 17, 2013).

28. Ibid., 1.

29. See the Federation of American Scientists website for the listing of National Presidential Security Decisions and the title and release date of NSPD 54. Available at http://www.fas.org/irp/offdocs/nspd/index.html.

30. National Presidential Security Directive #54, 2.

31. Ibid., 4.

32. Ibid., 4–5.

33. White House. February 19, 2013. Executive Order 13636, "Improving Critical Infrastructure Security." *Federal Register*, vol. 78, no. 33, 11740.

34. Ibid., 11739.

35. Eisner, R., Waltzman, H. W. and Shen, L. "United States: The 2013 Cybersecurity Executive Order: Potential Impacts on The Private Sector." Available at http:// www.mondaq.com/unitedstates/x/258936/technology/The+2013+Cybersecurity +Executive+Order+Potential+Impacts+on+the+Private+Sector (accessed March 2, 2014).

36. White House. February 19, 2013. Executive Order 13636, "Improving Critical Infrastructure Security." *Federal Register*, vol. 78, no. 33, 11740.

37. White House. February 12, 2013. Presidential Policy Directive 21, 3.
38. White House. February 19, 2013. Executive Order 13636, "Improving Critical Infrastructure Security." *Federal Register,* vol. 78, no. 33, 11739.
39. White House. February 12, 2013. Presidential Policy Directive 21, 12.
40. Ibid., Presidential Policy Directive, 11.
41. Department of Homeland Security. Available at https://www.dhs.gov/enhanced -cybersecurity-services (accessed March 8, 2014).
42. Department of Homeland Security. April 19, 2013. "Privacy Impact Assessment for EINSTEIN 3 Accelerated (E³A)." Available at http://www.dhs .gov/sites/default/files/publications/privacy/PIAs/PIA%20NPPD%20E3A%20 20130419%20FINAL%20signed.pdf (accessed March 8, 2014).
43. Ibid., 3.
44. See http://www.us-cert.gov.
45. Radack, J. July 14, 2009. "NSA's Cyber Overkill." Available at http://articles.la times.com/2009/jul/14/opinion/oe-radack14 (accessed March 14, 2014).
46. For a more comprehensive discussion of the NSA involvement in the development of various versions of EINSTEIN, please refer to Bellovin, S. M., Bradner, S. O., Diffie, W., Landau, S. and Rexford, J. 2011. "Can It Really Work? Problems with Extending EINSTEIN 3 to Critical Infrastructure." *Harvard National Security Journal,* vol. 3, 4–6.
47. U.S. Computer Emergency Readiness Team. n.d. Available at http://www.us -cert.gov/ (accessed March 14, 2014).
48. Messmer, E. April 20, 2013. "US Government's Use of Deep Packet Inspection Raises Serious Privacy Questions." Available at http://news.techworld.com /security/3444019/dhs-use-of-deep-packet-inspection-technology-in-new -net-security-system-raises-serious-privacy-questions/ (accessed March 14, 2014).
49. Department of Homeland Security. April 19, 2013. "Privacy Impact Assessment for EINSTEIN 3 Accelerated (E³A)." Available at http://www.dhs .gov/sites/default/files/publications/privacy/PIAs/PIA%20NPPD%20E3A%20 20130419%20FINAL%20signed.pdf (accessed March 8, 2014).
50. National Institute of Standards and Technology. February 12, 2014. "NIST Releases Cybersecurity Framework Version 1.0." Available at http://www.nist .gov/itl/csd/launch-cybersecurity-framework-021214.cfm (accessed March 14, 2014).
51. Ibid., 1.
52. National Institute of Standards and Technology. loc. cit., 1.
53. Ibid., 5.
54. Table of U.S. Laws adapted from Congressional Research Services. June 2013. "Federal Laws Relating to Cybersecurity: Overview and Discussion of Proposed Revisions. Report 7-5700, Laws Identified as Having Relevant Cybersecurity Provisions."
55. For example, see Association of Southeast Asian Nations and the Union of South American Nations.
56. North Atlantic Treaty Organization Website. Available at http://www.nato.int /cps/en/natolive/75747.htm (accessed March 23, 2014).
57. United Nations Website. Available at http://www.un.org/en/aboutun/index .shtml (accessed March 21, 2014).

58. Maurer, T. September 2011. "Cyber Norm Emergence at the United Nations—An Analysis of the UN's Activities Regarding Cyber-security." Discussion Paper 2011-11. Massachusetts: Belfer Center for Science and International Affairs, Harvard Kennedy School, 11.

59. United Nations. Available at http://www.un.org/en/documents/charter/chapter3.shtml (accessed March 21, 2014).

60. United Nations. Available at http://www.un.org/en/documents/charter/chapter4.shtml (accessed March 21, 2014).

61. United Nations. Available at http://www.un.org/en/documents/charter/chapter9.shtml (accessed March 21, 2014).

62. United Nations. Available at http://www.un.org/en/documents/charter/chapter10.shtml (accessed March 21, 2014).

63. Internet Governance Forum. Available at http://www.intgovforum.org/cms/aboutigf (accessed March 21, 2014).

64. United Nations. Available at http://www.un.cv/agency-itu.php (accessed March 21, 2014).

65. Internet Governance Forum. Available at http://www.intgovforum.org/cms/aboutigf (accessed March 21, 2014).

66. Internet Governance Forum Website. loc. cit.

67. International Telecommunication Union. Available at http://www.itu.int/net/about/basic-texts/constitution/chapteri.aspx (accessed March 31, 2014).

68. International Telecommunication Union Website. loc. cit.

69. International Telecommunication Union Website. loc. cit.

70. International Telecommunication Union Website. loc. cit.

71. International Telecommunication Union Website. loc. cit.

72. International Telecommunication. Available at http://www.itu.int/en/wcit-12/Pages/default.aspx (accessed March 31, 2014).

73. For an introspective and detailed account of the history of the ITU and ITR, see Hill, R. 2014. *The New International Telecommunication Regulations and the Internet: A Commentary and Legislative History*. Berlin, Heidelberg: Springer.

74. European Parliament. November 19, 2012. "Motion for a Resolution B7-0499/2012." Available at http://www.europarl.europa.eu/sides/getDoc.do?pubRef=-//EP//NONSGML+MOTION+B7-2012-0499+0+DOC+PDF+V0//EN (accessed March 31, 2014).

75. Pfanner, E. December 13, 2012. "U.S. Rejects Telecommunications Treaty." Available at http://www.nytimes.com/2012/12/14/technology/14iht-treaty14.html?pagewanted=1&_r=0 (accessed March 31, 2014).

76. See questions and answers at the ITU. Available at http://www.itu.int/en/wcit-12/Pages/treaties-signing.aspx (accessed April 21, 2014).

77. Maurer, T. op. cit., 5.

78. Ibid., 16.

79. NATO. Available at http://www.nato.int (accessed March 23, 2014).

80. North Atlantic Treaty. April 4, 1949, 1. http://www.nato.int/nato_static/assets/pdf/stock_publications/20120822_nato_treaty_en_light_2009.pdf (accessed March 23, 2014).

81. NATO. Available at http://www.nato.int/cps/en/natolive/topics_78170.htm (accessed March 23, 2014).

82. NATO Cooperative Cyber Defence Centre of Excellence. Available at http://ccdcoe.org/328.html (accessed March 23, 2014).
83. U.N. General Assembly Resolution 68/243. December 27, 2013. "Developments in the Field of Information and Telecommunications in the Context of International Security."
84. European Parliament. Available at http://europa.eu/about-eu/institutions-bodies/european-parliament/index_en.htm (accessed May 20, 2014).
85. European Parliament. Available at http://europa.eu/about-eu/institutions-bodies/council-eu/index_en.htm (accessed May 20, 2014).
86. European Parliament Website. loc. cit.
87. European Parliament. Available at http://europa.eu/eu-law/decision-making/legal-acts/index_en.htm (accessed May 24, 2014).
88. The Treaty on European Union, 5. Available at http://www.eurotreaties.com/lisbontext.pdf (accessed May 24, 2014).
89. Directive 95/46 Data Protection. November 23, 1995. Available at http://eur-lex.europa.eu/LexUriServ/LexUriServ.do?uri=OJ:L:1995:281:0031:0050:EN:PDF (accessed December 29, 2013).
90. European Commission. January 25, 2012. Proposal for a Regulation of the European Parliament and Council. Available at http://ec.europa.eu/justice/data-protection/document/review2012/com_2012_11_en.pdf (accessed December 29, 2013).
91. Directive 95/46 Data Protection. November 23, 1995. Available at http://eur-lex.europa.eu/LexUriServ/LexUriServ.do?uri=OJ:L:1995:281:0031:0050:EN:PDF (accessed December 29, 2013).
92. See the European Commission website page, which contains a list of and links to the data protection laws for each member nation. Available at http://ec.europa.eu/dataprotectionofficer/dpl_transposition_en.htm (accessed May 24, 2014).
93. Directive 95/46 Data Protection. November 23, 1995. Available at http://eur-lex.europa.eu/LexUriServ/LexUriServ.do?uri=OJ:L:1995:281:0031:0050:EN:PDF (accessed December 29, 2013).
94. Council Framework Decision 2008/977/JHA. November 27, 2008. Available at http://eur-lex.europa.eu/legal-content/EN/TXT/PDF/?uri=CELEX:32008F0977&from=EN (accessed May 24, 2014).
95. Regulation (EC) No 45/2001. December 18, 2000, 1. Available at http://eur-lex.europa.eu/legal-content/EN/TXT/PDF/?uri=CELEX:32001R0045&from=EN (accessed May 24, 2014).
96. Charter of Fundamental Rights of the European Union. December 18, 2000, 10. Available at http://www.europarl.europa.eu/charter/pdf/text_en.pdf (accessed May 24, 2014).
97. See Case Number C-468/10–ASNEF. Available at http://curia.europa.eu/juris/liste.jsf?language=en&jur=C,T,F&num=C-468/10&td=ALL (accessed May 25, 2014).
98. European Commission. January 25, 2012. "Proposal for a Regulation of the European Parliament and of the Council." Available at http://ec.europa.eu/justice/data-protection/document/review2012/com_2012_11_en.pdf (accessed December 29, 2013).
99. European Commission. November 27, 2013. "Restoring Trust in EU-US Data Flows—Frequently Asked Questions." Available at http://europa.eu/rapid/press-release_MEMO-13-1054_en.htm (accessed July 5, 2014).
100. European Commission. loc. cit.

101. Ibid., 5.
102. Connolly, C. 2008. "Introduction to The U.S. Safe Harbor—Fact or Fiction." Available at http://www.galexia.com/public/research/assets/safe_harbor_fact _or_fiction_2008/safe_harbor_fact_or_fiction-Introduc.html (accessed July 5, 2014).
103. Connolly, C. loc. cit.
104. Letter dated April 10, 2014, addressed to Viviane Reding, Vice President. "Commissioner for Justice, Fundamental Rights and Citizenship for the European Commission from Article 29 Data Protection Working Party." Available at https:// www.huntonprivacyblog.com/files/2014/04/20140410_wp29_to_ec_on_sh_rec ommendations.pdf (accessed July 5, 2014).
105. Hunton and Williams, LLP. March 12, 2014. "European Parliament Adopts Draft General Data Protection Regulation; Calls for Suspension of Safe Harbor." Available at https://www.huntonprivacyblog.com/2014/03/articles/european -parliament-adopts-draft-general-data-protection-regulation-calls-suspen sion-safe-harbor/ (accessed July 5, 2014).
106. European Commission. January 25, 2012. "Proposal for a Regulation of the European Parliament and of the Council." Available at http://ec.europa .eu/justice/data-protection/document/review2012/com_2012_11_en.pdf (accessed December 29, 2013).
107. Ibid., 51.
108. See an excellent discussion concerning the dilemma of how the Internet does not forget and its effect on personal lives in Rosen, J. 2012. "The Right to Be Forgotten." 64 Stan. L. Rev. Online 88. Available at http://www.stanfordlaw review.org/sites/default/files/online/topics/64-SLRO-88.pdf.
109. For a discussion of the practical implications of the "right to be forgotten" in U.S. and EU contexts, see Bennett, S. C. 2012. "The 'Right to Be Forgotten': Reconciling EU and US Perspectives." 30 Berkeley J. Int'l Law. 161. Available at http://scholarship.law.berkeley.edu/bjil/vol30/iss1/4.
110. Order of the Court of Justice. May 13 2014. Case C 131/12. Available at http://curia.europa.eu/juris/documents.jsf?num=C-131/12 (accessed May 18, 2014).
111. Order of the Court of Justice. loc. cit.
112. Ibid., paragraph 88.
113. Ibid., paragraph 99.
114. See Dixon, H. and Warman, M. May 13, 2014. "Google Gets 'Right to Be Forgotten' Requests Hours After EU Ruling." Available at http://www .telegraph.co.uk/technology/google/10832179/Google-gets-right-to-be-for gotten-requests-hours-after-EU-ruling.html (accessed May 25, 2014); and Williams, R. May 15, 2014. "Eric Schmidt: ECJ Struck Wrong Balance Over Right to Be Forgotten." Available at http://www.telegraph.co.uk/technology /google/10833257/Eric-Schmidt-ECJ-struck-wrong-balance-over-right-to-be -forgotten.html (accessed May 25, 2014).
115. See the Electronics Communications Privacy Act: Wire and Electronic Communications Interception and Interception of Oral Communications, Title, 18 U.S.C. § 2510 et. seq.; Pen Register and Trap and Trace Statute, Title, 18 U.S.C. § 3121–3126; and the Foreign Intelligence Surveillance Act, Title, 50 U.S.C. § 1801 et. seq.

116. See Title, 18 U.S.C. § 2522, Enforcement of the Communications Assistance for Law Enforcement Act.

117. Stored Communications Act, Title, 18 U.S.C. § 2701–2712.

118. Directive 95/46 Data Protection. November 23, 1995. Available at http://eur-lex .europa.eu/LexUriServ/LexUriServ.do?uri=OJ:L:1995:281:0031:0050:EN:PDF (accessed December 29, 2013).

119. Council Framework Decision 2008/977/JHA. November 27, 2008. Available at http://eur-lex.europa.eu/legal-content/EN/TXT/PDF/?uri=CELEX:32008F097 7&from=EN (accessed May 24, 2014).

120. See the Judgment of the Court in Joined Cases C-317/04 and C-318/04, issued on May 30, 2006, for a recitation of the facts and circumstances of the DHS agreement. Available at http://curia.europa.eu/juris/showPdf.jsf?text=&docid =57549&pageIndex=0&doclang=EN&mode=lst&dir=&occ=first&part=1 &cid=51728 (accessed May 25, 2014).

121. Memorandum and Order in the Matter of a Warrant to Search a Certain E-Mail Account Controlled and Maintained by Microsoft Corporation in: 13 Mag. 2814, U.S. District Court for the Southern District of New York, April 25, 2014. Available at http://www.ediscoverylawalert.com/wp-content/uploads /sites/243/2014/04/WarrantSCA.pdf (accessed May 25, 2014).

122. Ibid., 3.

123. Ibid., 8–9.

124. Ibid., 9.

125. Ibid., 11–12.

126. Ibid., 12.

127. Ibid., 13.

128. Ibid., 13.

129. Ibid., 26.

130. Ibid., 26.

131. See David Callahan's article, "US law in European Data Centers: Microsoft in Federal Court." Available at http://www.duquesneadvisory.com/US-law-in -European-datacenters-Microsoft-in-federal-court_a291.html (accessed July 4, 2014).

132. Kerr, O. S. August 2004. "A User's Guide to the Stored Communications Act— And a Legislator's Guide to Changing It." The George Washington University Law School, Public Law and Legal Theory Working Paper No. 68, George Washington Law Review, vol. 72, no. 6, 1–41.

133. Bowman, C. M. 2012. "A Way Forward After Warshak: Fourth Amendment Protections for E-Mail." Berkeley Technology Law Journal, vol. 27, Annual Review Online, 809–836.

134. Ibid., 813.

135. Factsheet E.U.-U.S. Negotiations on Data Protection. June 2014. Available at http://ec.europa.eu/justice/data-protection/files/factsheets/umbrella_factsheet _en.pdf (accessed July 5, 2014).

136. Ibid., 2.

137. Ibid., 2.

138. Association of Certified Fraud Examiners. 2014. "Report to the Nations on Occupational Fraud and Abuse," 4.

139. Ibid., 21.

140. Cummings, A., Lewellen, T., McIntire, D., Moore, A. P. and Trzeciak, R. 2012. "Insider Threat Study: Illicit Cyber Activity Involving Fraud in the U.S. Financial Services Sector." Software Engineering Institute, Carnegie Mellon University. Available at http://www.sei.cmu.edu/reports/12sr004.pdf (accessed July 6, 2014).

141. Ibid., vii.

142. Cappelli, D. M., Moore, A. P., Trzeciak, R. F. and Shimeall, T. J. 2009. *Common Sense Guide to Prevention and Detection of Insider Threat*, 3rd Edition—Version 3.1. Software Engineering Institute, Carnegie Mellon University and CyLab. Available at http://www.cert.org/archive/pdf/CSG-V3.pdf (accessed July 6, 2014).

143. Charge Sheet in U.S.A. v. Pfc.Bradley Manning dated May 10, 2010. Available at http://fas.org/irp/news/2010/07/manning070510.pdf (accessed July 6, 2014).

144. Elsea, J. K. September 9, 2013. "Criminal Prohibitions on the Publication of Classified Defense Information." Congressional Research Services, Report R41404. Available at http://fas.org/sgp/crs/secrecy/R41404.pdf (accessed July 5, 2014).

145. Charge Sheet in U.S.A. v. Pfc. Bradley Manning dated May 29, 2010. Available at http://fas.org/sgp/news/2011/03/manning-charges.pdf (accessed July 6, 2014).

146. Elsea, J. K. September 9, 2013. "Criminal Prohibitions on the Publication of Classified Defense Information." Congressional Research Services, Report R41404, 1. Available at http://fas.org/sgp/crs/secrecy/R41404.pdf (accessed July 5, 2014).

147. Greenwald, G. "Edward Snowden: The Whistleblower Behind the NSA Surveillance Revelations." *The Guardian*. Available at http://www.theguardian.com/world/2013/jun/09/edward-snowden-nsa-whistleblower-surveillance (accessed July 16, 2014).

148. Criminal Complaint, U.S.A. v. Edward Snowden, Case No. 13-CR-265 (CMH) filed in the U.S. District Court for the Eastern District of Virginia. Available at http://fas.org/sgp/jud/snowden/complaint.pdf (accessed July 6, 2014).

149. Statement of Bradley Manning dated January 29, 2013, in U.S.A. v. Pfc. Bradley Manning. Available at http://fas.org/sgp/jud/manning/022813-statement.pdf (accessed July 6, 2014).

150. See NBC News Exclusive Interview of Edward Snowden by reporter Brian Williams aired on May 28, 2014. Available at http://www.nbcnews.com/feature/edward-snowden-interview/watch-primetime-special-inside-mind-edward-snowden-n117126 (accessed July 16, 2014).

151. Blaylock, D. December 13, 2013. "GAP Praises House Approval of Military Whistleblower Protection Act Makeover." Available at http://coffman.house.gov/media-center/in-the-news/gap-praises-house-approval-of-military-whistleblower-protection-act (accessed July 6, 2014).

152. Project on Government Oversight. June 16, 2014. "Senate Approves Intelligence Whistleblower Rights." Available at http://www.pogo.org/about/press-room/releases/2014/senate-approves-intelligence-whistleblower-rights.html (accessed July 5, 2014).

153. Whistleblower Protection Act Makeover. Available at http://coffman.house.gov/media-center/in-the-news/gap-praises-house-approval-of-military-whistleblower-protection-act (accessed July 6, 2014).

154. Elsea, J. K. September 9, 2013. "Criminal Prohibitions on the Publication of Classified Defense Information." Congressional Research Services, Report R41404, 3. Available at http://fas.org/sgp/crs/secrecy/R41404.pdf (accessed July 5, 2014).
155. See Alexa O'Brien's. Available at http://www.alexaobrien.com/secondsight /archives.html for archived pleadings, transcripts, and commentary relating to U.S.A. v. Pfc. Bradley Manning, which O'Brien compiled during the course of her media coverage of the trial.
156. For a succinct discussion about retaliation faced by whistleblowers and the less than successful remedies available to them, see Sagar, R. 2013. *Secrets and Leaks: The Dilemma of State Secrecy.* New Jersey: Princeton University Press, 144–149.
157. See *Smithsonian Magazine.* August 2011. "Leaks and the Law: The Thomas Drake Story." Available at http://www.smithsonianmag.com/history/leaks-and-the -law-the-story-of-thomas-drake-14796786/ (accessed July 7, 2014), for details concerning Thomas Drake, a former NSA official who reported his concerns to the appropriate audiences, with no result, and ultimately leaked nonclassified information to the media, for which he was unsuccessfully prosecuted under the 1917 Espionage Act, and mention of Timothy Tamm, Justice Department attorney, against whom no charges were ever brought.
158. Elsea, J. K. September 9, 2013. "Criminal Prohibitions on the Publication of Classified Defense Information." Congressional Research Services, Report R41404, 5–7. Available at http://fas.org/sgp/crs/secrecy/R41404.pdf (accessed July 5, 2014).
159. Ibid., 8.
160. For a discussion on the potential penalty enhancements available to the government where military personnel are the violators, see Elsea, J. K. September 9, 2013. "Criminal Prohibitions on the Publication of Classified Defense Information." Congressional Research Services, Report R41404, 11–13. Available at http://fas.org/sgp/crs/secrecy/R41404.pdf (accessed July 5, 2014).
161. See Sagar, R. 2013. *Secrets and Leaks: The Dilemma of State Secrecy.* New Jersey: Princeton University Press, for a comprehensive and well-researched discussion about the history of state secrets, their purpose and role, and a proposed framework for their appropriate use and regulation.
162. Anderson, R. 2014. "Privacy versus Government Surveillance: Where Network Effects Meet Public Choice." Available at http://weis2014.econinfosec.org /papers/Anderson-WEIS2014.pdf (accessed May 27, 2014).

Bibliography

Bellovin, S. M., Bradner, S. O., Diffie, W., Landau, S., and Rexford, J. 2011. "Can It Really Work? Problems with Extending EINSTEIN 3 to Critical Infrastructure." *Harvard National Security Journal*, vol. 3, 1–38.
Bennett, S. C. 2012. "The 'Right to Be Forgotten': Reconciling EU and US Perspectives." 30 *Berkeley J. Int'l Law.* 161. Available at http://scholarship.law.berkeley.edu /bjil/vol30/iss1/4 (accessed May 25, 2014).

Boulton, R., and Coskun, O. March 28, 2014. "Turkish Security Breach Exposes Erdoğan in Power Struggle." Available at http://www.reuters.com/article/2014/03/28 /us-turkey-election-idUSBREA2R12X20140328 (accessed March 28, 2014).

Bowman, C. M. 2012. "A Way Forward After Warshak: Fourth Amendment Protections for E-Mail." *Berkeley Technology Law Journal*, vol. 27, Annual Review Online, 809–836.

Cappelli, D. M., Moore, A. P., Trzeciak, R. F., and Shimeall, T. J. 2009. *Common Sense Guide to Prevention and Detection of Insider Threat*, 3rd Edition—Version 3.1. Software Engineering Institute, Carnegie Mellon University and CyLab, Pittsburgh, PA. Available at http://www.cert.org/archive/pdf/CSG-V3.pdf (accessed July 6, 2014).

Center for Strategic and International Studies. December 2008. "Securing Cyberspace for the 44th Presidency: A Report of the CSIS Commission on Cybersecurity for the 44th Presidency." Available at http://csis.org/files/media/csis/pubs/081208 _securingcyberspace_44.pdf (accessed August 17, 2013).

Contreras, J. L., DeNardis, L., and Teplinsky, M. June 2013. "America the Virtual: Security, Privacy, and Interoperability in an Interconnected World: Foreword: Mapping Today's Cybersecurity Landscape." *American University of Law Review*, vol. 62, no. 5, 1113–1130..

Cummings, A., Lewellen, T., McIntire, D., Moore, A. P., and Trzeciak, R. 2012. "Insider Threat Study: Illicit Cyber Activity Involving Fraud in the U.S. Financial Services Sector." Software Engineering Institute, Carnegie Mellon University, Pittsburgh, PA. Available at http://www.sei.cmu.edu/reports/12sr004.pdf (accessed July 6, 2014).

Department of Homeland Security. n.d. "Cybersecurity Results." Available at http:// www.dhs.gov/cybersecurity-results (accessed January 11, 2014).

Department of Homeland Security. n.d. "Enhanced Cybersecurity Services." Available at https://www.dhs.gov/enhanced-cybersecurity-services (accessed March 8, 2014).

Department of Homeland Security. April 19, 2013. "Privacy Impact Assessment for EINSTEIN 3 Accelerated (E^3A)." Available at http://www.dhs.gov/sites/default /files/publications/privacy/PIAs/PIA%20NPPD%20E3A%2020130419%20 FINAL%20signed.pdf (accessed March 8, 2014).

Eisner, R., Waltzman, H. W., and Shen, L. 2013. "United States: The 2013 Cybersecurity Executive Order: Potential Impacts on The Private Sector." Available at http:// www.mondaq.com/unitedstates/x/258936/technology/The+2013+Cybersecu rity+Executive+Order+Potential+Impacts+on+the+Private+Sector (accessed March 2, 2014).

Elsea, J. K. September 9, 2013. "Criminal Prohibitions on the Publication of Classified Defense Information." Congressional Research Services, Report R41404. Available at http://www.fas.org/sgp/crs/secrecy/R41404.pdf (accessed July 5, 2014).

European Parliament. November 19, 2012. Motion for a Resolution B7-0499/2012. Available at http://www.europarl.europa.eu/sides/getDoc.do?pubRef=-//EP //NONSGML+MOTION+B7-2012-0499+0+DOC+PDF+V0//EN (accessed March 31, 2014).

European Parliament and Council. November 23, 1995. Directive 95/46 Data Protection. Available at http://eur-lex.europa.eu/LexUriServ/LexUriServ.do?uri =OJ:L:1995:281:0031:0050:EN:PDF (accessed December 29, 2013).

European Parliament and Council. December 18, 2000. Regulation (EC) 45/2001. Available at http://eur-lex.europa.eu/legal-content/EN/TXT/PDF/?uri=CELEX :32001R0045&from=EN (accessed May 24, 2014).

European Parliament and Council. November 27, 2008. Council Framework Decision 200/977/JHA. Available at http://eur-lex.europa.eu/legal-content/EN/TXT /PDF/?uri=CELEX:32008F0977&from=EN (accessed May 24, 2014).

European Parliament, Directorate General for Internal Policies Policy Department A: Economic and Scientific Policy, Industry, Research and Energy. September 2013. "Data and Security Breaches and Cyber-Security Strategies in the E.U. and Its International Counterparts." IP/A/ITRE/NT/2013-5, PE 507.476. Available at http://www.europarl.euro.eu (accessed January 11, 2014).

European Union Court of Justice. November 24, 2011. Case Number C-468/10 ASNEF. Available at http://curia.europa.eu/juris/liste.jsf?language=en&jur=C,T,F&num=C -468/10&td=ALL (accessed May 25, 2014).

General Accounting Office. February 2013. "Cybersecurity: National Strategy, Roles and Responsibilities Need to Be Better Defined and More Effectively Implemented." Available at http://www.gao.gov/assets/660/652170.pdf (accessed September 29, 2013).

International Telecommunications Union. April 2008. "Series X: Data Networks, Open Systems Communications and Security."

Kerr, O. S. 2004. "A User's Guide to the Stored Communications Act—And a Legislator's Guide to Changing It." The George Washington University Law School, Public Law and Legal Theory Working Paper No. 68, George Washington Law Review, vol. 72, no. 6, 1–41.

Maurer, T. September 2011. "Analysis of the UN's Activities Regarding Cyber-security." Discussion Paper 2011-11. Massachusetts: Belfer Center for Science and International Affairs, Harvard Kennedy School.

Maurer, T. 2011. "Cyber Norm Emergence at the United Nations—An Analysis of the UNs Activities Regarding Cyber Security?" discussion Paper 2011-11, Cambridge, MA: Belfer Center for Science and International Affairs, Harvard Kennedy School, 47. Available at http://belfercenter.ksg.harvard.edu /files/maurer-cyber-norm-dp-2011-11-f.

Messmer, E. April 20, 2013. "US Government's Use of Deep Packet Inspection Raises Serious Privacy Questions." Available at http://news.techworld .com/security/3444019/dhs-use-of-deep-packet-inspection-technology-in-new -net-security-system-raises-serious-privacy-questions/ (accessed March 14, 2014).

Moore, J. March 27, 2014. "Turkey YouTube Ban: Full Transcript of Leaked Erdoğan Corruption Call with Son." International Business Times. Available at http://www .ibtimes.co.uk/turkey-youtube-bantranscript-leaked-erdogan-corruption-call -son-1442150 (accessed March 30, 2014).

National Institute of Standards and Technology. February 12, 2014. "Framework for Improving Critical Infrastructure Cybersecurity Version 1.0." Available at http:// www.nist.gov/cyberframework/upload/cybersecurity-framework-021214.pdf (accessed March 14, 2014).

National Institute of Standards and Technology. February 12, 2014. "NIST Releases Cybersecurity Framework Version 1.0." Available at http://www.nist.gov/itl /csd/launch-cybersecurity-framework-021214.cfm (accessed March 14, 2014).

NATO Cooperative Cyber Defence Center of Excellence. 2013. *Tallinn Manual on the International Law Applicable to Cyber Warfare.* Available at http://issuu.com/nato _ccd_coe/docs/tallinnmanual?e=5903855/1802381# (accessed July 15, 2014).

Radack, J. July 14, 2009. "NSA's Cyber Overkill." Available at http://articles.latimes .com/2009/jul/14/opinion/oe-radack14 (accessed March 14, 2014).

Rosen, J. 2012. "The Right to Be Forgotten." 64 Stan. L. Rev. Online 88. Available at http://www.stanfordlawreview.org/sites/default/files/online/topics/64-SLRO-88.pdf (accessed May 25, 2014).

Sagar, R. 2013. *Secrets and Leaks: The Dilemma of State Secrecy.* New Jersey: Princeton University Press.

Satola, D., and Judy, H. September 3, 2010. "Electronic Commerce Law: Towards a Dynamic Approach to Enhancing International Cooperation and Collaboration in Cybersecurity Legal Frameworks: Reflections on the Proceedings of the Workshop on Cybersecurity Legal Issues" at The 2010 United Nations Internet Governance Forum. *William Mitchell Law Review*, 37 Wm. Mitchell L. Rev. 1745.

Tehan, R., and Fischer, E. A. 2013. Table of U.S. Laws adapted from Congressional Research Services. June 2013. "Federal Laws Relating to Cybersecurity: Overview and Discussion of Proposed Revisions. Report 7-5700. Table 2, Laws Identified as Having Relevant Cybersecurity Provisions," 52–61.

The Daily Star. March 30, 2014. "Femen Stages Bare-Breasted Protest Against Turkish PM." *The Daily Star.* Available at http://www.dailystar.com.lb/News/Middle -East/2014/Mar-30/251709-femen-stages-bare-breasted-protest-against -turkish-pm.ashx#axzz2xTVdeiKJ (accessed March 30, 2014).

The Mitre Corporation. 2010. "Science of Cyber-Security." JASON Report JSR-10- 102. Available at http://www.fas.org/irp/agency/dod/jason/cyber.pdf (accessed January 11, 2014).

United Nations. December 27, 2013. "Developments in the Field of Information and Telecommunications in the Context of International Security." General Assembly Resolution 68/243.

United States Senate Bill 2105. 2012. "The CyberSecurity Act of 2012." Available at https:// www.govtrack.us/congress/bills/112/s2105/text (accessed January 13, 2014).

White House. February 2003. "The National Strategy to Secure Cyberspace." Available at http://www.us-cert.gov/sites/default/files/publications/cyberspace_strategy .pdf (accessed March 30, 2014).

White House. February 12, 2013. Executive Order 13636, "Improving Critical Infrastructure Security." *Federal Register*, vol. 78, no. 33, 11739–11744.

White House. February 12, 2013. Presidential Policy Directive 21. Available at https:// fas.org/irp/offdocs/ppd/ppd-21.pdf (accessed March 2, 2014).

Economic Cost of Cybersecurity

6

THOMAS A. JOHNSON

Contents

6.1 Introduction

Calculating the cost of cybersecurity is a very complex problem since there are a number of variables that must be included in any economic assessment. Another facet of the problem is to define what is being measured in calculating the economic cost. In addition, what economic model will be applied, and will it control for the statistical requirements of sampling and other research methodology requirements? How complete and accurate are computer breaches and computer criminal acts being reported and what is the variability between corporations, governmental agencies, and individual citizens? Further difficulties emerge as a result of the public media reporting the "cost of computer crime" from various sources, which, in many instances, are nonscientific sources and may contain undocumented sources as well as elevated cost estimates.

Listings of the factors that will be important in determining the economic cost of cybersecurity include the following:

1. Financial losses to business organizations
    Small businesses
    Corporations
2. Nongovernmental organizations (NGOs) and charitable organizations
3. Individuals
4. Governmental organizations
    Local, municipal, state
    Federal
    Military
5. Costs expended to protect against loss
    Antivirus software
    Cybersecurity and information technology (IT) information security personnel
    Defensive measures
    Corporate, governmental, military
    Offensive measures
    Military
    Cyber intelligence/counter intelligence
    Military
    Corporate
6. Insurance costs
7. Macroeconomic costs

It is critical to assess and measure the cost of cybersecurity and the range of issues that are required to prepare an adequate defense and prevention strategy for the security of information assets and intellectual property. An understanding of the scope of cyber crime when expressed in financial terms provides policymakers with a perspective as to how serious the cyber crime problem really is and what degree of investment of resources will be required to realistically address and defend against this growing problem. Since cyber activities have expanded beyond cyber crime to now include cyber espionage and cyber warfare challenges, we now have substantially increased a society's vulnerability, while also increasing their financial burden for defense and prevention of security breaches and attacks.

The economic analysis of cybersecurity costs now have to assess organizations and entities at the federal level, state, and municipal levels; corporate businesses; small businesses; NGOs; and the individual. As each of these entities has a vast array of organizations and individuals who may be victimized, a careful and sound research-based scientific study must be performed to determine the costs of victimization losses. Also, the cost of prevention and defense must be factored into the true cybersecurity costs. These costs will entail antivirus software, firewalls, intrusion prevention software, and a range of additional security devices and network software programs and services at a global level. In addition, the cost of cybersecurity professionals, managers, and executives at the C-level, including computer information security officers, will also be included in the economic cost modeling.

The cost of cyber crime is quite complicated, as all costs cannot be neatly summed up by reporting and totaling actual financial losses. It becomes very difficult to measure actual financial losses, since the loss of intellectual property has both immediate and long-term costs. The closure and bankruptcies of some businesses have been reported due to their loss of critical intellectual property. Another dimension of the difficulty in making an assessment of economic costs of cybersecurity has occurred when a security breach has resulted in the diminishing of a business's reputation and, in some cases, the loss of customers or the loss of an opportunity to serve other business partners. It is difficult to ensure the accurate assessment of the financial costs of a computer security breach, especially when there exists a series of interdependencies between the actions of a breach in terms of its initial impact and the subsequent incurred costs several weeks or months after the breach. Equally difficult is the cost accounting assessment of the financial loss incurred by the lost opportunity of serving business customers who fear returning to an organization that has suffered a major breach.

Computer security breaches occurring or targeted against our nation's military and our governmental agencies create additional cost factors that are incurred in the defense of our nation. Another important aspect of analyzing the cost of cybersecurity occurs in terms of the transformational costs involved in securing the defense of our nation. The increase in cyber espionage by nation-states as well as terrorist organizations has resulted in our military investing billions of dollars to provide a protective defense for our nation. In addition to cyber espionage, the threat of cyber warfare has created a need for cyber weapons and the defense against opposing offensive cyber weapons. There is a range of very complex costs of personnel, equipment, and hardware and software that are added to the long range responsibility and requirement that must also be considered in any true assessment of the cost of cybersecurity.

Many researchers and economists have expressed concern over the inflated estimates of the costs of cybersecurity and have even noted that many officials in the federal government are commenting on financial costs in the trillions of dollars without providing a basis for these cost figures. Interestingly, most of the economic research has been done by those corporations involved with the field of cybersecurity, and the criticism has been raised as to whether the effort is more of a "marketing" focus as opposed to a science-based approach committed to an economic analysis. In fairness to the past industry-based economic assessment, we can be grateful for their interest in pursuing this important information. Also, it should be noted that little focus on determining the economic costs of security breaches and computer crime was being performed by our nation's research universities. Even less effort was being expended by our governmental agencies.

6.2 Cost of Cybersecurity—Studies and Reports

There exist little consensus and even less satisfaction as to the current knowledge regarding the accurate cost of cybersecurity within our nation. There is little agreement as to the real cost of computer crime, and while great improvement is being made in the area of determining the cost of security breaches, much work remains to be completed. One of the problems is the absence of standard research methodologies for cost measurement and modeling. Another problem stems from no standardized protocol and requirement for the reporting of security breaches; in fact, there is great reluctance of business organizations to even report computer criminal and breach activities. As a result, we have very spotty empirical data on costs that are attributable to computer crime, security breaches, viruses, worms, and other attack mechanisms. Without solid empirical data, the challenge of calculating the cost of cybersecurity becomes speculative at best.

6.2.1 Past Computer Crime Studies and Reports

In an important study on the economic impact of cyber attacks, Brian Cashell, William Jackson, Mark Jickling, and Baird Webel reviewed several significant surveys, including the 2003 Computer Security Institute (CSI) and the Federal Bureau of Investigation (FBI) 8th Annual Survey, which was based on computer security practitioners in 530 U.S. corporations, financial institutions, government agencies, medical institutions, and universities. They also reviewed a study focused on worldwide economic damage estimates of all forms of digital attack by the British firm Mi2g. Another study they examined was the Computer Economics Institute (CEI) assessment of the financial impact of major virus attacks from 1995 to 2003. We will focus only on their comments, which were directed to research methodological issues, to highlight in a constructively critical fashion the areas that future studies will be well advised to consider as new studies are launched.[1]

Regarding the CSI/FBI Survey, the criticism was directed to the point that the respondents were not a representative sample of business organizations and other entities that would be exposed to cyber risk. Also, survey recipients were not randomly chosen, but were self-selected from among security professionals. As a result, there was no rigorous, statistically sound method for extrapolating the reports of a group of 530 to the national level. More significantly, 75% of respondents reported financial losses; however, only 47% could quantify the losses. Finally, the survey was deficient in the absence of a standardized method for quantifying the costs of cyber attacks.[2]

The Mi2g study on worldwide economic damage estimates for all forms of digital attacks was criticized on the basis that their conclusions were based on the collection of economic information from a variety of open sources and extrapolated to a global level using a proprietary set of algorithms. Since their model is proprietary, outside researchers cannot evaluate their model and its underlying assumptions. CEI's benchmarks and algorithms are the key to its cost estimates, and due to the proprietary nature, outside evaluators cannot attest to the models or the underlying assumptions.[3]

In 2002, a study by the World Bank criticized the existing base of information that supports projections about the extent of the electronic security problem to be flawed for two reasons. First, there are strong incentives that discourage the reporting of security breaches. Second, organizations are often not able to quantify the risks of the cyber attacks they face or to establish a dollar value on the costs of the attacks that have already occurred. It is interesting to note that incentives to not report security breaches still remain a problem to this day. The difficulty is that organizations in many cases have real economic incentives not to reveal information about security breaches because the costs of public disclosure may take several forms such as the following:

- Financial market impacts: The stock and credit markets and bond rating firms may react to security breach announcements. Negative reactions raise the cost of capital to reporting firms. Even firms that are privately held and not active in public securities markets may be adversely affected if banks and other lenders judge them to be more risky than previously thought.
- Reputation or confidence effects: Negative publicity may damage a reporting firm's reputation or brand or cause customers to lose confidence. These effects may give commercial rivals a competitive advantage.
- Litigation concerns: If an organization reports a security breach, investors, customers, or other stakeholders may use the courts to seek recovery of damages. If the organization has been open in the past about previous incidents, plaintiffs may allege a pattern of negligence.
- Liability concerns: Officials of a firm or organization may face sanctions under federal laws such as the Health Insurance Portability and Accountability Act of 1996 (HIPAA), the Gramm-Leach-Bliley Act of 1999 (GLBA), or the Sarbanes-Oxley Act of 2003, which require

institutions to meet various standards for safeguarding customer and patient records.

- Signal to attackers: A public announcement may alert hackers that an organization's cyber-defenses are weak and inspire further attacks.
- Job security. IT personnel may fear for their jobs after an incident and seek to conceal the breach from senior management.[4]

Another economic cyber risk model reviewed was the annual loss expectancy (ALE) model developed in the late 1970s by the National Institute of Standards and Technology. The ALE model creates a dollar figure, produced by multiplying the cost, or impact, of an incident (in dollars) by the frequency (or probability) of that incident. So the ALE cost model analyzes security breaches from the perspective of (1) how much the breach would cost and (2) how likely it is to occur. The ALE cost model combines probability and severity of computer attacks into a single number, which represents the amount that a firm could actually expect to lose in a given year. While ALE has become a standard unit of measure for talking about the cost of cyber attacks—it has not been used by many to assess cyber risk. One critique of the ALE cost model is the difficult nature of establishing cost measurements and the equal difficulty in specifying the likelihood of an attack.[5]

The importance of developing economic cost models to assess and measure security breaches is a method for an organization to assess the cyber risks they confront. Without these cost models, how can they make rational decisions about the appropriate amount of money and resources they should spend in security of their information systems and computer networks? In short, without these cost models, it is difficult, at best, and almost impossible to evaluate the effectiveness of the computer security efforts.[6] Organizations, particularly businesses and corporations should be quantifying the factors of security breaches and their frequency so they are capable of assessing the optimal amount to spend on computer security systems and to also measure the effectiveness of this financial investment and their computer security programs.

6.2.2 Contemporary Cost of Cyber Crime—Studies and Reports

While there is no single, overall inclusive economic assessment of the cost of cybersecurity that meets the level of acceptance of the scientific community, this documents a need for further research by both the academic and industry communities. We believe that there is increasing improvement in the efforts of the industry to sharpen their cost assessment of cybersecurity, and one very good example is the work being performed by the Ponemon Institute. The Ponemon Institute has been commissioned by corporations such as IBM, Hewlett-Packard, and Experian Corporation to focus on a number of studies involving security breaches, as well as a cost–benefit analysis study, and they have applied a research methodology to control for bias as well as pointed out the limitations of their study, thus providing readers with a clearer report than most previous reports have achieved.

The Ponemon Institute's studies of cyber crime included six nations: the United States, United Kingdom, Germany, Australia, Japan, and France. The study of these six nations involved field-based research as opposed to a more traditional survey research methodology. A total of 234 companies were included in the study, and it consisted of only larger organizations with more than 1000 enterprise seats, which was defined as the number of direct connections to the network and enterprise systems. The report stated that ten months of effort was required to recruit the companies and to build an activity-based cost model to analyze the data, collect source information, and complete the analysis. A total of 1935 interviews were conducted with company personnel, although each nation's individual study would be a number less than the total. For example, the Ponemon Institute's study of the United States was based on 561 interviews drawn from 60 U.S. companies. A total of 1372 attacks were used to measure the cost; however, again, the number of attacks reviewed in each nation varied both in number and type of attack that created a higher cost in one nation compared to another nation. For instance, in the study of the United States, 488 attacks were recorded at an average annualized cost of $11.56 million. The number of attacks and their average annualized cost for each of the surveyed nations reported the following data:

Nation	Companies	Total Attacks to Measure Cost	Average Annualized Cost
United States	60	488	$11.56 million
United Kingdom	36	192	2.99 million pounds
Germany	47	236	5.67 million euros
Japan	31	172	668 million yen
Australia	33	172	668 million yen
France	27	104	3.89 million euros
Average annualized cost (U.S.$)	234	1372	$7.22 million

The above data were collected from the seven studies performed by the Ponemon Institute's research in each nation.[7] There are a number of very interesting results and important data that are included in each of the seven reports, and these reports will stimulate a number of questions and hopefully additional research.

The focus of these field-based studies was to acquire useful data primarily for the industry and presumably any other interested parties. The data were collected within a cost framework that measured two cost streams, one pertaining to internal security related activities and the second to the external consequences and costs.

Internal Cost Activity	External Consequences and Costs
Detection	Information loss or theft
Investigation and escalation	Business disruption
Containment	Equipment damage
Recovery	Revenue loss
Ex-post response	

The Ponemon Institute's Cost of Cyber-Crime Study was unique in addressing the core systems and business-process-related activities that are responsible for creating a range of expenditures associated with a large company's response to cyber crime. The inclusion of direct, indirect, and opportunity costs associated with cyber crimes is a very essential and valuable framework of their seven studies.[8]

The study's definition of cyber crime was limited to cyber attacks and criminal activity conducted via the Internet. These attacks were defined as including the theft of intellectual property, confiscating online back accounts, creating and distributing viruses, posting confidential business information on the Internet, and disrupting a country's critical infrastructure.[9] It is useful to present the key findings of the Ponemon Institute's field-based cyber crime studies and to encourage further research in these vital areas of inquiry.

In reviewing the 2013 cost of cyber crime in the United States, the study is based on 60 U.S. companies that are considered large, with over 1000 enterprise seats. The key findings of the 2013 U.S. study reported an average annualized cost of $11.6 million per year with a range of $1.3 million to $58 million. The 60 companies in the study experienced 122 successful attacks per week, and the most costly cyber crimes were denial-of-service attacks, malicious insiders, and web-based attacks. The average time to resolve an attack was 32 days, with an average cost to participating organizations of $1,035,769 during this 32-day period. On an annualized basis, the detection and recovery combined for 49% of the total internal activity cost, with cash outlays and labor representing the majority of these costs.[10]

The Ponemon Institute was careful to identify the limitations of their research study by cautioning against extrapolation of their data beyond the field-based survey parameters of the size of the organizations reviewed and the exclusion of small business organizations as well as governmental organizations. The key findings of the Ponemon Institute's *2013 Cost of Cyber-Crime Study: Global Report*, which includes all six nations, reveals that the average annualized cost of cyber crime for the 234 organizations was $7.2 million per year, with a range of $375,387 to $58 million. The companies experienced 343 successful attacks per week, and the most costly cyber crimes were caused by malicious insiders, denial-of-service, and web-based attacks. The average time to resolve a cyber attack was 27 days, with an average cost to participating organizations of $509,665 during this 27-day period. On an annualized basis, the detection and recovery combined for 54% of the total internal activity cost, with the productivity loss and direct labor representing the majority of these costs.[11]

In another industry-based study, IBM's Managed Security Services Division reported that they continuously monitor tens of billions of events per day for their 3700 clients in more than 130 countries for the express purpose of identifying security breaches for interdiction and removal. In a one-year period between April 1, 2012, through March 31, 2013, and with normalizing data to describe an average client organization between 1000 and 5000 employees, they reported 81,893,882 security events for an average of 73,400 security attacks to a single organization. These 73,400 attacks were identified by correlation and analytic tools as malicious activity attempting to collect, disrupt, deny, degrade, or destroy information systems resources or the information. The monthly average to an IBM single organization client amounted to 6100 attacks, with 7.51 security incidents requiring action on a monthly basis. The two types of incidents that represented the most common attack types were malicious code and sustained probe/scans. It is interesting to note that 20% of the attackers were considered as malicious inside attacks.[12] While this report did not note any cost factors, we included it to represent the global nature of the problem of cybersecurity and its continuing expansion in both numbers of incidents that must be monitored to ensure for due diligence in protecting an organization.

6.2.3   Global Data Breach Study

The 2014 Cost of Data Breach Benchmark Research Study sponsored by IBM and independently conducted by the Ponemon Institute was the ninth annual study and included 314 companies from ten countries participating in this research. Those nations who participated were the United States, the United Kingdom, Germany, Australia, France, Brazil, Japan, Italy, and, for the first time, the United Arab Emirates and Saudi Arabia. For purposes of this research, a data breach was defined as an event in which an individual's name plus a medical record and/or a financial record or debt card was put at risk either in electronic or paper format. The three main causes of a data breach were malicious or criminal attack, system glitch, or human error. The research methodology to perform this study was quite impressive as the researchers collected in-depth qualitative data through 1690 interviews conducted over a ten-month study, which entailed 314 participating organizations. Those people interviewed were IT personnel, compliance and information security practitioners who were knowledgeable about the organization's data breach and costs associated with resolving the breach. It is important to mention that the costs presented in this study are from actual data loss incidents and are not hypothetical. The methodology used to calculate the cost of a data breach as well as their stated limitations of the research is worthy of inclusion as it will serve as a comprehensive guideline for future research projects.

The importance of the Ponemon's Institute field research conclusions are reinforced by their publishing of the methodological approach they employed in the calculation of security breaches in the ten nations studied. The activity-based cost methodology utilized in their study merits further highlighting, as we believe it will benefit future researchers as additional studies on computer security breaches are pursued:

> To calculate the cost of data breach, we use a costing methodology called activity-based costing (ABC). This methodology identifies activities and assigns a cost according to actual use. Companies participating in this benchmark research are asked to estimate the cost for all the activities they engage in to resolve the data breach.

> Typical activities for discovery and the immediate response to the data breach include the following:
>   - Conducting investigations and forensics to determine the root cause of the data breach
>   - Determining the probable victims of the data breach
>   - Organizing the incident response team
>   - Conducting communication and public relations outreach
>   - Preparing notice documents and other required disclosures to data breach victims and regulators
>   - Implementing call center procedures and specialized training

> The following are typical activities conducted in the aftermath of discovering the data breach:
>   - Audit and consulting services
>   - Legal services for defense
>   - Legal services for compliance
>   - Free or discounted services to victims of the breach
>   - Identity protection services
>   - Lost customer business based on calculating customer churn or turnover
>   - Customer acquisition and loyalty program costs

> Once the company estimates a cost range for these activities, we categorize the costs as direct, indirect and opportunity as defined in the following:

- *Direct cost*—the direct expense outlay to accomplish a given activity.
- *Indirect cost*—the amount of time, effort and other organizational resources spent, but not as a direct cash outlay.
- *Opportunity cost*—the cost resulting from lost business opportunities as a consequence of negative reputation effects after the breach has been reported to victims (and publicly revealed to the media).

Our study also looks at the core process-related activities that drive a range of expenditures associated with an organization's data breach detection, response, containment and remediation. The costs for each activity are presented in the Key Findings section. The four cost centers are:

- Detection or discovery: Activities that enable a company to reasonably detect the breach of personal data either at risk (in storage) or in motion.
- Escalation: Activities necessary to report the breach of protected information to appropriate personnel within a specified time period.
- Notification: Activities that enable the company to notify data subjects with a letter, outbound telephone call, email or general notice that personal information was lost or stolen.
- Post data breach: Activities to help victims of a breach communicate with the company to ask additional questions or obtain recommendations in order to minimize potential harm. Post data breach activities also include credit report monitoring or the reissuing of a new account (or credit card).

In addition to the above process-related activities, most companies experience opportunity costs associated with the breach incident, which results from diminished trust or confidence by present and future customers. Accordingly, our Institute's research shows that the negative publicity associated with a data breach incident causes reputation effects that may result in abnormal turnover or churn rates as well as a diminished rate for new customer acquisitions.

To extrapolate these opportunity costs, we use a cost estimation method that relies on the "lifetime value" of an average customer as defined for each participating organization.

- Turnover of existing customers: The estimated number of customers who will most likely terminate their relationship as a result of the breach incident. The incremental loss is abnormal turnover attributable to the breach incident. This number is an annual percentage, which is based on estimates provided by management during the benchmark interview process.
- Diminished customer acquisition: The estimated number of target customers who will not have a relationship with the organization as a consequence of the breach. This number is provided as an annual percentage.

Limitations

Our study utilizes a confidential and proprietary benchmark method that has been successfully deployed in earlier research. However, there are inherent limitations with this benchmark research that need to be carefully considered before drawing conclusions from findings.

- Non-statistical results: Our study draws upon a representative, non-statistical sample of global entities experiencing a breach involving the loss or theft of customer or consumer records during the past 12 months. Statistical inferences, margins of error and confidence intervals cannot be applied to these data given that our sampling methods are not scientific.
- Non-response: The current findings are based on a small representative sample of benchmarks. In this global study, 314 companies completed the benchmark process. Non-response bias was not tested so it is always possible companies that did not participate are substantially different in terms of underlying data breach cost.
- Sampling-frame bias: Because our sampling frame is judgmental, the quality of results is influenced by the degree to which the frame is representative of the population of companies being studied. It is our belief that the current sampling frame is biased toward companies with more mature privacy or information security programs.
- Company-specific information: The benchmark information is sensitive and confidential. Thus, the current instrument does not capture company-identifying information. It also allows individuals to use categorical response variables to disclose demographic information about the company and industry category.
- Unmeasured factors: To keep the interview script concise and focused, we decided to omit other important variables from our analyses such as leading trends and organizational characteristics. The extent to which omitted variables might explain benchmark results cannot be determined.
- Extrapolated cost results: The quality of benchmark research is based on the integrity of confidential responses provided by respondents in participating companies. While certain checks and balances can be incorporated into the benchmark process, there is always the possibility that respondents did not provide accurate or truthful responses. In addition, the use of cost extrapolation methods rather than actual cost data may inadvertently introduce bias and inaccuracies.[13]

This study reported that the average cost paid for each lost or stolen record containing sensitive and confidential information was $145.00. The most expensive breaches occurred in the United States, at $201.00 per record, and Germany, at $195.00 per record. The United States experienced the highest total loss at $5.85 million and Germany at $4.74 million. On average, the United States had 29,087 exposed or compromised records. The two countries that spent the most to notify customers of a data breach were the United States and Germany, which, on average, spent $509,237 and $317,635, respectively. Typical notification costs included IT activities associated with the creation of contact databases, determination of satisfying all regulatory requirements, engagement of outside experts, and other related efforts to alert victims to the fact their personal information had been compromised.[14]

The average post-data-breach costs included help desk activities, inbound communications, special investigative activities, remediation, legal expenditures, product discounts, identity protection services, and regulatory interventions. The cost to the United States was $1,599,996; Germany, $1,444,551; France, $1,228,373; and the United Kingdom, $948,161.[15]

In terms of the average lost business cost because of data breaches, which included loss of reputation and diminished goodwill plus abnormal turnover of customers, the average business costs as measured in U.S. dollars were as follows:

United States	$3,324,959
France	$1,692,192
Germany	$1,637,509
United Kingdom	$1,587,463

Only 32% of the organizations in this research study had a cyber insurance policy to manage the risks of attacks and threats and 68% did not have a data breach protection clause or cyber insurance policy to address the above identified costs.[16]

There is a vast amount of data in the 2014 Cost of Data Breach Study that provides an interesting foundation on which future research will continue not only by the Ponemon Institute but also for other interested parties and researchers. The increasing cost of data breaches to organizations has resulted in the emergence of the cyber insurance industry, as many businesses simply recognize the need for additional protection.

6.3 Cybersecurity Insurance

One of the advantages of organizations seeking cyber insurance is that the effect of qualifying for insurance actually means a company will have to meet the requirements for cyber resilience as mandated by the insurance carrier's underwriters. In short, the insurance company is going to issue a cyber insurance policy only if reasonable security programs and policies are in place. This has the advantage of offering greater security to all concerned. However, establishing sound cyber resilience programs means that an organization is providing protection of its networks, computers, and data systems beyond the typical cybersecurity programs. So, the higher number of organizations seeking cyber insurance, the greater the possibility of our nation improving its overall cybersecurity.

6.3.1 Cyber Resilience Program Policies

It should be mentioned that as organizations seek cyber insurance, there will be increased costs involved in both their financial outlays for additional personnel, as well as new security software and other devices. An example of the increase of cybersecurity can be viewed in the following document on the development of "securing protected data on university owned mobile and non-mobile devices policy/use of personal devices." Note the requirements for compliance with important federal and state regulatory agencies that are listed and described within this policy. Compliance with these regulatory agencies and the encryption/password policy as well as the policy on data protection all result in an organization that is more prepared to defend itself against breaches. Of course, at the same time, this results in the need for employing additional personnel to implement these policies and to assist in the monitoring of requirements. An example of this policy is presented in the following:

Securing Protected Data on University-Owned Mobile and Non-Mobile Devices Policy/Use of Personal Devices

POLICY PURPOSE

The purpose of this policy is to provide guidance to all users to appropriately secure any Protected Data from risks including, but not limited to, unauthorized access, use, disclosure, and removal as well as to adhere to regulatory and compliance requirements.

SCOPE

This policy applies to all users who have access to/store/transmit Protected Data on University business.

DEFINITIONS

University—refers to University

User—Anyone with authorized access to the University business information systems. This includes employees, faculty, students, third party personnel such as temporaries, contractors or consultants and other parties with valid University access accounts.

University Owned Mobile Devices—these include, but are not limited to, Personal Digital Assistants (PDAs), notebook computers, Tablet PCs, iPhones, iPads, Palm Pilots, Microsoft Pocket PCs, RIM

Blackberry, MP3 players, text pagers, smart phones, compact disks, DVD discs, memory sticks, flash drives, floppy disk and other similar devices.

University Owned Non-Mobile Devices—these include, but are not limited to, computing devices that are not capable of moving or being moved readily such as desktop computers.

Data—information stored on any electronic media throughout the University.

Protected Data—Any data governed under Federal or State regulatory or compliance requirements such as HIPAA, FERPA, FISMA, GLBA, PCI/DSS, Red Flag, PII as well as data deemed critical to business and academic processes which, if compromised, may cause substantial harm and/or financial loss.

HIPAA: The Health Insurance Portability and Accountability Act with the purpose of protecting the privacy of a patient's medical records.

FERPA: The Family Educational Right and Privacy Act with the purpose of protecting the privacy of student education records.

FISMA: The Federal Information Security Management Act recognizes the importance of information security to the economic and national security interests of the United States and as a result sets forth information security requirements that federal agencies and any other parties collaborating with such agencies must follow in an effort to effectively safeguard IT systems and the data they contain.

GLBA: The Gramm-Leach-Bliley Act, also known as the Financial Services Modernization Act of 1999, contains privacy provisions requiring the protection of a consumer's financial information.

PCI/DSS: Payment and Credit Card Industry Data Security Standards is guidance developed by the major credit card companies to help organizations that process card payments, prevent credit card fraud, hacking and various other security issues. A company processing card payments must be PCI compliant or risk losing the ability to process credit card payments.

Red Flag: A mandate developed by the Federal Trade Commission (FTC) requiring institutions to develop identity theft prevention programs.

PII: Personally Identifiable Information that can potentially be used to uniquely identify, contact, or locate a single person such as health information, credit card information, social security number, etc.

IP: Intellectual Property Information is a work or invention that is the result of creativity, such as research or a design, to which one has rights and for which one may apply for a patent, copyright, trademark, etc.

Encryption/Password Protection—A process of converting Data in such a way that eavesdroppers or hackers cannot read the Data but authorized parties can.

Screen Lock—A password-protected mechanism used to hide Data on a visual display while the device continues to operate.

Screen Timeout—A mechanism which turns off a device after the device has not been used for a specified time period.

Personal Devices—Non University owned devices used by employees, at the employee's option, to access, store or transmit Protected Data on University business. This includes personal telephones whether or not the person is receiving a telephone allowance from the University. The University Information Technology Department does not support Personal Devices.

POLICY STATEMENT

User's must take appropriate steps to secure any protected data they access, create, possess, store, or transmit and must be in compliance with the following requirements:

- Protected data should only be accessed on University-owned mobile or non-mobile devices, and should include paper documents. In addition, attached policies should address the issues of security patches, password enabled, 2 factor authentication, containerized mobile phones, secure wireless points, (black-listed apps), and how and who will be responsible for the network monitoring. The University will provide all individuals with a University owned mobile or non-mobile device when it is determined such a device is required for the performance of the individual's position responsibilities. Accordingly, use of personal Devices is discouraged; however, should an individual use a personal Device on University business, the same procedures in this Policy for University Owned Devices applies to any Personal Device and all cybersecurity risks associated with use of personal Devices are the responsibility of the User.
- Protected data must be encrypted or password protected when stored on or transmitted over University-owned mobile or non-mobile devices and email. An additional plan which specifies the method of encryption, the cost to train user's, and the IT group tasked with these and other like responsibilities will be attached to the final approved document. The personnel responsible for this policy must be provided resources to address and implement this and other similar policies contained in this document.
- Protected data must not be sent through insecure public instant messaging networks including, but not limited to, AOL Instant Messenger, Yahoo Messenger, MSN Messenger, and Google Talk.
- University-owned mobile or non-mobile devices must be logged off when not in use during non-work hours. Mobile devices shall be

kept within the personal possession of the User whenever possible. Whenever a device is left unattended, the device shall be stored in a secure place preferably out-of-sight.

- A password protected Screen Timeout/Screen Lock must activate within a maximum of 30 minutes of inactivity.

Basic Security protection including, but not limited to, authentication, network configuration, firewall, anti-virus protection and security patches must be installed and actively maintained on an ongoing basis on all University-owned mobile or non-mobile devices.

Before university-owned mobile or non-mobile devices are connected to the University systems, they shall be scanned for viruses and all viruses must be appropriately deleted. Completely and securely remove all Protected Data from all University-owned mobile or non-mobile devices upon replacement, exchange or disposal. Assistance with these processes is available through the University's Information Technology Department.

The physical security of University-owned mobile or non-mobile devices is the responsibility of the user. If a University-owned mobile or non-mobile device is lost or stolen, user must promptly report the incident to supervisor, Public Safety, and Information Technology Department. This report should include the serial number if the device has one, and the university should maintain a listing of these serial numbers.

ENFORCEMENT

Users must take the mandatory University training along with periodic updates as available. However, a plan with a phased implementation process must be provided which is tied to both personnel and financial targets for addressing the main campus, regional and extended campus sites, as well as international campus locations.

Users who do not comply with this policy may temporarily be denied access to University computing resources and upon notice, may be subject to other penalties and disciplinary action. Depending on the circumstances, federal or state law may permit civil or criminal litigation and/or restitution, fines and/or penalties for actions that violate this policy.

Non-compliant devices may be disconnected from the University data network and departmental units until the device is brought into compliance.

Of course, there are additional areas other than the "bring your own device" that must be addressed relative to a decision as to the degree of cyber resilience programs that will best fit an organizations cybersecurity needs.

6.3.2 Cyber Liability, First-Party, and Third-Party Insurance

The degree of cyber insurance that your organization is interested in acquiring is based on the sensitivity of the data they are responsible for maintaining.

Other issues that an organization may be concerned about and need cyber insurance are the following cyber liability issues:

- Unauthorized access to data
- Disclosure of confidential data
- Loss of data or digital assets
- Introduction of malware, viruses, and worms
- Ransomware or cyber extortion
- Denial-of-service attacks
- Advanced persistent threat attacks
- Identity theft
- Invasion of privacy lawsuits
- Defamation from an employee's email
- Failure of notification of breach

In addition to cyber liability insurance, there is also optional insurance coverage from some insurance carriers that address first-party cyber crime expenses, which may include the following:

Crisis management expenses to include the
- Cost of cybersecurity forensic experts to assist in cyber extortion cases
- Public relations consultants to work with local media, providing appropriate information to maintain goodwill of the customers

Insurance carriers may also be prepared to offer additional first-party lines of coverage; the organization's risk manager can negotiate any number of concerns to create the type of cyber insurance policy that best fits the needs of the organization and the people they serve.

A more critical cyber insurance policy coverage would fall under third-party liability, where the claims of breach arising from cybersecurity failures result in damage to third-party systems. Typical problems arising in this area are when a company's credit card and point of sales systems are below the standards of the major credit card company mandate for compliance with industry-based standards. Two recent cases that highlight this problem are the attacks against the Schnucks Markets and also the attack against Target.

Kavita Kumar reported on the proposed class action settlement stemming from the 2014 Schnuck's Markets computer system breach in which an estimated 2.4 million payment cards were compromised.

Under the proposed settlement, Schnucks would pay up to $10 to customers for each credit or debit card that was compromised and had fraudulent charges posted on it that were later credited or reversed.

Schnucks also would pay customers for certain unreimbursed out-of-pocket expenses such as bank, overdraft and late fees as well as up to three hours for documented time spent at the rate of $10 an hour for dealing with security breach. There would be a cap on these expenses of up to $175 per class member.

The aggregate cap that Schnucks would pay on the above claims would be $1.6 million. If claims exceed that amount, customers would still be guaranteed at least $5 for each compromised card.

Furthermore, Schnucks would pay: up to $10,000 for each related identity theft loss, with the total capped at $300,000; up to $635,000 for the plaintiff and settlement attorney's fees; and $500 to each of the nine named plaintiffs in the lawsuit.[17]

While Schnucks denied any wrongdoing, the cost of the litigation was substantial, and they want to bring closure to the case to avoid further expense, business disruption, and reputational loss. The basis for the class action claim against the Schnucks Markets centered on their alleged failure to secure customers personal financial data and their failure to provide notification that their customer's personal information had been stolen. It is interesting to note that little focus was placed on those responsible for the malicious breach, and the burden of responsibility was transferred to the victims, whose losses are still being calculated by the credit card companies who are also suing Schnucks Markets for their third-party loss.

The class action litigation filed against the Target store was based on a breach of security that permitted the attackers to place malicious software on thousands of cash registers in various Target stores and gain access to 70 million records that contained names and e-mail addresses of customers. In addition to the class action suit by Target customers, the Jefferies investment bank estimates that Target may also face a bill of $1.1 billion to the payment card industry as a result of this breach.[18] The level of security and its quality will be a key in the Target litigation, as will the timing of its notification of this breach to its customers and to the regulators.

The importance of notification is clearly a critical factor for any organization suffering a security breach. Regulatory agencies at both the federal and state levels have imposed standards that companies must adhere to in reporting security breaches to those whom they suspect might be compromised by the breach. In 2011, the Securities and Exchange Commission issued guidelines stating that publicly traded companies must report significant instances of cyber theft and cyber attacks and even the material risk of such a security event. California was the first state to require data breach notifications in 2003. In 2012, companies and governmental agencies were required to notify the California Attorney's General Office of any data breach that involved more than 500 Californians.[19]

Cyber insurance can be a valuable investment, particularly third-party insurance protection against litigation brought by the payment card industry against businesses that fail to comply with the Payment Card Industry Data Security Standard, which requires that businesses who use online transactions abide by certain procedures. Today, businesses, organizations, and even universities should examine their business partners to be certain their respective security processes are in compliance with payment card standards or they may be vulnerable as a result of security breaches by a business partner.

6.3.3 Cybersecurity as a Business Risk

An important study sponsored by Experian Data Breach Resolution and independently conducted by the Ponemon Institute surveyed risk management professionals who either considered or adopted cyber insurance policies. According to survey question responses, many risk managers understand that security is a clear and present risk, and a majority of the surveyed companies now rank cybersecurity risks as greater than natural disasters and other major business risks. The increasing cost and number of data breaches are forcing business executives to reconsider cybersecurity from a purely technical issue to a more complex major business risk issue.[20] Corporate boards of directors and trustees are also expecting their chief executive officers (CEOs) to become more fully engaged in this new and potentially devastating risk.

The noteworthy findings of the study titled "Managing Cyber Security as a Business Risk: Cyber Insurance in the Digital Age" revealed that the concerns about cyber risks are now moving outside of the corporate IT teams and becoming more engaged by risk managers. As a result of risk managers becoming more engaged in cybersecurity issues and data breaches, there has been an increased interest in corporations acquiring cyber insurance policies. Of those participating in the study's survey, 31% currently have a cyber insurance policy and another 39% stated that their organizations plan to purchase a cyber insurance policy. Despite increasing interest in acquiring cyber insurance policies, the study did identify the main reasons respondents gave for not purchasing cybersecurity insurance, and those reasons, in order of frequency of response, were as follows:

- Premiums are too expensive.
- There are too many exclusions, restrictions, and uninsurable risks.
- Property and casualty policies are sufficient.
- They are unable to get insurance underwritten because of current risk profile.
- Coverage is inadequate based on exposure.
- Risk does not warrant insurance.
- Executive management does not see the value of this insurance.[21]

Of those respondents who stated that their company did have cyber insurance, 40% stated that risk management was most responsible for evaluating and selecting the insurance provider. Interestingly, the study reported that the chief information officer and chief information security officer had little involvement and influence in the purchase decision and policy coverage even though one naturally assumed that their views and input had been seriously considered. For those companies that did report having cyber insurance coverage, their policies covered the following types of incidents:

- Human error, mistakes, and negligence
- External attacks by cyber-criminals
- System or business process failures
- Malicious or criminal insiders
- Attacks against business partners, vendors, or other third parties that had access to the company's information assets[22]

The study also reported the following protections or benefits covered by the cyber insurance policy, and again the responses are ranked by the frequency of respondent answers, with the highest response to the lowest response as follows:

- Notification costs to data breach victims
- Legal defense costs
- Forensic and investigative costs
- Replacement of lost or damaged equipment
- Regulatory penalties and fines
- Revenue loss
- Third-party liability
- Communication costs to regulators
- Employee productivity losses
- Brand damage[23]

The above listing of areas to seek cyber insurance protection is consistent with most companies' concerns after experiencing a breach.

One very interesting result of this study revealed that companies rarely use formal risk assessments by in-house staff to determine how much coverage should be purchased. Instead, companies rely on the insurer to do a formal risk assessment.[24] What we find most striking about this situation is the fact that insurance carriers are only recently becoming involved with cybersecurity issues, so their level of experience and knowledge is probably not much deeper than that of the company's risk managers. Clearly, both groups will need further training and education as the field of cyber insurance develops. While corporations view the cybersecurity issues in terms of breaches, the insurance carriers view cybersecurity issues in terms of claims. Settled claims are determined by the company's cyber resilience defense against security breaches, as well as a host of other factors. So both groups must begin to learn a great deal more about cybersecurity since the costs of security breaches are increasing both in frequency and in costs measured into the millions of dollars and the insurance premiums as measured into the billions of dollars.

6.3.4 Security Breaches, Insurance Claims, and Actuarial Tables

The NetDiligence study "Cyber Liability and Data Breach Insurance Claims" is one of the more comprehensive examinations of the actual insurance payouts on claims for data breaches. The study was interested in comparing the actual cyber payouts to the anecdotal breach information that is reported in the media and industry reports. This study reported the real costs of cyber insurance payouts from an insurance company's perspective. Perhaps the most significant contribution of this study was the focus on improving the actuarial tables by encouraging risk managers and those working in the data security field to perform more accurate risk assessment reviews and to implement more effective safeguards to protect their organizations from data breaches. As the improvement of safeguards and risk assessments make progress in their respective areas, the insurance industry will be in a position to improve the actuarial tables, which will result in more precise price modeling of the cyber insurance policies. The NetDiligence study also compared their results to the work of the Ponemon study:

> Major underwriters of cyber liability provided information about 137 events that occurred between 2009 and 2011, which we analyzed for emerging patterns. Among our findings: PII (personal identification information) is the most typically exposed data type, followed by PHI (private health information). Topping the list of the most frequently breached sectors are health care and financial services. The average cost per breach was $3.7 million, with the majority devoted to legal damages.
>
> When compared with the Ponemon Institute's Seventh Annual U.S. Cost of a Data Breach Study, our figures appear to be extremely low. The institute reported an average cost of $5.5 million per breach and $194 per record. However, Ponemon differs from our study in two distinct ways: the data they gather is from a consumer perspective and as such they consider a broader range of cost factors such as detection, investigation and administration expenses, customer defections, opportunity loss, etc. Our study concentrates strictly on costs from the insurer's perspective and therefore provides a more focused view of breach costs.

The NetDiligence study also focuses primarily on insured per-breach costs, rather than per-record costs. As explained by Thomas Kang, Senior Claims Specialist at ACE USA, "You have to be careful in correlating too closely the cost of a breach response to the number of records. Certainly, it will cost more to notify and offer credit monitoring to more people, and there is greater risk of potential third-party claims for incidents involving a higher number of records. However, the legal and forensic costs can vary significantly depending on the complexity of the incident and the specific requirements in the policyholders industry, independent of the number of records. There appears to be an expectation in the marketplace for a breach to cost a certain amount simply based on the number of records, but our policyholders have been surprised to find that the actual response costs generally will be unique to the specifics of the breach. For example, we have breach incidents involving less than 5 thousand records, with remediation costs in six figures because of the policyholders' industry and the complexity of the breach."[25]

The NetDiligence study described their methodology in which they specifically worked with insurance underwriters and requested information on the data breaches and the claim losses sustained as follows:

Study Methodology

This study, although limited, is unique because it focuses on covered events and actual claims payouts. We asked the major underwriters of cyber liability to submit claims payout information based on the following criteria:

- The incident occurred between 2009 and 2011
- The victimized organization had some form of cyber or privacy liability coverage
- A legitimate claim was filed

We received claims information for 137 events that fit our selection criteria. Of those, 58 events included a detailed breakout of what was paid on the claim. Many of the events submitted for this year's study were recent, which means the claims are still being processed and actual costs have not yet been determined.

We used our entire sampling of 137 events to analyze the type of data breached, the cause of data loss and the business sectors affected. We used the smaller sampling (58 events) to evaluate the payouts associated with the events—again based on type of data breached, the cause of data loss and the business sectors affected.

As a result, readers should keep in mind the following:

- Our sampling is a small subset of all breaches
- Our numbers are lower than other studies because we focused on claims payouts rather than expenses incurred by the victimized organizations

- Our numbers are empirical as they were supplied directly by the underwriters who paid the claims
- Most claims were reported for total losses. Of those that mentioned retentions, these ran anywhere from $50 thousand to $1 million[26]

While this study reported on claims dated in 2011, they reported an average cost per incident of $3.7 million. The average cost for legal defense was $582,000, and the average legal settlement was $2.1 million. The average cost for crisis services, which included forensics, notification, call center expenses, credit monitoring, and legal guidance, was $983,000, and the business sectors most affected were financial services, health care, and retail stores.[27]

The 2013 Third Annual NetDiligence "Cyber Liability and Data Breach Insurance Claims Study" provided an update on the data from the 2011 figures, and they reported health care as the most frequently breached business sector, followed by the financial industry. The claims submitted ranged from $2500 to $20 million; however, the most typical range of claims was $25,000 to $400,000. Of the 140 claims submitted, 88 reported a total payout of $84 million; however, claims not reporting a total payout were still in litigation and a settlement had not yet been reached, so these figures will increase as the settlements are closed.[28]

The objective of both NetDiligence studies was to help risk management professionals and insurance underwriters understand the impact of security breaches. These two NetDiligence studies consolidated claims from multiple insurance carriers so that the combined pool of claims would permit real costs and possible future trends. The insurance industry studies alongside of industry reports by the Ponemon Institute and several other industry reports will be necessary to establish more precise actuarial tables.

6.4   Challenges to Current Cybersecurity Models

Based on the numerous industry-driven surveys on security breaches, especially those Ponemon Institute commissioned cybersecurity surveys from throughout the world, and coupled with the NetDiligence surveys on actual cyber insurance claims, it is abundantly clear that cybersecurity breaches are a global problem that is growing both in volume and cost.

6.4.1   Financial Services Sector

One of the areas in which growth continues to be targeted by cyber-criminals is the financial services sector. Financial service companies in the United States lost, on average, $23.6 million in 2013, and this represented a 44%

increase in average loss from the previous year of 2012.[29] In fact, financial institutions are experiencing such an increase in cyber threats that an assumption by most, if not all, financial institutions is that their customer personal computers (PCs) are infected with viruses. The thought that is beginning to underscore this assumption centers on Internet-based banking systems that are accessed through smart phones, which typically are insecure and open to multiple viruses due to their having use in social media sites. Another factor supporting this belief of customer widespread infected PCs is the abundant number of viruses targeting the financial community, which include ZeuS, SpyEye, Conficker, DNS Changer, Gameover ZeuS, Black Hole Exploit Kit, and fake antivirus software. In a white paper on cyber threats and financial institutions, Josh Bradford reports on the eight cyber threats that the FBI notes are of concern for financial institutions as follows:

- Account takeovers
- Third-party payment processor breaches
- Securities and market trading company breaches
- Automated teller machine skimming breaches
- Mobile banking breaches
- Insider access
- Supply chain infiltration
- Telecommunication and network disruption

The important aspect about account takeovers is a new emerging trend in which the cyber-criminals refocus their attack on the customers as opposed to only the financial institution. This is accomplished through targeted phishing schemes via e-mail or text messages, and it is designed to compromise the customer's online banking information. The "high roller" malware is designed to specifically target the PCs of bank customers with high account balances, and the infected PC or smart phone will automatically transfer large sums of money into mule business accounts at the precise moment the customers log into their account. In addition, the proliferation of relatively cheap "do it yourself virus kits" available through the Internet is creating more problems for the financial services sector.[30]

Additional concerns to the financial services firms throughout the world are the increasing frequency, speed, and sophistication of cyber attacks. The Deloitte Center for Financial Services analyzed data from an investigative annual report by Verizon and discovered that in 2013, 88% of the attacks initiated against financial service companies were successful in less than 24 hours. The speed of the cyber attack, the significant lag time in discovery of the attack, and the longer restoration of system services highlight the challenges in both the cyber attack detection and response capabilities.[31] In short, the attacker's "skill to attack" and the financial service firm's "ability to defend" outpace both the discovery and restoration success, which is so necessary to the continued financial stability and health of the financial sector firm.

The increasing sophistication of cyber attacks, which are being directed at more than just the financial sector but at many others as well, can be seen in the June 2014 PricewaterhouseCoopers Survey, "U.S. Cyber Crime: Rising Risks, Reduced Readiness," where they reported that, "Recently, for instance, hackers engineered a new round of distributed denial-of-service (DDoS) attacks that can generate traffic rated at a staggering 400 gigabits per second, the most powerful DDoS assaults to date."[32]

6.4.2   Survey of Financial Institutions' Cybersecurity Programs

The New York State Department of Financial Services' concern on the number of cyber attacks against financial institutions in terms of both the increasing frequency and sophistication of attacks caused them to survey all 154 financial institutions within New York State. Their survey was designed to seek information on each of the 154 institutions' cybersecurity programs and its costs and future plans. The objective of the survey research was to obtain a horizontal perspective of the financial services industry's efforts to prevent cyber crime and protect consumer and clients in the event of a security breach. The total of 154 depository institutions that completed the survey included 60 community and regional banks, 12 credit unions, and 82 foreign branches and agencies. They were asked questions about their information security framework; use and frequency of penetration testing; budget costs associated with cybersecurity; the frequency, nature, cost of, and response to cybersecurity breaches; and future plans on cybersecurity.[33]

Almost 90% of the surveyed institutions reported having an information security framework, in which the key pillars of their information security program included the following:

- A written information security plan
- Security awareness education and employee training
- Risk management of cyber risk including trends
- Information security audits
- Incident monitoring and reporting[34]

The vast majority of institutions reported utilizing some or all of the following software security tools:

- Antivirus software
- Spyware and malware detection

- Firewalls
- Server-based access control lists
- Intrusion detection tools
- Vulnerability scanning tools
- Encryption for data in transit
- Encrypted files
- Data loss prevention tools

Also, most of the institutions used penetration testing as an additional important element to the above listing of defenses. However, more than 85% of the institutions participating in penetration testing used third-party consultants to perform the penetration tests. Another point of importance was the number of institutions participating in the Information Sharing and Analysis Centers (ISACs), which dropped off at the level of small-institution participation rate of 25% and large-institution participation rate of 60%. Institutions, particularly the smaller institutions, if not all, could achieve an advantage by participation in the F-ISACs, or Financial-ISACs. The federal government and Department of Homeland Security share a great deal of their information from the reports sent to the ISACs.[35]

It is interesting to note that virtually all surveyed institutions anticipate budgetary increases for their cybersecurity programs, and the three principal reasons for this are because of (1) compliance and regulatory requirements, (2) business continuity and disaster recovery, and (3) concern for reputational risk. Despite budgetary increases in their cybersecurity programs, their expressed concerns as to the primary barriers they will encounter in building cybersecurity programs for the future centered on the increasing sophistication of the threats and cyber attacks. They were also concerned about the emerging technologies and their ability to keep pace with these new technologies.[36]

6.4.3   New Cybersecurity Models

Despite all the efforts of institutions and organizations across all business sectors and regions, the risk of cyber attacks is a significant issue that could have major strategic implications for the global economy. McKinsey & Company prepared a report, "Risk and Responsibility in a Hyperconnected World," with the cooperation of the World Economic Forum as a joint research effort to develop a fact-based view of cyber risks and to assess their economic and strategic implications. They interviewed executives and reviewed data from more than 200 enterprises, and their main finding was despite years of effort and tens of billions of dollars spent annually, the global economy is still not sufficiently protected against cyber attacks and the risks are increasing and getting worse. They further concluded that the risk of cyber attacks could materially slow the pace of technology and business innovation with as much as $3 trillion in aggregate impact.[37]

While the major technology transformational advancements made by big data and cloud computing are expected to add $10 trillion dollars to the global economy, the potential drag on these technologies will continue to originate from the increasing volume and complexity of cyber attacks. Also, the introduction of big data offers a vast new opportunity for security breaches so each of the estimates is subject to major revision, and our fear is the losses will increase on a global scale while the anticipated revenue from the new transformational technologies of big data and cloud computing will decrease below anticipated estimates.

The McKinsey & Company report stated, "The defenders are losing ground to the attackers. Nearly 60% of technology executives said that they cannot keep up with attackers increasing sophistication." In short, current models of cybersecurity protection across so many business sectors are simply becoming less effective in protecting institutions from cyber attacks.[38] As a result, we need further thought and analysis on building very different cybersecurity operating models. Current models are very IT centric, and the complexity of these models deters the CEOs and other C-level administrators from more active participation. Therefore, new cybersecurity models should be designed to engage senior business leaders by transitioning from technology centric to view these breaches as strategic business risks.

The CEOs of the past were focused only on "revenue centers" and their quarterly returns. Now that the level of cyber attacks is capable of stealing intellectual property and totally devastating a business organization, the board of director's fiduciary responsibilities have resulted in a series of "wake-up calls" to the CEOs for full engagement in developing effective cybersecurity programs. Many boards of directors now expect quarterly progress reports and are holding the CEOs and leading C-level administrators responsible for the development of more effective programs.

In addition to the past nonengagement of senior business executives, the shortcomings of the IT-centric model was simply around a "reactive" model of audit and compliance, and at best, the fragmented approaches simply were not designed to anticipate the increasing sophistication of cyber attacks.

The Deloitte Center for Financial Services offers important suggestions for model development in their report "Transforming Cybersecurity: New Approaches for an Evolving Threat Landscape." One suggestion is to enhance security through a "defense-in-depth" strategy that involves a number of mutually reinforcing security layers both to provide redundancy and potentially slow down the progression of attacks in progress, if not prevent them. The improvement of a cybersecurity model is a three-stage process that includes (1) secure, (2) vigilant, and (3) resilient. By (1) secure, the focus is on enhanced risk-prioritized controls to protect against known and emerging threats in compliance with industry standards and regulations. (2) Vigilant is an emphasis on the detection of violations and anomalies through more effective situational awareness across the environment, which implies intelligence activities not only limited to collection of raw data on known threat indicators but also through the engagement of direct human involvement. (3) Resilient is the establishment of programs with the ability to rapidly return to normal operations and repair damage to the business by the cybersecurity breach. Thus, a well-rounded cybersecurity program model is based on the three components of secure, vigilant, and resilient. However, this model requires actionable threat intelligence premised on experience-based learning and situational awareness. The final level requirement is to model the cybersecurity program with a strategic organizational approach that includes top-level executive sponsorship, a dedicated threat-management team, renewed focus on analytics and not solely automation, and a strong emphasis on external collaboration from the ISACs and F-ISACs to other important intelligence sources.[39]

6.4.4 Summary

In summary, the increasing risks of cybersecurity attacks and the growing sophistication of these cyber breaches have now reached a point where business executives are acknowledging that their ability to keep pace with these breaches is not keeping pace with those attacking their companies. The costs of these attacks and the need for cyber insurance have reached a level where security breaches are simply not only a problem for the IT departments, as these cyber breaches have become a major strategic business risk. As such, there will be a need for cross-functional teams composed of the CEO and other C-level administrators, including the chief information officer, chief information security officer, chief operating officer, risk manager, compliance officer, and corporate council, to develop actionable programs that go beyond the "reactive" and audit-compliance aspects of the more traditional information security programs. The new cybersecurity and IT models must be guided by a new enriched business-driven risk management approach.

The costs of cyber attacks today are so serious that they are threatening the very sustainability of corporations throughout the world. In addition to the cyber attacks threatening the sustainability of our corporations and business community, other private and public entities are also being attacked, and their capability to withstand such serious cyber attacks is even less ensured than that of the corporate community. Hospitals, health care facilities, schools, and universities as well as most municipal and local governmental agencies simply do not have the personnel or capabilities to withstand the sophisticated level of attacks that could be directed at them, should they become targeted for such security attacks. Similarly, most states and many federal governmental agencies have minimal ability to cope with the number of attacks that could be directed at them for extended attack time periods. While our nation's military and intelligence community have developed both programs and personnel with new skills to defend against the enormous range of cyber attacks, the sheer number of daily attacks is coming perilously close to overwhelming their defensive capabilities. Our nation cannot afford for these important and critical agencies to confront security attacks that could potentially result in their loss of sustainable operational capability.

Notes and References

1. Cashell, Jackson, Jickling and Webel. *The Economic Impact of Cyber-Attacks*, CRS-1.
2. Ibid., CRS-8.
3. Ibid., CRS-11.
4. Ibid., CRS-13.
5. Ibid., CRS-17.
6. Ibid., CRS-14.
7. Ponemon Research Institute. *2013 Cost of Cyber Crime Study: United States*; and the *2013 Cost of Cyber Crime Study: United Kingdom*; and *2013 Cost of Cyber Crime Study: Germany*; and *2013 Cost of Cyber Crime Study: Japan*; and *2013 Cost of Cyber Crime Study: Australia*; and *2013 Cost of Cyber Crime Study: France*; and the *2013 Cost of Cyber Crime Study: Global Report*, 1.
8. Ponemon Research Institute. *2013 Cost of Cyber Crime Study: United States*, 1–2, 23.
9. Ibid., 1.
10. Ibid., 1, 4.
11. Ponemon Research Institute. *2013 Cost of Cyber Crime Study: Global Report*, 1, 3–4.
12. IBM Global Technology Services. *IBM Security Services Cyber Security Intelligence Index*, 1–2, 4–5.
13. Ponemon Institute Research Report. *2014 Cost of Data Breach Study: Global Analysis*, 3, 23–24, 27.
14. Ibid., 2.
15. Ibid., 16.
16. Ibid., 16, 22.
17. Kumar. "Schnucks Agrees to Proposed Settlement Over Data Breach," 1.
18. Business Section. "Cyber-Security: White Hats to the Rescue," 1.
19. Harris. *Cybersecurity in the Golden State*, 2.
20. Ponemon Institute. *Managing Cyber Security as a Business Risk: Cyber Insurance in the Digital Age*, 1.
21. Ibid., 4.
22. Ibid., 8–9.
23. Ibid., 10.
24. Loc. Cit.

25. Greisiger. *Cyber Liability and Data Breach Insurance Claims: A Study of Actual Payouts for Covered Data Breaches*, 4–5.
26. Ibid., 6.
27. Ibid., 7–8.
28. Greisiger. *Cyber Liability and Data Breach Insurance Claims: A Study of Actual Claim Payouts*, 1–3.
29. Deloitte Center for Financial Services. *Transforming Cybersecurity: New Approaches for an Evolving Threat Landscape*, 1.
30. Bradford. *Cyber-Threats and Financial Institutions: Assume All Networks are Infected...Is This the New Normal?*, 2–5, 7.
31. Deloitte Center for Financial Services. op. cit., 4–5.
32. PricewaterhouseCoopers. *U.S. Cybercrime: Rising Risks, Reduced Readiness: Key Findings from the 2014 U.S. State of Cybercrime Survey*, 4.
33. Cuomo and Lawsky. *Report on Cyber Security in the Banking Sector*, 1.
34. Ibid., 2.
35. Ibid., 3–5.
36. Ibid., 6, 10.
37. Chinn, Kaplan and Weinberg. "Risk and Responsibility in a Hyperconnected World: Implications for Enterprises." Also see, *The Rising Strategic Risks of Cyber Attacks*, McKinsey Quarterly, 1.
38. Loc. Cit.
39. Deloitte Center for Financial Services, 6–8.

Bibliography

Bradford, J. *Cyber-Threats and Financial Institutions: Assume all Networks are Infected... Is This the New Normal?* A White Paper. Sponsored by Chartis, Advisen Ltd, Washington, DC, 2012.

Business Section. "Cyber-Security: White Hats to the Rescue." In *The Economist*, New York: Print Edition, 2014.

Cashell, B., Jackson, W. D., Jickling, M., and Webel, B. *The Economic Impact of Cyber-Attacks*. CRS Report for Congress; Congressional Research Service: The Library of Congress, Washington, DC, RL32331, 2004.

Chinn, D., Kaplan, J., and Weinberg, A. "Risk and Responsibility in a Hyperconnected World: Implications for Enterprises," also see *The Rising Strategic Risks of Cyber Attacks*, McKinsey Quarterly, 2014.

Cuomo, A. M., and Lawsky, B. M. *Report on Cyber Security in the Banking Sector*. Albany: New York State Department of Financial Services, 2014.

Deloitte Center for Financial Services. *Transforming Cybersecurity: New Approaches for an Evolving Threat Landscape*. New York: Deloitte Development, 2014.

Greisiger, M. *Cyber Liability & Data Breach Insurance Claims: A Study of Actual Payouts for Covered Data Breaches, NetDiligence*. Pennsylvania: A Company of Network Standard Corporation, 2012.

Greisiger, M. *Cyber Liability & Data Breach Insurance Claims: A Study of Actual Claim Payouts*. Pennsylvania: Sponsored by AllClear ID, Faruki, Ireland and Cox PLL, Kivu Consulting; NetDiligence: A Company of Network Standard Corporation, 2013.

Harris, K. D. *Cybersecurity in the Golden State.* California: Department of Justice, 2014.

IBM Global Technology Services. *IBM Security Services Cyber Security Intelligence Index,* 2013. Available at IBM.COM/Services/Security.

Kumar, K. "Schnucks Agrees to Proposed Settlement Over Data Breach." In *St Louis Post-Dispatch.* Missouri: Kevin D. Mowbray, 2013.

Ponemon Institute. *Managing Cyber Security as a Business Risk: Cyber Insurance in the Digital Age.* Michigan: Sponsored by Experian Data Breach Resolution, Ponemon Institute, LLC, 2013.

Ponemon Institute Research Report. *2014 Cost of Data Breach Study: Global Analysis.* Michigan: Sponsored by IBM Benchmark Research, Ponemon Institute, LLC, 2014.

Ponemon Research Institute. *2013 Cost of Cyber Crime Study: Global Report.* Michigan: Sponsored by HP Enterprise Security, Ponemon Institute, LLC, 2013.

Ponemon Research Institute. *2013 Cost of Cyber Crime Study: United States;* and the *2013 Cost of Cyber Crime Study: United Kingdom;* and *2013 Cost of Cyber Crime Study: Germany;* and *2013 Cost of Cyber Crime Study: Japan;* and *2013 Cost of Cyber Crime Study: Australia;* and *2013 Cost of Cyber Crime Study: France;* and the *2013 Cost of Cyber Crime Study: Global Report.* Michigan: Sponsored by HP Enterprise Security, Independently conducted by Ponemon Institute, LLC, 2013.

Ponemon Research Institute Report. *2013 Cost of Cyber Crime Study: United States.* Michigan: Sponsored by HP Enterprise Security, Ponemon Institute, LLC, 2013.

PricewaterhouseCoopers. *U.S. Cybercrime: Rising Risks, Reduced Readiness: Key Findings from the 2014 U.S. State of Cybercrime Survey.* Delaware: Co-sponsored by the CERT Division of Software Engineering Institute at Carnegie Mellon University; CSO Magazine; United States Secret Service, 2014.

Cybersecurity Threat Landscape and Future Trends

7

THOMAS A. JOHNSON

Contents

7.1 Introduction

This chapter will explore the transformational changes that will impact the entire field of information assurance and computer security as a result of five major trends throughout the world. These five trends are the following:

- Virtualization
- Social media

- Cloud computing
- Internet of Things (IoT)
- Big data

Each of these trends provides clear enhancements and cost-effective strategies for improving business operations and revenue streams for corporations. However, collectively, these trends introduce a transformational challenge to computer security professionals because the field has not yet been confronted with such a fundamental change in providing security to the volume and velocity of data that is being created in terms of exabyte capacities. The entire data and computer industry is confronting a change at a level few are prepared to address.

The increasing number of breaches throughout our global community of businesses, government, and citizens has occurred within a threat landscape of attack mechanisms far beyond the current computer security defense capabilities. The potential volume of new data in both structured and unstructured formats will introduce new threat attacks and will deeply impact corporations, governments, and military institutions throughout the world.

The cost of securing information and the incredible size of databases will increase in both financial terms as well as in risk and vulnerability. New skill sets and the training and education of computer security and data professionals will be required to become prepared for the massive changes that will impact virtually all industries, governments and nations.

7.2   Breaches—Global Data

The number and types of breaches occurring globally can best be ascertained by going directly to the source of those corporations and entities that are offering security services, and obtaining their conclusions on the range of current breach activity.

The Symantec Corporation has compiled an impressive data report in their "Internet Security Threat Report 2014," and they have perhaps the most comprehensive source of Internet threat data in the world. Their data are captured by the Symantec Global Intelligence Network of over 41.5 million attack sensors, which record thousands of events per second. The Symantec Network monitors threat activity in 157 countries and territories. In addition to their real-time monitoring of events, Symantec also maintains one of the world's most comprehensive vulnerability databases consisting of over 60,000 identified vulnerabilities over 20 years and from over 19,000 vendors representing 54,000 products. The Symantec Probe Network, which includes a system of more than 5 million decoy accounts, collects data on spam, phishing, and malware data. Symantec's Skeptic Cloud proprietary system for heuristic technology is designed to detect new sophisticated targeted threats before they reach the networks of their clients. The scope of this system is impressive, as over 8.4 billion e-mail messages are processed each month along with more than 1.7 billion web requests filtered each day across 14 data centers.[1]

The data collected over 2013 recorded eight mega breaches in which over 10 million identities were exposed and the targeted attacks of spear-phishing attacks increased by 91%. In addition, there was a dramatic increase in watering-hole attacks and attacks based on a legitimate website having malware being installed by attackers with the purpose of advancing an advanced persistent threat (APT) attack. So both spear-phishing and watering-hole attacks increasing in frequency suggest an increase in APT attacks. Symantec's research suggested that 77% of legitimate websites had exploitable vulnerabilities and 16% of all websites had a critical vulnerability installed by an individual or group focused on targeting victims visiting these websites.[2]

There was a 500% increase in Ransomware attacks where the attacker pretends to be a law enforcement agent and demands $100 to $500 to unlock the victim's computer from the encryption planted surreptitiously on the victim's computer. This attack evolved into the CryptoLocker attack, in which the user's files and entire hard drive were encrypted and the attacker would decrypt the files only if a ransom fee was paid.[3]

Other conclusions reached by the extensive Symantec Internet Threat Report were the increase in social media scams and the increase in malware targeting mobile applications and devices. Also for the first time, attackers began attacking devices through the IoT, such as baby monitors, security cameras, smart televisions, automobiles, and even medical equipment. The IoT will become a prime attack vector in which we are clearly not prepared to provide security.[4] As the volume of data increases as a result of a proliferation of devices connected to the IoT, we will also experience a phenomenal number of new threats and attacks.

Another important source of global data is provided by FireEye and Mandiant, a FireEye company. Their data are gathered from more than 1216 organizations in 63 countries across more than 20 industries. In addition to their collection of autogenerated data, they also surveyed 348 organizations and they concluded that no nation or no corner of the world is free from attack vulnerabilities. Also, they concluded that the two most vulnerable vertical industries to attack were higher education and financial services. Higher education is a prime target because of the vast amount of valuable intellectual property and their open network philosophy, which makes them quite vulnerable and easy to breach. The financial services industry is vulnerable due to their vast amount of cash and the physical resources they possess.[5]

The "Verizon 2013 Data Breach Investigations Report" was based on data collected from the following 18 contributors:

Complete List of 2013 DBIR Partners
- Australian Federal Police
- CERT Insider Threat Center at the Carnegie Mellon University Software Engineering Institute (United States)
- Consortium for Cybersecurity Action (United States)
- Danish Ministry of Defence, Center for Cybersecurity
- Danish National Police, NITES (National IT Investigation Section)
- Deloitte (United States)
- Dutch Police: National High Tech Crime Unit
- Electricity Sector Information Sharing and Analysis Center (United States)
- European Cyber Crime Center
- G-C Partners, LLC (United States)
- Guardia Civil (Cybercrime Central Unit) (Spain)
- Industrial Control Systems Cyber Emergency Response Team
- Irish Reporting and Information Security Service (IRISS-CERT)
- Malaysia Computer Emergency Response Team, CyberSecurity Malaysia
- National Cybersecurity and Communications Integration Center (United States)
- ThreatSim (United States)
- U.S. Computer Emergency Readiness Team
- U.S. Secret Service

The Verizon combined data set for 2013 reflected 2012 numbers in which 47,000 reported security incidents resulted in 621 confirmed data disclosures, which resulted in 44 million compromised records. In the nine-year period Verizon has been collecting these data, they have reported on 2500 data disclosures and over 1.1 billion compromised records.[6]

The impressive amount of data collected by Symantec, FireEye, and Verizon provides an important perspective on the extraordinary challenges confronting computer security professionals. Also, the attacks reported are only those attacks known and discovered. There are many successful attacks that remain unknown for a vast period of time, and in the case of APT attacks, the normative range is approximately 243 days before the victim is aware of the attack. Some attacks have resulted in the attacker's presence on the targeted system for as long as four years. We have no way of knowing how many systems have been attacked without the knowledge of the victim.

The most sophisticated form of a targeting attack in 2013 made use of the watering-hole attack, in which the attackers infiltrated a very legitimate website and planted malicious code and then simply waited for their target to access the website since the attacker was able to monitor the logs of the compromised website. The attacker's process of reconnaissance of the potential target enables the attacker to select a number of legitimate websites that the victim is liable to visit as a result of the victim's interest in the nature of the website. This attack technique is effective because the victim is not suspicious of legitimate websites and is totally unaware that someone may have planted malicious code on the websites.[7]

Another interesting industry that has been targeted in 2013 is the health care industry, and the purpose for these attacks is a result of the enormous number of people with absolutely valid personal identification information that will be valuable to the attacker in using or selling this compromised information to other cyber-criminals. This tactic will certainly increase in volume as a result of the Affordable Health Care Act (Obama Care) since there are millions of people adding their medical information to databases that have operated in a most ineffective fashion during the first four months leading up to its full implementation. Another reason this will become a high-valued target is the potential access points that attackers will have to the U.S. Treasury databases, since those signing up and enrolling in the Affordable Health Care Act must be qualified by the level of their income. Therefore, health care databases interacting with Treasury and Internal Revenue Service databases will provide an opportunity for potential targeting by attackers who no doubt are already developing malicious code and malware which will be targeted at these areas.

The business model for the delivery of toolkits such as the Black Hat exploit kit, Magnitude Exploit, and the authors of the Ransomware threats such as Revention (Trojan.Ransomlock.G) have moved to the Whitehole kit. The new business model now permits the developers of the malware to retain ownership as they do not sell the kits outright, but they offer their kits as a service in which they maintain full control of the code and they administer the tool kit by offering their services for a fee to anyone wishing to compromise another person's computer system.[8] Some attackers now advertise their services on the Silk Road and the Dark Web. Some even have been emboldened to offer their services on the Internet.

FireEye and Mandiant reported on the new generation of attacks including high-end cyber crime and state-sponsored campaigns known as APT attacks. Common to these attacks is the organizational method in which multiple teams of people are involved and each with assigned specific tasks. Another unique facet of an APT attack is that it is not a single, one-step attack but is coordinated through multiple steps. The process of the attack is described as follows:

1. External reconnaissance. Attackers typically seek out and analyze potential targets—anyone from senior leaders to administrative staff—to identify persons of interest and tailor their tactics to gain access to target systems. Attackers can even collect personal information from public websites to write convincing spear-phishing e-mail.

2. Initial compromise. In this stage, the attacker gains access to the system. The attacker can use a variety of methods, including well-crafted spear-phishing e-mails and watering-hole attacks that compromise websites known to draw a sought-after audience.

3. Foothold established. The attackers attempt to obtain domain administrative credentials (usually in encrypted form) from the targeted company and transfer them out of the network. To strengthen their position in the compromised network, intruders often use stealthy malware that avoids detection by host-based and network-based safeguards. For example, the malware may install with system-level privileges by injecting itself into legitimate processes, modifying the registry, or hijacking scheduled services.

4. Internal reconnaissance. In this step, attackers collect information on surrounding infrastructure, trust relationships, and the Windows domain structure. The goal: move laterally within the compromised network to identify valuable data. During this phase, attackers typically deploy additional backdoors so they can regain access to a network if they are detected.

5. Mission completed? Once attackers secure a foothold and locate valuable information, they exfiltrate data such as e-mails, attachments, and files residing on user workstations and file servers. Attackers typically try to retain control of compromised systems, poised to steal the next set of valuable data they come across. To maintain a presence, they often try to cover their tracks to avoid detection.[9]

Tony Flick and Justin Morehouse's book, *Securing the Smart Grid: Next Generation Power Grid Security*, discusses what security professionals expect and what they predict particularly in the emergence of an all-encompassing smart grid. Clearly, the electrical power grid has received the most attention, and in California, the PG&E has established a smart grid for customer's use of electricity. Some areas are moving their natural gas and water systems through this same transformation, so they may also operate within a smart grid. The creation of a metering infrastructure will require advanced sensor networks to be deployed, and this will enable the utility workers to locate water and gas leaks faster and even remotely. This system of smart grids will assist customers in more effectively regulating their use of these utilities in a more cost-effective manner. However, security professionals are concerned that their new smart grids and their supporting infrastructure will offer security vulnerabilities that could cause a local or potential national catastrophe if they become targeted by cyber-criminals or nation-state's focused on causing harm for the United States. Interestingly, the city of Tallahassee, Florida, is creating a smart grid that includes the electricity, gas, and water utilities, and while this will be more convenient for the citizens to see the total cost of their utility services in real-time on one system, it does, on the other hand, present itself as a single point of failure in which all utility service could be lost.[10]

The possibility of failure is consistent with our nation's concern for the safety and reliability of our critical infrastructure. On May 1, 2013, Bill Gertz reported in The Washington Free Beacon that U.S. Intelligence Agencies traced a recent cyber intrusion into a sensitive infrastructure database to the Chinese government or their military cyber warriors. The compromise of the U.S. Army Corps of Engineers National Inventory of Dams suggest that China might be preparing to conduct a future cyber attack against our electrical power grid, including the electricity produced by our hydroelectric dams. Evidently, the database hacked contains sensitive information on vulnerabilities of every major dam in the United States. The database also contains information on the number of people who might be killed if the dam failed, so it included significant and high-hazard level dams.[11]

General Keith Alexander has repeatedly warned our nation that potential adversaries are increasing their level of sophistication in their offensive cyber capabilities and tactics. Since cyber warfare is moving well beyond simply the disruption of networks to the era in which malware and malicious code can be planted within computer systems, we now face the enhanced risk of destruction of hydroelectric generators at dams with the potential for cyber attacks on the electrical power controllers as well.[12]

Clearly, the Chinese and the Russians have military cyber capabilities to clandestinely implant malicious code and malware into the U.S. electrical power grid system. We have already noted attempts at penetration of these critical infrastructures, and we must remain vigilant to protect against further attempts.

7.3   Threat Landscape

The increasing number of breaches occurring globally as reported by Symantec, FireEye, and Verizon is most alarming as it represents a significant threat to all nations. The loss of intellectual property and damage to information systems is a cost that is causing a great deal of alarm to both the corporate suites of major corporations as well as to governmental leaders throughout the world. The increasing number of breaches is causing the retargeting of limited resources from new developmental projects to firming up the cybersecurity defense programs.

The breaches that have occurred over the years have evolved and increased as a result of the numerous attack tools and exploit techniques that are too easily available for free from the Internet or by sale from cyber-criminals and hactivists. Despite the thousands of different computer and network attacks that have been developed and used since the very first computer attack tools were identified in 1981, we believe that analysis of the threat landscape provides an organizational framework of great value.

Steve Piper's *Definitive Guide to Next Generation Threat Protection* is an excellent resource available from the CyberEdge Group, and we recommend building on his framework as it will be extremely useful in analyzing vulnerabilities and developing defense strategies against breaches.[13]

7.3.1   Traditional Threats

Worm
- A stand-alone malware program that replicates itself
- Harms networks by consuming bandwidth
- A lateral attack vector that can exfiltrate data

Trojan
- Typically masquerades as a helpful software application
- Can be initiated by spam mail, social media, or a game application

Computer virus
- Is a malicious code that attaches itself to a program or file, enabling it to spread from one computer to another, leaving infections as it travels

Spyware
- Covertly gathers user information without the user's knowledge, usually for advertising called "Adware"

Botnet
- Is a collection of compromised Internet-connected computers on which malware is running command and control servers; can launch distributed denial-of-service (DDoS) attacks using these botnets

7.3.2   Social Engineering Threats

Social engineering attacks
- An example is phishing, in which the purpose is to obtain user names, passwords, credit card information, and social security information.

- After clicking on a (seemingly innocent) hyperlink, the user is directed to enter personal details on a fake website that looks almost identical to a legitimate website.

Spear phishing
- Targets a specific person within an organization.

Whaling
- Is directed specifically toward senior executives and other high-profile targets.

Baiting
- A criminal casually and purposefully drops a USB-thumb drive or CD-ROM in a parking lot or Cyber Café. The drive is prominently labeled with words, such as, "Executive Compensation" or "Company Confidential" to pique the interest of whoever finds it. When the victim accesses the media in their computer it installs the malware.

7.3.3 Buffer Overflow and Structured Query Language Injection

Buffer overflow
- The hacker writes more data into a memory buffer than the buffer is designed to hold. Some of the data spill into adjacent memory, causing the desktop or web-based application to execute arbitrary code with escalated privileges or to crash.

Structured query language (SQL) injection
- Attacks databases through a website or web-based application. The attacker submits SQL statements into a web form in an attempt to get the web application to pass the rogue SQL command to the database. A successful SQL injection attack can reveal database content such as credit card numbers and social security numbers and passwords.

7.3.4 Next-Generation Threats

Polymorphic threats
- A cyber attack such as a virus, worm, spyware, or Trojan that constantly changes (morphs), making it impossible to detect using signature-based defenses.
- Vendors who manufacture signature-based security products must consistently create and distribute new threat signatures.

Blended threats
- A cyber attack that combines elements of multiple types of malware and usually employs multiple attack vectors (varying paths

and targets of attack) to increase severity of damage. Examples
are Nimda virus, Code Red virus, Conficker virus.

Zero-Day Attack

- Zero-Day threat is a cyber attack on an application or an
  unknown publicly operating system application vulnerability so
  named because the attack is launched on or before "day zero" of
  public awareness of the vulnerability.

APTs

- Sophisticated network attacks in which an unauthorized person
  gains access to a network and stays undetected for a long period
  of time. The intention of the APT is to exfiltrate data rather than
  cause damage.
- The APT attack process is as follows:

  Stage 1—Initial intrusion through system exploitation.

  Stage 2—Malware is installed on the compromised system.

  Stage 3—Outbound connection initiated.

  Stage 4—Attack spreads laterally.

  Stage 5—Compromised data are extracted via tunneling and
  encryption.

  Stage 6—Attacker covers their tracks—remains undetected.

Eric Cole describes APT attacks as being targeted, data focused, and
seeking high-valued information and intellectual property from the victim organization being probed. If the APT attack is successful, the amount
of damage to the organization will be very significant. Cole reports on the
characteristics of the APT attack as being a nonstop attack, and signature
analysis will be ineffective in protecting against the attack. Attackers, once
obtaining access, will not simply get in and then leave, as they want long-term access and will remain as long as possible. Several researchers have discovered that a norm of 243 days before discovery of the attack was reported,
with some attacks lasting as long as four years before discovery of the APT
attack. Cole also reports that the APT attack is not based on an individual
or small hacker cell but a well-organized and very structured organization in which there are an attack protocol and methodology that are very
detailed and sophisticated. Cole also indicates that one of the most frightening features of the APT is that it turns our biggest strength into our biggest
weakness. So by using encryption that was designed to protect and prevent
attackers from accessing critical information, the attacker uses encryption
to establish an outbound tunnel from the targeted victim's organization
to the attacker's site and exfiltrates data in an encrypted format virtually
undetected, as most security devices are not capable of reading encrypted
packets.[14]

Additional new threat attacks such as CryptoLocker and Ransomware permit the cyber-criminal to encrypt and prevent access to all files unless the victim pays the extortion fee to have their computer files decrypted and regain access to the files. Donna Leinwand Leger reports that small groups of anonymous hackers once went after individual victims, but now, we are experiencing how they have organized into crime syndicates that launch massive attacks against entire companies. Also, computer threat researchers at Dell Secure Works estimated that the CryptoLocker virus struck over 250,000 computers in its first 100 days. The virus is being sent through "the onion router," (TOR), and it comes to the victim via an infected e-mail that appears to come from the local police or the Federal Bureau of Investigation, a package delivery service such as FedEx or UPS, or in PDF attachments. Once the victim's computer is infected, a pop-up screen appears with instructions to pay the ransom through an anonymous payment system such as Ukash, PaySafe, MoneyPak, or Bitcoin. In some cases, the pop-up screen has a clock running, which notifies the victim to pay within so many hours or the ransom price will be increased. CryptoLocker is one of the few mainstream attacks where security companies do not have a method for decrypting the virus. Kaspersky Lab in North America reported no effective cure for the CryptoLocker virus, at least at the time this book is being written.[15] The range of victims not only includes individuals, and companies but also police departments. We anticipate that any organization with data may be targeted.

7.3.5 Attacker's Need for Information

Irrespective of the type of computer attack or exploit techniques that an attacker would plan to use, the one item absolutely necessary for the attacker is information. The source of information to the attacker would be the servers at the targeted victim's organization. To acquire this information, the attacker needs an Internet protocol (IP) address, and since ports are the entry point into a computer system, the attacker will be looking for open ports. Ultimately, for an attacker to compromise a system, there must be vulnerability present on the system and the attacker will attempt to discover this vulnerability. To acquire the IP information, the attacker will use a Whois search to find the name servers for the domain. Once the name servers are identified, the attacker will use Nslookup to identify the IP. The Nslookup will identify the organization's IP address, and if it is a U.S. address, the American Registry for Internet Numbers (ARIN) will provide the range of the address to the target. Once the attacker knows the IP range, the attacker will scan the range to discover visible IP addresses and open ports, and this process can be accomplished with tools such as NMap and Zenmap, both software tools used as security scanners to discover hosts or services on a computer network. The next step in an attack on a targeted organization is to locate vulnerabilities, and the attacker will use a vulnerability scanner such as OpenVas to identify vulnerabilities or exposures. The next step the attacker will implement is to use a tool such as Core Impact, as this tool will actually find system vulnerabilities and, if vulnerable, will exploit the service and provide the attacker access to the system. Eric Cole recommends that an organization should apply this same technique to discover and identify their exposure points, to increase their own security.[16]

The classic book on computer attacks and one of the most outstanding orientations to the common phases of an attack on computers and networks is provided by Ed Skoudis and Tom Liston in their book *Counter Hack Reloaded*, where they provide a step-by-step guide to both attacks and the defense to such attacks. Skoudis and Liston note that most attacks follow a general five-phase approach, which includes reconnaissance, scanning, gaining access, maintaining access, and covering the tracks of the attack. They outline the process as follows:

Typical Phase of the Computer Attack
   Phase 1—Reconnaissance
   Phase 2—Scanning
   Phase 3A—Gaining Access at the Operating System and Application
      Level
   Phase 3B—Gaining Access at the Network Level
   Phase 3C—Gaining Access and Denial-of-Service Attacks
   Phase 4—Maintaining Access
   Phase 5—Covering Tracks and Hiding

The exceptional contribution of their book centers on the comprehensive description of each attack phase and the tools and techniques used during each stage of the attack.[17]

Eric Cole considers APT attacks so significant and such a transformational attack on our traditional cybersecurity products, programs, and systems that he was moved to write his excellent book *Advanced Persistent Threat* on this subject because it quite simply changed the rules as to how we secure our systems. For example, over the years, worms and viruses adapted and changed, but the fundamental way they worked remained the same. The APT is no longer software that is programmed to perform a certain function; now, it is a person, group, or a nation that is an organized adversary that will not give up until they obtain or exfiltrate the information or intellectual property they are seeking. Therefore, to defend against an APT attack, you will not find a product that will protect your organization. Instead, it will be necessary to develop a strategy that implements a variety of solutions that can be adaptive and be prepared for future changes in the APT threat. This new strategy must be more than the past approach of reactive security, and we now must have a proactive security approach that goes beyond the binary decision of allowed or denied. Today, our cybersecurity environment operates within social media, cloud computing, bring your own devices (BYOD), the machine-to-machine IoT (M2M-IoT), and big data, all areas in which there will be different levels of trust and access which will be required. Therefore, access has to be based on overall risk and not simply static rules. The overarching reality is quite simply: whether you are an individual, small company, a major corporation, government organization, or a university, you will be targeted and you will be attacked.[18]

7.4   Transformational Changes for Cybersecurity

The challenges confronting information assurance and cybersecurity have become greatly pronounced as a result of five major transformational changes in how data are produced, processed, collected, stored, and utilized. These five transformational changes are as follows:

- Virtualization
- Social media
- Cloud computing
- M2M-IoT
- Big data

These five major movements are creating both major advancements and increased productivity in the industries and governmental entities utilizing one or more of them. While the corporate community embraces the increased revenue streams that each may produce, they will also experience increased costs in the information technology (IT) and computer security created by these transformational movements. In addition to enhanced data security problems creating a need for more skilled personnel, there will also be increased needs for data analytics personnel.

The five transformational movements have an interesting relationship in terms of their interdependencies. For example, the virtualization of computer server provisioning has created the need for cloud computing. The explosive growth in social media provided an enhanced need for virtualization and also created a need for cloud computing. The presence of cloud computing and its availability as either a public cloud, private cloud, community cloud, or hybrid cloud provide a menu suitable to a reduced cost structure to those corporations or governments adopting one of these models. Cloud computing also requires the advances made in virtualization, and while there are cost savings in computer hardware, the challenges of computer security of the cloud environment is considered a challenge. The IoT, which is based upon M2M integration of automatic data stream processing from one computer sensor to another sensor, as an example your home heating and cooling thermostat to your smart phone as well as other appliances, is representative of the enormous increase in the processing of data. The IoT will include all forms of digital data, which include voice, video, and text, and its growth is at an exponential level. Since these data streams are being processed through the Internet, the processing requires a new format of unstructured data that differ from the traditional SQL for accessing relational databases. So this movement of IoT has created the need for big data and the introduction of Hadoop and NoSQL to process the phenomenal volume and velocity of these new data streams. Big data will also require new personnel in the data analytics field, as well as increased cybersecurity provisioning.

The cumulative interdependencies of these five transformational movements have resulted in major advancements for the entire computer industry. We will describe some of the emerging challenges and provide a brief overview of the contributions that each of the five movements has made to the overall computer industry.

7.4.1 Virtualization

Virtualization is best defined as a strategy that permits and enables the provisioning of multiple logical servers on one physical server. In virtualization, you will always require a physical server, but by being able to manage this physical server through a logical process, one can consolidate applications and workloads on one physical server as opposed to requiring multiple physical servers. For example, if your organization has 16 separate computer servers hosting critical infrastructures, the virtualization process would enable all 16 separate servers to be hosted on one physical server. While this process is very cost effective in terms of reducing capital expenditures for multiple equipment, it does provide vulnerability should a hardware failure occur on the physical server that contains all the virtual machines (VMs). Another aspect of virtualization is the need for more memory since the increase in logical connections has increased the volume of data. Also, the number of software licenses may be increased since multiple applications are being delivered through one physical server.[19]

Virtualization really became mainstream in 2011–2012, despite its early appearance in 1999. Another advantage of virtualization centers on the fact that it enables IT departments to confront one of their most difficult challenges of infrastructure sprawl that consumes 70% of the IT budget for maintenance while leaving few resources to focus on building new business innovations.[20]

In essence, virtualization is the key technology that enables cloud computing, and both cloud computing and the new "software-defined" data centers are examples of IT assets that have been virtualized.[21] Thus, the interdependency of virtualization, cloud computing, and big data is in an integral relationship.

Despite the recent emergence of virtualization, threats to the virtualized infrastructure have already occurred, and since virtualization now occupies such an important role in cloud computing, it is imperative to enhance our management of the security environment in our virtualized infrastructure. Ronald Krutz and Russell Dean Vine's excellent book, *Cloud Security: A Comprehensive Guide to Secure Cloud Computing*, provides an outstanding framework to understand the security threats to the different types of virtualized environments. Their listing of virtual threats emphasizes the range of vulnerabilities stemming from the fact that vulnerability in one VM system can be exploited to attack other VM systems or the host system, since multiple virtual machines share the same physical hardware or server.[22] Additional important virtual threats they describe are the following:

Shared Clip Board—this technology allows data to be transferred between VMs and the host, providing a means of moving data between malicious programs in virtual machines of different security realms.

Keystroke Logging—some virtual machine technologies enable the logging of key strokes and screen updates to be passed across virtual terminals in the virtual machine, writing to host files and permitting the monitoring of encrypted terminal connections inside the virtual machine.

VM Monitoring from the Host—since all network packets coming from or gaining to a VM pass through to the host, the host may be able to affect the virtual machine in any number of ways.

Virtual Machine Monitoring from Another VM—usually, virtual machines should not be able to directly access one another's virtual disks on the host. However, if the VM platform uses a virtual hub or switch to connect the VMs to the host, then intruders may be able to use a hacker technique known as "ARP Poisoning" to redirect packets going to or from the other VM for sniffing.

Virtual Machine Backdoors—a backdoor, covert communication channel between the guest and host could allow intruders to perform potentially dangerous operations.

Hypervisor Risks—the hypervisor is the part of the virtual machine that allows host resource sharing and enables VM/host isolation. Therefore, the ability of the hypervisor to provide the necessary isolation during an intentional attack determines how well the virtual machine can survive risk.

The Hypervisor is susceptible to risk because it is a software program, and risk increases as the volume and complexity of application code increases.

Rogue Hypervisor and root kits are all capable of external modification to the Hypervisor, and can create a covert channel to dump unauthorized code into the system.[23]

In addition to identifying virtualization risks, Krutz and Vines also provide an extensive list of VM security recommendations and best practice security techniques, which include the following:

- Hardening the host operating system
- Limiting physical access to the host
- Using encrypted communications
- Disabling background tasks
- Updating and patching of systems
- Enabling perimeter defense on the VM
- Implementing file integrity checks
- Maintaining back-ups
- Hardening the VM
- Harden the hypervisor
- Root secure the monitor
- Implement only one primary function per VM
- Firewall any additional VM ports
- Harden the host domain
- Use Unique Nic's for sensitive VMs
- Disconnect unused devices
- Secure VM remote access[24]

Clearly, virtualization is an enabling and transformational trend that has already impacted many industries, as well as the computer field itself. We can anticipate additional advancements in the virtualization infrastructure, and these will impact each of the five major trends we have identified.

7.4.2 Social Media

In today's current environment, the number of people using and participating in social media is exploding at a level so intense that businesses and the corporate community are moving head long into these environments. Business organizations see an opportunity to more effectively market their products especially given the enormous number of people who are so totally engaged in social media. Also, the low cost of marketing products or services over social media compared with the more expensive cost of traditional marketing media is another driving force behind the acceptance of social media by corporations and the business communities.

One of the major pillars supporting the emergence of social media has been the function of mobility of various computing devices. Thus, the mobile telephone, smart phone, and the tablets have all provided a means for people to engage in social media wherever they are located. The desktop computer as well as the laptop, once the primary tools of the individual at home or at work, are now being replaced by smart phones and tablets, and this allows easier and more frequent access to an increasing number of social media sites. While this access has been welcomed by the individual and to a large degree by corporations and the business community, there are many aspects of social media that present a challenge to the security of data that reside in our corporations and businesses.

So the factor of mobile devices such as smart phones and tablets, which are increasingly being brought to the individual's workplace and, in many cases, with or without the knowledge of the employer, has prompted concerns, especially when the individual uses the personal device to access the employer's websites or database and other applications. The concern for the organization, whether it is a business, a governmental, or a nongovernmental organization, all centers on the possibility of the individual device introducing malicious code such as a virus or worm into the employer's data system. This, in turn, has introduced the BYOD concern, and what policies and programs should be developed to respond to this major trend?

Business organizations as well as universities, governmental entities, and virtually any organization that employs people will, at some point, have to consider the creation of policies for employees or those who bring their own devices to work. Thus, the creation of a BYOD policy will have to entail not only a policy but also programs for informing and training employees as to the safe use of their devices in the employers work environment. Obviously, the first decision is whether to permit employees to use their personal devices with the organizations business applications, data, and other internal digital information. Clearly, there are some organizations that have classified information such as our military, federal law enforcement agencies, and our national laboratories that already have articulated policies in place precluding BYOD into designated areas. Also, some businesses, financial institutions and health care organizations may be precluding their employees from bringing their personal devices or using their personal devices due to stringent legal, regulatory, and compliance rules.

Those organizations that are able to consider authorization of their employees' use of personal devices should develop a BYOD set of policies and programs. Since the major concern of any organization will be on maintaining the security of their data, it will be imperative that such policies and programs are created not simply by top management but through the inclusion of the IT leadership, the legal department, and the human resources department. The creation of such a policy will, by its specific intent, generate programs that will be implemented and will have to be monitored for employee approved usage. In addition to employee usage, what policies will exist for violations of the approved personal device use? Since businesses must address concerns related to secure access, malware prevention from third-party users, and exfiltration of their intellectual property, it is necessary and incumbent to establish policies that will secure the data of the organization from exploitation or modification.

Smart phones, which, in many cases, are equipped with near-field communication (NFC), allow one smart phone to share information with another NFC device and to very easily transfer payment information or photos and other contact information. This is technology that hackers can use to gain access to an employee's information and entire digital personality, including information as to the employer and the employer's databases. In addition to NFC technology, the recent malware known as Ransomware can encrypt an individual's smart phone and prevent the user from using it unless a ransom is paid. This could also impact the corporation if the employee passes data from the corporate databases. In this case, both the user of the smart phone and their employer could be susceptible to extortion unless the money is paid to the cyber-criminal. Also, since smart phone users maintain photos on their device, this becomes another target for extortion, with the attacker threatening either to delete the photos or to post them on various public sites, causing the owner a loss of privacy.

One of the difficult issues that confront organizations in creating BYOD policies, whether these are focused on smart phones, tablets, or other devices, is related to the issue of privacy. In essence, how do you maintain a balance between the need to protect your organization's data and resources and responding to the individual user's personal data on that same device that may or may not be owned by the user? In the event the employee visits sites that may be blacklisted by the organization, what recourse is open to the human resources department? Indeed, how will this be monitored, and what recourse is open to the organization for the user's noncompliance with the BYOD policy?

Additional issues that must be carefully considered are as follows:

- Will employee's smart phones require some form of security or mobile security software?
- Will encryption be required?
- Will phones be containerized to separate the business from the personal data?
- Will certain "blacklisted" applications be blocked from the user's phone?
- Will monitoring be instituted? If so, by whom?
- Will file sync be authorized where documents are uploaded to the cloud? While a convenient application use for the individual, it adds a significant vulnerability to the organizations database.
- Will e-mail encryption policies be implemented?
- Will certain Apps be permitted, and from what devices or operating systems?[25]

Eric Cole, in discussing top security trends, reports that the exponential growth of smart phones, tablets, and other mobile devices has opened additional opportunities for cyber attacks as each has created vulnerable access points to networks. This expanding use of social media contributes to the cybersecurity vulnerabilities and expanded threats, and in particular when assessing the smart phones, it is clear that at least 80% do not have appropriate mobile security in place.

> If a laptop, tablet and mobile phone all contain the same data, why does one have fifteen character passwords and another only a four digit pin? Why does one have endpoint security and patching and the other device has nothing? The policy should be written for the sensitivity of the data and any device that contains that information should have the same level of protection.

What Cole quite astutely points out is that security should be based on the data and not on the type of device.[26]

In analyzing APT attacks, it is the targeting of humans and the reconnaissance of social media information found on sites such as Facebook, LinkedIn, and others that allow APT attackers to become so successful in their operations.

> An APT attacker would scan social media sites looking for a list of people who work at a target organization. They would also go to the organizations website and see who is listed on the webpage. Press releases, job vacancy sites and other open source information are all used to obtain a list of employees. Subcontractors would also be targeted as a potential access point. Once a list of employees is gained, Google alerts are set-up on those individuals tracking all postings and any information that is publicly available about those people. Correlations analysis is done to try and find out the bosses including the overall structure of the organization. Once a threat actor finds out about a person's job, their interest, and co-workers, they begin to put together a plan.[27]

In essence, the attacker has socially engineered a plan to attack a target organization on the basis of social media and mobility and, in the process, has benefited by numerous vectors, which must now be analyzed by cybersecurity professionals to neutralize those weak points and vulnerabilities.

7.4.3   Internet of Things

As a result of the transformational developments in virtualization, social media, and mobility, we now encounter the M2M connectivity, and we are entering a new era that is termed the *Internet of Things*.

The M2M movement made possible by Wi-Fi and sensors has enabled direct connectivity between machine and machine without human interface.

While the M2M movement began in the 1990s, it has gained incredible expansion particularly through its connectivity via cellular networks, and projections are now being estimated that within the next five years, there will be 25 billion to 50 billion devices connected, and each providing a stream of data that will increase the IoT era. The cellular network is growing since the data exchange from one device to another device is being accomplished wirelessly and on a mobile basis.[28] The point for which these devices are becoming Internet connected is to improve the homeowner's convenience and ability to use some devices more economically. For example, the ability of a smart telephone to be able to receive data from the homeowner's heating and cooling units provides the homeowner the opportunity to either reduce or elevate the thermostat, which will lower the cost of the utility bills, conserve limited resources that produce this energy, and also provide a convenience to the homeowner. This same process can be applied to lighting and security issues around the home as well.

The growing applications of M2M are providing a shift in business models that now permit more than simply selling products and are now expanded to also sell services. An example can be viewed by those companies that deal with commercial trucking operations. Now, they can sell more than the truck tire; they can provide a service that permits them to dispatch their service vehicles to the truck when the truck tire wear reaches a critical level. Another example is a manufacturing company, a produce shipping company, or a garden supply or florist operation, who can all install devices that not only track the location of the vehicle but also record the inside temperature to guard against spoilage. There are other business sectors such as health care, security services, energy companies, construction, automotive, and transportation that are all in the process of connecting M2M devices and creating this incredible expansion of the IoT.[29]

The Wall Street Journal reported on an application that even involved a smart-phone-controlled Crock-Pot cooker to adjust the heat and cooking time from a remote site. Ironically, the typical selling point of Crock-Pots is to permit the remote preparation of a meal; so is the M2M connectivity really representative of the type of devices that will become an important part of the IoT, or is this simply an application that is more of a gimmick or marketing ploy?[30]

A more serious application that actually has benefits but also possible downsides is the incorporation of the Livestream video sharing App to the Google Glass eyepiece. This software application allows Google Glass wearers to share with another exactly what they are seeing and hearing simply by issuing the verbal command, "OK glass, start broadcasting." The application and use of this technology can be most useful to physicians, especially during a surgical operation, as it can provide incredibly focused instruction to interns and other physicians interested in the particular surgical intervention.

On the other hand, there are potential incursions on one's privacy should you be the target of the particular video broadcast. There are even more serious potential situations that could involve broadcasting obscene, pornographic, or even sexual assaults via this medium.[31] Certainly, both Google as well as Livestream are concerned about potential abuses and should take steps to guard against violations of their licensed application.

The range of applications that are proliferating and creating this IoT continues to expand to the point that all the data being processed are now being created as unstructured data that is creating the need for the emergence of big data and new methods to store and process this IoT environment. At the same time, the processing of these data as they achieve the volume and velocity that billions of these devices are creating has also generated the need for both virtualization and for cloud computing.

7.4.4 Cloud Computing

Cloud computing, while a new paradigm shift, originated based on the time sharing model of computing from the 1960s as a result of IBM developing a four-processor mainframe and software that permitted the time sharing computing model. The introduction of the personal computer led to the client server computing model, which was an important facet of the eventual emergence of cloud computing. The major event that really enabled cloud computing was the introduction of the virtualization computing model. These items, plus the addition of the Internet, high-speed networks, Wi-Fi, cellular models, and the smart chips enabling mobility, have all come together to spawn this new transformational change in computing.

The attractiveness of cloud computing to organizations, governmental agencies, small businesses, and individuals centers on the fact that the cost of one's computing is on a metered basis, and you pay only for what you are actually using. This means one can go to a cloud provider and rely on the cloud provider's computing infrastructure. The cloud providers already possess the computers, servers, network bandwidth, Internet and network access, storage capability, the facility with cooling and heating, and other related items that permit a service contract that enables the user to acquire computing services without any capital investment of equipment, buildings, heating and cooling, and personnel to operate their computing needs. While there are many excellent attributes to cloud computing, there are also some very negative aspects that must also be reviewed and assessed by those interested in cloud computing.

Perhaps, the most appropriate manner in presenting our discussion of cloud computing is to present the definition of cloud computing and related cloud models as defined by the U.S. government agency the National Institute of Standards (NIST):

As defined by NIST, cloud computing is a model for enabling ubiquitous, convenient, on-demand network access to a shared pool of configurable computing resources (e.g., networks, servers, storage, applications, and services) that can be rapidly provisioned and released with minimal management effort or service provider interaction. Cloud computing services can be described by their shared characteristics, by the computing resources provided as a service, and by the method of deployment.[32]

The generally agreed classification scheme for cloud computing is termed the *SPI Framework*, which means the Software–Platform–Infrastructure model. This represents the three major services provided through the cloud: SaaS, or Software as a Service; PaaS, referring to Platform as a Service; and IaaS, which is Infrastructure as a Service. The three cloud service delivery models as defined by NIST are as follows:

Service Models

Software as a Service (SaaS): The capability provided to the consumer is to use the provider's applications running on a cloud infrastructure. The applications are accessible from various client devices through either a thin client interface, such as a web browser (e.g., web-based email), or a program interface. The consumer does not manage or control the underlying cloud infrastructure including network, servers, operating systems, storage, or even individual application capabilities, with the possible exception of limited user-specific application configuration settings.

Platform as a Service (PaaS): The capability provided to the consumer is to deploy onto the cloud infrastructure consumer-created or acquired applications created using programming languages, libraries, services, and tools supported by the provider. The consumer does not manage or control the underlying cloud infrastructure including network, servers, operating systems, or storage, but has control over the deployed applications and possibly configuration settings for the application-hosting environment.

Infrastructure as a Service (IaaS): The capability provided to the consumer is to provision processing, storage, networks, and other fundamental computing resources where the consumer is able to deploy and run arbitrary software, which can include operating systems and applications, the consumer does not manage or control the underlying cloud infrastructure but has control over operating systems, storage, and deployed applications; and possibly limited control of select networking components (e.g., host firewalls).[33]

Cloud computing offers four major types of cloud models, termed *private cloud*, *public cloud*, *community cloud*, and *hybrid cloud*. Each of these deployment models provides a range of services and capabilities that have different cost structures as well as different specifications depending upon the needs of the organization seeking a cloud service contract. For example, if security was an issue to the customer, the cloud model of choice would be a private cloud, whereas a customer requiring less security could select a public cloud. The four cloud models as defined by the NIST are as follows:

Cloud Models

Private Cloud: The cloud infrastructure is provisioned for exclusive use by a single organization comprising multiple consumers (e.g., business units). It may be owned, managed, and operated by the organization, a third party, or some combination of them, and it may exist on or off premises.

Public Cloud: The cloud infrastructure is provisioned for open use by the general public. It may be owned, managed, and operated by a business, academic, or government organization, or some combination of them. It exists on the premises of the cloud provider.

Community Cloud: The cloud infrastructure is provisioned for exclusive use by a specific community of consumers from organizations that have shared concerns (e.g., mission, security requirements, policy and compliance considerations). It may be owned, managed, and operated by one or more of the organizations in the community, a third party, or some combination of them, and it may exist on or off premises.

Hybrid Cloud: The cloud infrastructure is a composition of two or more distinct cloud infrastructures (private, community, or public) that remain unique entities, but are bound together by standardized or proprietary technology that enables data and application portability (e.g., cloud bursting for load balancing between clouds).[34]

There are a number of benefits provided by the cloud environment, irrespective of which cloud model is selected. Typically, these benefits permit an organization the ability to rapidly deploy business and research applications in a cost-effective manner. Also, the cloud computing model relieves the customer from the concerns about updating servers or having to install the latest software patches, and it enables the customer to acquire increased or additional services on an as-needed basis. The cloud model also permits customers to focus on the innovation of their business computing solutions instead of dealing with the operation and maintenance of their computing infrastructure. In general, the cloud paradigm provides a cost savings since the customer is only incrementally paying for the computing services metered or used, and this avoids the large capital investment in equipment and personnel were they to create their own computing infrastructure.[35]

While cloud computing offers several attractive reasons for its consideration, there are also some concerns to weigh before concluding on a decision as to selecting a cloud model, or for that matter even deciding as to whether it is appropriate for your organization to move into the cloud paradigm at all. Clearly, the issue of security is a major concern, as well as where your data are being housed and located. Each of these issues might be addressed in a service level agreement with the cloud provider.

Perhaps one of the most serious drawbacks centers on the fact that most cloud providers' traditional level agreements state that the cloud provider takes control and has potential ownership of the information, yet the customer organization still has full liability if proper security is not managed. Since cloud providers seek to retain the customer's business, the control of the customer's information is a way to deter the customer from changing cloud providers. In addition to the issue of ownership of the information, liability is another major issue to be aware of or resolve. For example, in many cloud agreements, if the cloud provider does not provide proper security and there is a breach of critical information or regulatory data, the customer is liable and not the cloud provider.[36]

Any organization considering a business relationship with a cloud provider should be certain that contractual language specifies and requires the cloud provider to adhere to the legal requirements of public privacy laws and other regulatory issues, including the following:

- The Health Insurance Portability and Accountability Act
- The Fair Credit Reporting Act of 2003
- The Gramm-Leach-Bliley Act of 1999
- The Federal Information Security Act
- The PCI/DSS Payment and Credit Card Industry Data Security Standards
- Red Flag, a mandate by the Federal Trade Commission requiring institutions to develop identity theft prevention programs
- Patent assurance that the cloud provider is the rightful and legal owner of the technologies they are providing and that they will indemnify the customer against any patent infringement litigation

Krutz and Vines also suggest that service level agreements be created that acknowledge mutual commitments for both the customer and the cloud provider and that the cloud provider should have a clear understanding of the customer's expectations and concerns. The following elements are typically included in a service level agreement:

- Intellectual property protection
- Application security
- Termination
- Compliance requirements

- Customer responsibilities
- Performance tracking
- Problem resolution
- Lead time for implementation[37]

Now that we have provided an overview of the cloud computing paradigm, we shall now examine several of the issues that the U.S. Department of Defense (DoD) addressed as it moved its entire information infrastructure into a cloud environment.

The scope of any organization moving into a cloud environment entails a number of challenges and the need for a very well-planned program; however, the enormous challenge that confronted the DoD was both unique and without precedent. The DoD had to address the same issue that most organizations confront, namely, their concern about the security of the cloud model. The DoD has a need for world-class security as a result of their military and intelligence missions, as well as its dependence of operations within cyberspace.

An example of the DoD's reliance on cyberspace is documented by the 15,000 networks and 7 million computing devices across hundreds of installations in dozens of countries throughout the world. DoD networks are probed millions of times every day, and successful penetrations have resulted in the loss of thousands of files and important information on our weapons systems. The number of foreign nation attacks and efforts to exploit our DoD unclassified and classified networks have increased not only in number but also in sophistication. Equally of concern are the attacks by nonstate actors who also seek to penetrate and disrupt DoD networks. The global scope of DoD networks offers adversaries numerous targets to attack, and as a result, the DoD must defend against not only external threat actors but also internal threats. In addition, since a great deal of software and hardware products are manufactured and assembled in foreign countries, the DoD must also develop strategies for managing these risks at both the design, manufacture, and service distribution points as they can represent supply chain vulnerabilities and threats to the operational ability of the DoD.[38]

In view of these challenges, it was a bold and decisive move on the part of the Joint Chiefs of Staff to authorize the chief information officer of the DoD to develop a cloud computing strategy. This action was designed to reengineer the DoD information infrastructure and improve its mission effectiveness in cybersecurity. The result of this transformation was to create the Joint Information Environment, known today as the JIE. The DoD cloud computing strategy was focused on eliminating the duplicative, cumbersome, and expensive set of application silos to a more robust, secure, and cost-effective joint service environment that is capable of fully responding to the changing mission needs of the DoD.

The DoD identified a four-step process that guided the movement into the cloud computing infrastructure.

Step 1: Foster Adoption of Cloud Computing
- Establish a joint governance structure to drive the transition to the DoD Enterprise Cloud environment
- Adopt an Enterprise First approach that will accomplish a cultural shift to facilitate the adoption and evolution of cloud computing
- Reform DoD IT financial, acquisition, and contracting policy and practices that will improve agility and reduce costs
- Implement a cloud computing outreach and awareness campaign to gather input from the major stakeholders, expand the base of consumers and providers, and increase visibility of available cloud services throughout the Federal Government

Step 2: Optimize Data Center Consolidation
- Consolidate and virtualize Legacy applications and data

Step 3: Establish the DoD Enterprise Cloud Infrastructure
- Incorporate core cloud infrastructure into data center consolidation
- Optimize the delivery of multi-provider cloud services through a Cloud Service Broker
- Drive continuous service innovation using Agile, a product-focused, iterative development model
- Drive secure information sharing by exploiting cloud innovation

Step 4: Deliver Cloud Services
- Continue to deliver DoD Enterprise cloud services
- Leverage externally provided cloud services, i.e., commercial services, to expand cloud offerings beyond those offered within the Department[39]

The specific objectives the DoD sought to achieve by moving into the cloud computing infrastructure were designated as follows:

- Reduced Costs/Increased Operational Efficiencies
  - Consolidating systems, which reduces the physical and energy footprint, the operational, maintenance, and management resources, and the number of facilities
  - Using a pay-as-you-go pricing model for services on demand rather than procuring entire solutions
  - Leveraging existing DoD cloud computing development environments to reduce software development costs
- Increased Mission Effectiveness
  - Enabling access to critical information
  - Leveraging the high availability and redundancy of cloud computing architectures to improve options for disaster recovery and continuity of operations

- Enhancing Warfighter mobility and productivity through device and location independence, and provision of on-demand, yet secure, global access to enterprise services
- Increasing, or scaling up, the number of supported users as mission needs surge, optimizing capabilities for the joint force
- Enabling data to be captured, stored, and published almost simultaneously, decreasing the time necessary to make data available to users
- Enabling the ability to create and exploit massively large data sets, search large data sets quickly, and combine data sets from different systems to allow cross-system data search and exploitation
- Cybersecurity
  - Leveraging efforts such as FedRAMP that help standardize and streamline Certification and Accreditation (C&A) processes for commercial and Federal Government cloud providers, allowing approved IT capabilities to be more readily shared across the Department
  - Moving from a framework of traditional system-focused C&A with periodic assessments to continual reauthorization through implementation of continuous monitoring
  - Moving to standardized and simplified identity and access management (IdAM)
  - Reducing network seams through network and data center consolidation and implementation of a standardized infrastructure[40]

The DoD cloud environment had to support Legacy applications as well as develop new applications. The cloud environment also is required to be closely aligned with the initiatives of the intelligence community and support information sharing with the Joint Worldwide Intelligence Communication System (JWICS). The DoD chief information officer will lead unclassified but sensitive Internet Protocol Router Network (NIPRNET) and Secret Internet Protocol Router Network (SIPRNET) efforts. The Director of National Intelligence will designate their chief information officer to lead the Top Secret Sensitive Compartmentalized Information (TS SCI), and both the DoD and the National Intelligence Agency will be required to evaluate data and information sensitivity as to low risk, moderate risk, and high risk. Cloud model deployment will incorporate data on the basis of risk in which some commercial cloud providers will manage low-risk and, in selected cases, moderate-risk data and information. High-risk data, which if breached would result in having a severe or catastrophic effect on organizational operations, organizational assets, or individuals, will not be placed within a commercial cloud provider that is generally available to the public and will remain within the DoD. Protecting mission-critical information and systems requires the most stringent protection measures including highly classified tools, sophisticated cyber analytics, and highly adaptive capabilities that must remain within the physical and operational control of the DoD.[41]

The transformation of the DoD to a cloud infrastructure for its information network, and cyberspace activities resulting in the current JIE has been an incredible journey relying on the expertise of some of our nation's most professional, knowledgeable, and highly skilled personnel.

7.4.5 Big Data

As pointed out earlier, social media and the enormous number of mobile devices, as well as the M2M connectivity and the IoT with the increasing number of sensors, have created an environment in which we are experiencing an explosion of data. As a result of cloud computing and virtualization, we are now capable of entering the new environment of big data. The data being produced today are so large and complex that they cannot be processed by traditional relational database management programs. The reason new processes are necessary is due to the nature of the data appearing in both an unstructured and semistructured format, which totally deviates from the structured data format, which is based on the SQL, an international standard for defining and accessing relational databases.

7.4.5.1 *Structured and Unstructured Data*

Structured data consist of the ordinary processing of documents such as customer invoices, billing records, employee pay information, and any number of typical business transactions that have been traditionally managed in spreadsheets and databases. In contrast to the structured data, the form of unstructured data consists of photographs, videos, social network updates, blog entries, remote sensor logs, and other remote and diverse types of information that are more difficult to process, categorize, and analyze with traditional tools. Naturally, the question that comes to the forefront is if big data cannot be processed by the traditional relational database management programs, how then is this new enormous volume of data being processed? The answer typically revolves around two big data components. The first is Hadoop, which is an open source technology framework that provides a storage capability for these large unstructured and semistructured data sets and, through its MapReduce processing engine, offers a shared file system with analysis capability. The Hadoop solutions are available through a number of vendors such as IBM, HP, Apache, Cisco, and others. The second component is NoSQL, which provides the capability to capture, read, and update in real-time the large influx of unstructured data and data without schemes; examples include click streams, social media, log files, event data, mobility trends, sensor, and M2M data.[42]

An example of a big data technology ecosystem would include a big data platform that provides storage of the data. The data can include images and videos, social media, web logs, documents, an operational system from a Legacy system, and a data warehouse. This platform includes the capabilities to integrate, manage, and apply sophisticated computational processing to the data. Hadoop uses a processing engine named MapReduce to both distribute data and process the data in parallel across various nodes.[43]

An example of how big data would be used by health care providers would entail the use of big data technologies to track the patient's lifecycle with health care management capabilities, including all patient transactions, social media interactions, radiology images, pharmaceutical prescriptions, patient medical history, and any other related information important to the health care and lifecycle of the patient. These data are stored and are repopulated into operational systems or prepared for subsequent analytics through the data warehouse.[44]

7.4.5.2 Securing Big Data

Obviously, with data as important as a patient's medical data, there is a need for the assurance of the information and its security. Since big data consists of data sourced through the Internet, cloud computing, social media, mobile devices, as well as Legacy system data, this commingling of data provides vulnerability, and malicious hacking from some remote unknown source could create a threat problem. The security of these big data systems is critical and is very much a concern to those considering moving into this environment. One problem that was fairly well resolved by traditional IT systems was the "back-end systems," where the network's hosts, storage, and applications were within the enterprise server or the data center. Now because of virtualization, we have an IT infrastructure that is not solely on the premises, since it now is in the cloud computing environment. If you are in a public cloud or community cloud, there is a high probability that you do not even know where your data reside, and this means you may not even know if your data are in the same state or, for that matter, even what country. Another problem is termed *endpoints* and usually, in the past, referred only to the devices that were centrally procured, provisioned, and managed by the enterprise IT function. This is now obscured by BYODs, which are not owned by the organization but by the employee and which are highly susceptible to bringing malware into the data center. Also, user-generated unstructured data are so easy to share among many people, and it has become a very large problem in managing and protecting the data center from malicious software or some of these unpatched and low-level security mobile devices.[45]

The process and responsibility for providing security to the big data environment include many facets and responsibilities. Since big data adds substantial complexity to the entire IT infrastructure and since big data is widely distributed, it is important that it is protected in a secure manner. This means that judgments must be made as to the information that should be classified and what level of sensitivity should be provided to protect it. The information needs to be protected across applications and environments with periodic vulnerability tests. Also, the security measures should guard against any intrusions that could modify or change the data. Data that are assigned a higher risk level must be identified by its location. Obviously, data located within the IT infrastructure as well as the cloud environment must be protected. Users of the data must be monitored. Thus, the organization must have policies in place to govern how the organization will protect and ensure the big data environment. This means that there should be policies dealing with the security of the following:

- Structured information
- Unstructured data
- Device security
- Mobile application security
- Data transmission security
- Device information security
- Security monitoring and audit processes[46]

New security requirements that might be considered in the protection of information within the big data environment include the following:

- Need to encrypt sensitive data on big data platforms
- Need to flag sensitive data files in Hadoop and other NoSQL data stores
- Need to control who can access exploratory "sandboxes" built on Hadoop or other analytical database management systems
- Need to flag sensitive data files in Hadoop and other NoSQL data stores to control access to it
- Need to encrypt and redact sensitive data produced from analysis undetected in Hadoop
- Need to protect access to sensitive data in big data platforms from applications and tools using other database management systems
- Need to log and report on which users and applications accessed sensitive data on any big data platform
- Need to control access to sensitive data from MapReduce applications running on Hadoop
- On premises and cloud data need to be protected[47]

7.4.5.3 Security Analytics

The emerging new field of security analytics is the beginning of a new evaluation in how computer security will grow beyond the simple application of intrusion detection and intrusion prevention tools. Currently, organizations can purchase various security tools such as Security Incident and Event Management (SIEM), Data Loss Prevention (DLP), and Network Intrusion Prevention (NIP) and can take advantage of the tools built in algorithms. However, this approach is fundamentally reactive to the tools identifying an attack or a similar event. The new approach we hope security analytics will offer is to embrace the development of skill sets in computer security personnel that will enable them to both collect and analyze data logs, network flows, full packet capture, and endpoint execution and to extract useful insights by both applying data analysis algorithms as well as their own security analysis. The value of a well-educated and skillful security analytics expert lies in their ability to explore patterns and to offer correlation analysis of events tied to both anomaly detection as well as predictive event occurrences. The security analytics person can offer an enriching capability by constructing a new repository of collected log activity and network traffic data through the collection of Domain Name Server, Whois information, and threat intelligence alerts from all source sites and agencies, so that this repository can be data mined and analyzed for trends, patterns, and deviations from observed models. This new approach provides computer security personnel with the security analytical capabilities of detecting new attacks, investigating previous and past intrusions, and even being better prepared to encounter inside employee abuse or malicious activity. In short, the most important contribution of this new security analytics perspective is that we are now preparing computer security personnel to respond to events in real-time or at least near real-time with greater complexity than what is offered by signature-based intrusion detection tools.[48]

Currently, there exists a huge deficit of personnel who are skilled and trained in data analytics, and there simply is no existing field of computer security analytics. The need for personnel in both these fields is in such high demand particularly as a result of the emergence of big data.

In a 2013 survey focusing on detecting problems in real-time big data analytics, over 40% of the 260 enterprise security professionals stated that they were challenged by a lack of adequate staffing in security operations/incident response teams.[49] The Wall Street Journal reported that the McKinsey Global Institute estimated that the demand for employees skilled in data analysis will outstrip supply by 60% by 2018, and this does not even factor in the demand for security analytics personnel who are virtually nonexistent today.[50]

7.4.5.4 Big Data Applications

Perhaps the best way to appreciate the transformation that big data is introducing is to provide several examples of programs that have already been institutionalized. At the same time, it is appropriate to also present the amount of data that are being produced and why this challenge will continue to grow as additional programs are developed and institutionalized.

The amount of data being created in an unstructured format by social media, mobile devices, the IoT, and M2M sensors is truly remarkable. As of April 2013, IBM estimated that 2.5 quintillion bytes of data are created daily. The average amount of stored data per a U.S. company with more than 1000 employees exceeds 200 terabytes. There are 6 billion global cellphone subscriptions beaming location information back to networks. Amazon alone has more than 500,000 computer servers in their Elastic Computer Cloud. There are 4.5 million new URLs appearing on the web each month. There are 170 computing centers across 36 countries analyzing data from the CERN facility, and 25 million gigabytes of data are created annually by the large Hadron collider at CERN.[51] This amount of data is precisely why new technologies were created to store and process this information. However, what is missing is the personnel to work in the big data environment, and the Gartner Research Firm estimated that 85% of the Fortune 500 firms will be unprepared to leverage big data for a competitive advantage by 2015. In fact, estimates of the current shortage of U.S. managers with data analysis skills exceeds 1.5 million people.[52]

We have already discussed one application of big data that included patient lifecycle applications within the health care industry. Another fascinating application has transformed research capabilities in the field of geology through the use of big data. Most geological discoveries were reported in research journals, and over the history of the development of the field of geology worldwide, journals held vast amounts of research data. Some very good research that received little notice was consigned to oblivion and not accessible to contemporary geology researchers. Additionally, the volume and inaccessibility of past research were also hampered by the high cost of geological surveys and on-site discoveries. In 2012, Professor Shanan Peters, a geologist at the University of Wisconsin, teamed up with two computer science professors, Miron Livny and Christopher Re, to build a computer program that scanned pages from pre-Internet science journals, generations of websites, archived spreadsheets, and video clips to create a database comprising as nearly as possible the entire universe of trusted geological data. The massive piles of unstructured and overlooked data are now available for geology professors and students to query the database and to receive informative replies. This program was called Geo Deep Dive, and it has provided researchers access to a larger collection of geological data than ever before.

Another advantage of utilizing a query system is the ability to pose questions to the system that researchers may lack the expertise to answer on their own.[53]

This insightful program created by the University of Wisconsin Geology and Computer Science departments is an example of how other academic programs can enrich their fields of research. These gains were made possible as a result of virtualization, cloud computing, and big data, which allows the incorporation of valuable unstructured data that range from video to voice recordings and many other examples. The Hadoop and NoSQL components of big data permit rather advanced query capabilities resulting in the production of important new insights and directions for further research and knowledge building.

Examples of governmental programs that are embracing big data applications are in the National Weather Service and the Federal Emergency Management Association, where new data rich models are being developed to predict weather patterns. Also, the Centers for Medicare and Medical Services has created a system that permits their analysis of the 4 million claims it pays daily to search for fraudulent patterns of activity. Since federal requirements impose a 30-day obligation for paying all claims, a system to detect fraudulent behavior is necessary.[54]

Perhaps the most important and greatest long-term effects of big data applications are more than likely to be in the physical sciences, where big data has the capacity to assist researchers in formulating new hypotheses by the query development process capability. An example of an application of this type is in the work of the National Institutes of Health, where it has placed more than 1000 individual human genomes inside Amazon's Elastic Computer Cloud. Amazon is storing this massive amount of non-sensitive government information at no fee for the government. The information being stored currently amounts to 2000 terabytes of data, and when researchers want to use this database, they are charged to analyze the cloud-based data set only on the amount of computing time required to perform their research objective. This big data storage model has opened the field of research to large numbers of health and drug researchers, academics, and graduate students who could never have afforded this research before its inclusion in the cloud and by big data applications. More importantly, it has the potential to increase research and speed up the time for the development of treatments for diseases. The cost factor is really quite astonishing because research such as this would have entailed the use of a supercomputer and cost over $500,000. In less than seven years, the cost of sequencing an individual human genome in 2012 became $8000, and the cost at which sequencing an individual human genome that becomes part of a medical diagnosis at less than $1000.[55] So as the costs are reduced and greater opportunities for researchers to review the more than 1000 human genomes stored within the

Amazon Elastic Cloud continue to progress, we anticipate new discoveries and abilities to treat diseases.

Another interesting application of big data is found in some of the research in Canada, where researchers are interested in the identification of infections in premature babies before the appearance of overt symptoms. The research protocol is to convert 16 vital signs including heartbeat, blood pressure, respiration, and blood-oxygen levels into an information flow of more than 1000 data points per second to ascertain correlations between very minor changes and more serious problems. Over an extended period of time and as their database increases, it is projected that this will provide physicians with a deeper comprehension as to the etiology of such problems.[56]

One of the major changes in processing big data research questions centers on the issue of inference. The enormous volume of data being processed is being probed for inferential relationships and correlations. This approach is totally at variance to traditional research methodologies in which statistical samples of small amounts of data representing a larger population were analyzed for predictive and causal conclusions. The significance of this major research methodological change is to caution big data researchers that any causal conclusion they offer must be carefully reviewed and analyzed as the data sets they are including in their research are drawn from very unstructured data and are open to issues of scientific validity concerns and checks. However, if the results are framed within the perspective of correlation analysis, it will provide a rich set of previously unobserved opportunities to correlate event X with event Y or Z and even offer multiple correlative lines of research inquiry that later may be subject to more traditional causal analysis conclusions.

The University of California-Berkeley's Simons Institute for the Theory of Computing held their Fall 2013 program on the theoretical foundations of big data analysis, and their comments on big data are very instructive and they offer the following:

> We live in an era of "Big Data": science, engineering and technology are producing increasingly large data streams, with petabyte and exabyte scales becoming increasingly common. In scientific fields such data arise in part because tests of standard theories increasingly focus on extreme physical conditions (cf., particle physics) and in part because science has become increasingly exploratory (cf., astronomy and genomics). In commerce, massive data arise because so much of human activity is now online, and because business models aim to provide services that are increasingly personalized.[57]

Clearly, we are living in the era of big data, and data streams of petabyte and exabyte scales are increasingly becoming quite common. As organizations move to embrace and create more big data applications, it is important that the science surrounding these applications is more firmly based on the theories of computation, statistics, and related disciplines where continuing research in the topics of dimension reduction, distributed optimization, Monte Carlo sampling, compressed sensing, and low-rank matrix factorization are further researched.

The major transformational changes that big data is introducing to our society require a firmer application of science to guard against any latent, unanticipated, and dysfunctional consequences of this big data movement.

7.5 Preparing Future Generations for Cybersecurity Transformational Challenges

The challenges for cybersecurity professionals are both deep and longitudinal, as the era of big data, cloud computing, and the IoT has introduced so many fundamental security vulnerabilities. The threat landscape continues to grow, and both preventing and stopping breaches in real-time or near real-time are difficult at best.

The emergence of big data has spawned a need for increased research into the theoretical foundations for big data. The fields of engineering, computer science, and statistics will have to address the research challenges that confront inferential algorithms, while also providing additional research into the field of correlation analysis.

Our universities will be facing a need and challenge to locate and employ faculty and researchers who will provide the foundations for creating the academic instructional areas in security analytics, data analytics, decision science, predictive analytics, and correlation analysis.

The role of the university and its relationship to research collaborations with governmental agencies and the DoD will continue to grow in the importance of both providing skilled and educated next generation workers as well as providing a vigorous research program.

The fundamental role of defending our nation has dramatically changed as a result of the activities within the cyberspace environment. War as we once knew it is forever changed due to the digital advancements that continue to be made. Cyber weapons now exist and have the capability of decimating even the most prepared nations. The ability to design and prepare cyber weapons exceeds the current defense strategies of most nations.

The challenges in international law and in the area of individual privacy issues will continue to increase and require patient and sound educated judgments to guide both governments and nations.

Greater cooperation will be required between our universities, research institutes, and our industries as we prepare for the development of new advancements in science and the generation of new inventions.

Finally, our nation's commitment to an educational system that seeks to expand the boundaries of science, technology, and the advancement of knowledge is a strength that provides an environment for our children with unrivaled opportunities for growth and achievement. The dedication of teachers at our elementary and secondary school systems as well as the faculty of our colleges and universities all work in an effort to provide our nation with the next generation of citizen leaders and innovators. As we prepare our youth for the future and the transformational challenges they will encounter, our nation will be well advised to continue its investment in our education systems at all levels of society. The continuity and sustainability of our nation's commitment to these ideals, goals, and the highest of standards are fundamental parts of our heritage.

Notes and References

1. Wood, Editor, *Internet Security Threat Report 2014*, 4.
2. Ibid., 5–6.
3. Loc. Cit.
4. Wood, Ibid., 7.
5. FireEye and Mandiant, "Cybersecurity's Maginot Line: A Real-World Assessment of the Defense-in-Depth Model," 8–9.
6. Verizon Risk Team, *Verizon 2013 Data Breach Investigations Report*, 8–9.
7. Wood, op. cit., 34–37.
8. Ibid., 57.
9. FireEye and Mandiant, op. cit., 13.
10. Flick and Morehouse, *Securing the Smart Grid: Next Generation Power Grid Security*, 272–273.
11. Gertz, "The Cyber-Dam Breaks," 1–2.
12. Gertz, "Syria Facing U.S. Cyber Attacks in Upcoming Strikes," 3.
13. Piper, *Definitive Guide to Next Generation Threat Protection*, 5–9, 23.
14. Cole, *Advanced Persistent Threat: Understanding the Danger and How to Protect Your Organization*, 21–25.
15. Leger, "Hackers Holding Computers Hostage," 1, 6.
16. Cole, op. cit., 59–63.
17. Skoudis and Liston, *Counter Hack Reloaded: A Step-by-Step Guide to Computer Attacks and Effective Defenses*, Second Ed., xiii–xviii.
18. Cole, op. cit., 224–225.
19. Sloan and Schultz, "Virtualization 101," 16–18.
20. Essential Business Tech Editorial, "Redefining the Landscape: VM Ware is Reshaping Data Center Infrastructure through Virtualization," 15.
21. Sarna, *Implementing and Developing Cloud Computing Applications*, xxv.
22. Krutz and Vines, *Cloud Security: A Comprehensive Guide to Secure Cloud Computing*, 157.
23. Ibid., 158–160, 163–164.
24. Ibid., 165–173.

25. Essential Business Tech Report, "Total Mobility: Advice for Organizations Large and Small," 12–13.
26. Cole, op. cit., 46–47.
27. Ibid., 255.
28. Essential Business Tech Report, "Machine-to-Machine Networks," 29–30.
29. Ibid., 30–31.
30. Rothman, "The Crock-Pot Is Still Slow, but Now It's Smart," D3.
31. Drew-Fitzgerald, "Google Glass Can Turn You Into Live Broadcast," B4.
32. Taki, Chief Information Officer, "Cloud Computing Strategy," C.1.
33. Ibid., C.1–2.
34. Ibid., C.1.
35. Krutz and Vines, op. cit., 55–58.
36. Cole, op. cit., 217–218.
37. Krutz and Vines, op. cit., 26–27.
38. U.S. Department of Defense, *Department of Defense Strategy for Operating in Cyberspace*, 1–4.
39. Taki, op. cit., E-3.
40. Ibid., 5.
41. Ibid., 25–26.
42. Essential Business Tech Report, "Big Data FAQ," 32–33.
43. Davenport and Dyche, *Big Data in Big Companies*, 9–11.
44. Ibid., 18.
45. Essential Business Tech Report, "Securing Big Data: Security Issues Around Big Data Solutions," 23–25.
46. Ferguson, *Enterprise Information Protection—The Impact of Big Data*, 4–7, 10–12.
47. Ibid., 20–22.
48. Essential Business Tech Report, "Security Analytics: How Exposing Security-Related Data to Analytics Is Altering the Game," 32, 34.
49. Ibid., 33.
50. Ovide, "Big Data, Big Blunders," R-4.
51. Marks, "Welcome to the Data Driven World: The Governments Big Investment in Big Data is Changing What We Know and How We Know It," 22, 28.
52. Ibid., 23.
53. Marks, loc. cit.
54. Ibid., 26–27.
55. Ibid., 27.
56. Cukier and Mayer-Schoenberger, "The Rise of Big Data: How It's Changing the Way We Think About the World," 32.
57. Jordan, "Theoretical Foundations of Big Data Analysis," 1.

Bibliography

Cole, E. *Advanced Persistent Threat: Understanding the Danger and How to Protect Your Organization*. Massachusetts: Syngress Is an Imprint of Elsevier, 2013.
Cukier, K., and Mayer-Schoenberger, V. "The Rise of Big Data: How It's Changing the Way We Think About the World." In *Foreign Affairs*, vol. 92, no. 3, p. 32. New York: Council on Foreign Affairs, 2013.

Davenport, T. H., and Dyche, J. *Big Data in Big Companies*. Cary, NC: International Institute for Analytics: SAS Institute, 2013.

Essential Business Tech Report. "Big Data FAQ." In *PC Today*, Technology for Business, vol. 11, no. 12, pp. 32–34. Nebraska: Sandhills Publishing Company, 2013.

Essential Business Tech Report. "Machine to Machine Networks." In *PC Today*, vol. 11, no. 12, pp. 29–31. Nebraska: Sandhills Publishing Company, 2013.

Essential Business Tech Report. "Redefining the Landscape: VM Ware Is Reshaping Data Center Infrastructure through Virtualization." In *PC Today*, vol. 12, no. 2, p. 15. Nebraska: Sandhills Publishing Company, 2014.

Essential Business Tech Report. "Total Mobility: Advice for Organizations Large and Small." In *PC Today*, vol. 12, no. 2. Nebraska: Sandhills Publishing Company, 2014.

Essential Business Tech Report. "Securing Big Data: Security Issues Around Big Data Solutions." In *PC Today*, vol. 11, no. 12, pp. 32–33. Nebraska: Sandhills Publishing Company, 2013.

Essential Business Tech Report. "Security Analytics: How Exposing Security-Related Data to Analytics Is Altering the Game." In *PC Today*, vol. 12, no. 5. Nebraska: Sandhills Publishing Company, 2014.

Ferguson, M. *Enterprise Information Protection—The Impact of Big Data*. England: White Paper, Intelligent Business Strategies, 2013.

FireEye and Mandiant. "Cybersecurity's Maginot Line: A Real-World Assessment of the Defense-in-Depth Model." California: FireEye, 2014.

Fitzgerald, D. "Google Glass Can Turn You Into Live Broadcast." In *The Wall Street Journal, Sec. B-4*, Dow Jones and Company, 2014.

Flick, T., and Morehouse, J. *Securing the Smart Grid: Next Generation Power Grid Security*. Philadelphia, PA: Syngress is an Imprint of Elsevier, 2011.

Gertz, B. "Syria Facing U.S. Cyber Attacks in Upcoming Strikes." In *The Washington Free Beacon*, 2013.

Gertz, B. "The Cyber-Dam Breaks." In *The Washington Free Beacon*, 2013.

Jordan, M. "Theoretical Foundations of Big Data Analysis." California: Simons Institute for the Theory of Computing, University of California–Berkeley, 2013.

Krutz, R. L., and Vines, R. D. *Cloud Security: A Comprehensive Guide to Secure Cloud Computing*. Indiana: Wiley Publishing Inc., 2010.

Leger, D. L. "Hackers Holding Computers Hostage." In *USA Today*. Virginia: A Gannett Company, 2014.

Marks, J. "Welcome to the Data Driven World: The Governments Big Investment in Big Data Is Changing What We Know and How We Know It." In *Atlantic Media*, vol. 45, no. 2, pp. 22–28. Washington, 2013.

Ovide, S. "Big Data, Big Blunders." In *The Wall Street Journal*, Sec. R-4, Dow Jones and Company, 2013.

Piper, S. *Definitive Guide to Next Generation Threat Protection*. Annapolis, MD: CyberEdge Press, 2013.

Rothman, W. "The Crock-Pot Is Still Slow, but Now it's Smart." In *The Wall Street Journal*, Sec. D-3. Dow Jones and Company, 2014.

Sarna, D. E. Y. *Implementing and Developing Cloud Computing Applications*. Florida: CRC Press, Taylor and Francis Group, 2011.

Skoudis, E., and Liston, T. *Counter Hack Reloaded: A Step-by-Step Guide to Computer Attacks and Effective Defenses*, Second Ed. New Jersey: Prentice Hall, 2006.

Sloan, J., and Schultz, G. "Virtualization 101." In *PC Today*, vol. 11, no. 10, pp. 16–18. Nebraska: Sandhills Publishing Company, 2013.

Taki, T. M. "Cloud Computing Strategy." Washington: United States Government Printing Office, United States Department of Defense, 2012.

U.S. Department of Defense. *Department of Defense Strategy for Operating in Cyberspace*. Washington: United States Government Printing Office, United States Department of Defense, 2011.

Verizon Risk Team. *Verizon 2013 Data Breach Investigations Report*, New York: Verizon, 2013.

Wood, P., Editor. *Symantec Internet Security Threat Report 2014*, vol. 19. Mountain View, CA: Symantec, 2014.

Index

A

Abacus, 2
Activity-based costing (ABC), 264
Actuarial tables, 276–278
Actuators, 123
Ad Sense, 16
Advanced Persistent Threat, 298
Advanced persistent threats (APT) attacks,
    12, 159, 179–180, 289, 291, 296,
    298–299, 305
Advanced Research Projects Agency
    Network (ARPANET), 6–8
Affordable Health Care Act, 291
Afghanistan, 166
Agile, 312
Aiken, Howard, 3
Air Force Information Warfare Center, 171
Airlines flight 77, 184
Air transportation, 69–70
Alarm system, security design, 89, 90, 152
Alaska, 112, 118
ALE (annual loss expectancy), 100, 260
Alexander, Keith, 43, 172, 173, 189–190, 293
Al-Midhar, Khalid, 184
Al-Qaeda, 165, 166, 184, 188, 192
ALTAIR 8800 computer, 5
Altimeter Group, 20–21
Amazon, 318, 319, 320
"Amber Alert" system, 109
American Registry for Internet Numbers
    (ARIN), 297
Ammunition, 116
Amplification, in financial markets, 84–85
Analysis framework, in protection and
    engineering design, 142–144
Analytics, security, 317
Andreeson, Marc, 7–8
Android operating system, 14, 15
Annual loss expectancy (ALE), 100, 260
Antitrust Laws, 210
Apple's mobile operating system (iOS), 15
APT. *See* Advanced persistent threats (APT)

ARIN (American Registry for Internet
    Numbers), 297
Armed Forces—Military Intelligence, 163
Armored truck drivers, 116
ARPANET (Advanced Research Projects
    Agency Network), 6–8
"ARP Poisoning," 301
Arquilla, John, 158
Arsenal, of digital cyber threats, 57
Assange, Julian, 170
Association of Certified Fraud Examiners, 239
Attackers
    design issues in critical infrastructures,
        83–90
        capabilities and intents, 86–87
        intentional, intelligent, and malicious
            attackers, 83–86
        random stochastic models, 89–90
        system tolerance, redundancy design
            for, 87–89
    identification, 177
    need for information, 297–299
    signal to, 260
Attack graphs, 91–94
Attacks, 11–18. *See also* specific entries
    APT, 12, 159, 179–180, 289, 291, 296,
        298–299, 305
    botnets and cyber crime applications, 15–17
    CryptoLocker, 289, 297
    cyber, 158, 160
        contemporary cost, studies and
            reports, 260–263
        on critical infrastructures, 42–54
        economic impact, 258–260
    cyberspace, 54–58, 158, 160
    drone, 165, 166–167
    Flame, 13
    mobile malware, 14
    Ransomware, 289, 297, 304
    rootkit, 13
    RSA SecurID attack, 13
    spear-phishing, 12, 289, 292, 295
    toolkits, 13–14

Index

Printed in the United States
by Baker & Taylor Publisher Services

Printed in the United States
by Baker & Taylor Publisher Services